AF564636

Home Science as General Education

Home Science as General Education

Sangeeta Rani

RANDOM PUBLICATIONS
NEW DELHI (INDIA)

Home Science as General Education

ISBN 978-93-5111-843-5

Published in 2016 in India by

RANDOM PUBLICATIONS

4376-A/4B, Gali Murari Lal, Ansari Road
New Delhi-110 002
Phone : +9111-43580356, 011-23289044, 011-43142548
e-mail: sales@randompublications.com,
info@randompublications.com, randomexports@gmail.com

Reprinted 2025

Type Setting by : Friends Media, Delhi-110089
Digitally Printed at : Replika Press Pvt. Ltd.

COOKING TECHNIQUES

Baking

Baking is the technique of cooking food in an oven by dry heat applied evenly throughout the oven or only from the bottom element. Many household ovens in North America are usually provided with two heating elements, one in the bottom for baking, and one in the top for broiling. The person that does the baking is called a baker. Breads, desserts, and meat are often baked, and baking is the primary cooking technique used to produce cakes and pastry-based goods such as pies, tarts, and quiches. Such items are sometimes referred to as "baked goods," and are sold at a bakery. The dry heat of baking changes the structures of starches in the food and causes its outer surfaces to brown, giving it an attractive appearance and taste, while partially sealing in the food's moisture. The browning is caused by caramelization of sugars and the Maillard reaction. Moisture is never really entirely "sealed in," however; over time, an item being baked will become drier and drier.

This is often an advantage, especially in situations where drying is the desired outcome, for example in drying herbs or in roasting certain types of vegetables. The most common baked item is bread. Variations in the ovens, ingredients and recipies used in the baking of bread result in the wide variety of breads produced around the world. To compensate for moisture loss, some items (usually meats) are basted on the surface with butter or oil to slow the loss of moisture through the skin.

The term baking is not usually associated with the cooking of meats in this manner, it is instead termed roasting. Some foods are replenished with moisture during baking by placing a small amount of liquid (such as water or broth) in the bottom of the pan, and letting it steam up into or around the food, a method commonly known as braising. Over time baked goods become hard in a process known as going stale. This is not primarily due to moisture being lost from the baked products, but more a reorganization of the way in which the water and starch are associated over time, a process similar to recrystallization.

Ingredients often used in baking

- Butter, margarine or other shortening
- Flour
- Sugar
- eggs
- Leavening agents:
- Baking powder
- Yeast

Blind-baking

The term blind-baking (sometimes called "pre-baking") refers to the process of baking a pie crust or other pastry without the filling. Generally, the pie crust is lined with tin foil or parchment paper, then filled with dried peas, lentils, beans or other pulses, so that it will keep its shape when baking. (Metal or ceramic pie weights are also used.) After the pie crust is done, the pulses are replaced with the proper filling. Blind-baking is necessary if the pie filling can not be baked as long as the crust requires, or if the filling of the pie would make the crust too soggy if added immediately.

Broiling

Broiling is a process of cooking food with high heat with the heat applied directly to the food, most commonly from above. Heat transfer to the food is primarily via radiant heat. As it is a way of cooking without added oil, it is popular in low-fat diets. In electric ovens, broiling is accomplished by placing the food near the upper heating element, with the lower heating element off and the oven door partially open. Gas ovens often have a separate compartment for broiling, as a drawer below the flame. Similar to a broiler is a salamander, which is most frequently used in a professional kitchen. It is smaller than a standard broiler, and is used to finish off dishes, such as caramelizing the sugar on a Crème brûlée.

In American English, cooking done over an open flame on a grid-iron, barbecuing, or double-sided frying with something like a George Foreman Grill are all often called grilling, but in British English and Australian English "grilling" simply means "broiling".

FlashBake

FlashBake is a high tech cooking technology invented in 1993. A company (Quadlux, Inc. from Fremont, CA, USA) made an oven that cooks with intense infrared and visible light radiation. It can cook like a regular oven with a speed close to that of a microwave oven. This technology is not popular in the home market due to the high price. FlashBake is a registered trademark. This patented technology was licensed to various restaurant equipment suppliers, such as Wolf Stoves and Vulcan-Hart. Other licensees include home appliance manufacturer GE for their Advantium line of oven, and Bosch & Siemens in Europe. Amana developed their own *WAVE* ovens after failure to license the technology from Quadlux. Amana later lost in a law suit with Quadlux regarding this dispute. Some high end products still use the technology, but Quadlux ended production on 1st July 2000 because of production difficulties with the contract manufacturer Watertown Metal Products. They ceased research and development and dropped to a staff of four. It is unclear as to whether they are still in business.

Boiling

Boiling is the rapid vaporization of a liquid, which typically occurs when a liquid is heated to a temperature such that its vapor pressure is above that of the surroundings, such as air pressure. Thus, a liquid may also boil when the pressure of the surrounding atmosphere is sufficiently reduced, such as the use of a vacuum pump or at high altitudes. Boiling occurs in three characteristic forms, which are *nucleate*, *transition* and *film boiling*.

Nucleate boiling is the most common type of boiling and it is characterized by bubbles, which rise from discrete points on a surface, whose temperature is only slightly above the liquid's saturation temperature. In general, the number of nucleation sites are increased by an increasing surface temperature. An irregular surface of the boiling vessel can create additional nucleation sites, while an exceptionally smooth surface (such as glass) lends itself to superheating.

When the surface temperature reaches a maximum value, the critical superheat, vapor begins to form faster than liquid can reach the surface. Thus, the heated surface suddenly becomes covered with a vapor layer. Because of the vapor layer's lower thermal conductivity, this vapor layer insulates the surface. This condition of a vapor film insulating the surface from the liquid characterizes *film boiling*. *Transition boiling* may be defined as the unstable boiling, which occurs at surface temperatures between the maximum attainable in nucleate and the minimum attainable in film boiling.

Boiling in cookery

In cookery, boiling is cooking food in boiling water, or other water-based liquid such as stock or milk. Simmering is gentle boiling, while in poaching the cooking liquid moves but scarcely bubbles. Under special conditions, a heated liquid may show boiling delay when heated over its boiling point, by starting to boil suddenly and violently. In places where the available water supply is contaminated with disease-causing bacteria, boiling water (and allowing it to cool) before drinking it is a valuable health measure. Boiling water for a few minutes kills most bacteria, amoebas, and other microbial pathogens. It thus can help prevent cholera, dysentery, and other diseases caused by these organisms.

Increasing the temperature of a liquid already boiling by adding heat is impossible. Pressure and a change in composition of the liquid may alter the boiling point of the liquid. For this reason, high elevation cooking generally takes longer since boiling point is a function of atmospheric pressure. The boiling point is defined as the temperature at which the vapor pressure of the substance equals the pressure above the substance. Increasing the pressure as in a pressure cooker raises the temperature of the contents above the open air boiling point.

Adding salt also increases the boiling point. Due to variations in composition and pressure, the boiling point of water is almost never 212 F/ 100 C, but rather close enough for cooking.

Foods suitable for boiling include:

- Fish.
- Vegetables.
- Farinaceous foods such as pasta.
- Eggs.
- Meats.
- Sauces.
- Stocks and soups.

Advantages:

- Older, tougher, cheaper joints of meat and poultry can be made digestible.
- It is appropriate for large-scale cookery
- Nutritious, well flavoured stock is produced
- It is safe and simple
- Maximum colour and nutritive value is retained when cooking green vegetables, provided boiling time is kept to the minimum Disadvantages.
- There is a loss of soluble vitamins in the water.
- It can be a slow method
- Foods can look unattractive Method. Boiling can be done in two ways. The food can be placed into already rapidly boiling water and left to cook, the heat can be turned down and the food can be simmered. The food can also be placed into the pot, and cold water may be added to the pot. This may then be boiled until the food is satisfactory.

Blanching

Blanching is a cooking term that describes a process of food preparation wherein the food substance is rapidly plunged into boiling water and then removed after a brief, timed interval and then plunged into iced water or placed under cold running water. Blanching rapidly heats and then cools the food. This allows the food, usually fruits and vegetables, to firm up and makes the food's natural flavour more pronounced, and is often a preparative technique for freezing food. Blanching is also an effective method of loosening the skin on fruits or nuts that one may wish to peel, such as tomatoes, plums, peaches, or almonds. In addition, blanching enhances the color of some (particularly green) ingredients. Steam blanching is also used to neutralise bacteria and enzymes present in foods so that they may be processed and gain a greater shelf life, such as peanuts. Blanching can also describe deep frying in oil at a lower temperature as with the initial cooking of French fries ('chips' in EE).

Preface

"Home science education is worth life education". From time immoral down the ages of civilization, "Home and Family" has been the core of all human development and the society at large. By catering to the physical, emotional and spiritual needs of the members, the home gives meaning to life and refines the life of citizen leading to better living and thus building a healthy and developed country. Home science can be defined as "Education for better living". It explores the plausibility of the establishment of the perfections in the social orders starting from the home life to the community level.

On the whole, the goals of Home science can be spell out as "for prosperous living and achieving the highest happiness". The development of Home science education reflects social pressures that are evident around the turn of the century. It is a need-based, professionally oriented education to assist family and community towards improved living. In the context of growing pressures in the work environment and external world, the family assumes a significant role in shaping the citizens of tomorrow. The family is the main factor which protects the individuals from all external forces and provides the right type of atmosphere for children to grow into strong and independent personalities. Home science, then becomes the key subject in shaping the future course of our lives, as it equips the future citizens with relevant knowledge, competencies and prepares them to become efficient custodians of the nations future.

– Author

Contents

1

Food Science

FOOD SCIENCE PROCESSING

Food science processing is the set of methods and techniques used to transform raw ingredients into food for consumption by humans. The *food science processing industry* utilizes these processes. Food science processing often takes clean, harvested or slaughtered and butchered components and uses these to produce attractive and marketable food products. Similar process are used to produce animal feed. For Examples,

Following are common food processing techniques:

- Removal of unwanted outer layers, such as potato peeling or the skinning of Peaches
- Chopping or slicing, of which examples include potato chips, diced carrot, or candied peel.
- Mincing and macerating
- Liquefaction, such as to produce fruit juice
- Emulsification
- Cooking, such as boiling, broiling, frying, steaming or grilling
- Mixing
- Addition of gas such as air entrainment for bread or gasification of soft drinks
- Proofing
- Spray drying

Extreme examples of food processing include the delicate preparation of deadly fugu fish, preparing space food for consumption under zero gravity, winemaking, hot dogs, and chicken nuggets.

HISTORY

Food processing dates back to the prehistoric ages when crude processing incorporated slaughtering, various types of cooking, such as over fires, smoking, steaming, oven baking), fermenting, sun drying and preserving with salt. Foods preserved this way were a common part of warriors and sailor's diets up until the introduction of canned food. These crude processing techniques remained essentially the same until the advent of the industrial revolution. Modern food processing technology in the 19th and 20th century has largely been developed because of military needs.

Using newly discovered industrial age technology, Nicolas Appert developed a vacuum bottling process to supply troops in the French army with food, which would eventually lead to tinning and later, canning by Peter Durand in 1810. Although initially expensive and somewhat hazardous due to lead used in the cans, canned goods would later become a staple around the world. Another important advance of the 19th century was pasteurization, discovered by Louis Pasteur in 1862.

In the 20th century, World War II and the space race drove the development of food processing even further with advances such as spray drying, juice concentrates, freeze drying and the introduction of artificial sweetners, colorants, and preservatives such as sodium benzoate and saccharine. Late 20th century food processing would reach its peak with products like dried instant soups, reconstituted fruits and juices, and self cooking meals like the MRE food ration.

ADVANTAGES

Benefits of food processing includes toxin removal, preservation, improving flavor, easing marketing and distribution tasks, and increasing food consistency. In addition, it increases seasonal availability of many foods, enables transportation of delicate perishable foods across long distances, and makes many kinds of foodstuffs safe to eat by removing the microorganisms. Modern supermarkets would not be feasible without modern food processing techniques, long voyages would not be possible, and military campaigns would be significantly more difficult and costly to execute. Modern food processing also improves the quality of life for allergics, diabetics, and other people who cannot consume some common food elements. Food processing can also add extra nutrients.

DISADVANTAGES

Food processing frequently lowers nutritional value, and sometimes toxic chemicals are added or created in the food during processing such as nitrites, or aromatic hydrocarbons. Several food additives have been found to cause health problems and some techniques alter food flavor negatively. In addition, high quality and hygiene standards must be maintained to ensure consumer safety and not all food processors comply with these standards. Proponents of the raw food diet advocate consumption of foods prepared with very little food processing.

INDUSTRIES

Food processing industries and practices include the following:

- Meat packing plant
- Industrial rendering
- Slaughterhouse
- Vegetable packing plant
- Cannery

COOKING

Cooking is an act of preparing food for eating. It encompasses a vast range of methods, tools and combinations of ingredients to improve the flavour or digestibility of food. It generally requires the selection, measurement and combining of ingredients in an ordered procedure in an effort to achieve the desired result. Constraints on success include the variability of ingredients, ambient conditions, tools and the skill of the individual cooking.

The diversity of cooking worldwide is a reflection of the myriad nutritional, aesthetic, agricultural, economic, cultural and religious considerations that impact upon it.

Cooking requires applying heat to a food which usually, though not always, chemically transforms it, thus changing its flavor, texture, appearance, and nutritional properties. There is archaeological evidence of cooked foodstuffs, both animal and vegetable, in human settlements dating from the earliest known use of fire. The earliest use of cooking was possibly done by *Homo erectus*, although the evidence is in contention among paleoanthropologists.

Effects of Cooking

Food safety

If heat is used in the preparation of food, this can kill or inactivate potentially harmful organisms including bacteria and viruses. The effect will depend on temperature, cooking time, and technique used. The temperature range from 4°C to 57°C (41°F to 135°F) is the "food danger zone." Between these temperatures bacteria can grow rapidly. Under the correct conditions bacteria can double in number every twenty minutes. The food may not appear any different or spoiled but can be harmful to anyone who eats it. Meat, poultry, dairy products, and other prepared food must be kept outside of the "food danger zone" to remain safe to eat. Refrigeration and freezing do not kill bacteria, but only slow their growth.

Proteins

Much edible animal material is made of proteins, including muscle, offal, and egg white. Almost all vegetable matter also includes proteins although generally in smaller amounts. They may also be a source of essential amino acids. When proteins are heated to near boiling point they become de-natured and change texture. In many cases this causes the structure of the material to become softer or more friable-meat becomes *cooked*. In some cases proteins can form more rigid structures such as the production of stable foams using egg whites.

These are believed to be formed through the partial unravelling of the albumen protein molecules in response to beating with a whisk. The formation of a relatively rigid but flexible matrix from egg white provides an important component of much cake cookery and also underpins many desserts based on meringue.

Fat

Fats and oils come from both animal and plant sources. In cooking, fats provide tastes and textures but probably the most significant attribute is the wide range of cooking temperatures that can be provided by using a fat as the principal cooking medium rather than water. Commonly used fats and oils include butter, olive oil, sunflower oil, lard, beef fat-both dripping or tallow, rapeseed oil or Canola, and peanut oil. The inclusion of fats tend to add flavour to cooked food even though the taste of the oil on its own is often unpleasant.

This fact has encouraged the popularity of high fat foods many of which are classified as *junk* food such as hamburgers or convenience fried cereal snacks. Fats can also be blended with cereal flours to make a range of doughs and pastries. Roux made with heated fat and flour can also absorb large volumes of water-based liquids, including milk and water itself to form smooth sauces.

This relies on the properties of starches to create simpler mucilaginous saccharides during cooking, which causes the familiar thickening of sauces. Oils are commonly emulsified with water-based fluids such as vinegar or lemon juice to make mayonaises. In this the fatty content of egg yolk is used as the emulsification agent.

Carbohydrates

Carbohydrates used in cooking include a variety of sugars and starches including cereal flour, rice, arrowroot, and potato. Long chain sugars such as starch tend to break down into more simple sugars when cooked or made more acidic, such as with lemon juice or vinegar. Simple sugars can form syrups.

If sugars are heated so that all water of crystallisation is driven off, then caramelisation starts with the sugar undergoing thermal decomposition with the formation of carbon and other breakdown products producing caramel.

Braising

Braising is cooking with "moist heat", typically in a covered pot with a small amount of liquid. From the French "braiser". Braising relies on heat, time, and moisture to successfully break down tough connective tissue and collagens in meat. It is an ideal way to cook tougher cuts. Many classic braised dishes such as Coq au Vin are highly-evolved methods of cooking tough and unpalatable foods. Swissing, stewing and pot-roasting are all braising types. Most braises follow the same basic steps. The meat or poultry is first browned in hot fat. Aromatic vegetables are sometimes then browned as well. A cooking liquid that often includes an acidic element, such as tomatoes or wine, is added to the pot, which is covered. The dish cooks in relatively low heat in or atop the stove until the meat is fork-tender. Often the cooking liquid is finished to create a sauce or gravy.

A successful braise intermingles the flavors of the foods being cooked and the cooking liquid. Also, the dissolved collagens and gelatins from the meat enrich and add body to the liquid. Braising is economical, as it allows the use of tough and inexpensive cuts, and efficient, as it often employs a single pot to cook an entire meal. Familiar braised dishes include Murshed, pot roast, beef stew, Swiss steak, chicken cacciatore, goulash, braised tilapia and boeuf bourguignon, among others.

Coddling

In cooking, to *coddle* food is to heat it in water kept just below the boiling point. The eggs added to a Caesar salad should ideally be coddled. However, coddled eggs are in actual fact still raw and eggs prepared in this way present a salmonella risk

Double Steaming

Double steaming is a Chinese cooking technique to prepare delicate food such as bird nests, shark fins etc. The food is covered with water and put in a covered ceramic jar. The jar is then steamed for several hours. This technique ensures there is no loss of liquid or moisture (its essences) from the food being cooked, hence it is often used with expensive ingredients like Chinese herbal medicines.

Cantonese calls double steaming *dan* (Simplified Chinese: –p; Traditional Chinese: Éq; Pinyin: dùn). Note that the Cantonese usage of this Chinese character deviates from its original meaning which is simmer or stew in Mandarin. It is unclear if this cooking technique is common outside of Cantonese cuisine, thus, there may not be a non-Cantonese term for it.

Cantonese cuisine is famous for its slow cooked soup. One famous dish of this kind is called the *Winter melon urn* (¬QÜtÅv). It is prepared by emptying the inside of a winter melon to make an urn. The outside of the winter melon is often carved with artistic patterns. The inside is then filled with soup ingredients such as Chinese cured ham, and several Chinese herbs. Winter melon is believed to be nourishing and it is seldom cooked with ingredients that are believed to be too *yin* or too *yang*.

The whole urn completed with its original melon lid is double steamed for at least four hours. The flavor of the soup is soaked into the "flesh" of the melon. The whole melon and its content is brought to the dinner table. The soup is served by scooping out the liquid and the inside wall of the melon. In this case, the edible melon takes the place of the double steaming jar. This application is possible because winter melon has a waxy, thus waterproof, rind. There is another dessert dish called *double steamed frog ovaries in a coconut (also known as hasma)* designed for women.

The Chinese medicinal ingredients, rock sugar are placed inside a young coconut soaking in the original coconut juice. The filled coconut is then double steamed for several hours. The whole coconut is served whole at the table after dinner. The contents and the inside wall of the coconut are scooped out to be consumed.

Infusion

An Infusion is a method of preparing herbs in which 1 to 2 teaspoons of dried herb or 2 to 4 fresh herbs (flowers and berries are substitutable) is "infused" or placed in oil or boiling water, and then, after about ten minutes, is strained. Waiting too long before straining results in bitter tasting herbs. Short-term infusions are more popular today, made in 24 hours to 3 weeks. The herb/botanical is then removed from the oil and the oil is used in the many formulas that call for short-term infused oils. Using ceramic pots with lids, drinking one cup thrice daily, and preparing the infusion quickly, help treat colds and flus.

Long-term infusions

Long-term infused oils sit for a minimum of one year or longer before opening in order to have a more concentrated, infused oil that is used similar to an essential oil by the drop rather than by the ounce as one would use a short-term infused oil. Long-term infused oils are prized for their vibrant colors, concentration, and use with or without essential oils as well as their long shelf life.

History

It is unknown when infusions were first made, but the first recorded use of essential oils is in the 10th century by the Persian chemist Avicenna. Infusions were used by common men or women in daily life. Today the use of infusions is becoming common once again. Because infusions cannot be patented, there is little available research in regard to infusions.

Poaching (cooking)

Poaching is the process of gently simmering food in liquid, generally water, stock or wine.

Poaching is particularly suitable for fragile food, such as eggs, poultry, fish and fruit, which might easily fall apart or dry out. For this reason, it is important to keep the heat low and to keep the poaching time to a bare minimum, which will also preserve the flavour of the food. Poached eggs are generally cooked in water, fish in white wine, poultry in stock and fruit in red wine.

Pressure cooking

Fig. A Pressure Cooker

Pressure cooking is a method of cooking in a sealed vessel that does not permit air or liquids to escape below a preset pressure. Because water's boiling point increases as the pressure increases, the pressure built up inside the cooker allows the liquid in the pot to rise to a temperature higher than 100 °C (212 °F) before boiling. The higher temperature causes the food to cook faster. Cooking times can be reduced by a factor of three or four. For example, shredded cabbage is cooked in one minute, fresh green beans take about five, small to medium-sized potatoes (up to 200 g) may be ready in five minutes or so and a whole chicken takes no more than twenty-five minutes. It is often used to simulate the effects of long braising or simmering in shorter periods of time.

A safety valve releases steam when the pressure exceeds the safety limit for the cooker; usually the steam pressure lifts a weighted stopper allowing excess pressure to escape. There is usually a backup pressure release mechanism that may employ a number of different techniques to release pressure quickly if primary pressure release mechanism fails. One such method is in the form of a hole in the lid blocked by a plug of low melting-point alloy. If internal temperature (and hence pressure) gets too high, the metal plug will melt, resulting in a release of the pressure.

An early pressure cooker, called a *steam digester,* was invented by Denis Papin, a French physicist, in 1679. Larger volume pressure cookers are often referred as pressure canners. A pressure cooker is often used by mountain climbers to compensate for the low atmospheric pressure at a very high altitude. Without it, water boils off before reaching 100 °C, leaving the food improperly cooked, as described in Charles Darwin's *Voyage of the Beagle*: At the place where we slept water necessarily boiled, from the diminished pressure of the atmosphere, at a lower temperature than it does in a less lofty country; the case being the converse of that of a Papin's digester. Hence the potatoes, after remaining for some hours in the boiling water, were nearly as hard as ever. The pot was left on the fire all night, and next morning it was boiled again, but yet the potatoes were not cooked. I found out this, by overhearing my two companions discussing the cause, they had come to the simple conclusion, "that the cursed pot [which was a new one] did not choose to boil potatoes." A larger scale version of a pressure cooker, used by laboratories and hospitals to sterilise biological waste materials, surgical instruments etc. is known as an autoclave.

Simmering

Simmering is a cooking technique in which foods are cooked in hot liquids kept at or just barely below the boiling point of water (at average sea level air pressure), 100 °C (212 °F). To keep a pot simmering, one brings it to a boil and then adjusts the heat downward until just before the formation of steam bubbles stops completely.

Water normally begins to simmer at about 94 °C or 200 °F. Professional chefs debate the appropriate temperature and appearance of simmering liquids constantly, with some saying that a simmer is as low as 180°F. If you are in culinary school or a professional kitchen, you should always use the chef's definition of simmering. Simmering ensures gentler treatment than boiling to prevent toughening and prevent food from breaking up. Simmering is usually a rapid and efficient method of cooking.

In Japanese cuisine, simmering is considered one of the four essential cooking techniques (along with grilling, steaming, and deep frying). In Argentina, simmering is considered the essential method to heat the water to experience "El Maté" in the perfect quality to taste the flavor of this worldwide known Argentinian tradition.

Steaming

Steaming is a method of cooking using steam.

Two types of steaming utensils

Steaming is a preferred cooking method for health conscious individuals because no cooking oil is needed, thus resulting in a lower fat content. Steaming also results in a more nutritious food than boiling because fewer nutrients are destroyed or leached away into the water (which is usually discarded). It is also easier to avoid burning food.

Steaming works by first boiling water, causing it to evaporate into steam; the steam then carries heat to the food, thus cooking the food. In western cooking, steaming is most often used to cook vegetables, and only rarely to cook meats. By contrast, vegetables are seldom steamed in Chinese cuisine; vegetables are mostly stir fried or blanched instead. In Chinese cooking, steaming is used to cook many meat dishes, for example, steamed whole fish, steamed pork spare ribs, steamed ground pork or beef patties, steamed chicken, steamed goose etc. Other than meat dishes, many Chinese rice and wheat foods are steamed too. Examples include buns, Chinese steamed cakes etc. Steamed meat dishes (except some dim sum) are less common in Chinese restaurants than in traditional home cooking because meats usually require longer cooking time to steam than to stir fry.

The Chinese chefs developed an efficient method of restaurant cooking: Big bamboo steaming baskets, each three feet in diameter and four inches tall, can be stacked up on top of a wok like a chimney. The bottom of each basket is a grid which allows the steam from the wok to rise all the way to the top of the stack. In the kitchen of some dim sum restaurants, a steaming stack can be 20 levels high. The bottom level is removed when done and the entire stack simply shifted downward. This technique ensures a constant supply of freshly steamed dim sum.

Steaming at home can also be done with a wok. A shelf is put on the bottom of the wok, and a small steam basket or a dish of food is put on the shelf. Water is then filled to just below the dish or basket. The water is kept boiling, and a lid is placed over. Most vegetable dishes can be cooked in approximately five minutes using this method; most meat dishes, however, take longer than 20 minutes.

A common alternative is to put the dish to be steamed on top of rice which is being cooked. A pot of rice which takes about 30 minutes to cook will then be ready at the same time as the steamed food. Specialized steamers are often available for purchase; however, although they are more convenient, they are not necessarily better. A related technique is enclosing food in a container or material that will release steam when heated, such as clay pot cooking. A kind of steaming can be done outdoors by wrapping meat, poultry, or fish in banana leaves and burying it in hot sand or ash. Another form of outdoor steam cooking is covering a large piece of meat, poultry or fish in wet clay and placing it in a fire.

Steeping

- Steeping may mean:
- Soaking in liquid until saturated with a soluble ingredient.
- Soaking to remove an ingredient; Example—salt from smoked ham or salted cod.

One example is the steeping of corn, part of the milling process. As described by the US Corn Refiners Association, harvested kernels of corn are cleaned and then steeped in water at a temperature of 50 degrees for 30 to 40 hours. In the process their moisture content rises from 15% to 45% and their volume more than doubles. The gluten bonds in the corn are weakened and starch is released.

The corn is then ground to break free the germ and other components, and the water used (steepwater), which has absorbed various nutrients, is recycled for use in animal feeds.

Stewing

In cooking, stewing means preparing meat cut into smaller pieces or cubes by simmering it in liquid, usually together with vegetables. A stew may be either simmered in a pot on the stove top or cooked in a covered casserole in the oven. Stewing is suitable for the least tender cuts of meat that become tender and juicy with the slow moist heat method. Cuts having a certain amount of marbling and gelatinous connective tissue give moist, juicy stews, while lean meat may easily become dry.

White stews, also known as *blanquettes* or *fricassées*, are made with lamb or veal that is blanched, or lightly seared without browning, and cooked in stock. Brown stews are made with pieces of red meat that are first seared or browned, before a browned mirepoix, sometimes browned flour, stock and wine are added.

Stews may be thickened by reduction, but are more often thickened with flour, either by coating pieces of meat with flour before searing, or by using a roux or *beurre manié*, a dough consisting of equal parts of butter and flour. They are very traditional in the cooking of Iran, wherein they are called khoresh, and have evolved both parallel and with influence from Indian dishes such as mughal stews and the plentiful torkaris of Bengal.

Vacuum flask cooking

Vacuum flask cooking is an invention introduced to the Asian market in the mid-1990s. The vacuum cooker (ÜqÒqK“) is a stainless steel vacuum flask. The flasks come in various sizes ranging from 20-40 cm (8-16 in) in diameter and 25 cm (10 in) tall. A removable pot, with handle and lid, is inside the vacuum flask.

Food is cooked in the pot on a regular stove at a high heat. After the food is fully cooked, the pot's lid is put on and the pot is inserted into the vacuum flask. The heavily insulated lid of the flask is closed and locked air-tight. The pot and food are left in the vacuum flask for several hours. The food continues cooking in its own heat, and stays warm. A typical user prepares a meal in the morning, heats the meal in the pot, places the pot in the vacuum cooker and returns home after work to enjoy a hot meal. Normally, reheating is not needed as the food remains hot enough for consumption after 6 to 8 hours. The main advantages are carefree operation, and zero power consumption during the prolonged cooking process. However, the reduction in power consumption is due entirely to possibly greater efficiency (*i.e.* reduced loss of heat to the environment during cooking), as the same amount of heat energy is required to transform uncooked food into cooked food in either case.

The main difference is whether the heat escapes or goes into the transformation of the food. Even given the same amount of heat energy, in the insulated environment, the prolonged chemical reaction more than cooks the food; it breaks down the food so much as to alter the texture of the dish. In order to achieve the same texture of the food, a regular stove might need to be burning for 6 hours or more. With the vacuum flask, the food is cooked on the stove for 20 minutes and then kept hot for 6 hours. The energy saving can be 10 to 20 fold.

The main disadvantage is the risk of food poisoning as the food temperature slowly decreases to levels which may allow bacteria growth in the food. The danger of food poisoning can be reduced, but not eliminated, by thoroughly cooking the food at high temperatures before putting it in the vacuum flask.

Also, it is important to buy a vacuum cooker that seals and insulates effectively, so the food temperature will be less likely to drop below a level sufficient to kill micro organisms. Vacuum flasks appeal to Cantonese cooks because many Cantonese dishes require prolonged braising or simmering. When these cookers were first introduced in the US, they sold very quickly in the larger Asian supermarkets. The vacuum flask approach is reminiscent of the familiar crock pot, in that food cooks unattended for extended periods. The differences are significant enough that neither is quite a replacement for the other. Haybox cooking is an earlier form of retained heat cooking.

Note that the food is NOT cooked in a vacuum. It is cooked inside a vacuum flask. The vacuum in the wall of the cooker insulates the pot, so the food in the pot remains hot over several hours. Note that a different kind of vacuum cooker is used in the candy manufacturing industry to cook candies at low air pressures. That is a different topic altogether.

Frying

Frying is the cooking of food in oil or fat. Chemically, oils and fats are the same, differing only in melting point, but the distinction is only made when needed. In commerce, many fats are called oils by custom, *e.g.* palm oil and coconut oil, which are solid at room temperature. Fats can reach much higher temperatures than water at normal atmospheric pressure. Through frying, one can sear or even carbonize the surface of foods while caramelizing sugars. The food is cooked much more quickly and has a special crispness and texture. Depending on the food, the fat will penetrate it to varying degrees, contributing richness, lubricity, and its own flavour. Frying techniques vary in the amount of fat required, the cooking time, the type of cooking vessel required, and the manipulation of the food. Sautéing, stir frying, pan frying, shallow frying, and deep frying are all standard frying techniques.

Sautéing and stir-frying involve cooking foods in a thin layer of fat on a hot surface, such as a frying pan, griddle, wok, or sauteuse. Stir frying involves frying quickly at very high temperatures, requiring that the food be stirred continuously to prevent it from adhering to the cooking surface and burning. Shallow frying is a type of pan frying using only enough fat to immerse approximately one-third to one-half of each piece of food; fat used in this technique is typically only used once. Deep-frying, on the other hand, involves totally immersing the food in hot oil, which is normally topped up and used several times before being disposal. Deep-frying is typically a much more involved process, and may require specialized oils for optimal results.

Deep frying is now the basis of a very large and expanding world-wide industry. Fried products have great consumer appeal in all age groups, and the process is quick, can easily be made continuous for mass production, and the food emerges sterile and dry, with a relatively long shelf life. The end products can then be easily packaged for storage and distribution. Examples are potato crisps, French fries, nuts, doughnuts, instant noodles, etc. There is some criticism of fried food for their low nutritional value. Frying, especially deep frying, imbues the food with fat from the oil, lowering their nutrient density.

Deep frying

An advertisement for an automated deep fryer from 19731

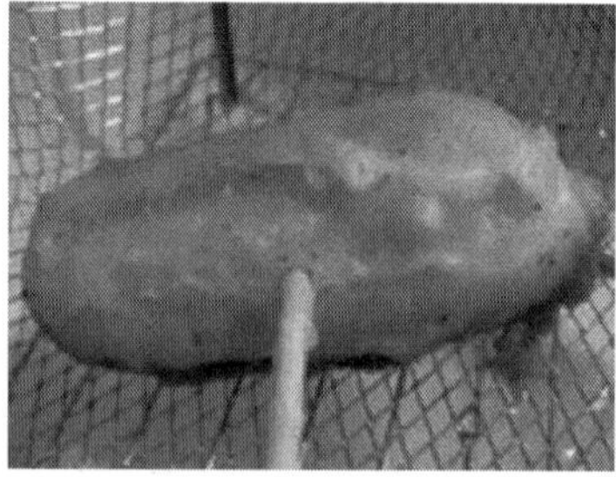

Fig. A Deep fried Twinkie.

Deep frying is a cooking method whereby food is submerged in hot oil or fat. Because of the high temperature involved and the high heat transfer rate, it is extremely fast. Although submersion in liquid oil is involved, no water is used and so deep frying is best classified as a dry cooking method. If performed properly, deep frying does not make food excessively greasy because the moisture in the food repels the oil. The hot oil heats the water within the food, and steams it from the inside out. As long as the oil is hot enough and the food is not immersed in the oil too long, oil penetration will be confined to the outer surface layer and none will actually reach the center the food.

If the food stays in the oil too long, too much of the water will be lost and the oil will begin to penetrate the food. If the oil is not hot enough, the surface of the food will take much longer to brown, allowing the centre to dehydrate excessively and allow more oil to penetrate. The correct frying temperature depends on the thickness and type of food as found by experience, but in most cases it lies between 175 and 190°C (345- 375°F) Some fried foods are given a coating of batter or breading prior to frying. The effect of these is that the outside of the food becomes crispy and browned while the inside becomes tender, moist, and steamed. Some foods, such as potatoes or whole, skin-on poultry, produce a natural skin and do not require breading.

In Japanese cuisine, deep frying is considered one of the four essential cooking techniques (along with grilling, steaming, and simmering). Although correctly produced fried foods are perfectly wholesome, correct management of the oil is essential. Abusing the frying oil by overheating, excessive use or undue exposure to air while hot leads to formation of oxidation products, polymers and other deleterious or even toxic compounds such as acrylamide (in starchy foods). Researchers in many countries have found that of the three major market sectors, the most abused frying oils were (in order from the worst) those in the catering, domestic and industrial sectors.

Some useful tests and indicators of excessive oil deterioration are the following: Sensory: Darkening, smoke, foaming, thickening. Laboratory: Acidity (FFA), anisidine value, viscosity, total polar compounds, polymeric triglycerides. Note that there are now on the market simple, resonably priced instruments reading the total polar compounds (the best single test), with sufficient accuracy for restaurant and industry use.

Examples of deep fried food

Bananas or plantains-popular in Southeast Asia and the Caribbean. Black Pudding-(AKA Blood Pudding) is delicacy popular in Scotland. Individual small puddings are battered and deep fried, mostly served with chips and sold in fish and chip shops as a take-away.

- Canapés: Deep frying is also a technique used to prepare bread pieces for these.
- Cheese curds: a breaded or battered deep-fried cheddar cheese curd, similar to Mozzarella sticks. They are found mainly in Wisconsin.

- Chicken fried steak
- Chicken wings
- Corn dogs
- Doughnut: a deep-fried piece of dough or batter.
- Fish and chips
- French fries (or chips in British English, or *pommes frites* in French): deep fried potato strips.
- French Toast- usually served in Hong Kong style cafes.
- Fried chicken
- Fried shellfish: shrimp, clams, scallops, and oysters are either battered or breaded then deep fried. Usually served with cocktail sauce and a lemon wedge, tartar sauce, and sometimes clarified butter.
- General Tso's chicken
- Mars bars: a delicacy of the North of England and Scotland. These are a popular candy (US) bar that has been dipped in batter first.
- Mozzarella sticks-a breaded or battered deep-fried mozzarella.
- Panelle e crocchè are a Sicilian typical dish, made by boiling vegetables then deep frying them.
- Pakora: various vegetables dipped in a batter of chick peas before frying.
- Potato chips (crisps in British English): thin slices of potato.
- Red pudding: a delicacy especially in Fife, Scotland. Individual puddings are battered and deep-fried, mostly served with chips and sold in fish and chip shops as a take-away.
- Scotch eggs
- Tempura: a Japanese technique consisting of a special batter and oil
- Turkey, deep fried whole in large vats of oil.
- Twinkie
- White pudding: a delicacy popular in Scotland and Ireland. Individual puddings are battered and deep-fried, mostly served with chips and sold in fish and chip shops as a take-away.

Hot salt frying

Hot salt frying is a technique used by street side food vendors in China. Coarse sea salt is placed in a large wok and heated to high temperature. Dry food items, such as eggs in shell, are buried in the hot salt and occasionally turned with a spatula.

This technique was also observed in San Blas, Nayarit, Mexico, along the *zocalo*, in July of 1991. A vendor had placed a large clay cazuela on top of a 4-legged, waist high charcoal brazier. The cazuela was filled with coarse salt. After the salt became hot, the vendor toasted/fried pepitas, or pumpkin seeds in their shells in the hot salt, stirring them with a slotted spoon. When the seeds were "done", the vendor spooned them into tiny paper bags and sold them to strollers in the zocalo for an afternoon or evening snack. This technique is also seen in India where street vendors sell shelled peanuts or popcorn cooked in salt heated in an iron wok.

Hot sand frying

Hot sand frying is a common technique for street side food vendors in China and India to cook chestnuts and peanuts. A large wok is filled with black sand and heated to high temperature. Nuts are buried in the hot sand and occasionally turned with a spatula, then the sand and nuts are separated through a wire-mesh screen.

Pan frying

Pan frying is a form of frying characterized by the use of less cooking oil than deep frying; enough oil to, at most, cover the food to be cooked only half way. As a form of frying, pan frying relies on oil as the heat transfer medium and on correct temperature to retain the moisture in the food. The exposed topside allows, unlike deep frying, some moisture loss (which may or may not be desirable) and contact with the pan bottom creates greater browning on the contact surface (which may or may not be desirable.) Because of the partial coverage, the food must be flipped at least once to cook both sides.

The advantages of using less oil are practical: less oil is needed on hand and time spent heating the oil is much shorter. The chief disadvantage of using less oil is that it is more difficult to keep the oil at an even temperature. The moisture loss and increased browning can be beneficial or detrimental depending on the item cooked and its preparation and should be taken into account if there is a choice to be made between pan frying and deep frying. Generally, a shallower cooking vessel is used for pan frying than deep frying. Using a deep pan with a small amount of oil does reduce spatter but the increased moisture around the cooking food is generally detrimental to the preparation. A denser cooking vessel—the pan should *feel* heavy for its size—is necessarily better than a less dense pan since that mass will improve temperature regulation. An electric skillet can be used analogously to an electric deep fryer and many of these devices have a thermostat to keep the liquid (in this case, oil) at the desired temperature. A popular entree that would be described as "pan fried" would be fish or seafood.

Pressure frying

In pressure frying, meat and cooking oil are brought to high temperatures while pressure is held high enough that the water within is prevented from boiling off. This leaves the meat very hot and juicy. It is a variation on pressure cooking and is mostly done in industrial kitchens. This should be only attempted with specialized equipment made for pressure frying. It is not safe in a household pressure cooker.

Sautéing

Sautéing is a method of cooking food using a small amount of fat in a shallow pan over relatively high heat. *Sauter* means "to jump," in French, and the food being sautéed is kept moving, not unlike the stir fry technique using a wok.

Food that is sautéed is usually cooked for a relative short period of time over high heat in order to brown the food, while preserving its color, moisture and flavor. This is very common with more tender cuts of meat, *e.g.* tenderloin and filet mignon. Sautéeing differs from searing in that the sautéed food is thoroughly cooked in the process. One may sear simply to add flavor and improve appearance before another process is used to finish cooking it.

Olive oil or clarified butter are commonly used for sautéeing, but most fats will do. Regular butter is less well suited for sautéeing, because it will burn at a lower temperature due to the presence of milk solids.

Sweating

A related cooking method, called a *sweat*, starts with the same raw materials as a sauté (a pan and some fat), but uses a low heat. The purpose of the sweat is simply to soften the food, not brown it as in a sauté. The food being sweated is sometimes salted, to allow some of the food's moisture to "sweat" out.

Performing a sauté

To sauté, a hot pan is required, large enough to hold all of the food in one layer. A kind of frying pan known as a *sauté pan* is ideal; it has straight sides, to maximize the surface area available for the sauté. Only enough fat to lightly coat the bottom of the pan is needed. Using too much fat will cause the food to fry rather than to sauté. The food is spread across the hot fat in the pan, and left to brown, turning occasionally for even cooking. Tossing or stirring the items in the pan by shaking the pan can cause the pan to cool faster, and make the sauté take longer, possibly producing a lower quality result.

The two most important items to watch are that the pan is very hot, and that the food is not crowded into the pan. This ensures that the food browns well without absorbing the fat or stewing in its own juices. Furthermore, the food must be completely dry in order to keep the pan from cooling and to keep the moisture from building up in the pan; moisture will steam or stew the food. This is particularly important in the case of food that has been marinated.

Stir frying

Stir frying is a common Chinese cooking technique used because of its fast cooking speed. Cantonese restaurant patrons judge the chefs by their "wok hei" (their ability to bring out the qi of the wok, which shows in the food as the look, smell, and taste).

A traditionally round-bottom iron pan called a wok is heated to a very high temperature. A small amount of cooking oil is then poured down the side of the wok (a traditional expression in China regarding this is "hot wok, cold oil"), followed by dry seasonings (including ginger and garlic), then at the first moment the seasonings can be smelled, meats are added and tossed, then once the meat is seared, vegetables, rice and/or noodles, along with liquid ingredients (for example often including premixed combinations of some of soy, vinegar, wine, salt, sugar, and cornstarch) are added and the wok may be covered for a moment so the water in the liquid ingredients can warm up the latest additions as it steams off. In some dishes, or if the cooking conditions are inadequate, different components may be stir fried separately before being combined in the final dish (if, for example, the chef desires the taste of the stir fried vegetables and meats to remain distinct).

The food is stirred and tossed very quickly using wooden or metal cooking utensils. Some chefs will lift the wok to the side to let the flame light the oil or add a dash of wine spirit to give the food extra flavor. Using this method, many dishes can be cooked extremely quickly (within a minute).

Some dishes that require more time are cooked by adding a few dashes of water after the stirring. Then the wok is covered with a lid. As soon as steam starts to come out from under the lid, the dish is ready. In this case, the food is stir fried on high heat for flavor and then steamed to ensure that it is fully cooked.

Cultural differences

Most home kitchens in the West are poorly equipped to stir fry properly. The average kitchen is not designed to handle the large amount of oil vapour produced as a byproduct of proper stir frying. Those stir frying at home cannot achieve the same flavor as in restaurants because the wok is neither hot enough nor big enough to allow fast tossing. By contrast, most Chinese home kitchens are designed with stir frying in mind. The kitchen itself is either in a separate building or in a room with access to the outside. The stove is usually separated from the rest of the kitchen and near a large window to allow for ventilation. The kitchen itself usually is lined with tile or brick for easy cleaning. In the western world, remedies can be to purchase specially designed vents to direct the oil vapour out of the house better.

Western-marketed woks with non-stick coating are not considered appropriate for proper stir-frying because the Teflon coating usually disintegrates after exposure to high heat. By contrast, low heat non-stick stir-frying is an oxymoron according to Cantonese cooking standards. Teflon woks also require the use of Teflon-safe utensils made of plastic or wood, which some traditional Chinese stir fryers deem are not as effective as metal utensils. Western woks are also usually flat-bottomed to accommodate for western stove tops that are flat, where a round-bottomed wok would roll around.

Many Western cooks on TV demonstrate stir frying on low heat with a small wok and a stirring motion comparable to tossing a salad. This is a western adaptation of stir frying, but is different from the traditional Chinese method.

Microwave

Fig. Microwave oven

A microwave oven, or microwave, is a kitchen appliance employing microwave radiation primarily to cook or heat food. Microwave ovens have revolutionized cooking since their use became widespread in the 1970s.

History

Cooking food with microwaves was discovered by Percy Spencer while building magnetrons for radar sets at Raytheon. He was working on an active radar set when he noticed a strange sensation, and saw that a peanut candy bar he had in his pocket started to melt. Although he was not the first to notice this phenomenon, as the holder of 120 patents, Spencer was no stranger to discovery and experiment, and realized what was happening. The radar had melted his candy bar with microwaves. The first food to be deliberately cooked with microwaves was popcorn, and the second was an egg (which exploded in the face of one of the experimenters). In North America, microwave popcorn is now one of the most commonly cooked items in microwave ovens, virtually to the exclusion of other home cooking methods such as hot air and oil popping. Most microwaves sold in North America today have a specific "popcorn button" which is solely used to cook premeasured packages of popcorn, several billion of which are produced annually in the U.S. alone.

In 1946 Raytheon patented the microwave cooking process and in 1947, the company built the first microwave oven, the Radarange. It was almost 6 feet (1.8 m) tall and weighed 750 pounds (340 kg). It was water-cooled and produced 3000 watts, about three times the amount of radiation produced by microwave ovens today. An early commercial model introduced in 1954 generated 1600 watts and sold for $2,000 to $3,000. Raytheon licensed its technology to the Tappan Stove company in 1952. They tried to market a large, 220 volt, wall unit as a home microwave oven in 1955 for a price of $1,295, but it did not sell well. In 1965 Raytheon acquired Amana, which introduced the first popular home model, the countertop Radarange in 1967 at a price point of $495.

In the 1960s, Litton bought Studebaker's Franklin Manufacturing assets, which had been manufacturing magnetrons and building and selling microwave ovens similar to the Radarange.

Litton then developed a new configuration of the microwave, the short, wide shape that is now common. The magnetron feed was also unique. This resulted in an oven that could survive a no-load condition indefinitely. The new oven was shown at a trade show in Chicago, and helped begin a rapid growth of the market for home microwave ovens. Sales figures of 40,000 units for the US industry in 1970 grew to one million by 1975. Market penetration in Japan, which had learned to build less expensive units by re-engineering a cheaper magnetron, was more rapid.

A number of other companies joined in the market, and for a time most systems were built by defense contractors, who were the most familiar with the magnetron. Litton was particularly well known in the restaurant business. By the late 1970s the technology had improved to the point where prices were falling rapidly. Formerly found only in large industrial applications, "microwaves" were increasingly becoming a standard fixture of most kitchens. The rapidly falling price of microprocessors also helped by adding electronic controls to make the ovens easier to use. By the late 1980s they were almost universal, and current estimates hold that nearly 95% of American households have a microwave.

Description

A microwave oven consists of:

- A magnetron,
- A magnetron control circuit (usually with a microcontroller),
- A waveguide, and
- A cooking chamber

A microwave oven works by passing microwave radiation, usually at a frequency of 2450 MHz (a wavelength of 12.24 cm), through the food. Water, fat, and sugar molecules in the food absorb energy from the microwave beam in a process called dielectric heating. Most molecules are electric dipoles, meaning that they have a positive charge at one end and a negative charge at the other, and therefore vibrate as they try to align themselves with the alternating electric field induced by the microwave beam. This molecular movement creates heat. Microwave heating is most efficient on liquid water, and much less so on fats, sugars, and frozen water. Microwave heating is sometimes incorrectly explained as resonance of water molecules, which only occurs at much higher frequencies, in the tens of gigahertz.

Most microwave ovens allow the user to choose between several power levels, including one or more defrosting levels. In most ovens, however, there is no change in the intensity of the microwave radiation; instead, the magnetron is turned on and off in cycles of several seconds at a time. This can actually be observed when microwaving airy foods like Krembos (An Israeli confection): it blows up during heating phases, while it deflates when the magnetron is turned off.

The cooking chamber itself is a Faraday cage enclosure which prevents the microwaves from escaping into the environment. The oven door is usually a glass panel for easy viewing, but has a layer of conductive mesh to maintain the shielding. Because the size of the perforations in the mesh is much less than the wavelength of 12 cm, the microwave radiation can not pass through the door, while visible light (with a much shorter wavelength) can.

Professional chefs generally find microwave ovens to be of limited usefulness. On the other hand, people who are lacking in free time, or not comfortable with their cooking skills, can use microwave ovens to reheat stored food (including commercially available pre-cooked frozen dishes) in only a few minutes.

A variant of the conventional microwave is the convection microwave. A convection microwave is a combination of a standard microwave and a convection oven. It allows food to be cooked quickly, yet come out browned or crisped, as from a convection oven. Convection microwaves are more expensive than a conventional microwave. They are not considered cost-effective if primarily used just to heat drinks or frozen food. They are usually used for cooking a prepared dish.

More recently, certain manufacturers have added a high power quartz halogen bulb to their convection microwave models while marketing them under names such as “Speedcook” and “Optimawave” to emphasize their ability to cook food rapidly and with the same browning results typically expected of a conventional oven. This is achieved using the high intensity halogen lights at the top of the microwave to deposit large amounts of infrared radiation to the surface of the food. The food browns while also being heated internally by the microwave radiation and heated through conduction and convection by contact with heated air-produced by the conventional convection portion of the unit. The IR energy which is rapidly delivered to the outer surface of food by the lamps is sufficient to initiate browning and caramelization reactions in a particular food’s proteins and carbohydrates, producing a texture and taste much more similar to that typically expected of conventional oven cooking rather than the bland boiled and steamed taste that microwave-only cooking tends to create. With wireless computer networks gaining in popularity, microwave interference has become a concern near wireless networks. Microwave ovens are capable of disrupting wireless network transmissions because the oven generates radio waves of about 2450 MHz, near the 802.11b/g frequency band.

Efficiency

A microwave oven does not convert all electrical energy into microwaves. A typical consumer microwave oven consumes 1100 W but delivers only 700 W of microwave power, yielding 64% efficiency. The lost 400 W are dissipated as heat by components of the oven. The main source of energy loss is the magnetron tube, which is much less than 100% efficient at generating microwave output from the power source. Lesser amounts of power are consumed by the oven lamp, AC power transformer losses, magnetron cooling fan, food turntable motor and control circuits. This waste heat does not end up in the food but is mostly expelled from the cooling vents on the oven and heats the air in the kitchen.

Of the microwave power that the oven generates, about 77% is typically used to heat the food, compared with 10% to 60% in conventional ovens. (Data collected by boiling water in microwave and measuring temperature change.) Conversely, conventional ovens can use fuel such as natural gas which may or may not be cheaper than the same amount of electrical energy.

Safety and controversy

Microwaving food is fast and popular, but there are potential hazards.

Uneven heating

Food is heated for so short a time that it is often cooked unevenly. Microwave ovens are frequently used for reheating previously cooked food, and bacterial contamination may not be killed by the reheating, resulting in foodborne illness. The uneven heating is partly due to the uneven distribution of microwave energy inside the oven, and partly due to the different rates of energy absorption in different parts of the food.

The first problem is reduced by a stirrer, a type of fan that reflects microwave energy to different parts of the oven as it rotates, and by a turntable or carousel that turns the food. It is also important not to place food or a container in the center of a microwave's turntable. That actually defeats its purpose. Rather, it should be placed a bit off-center so that the item travels all around the area of oven's cooking cavity, thus assuring even heating.

The second problem must be addressed by the cook, who should arrange the food so that it absorbs energy evenly, and periodically test and shield any parts of the food that overheat. In some materials with low thermal conductivity, where dielectric constant increases with temperature, microwave heating can cause localized thermal runaway. Many microwave ovens' performance drops after about 15 minutes of continuous usage, which means food takes longer to cook. When heating several meals, the last meal to be cooked may not be heated properly as a result. Defrosting is another common weakness, as many microwave ovens may start to cook the edges of the frozen food, while the inside of the food remains frozen.

Acute dangers

Liquids, when heated in a microwave oven in a container with a smooth surface, can superheat; that is, reach temperatures that are a few degrees Celsius above their normal boiling point without actually boiling. The boiling process can start explosively when the liquid is disturbed, such as when the operator grabs hold of the container to take it out of the oven, which can result in severe burns. A common myth states that only distilled water can exhibit this behavior; this is not true.

Closed containers and eggs can explode when heated in a microwave oven due to the pressure build-up of steam. Products that are heated too long can catch fire. Manuals of microwave ovens warn of such hazards.

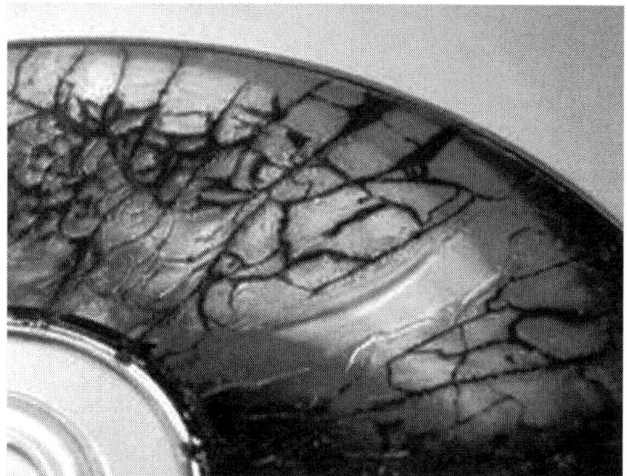

A microwaved DVD-R showing the effects of electrical discharge through its metal film. Tin foil, aluminium foil, ceramics decorated with metal, and products containing other metals can cause sparks when they are used in a microwave. Microwaving small, smooth, solid metal objects without pointed ends (for example, a spoon) can sometimes be safe, and usually does not produce sparking (putting a spoon into a liquid also helps prevent superheating).

Forks, however, will readily produce sparks when placed in the microwave. This is because while it acts as an antenna, absorbing microwave radiation just like other metal objects such as the spoon, the pointed ends of the fork will act to concentrate the electric field formed at the tips. This has the effect of exceeding the dielectric breakdown gradient of air, about 3 megavolts per meter (3×10^6V/m), causing sparks to form. This effect is somewhat analogous to the effect of St. Elmo's fire.

The effect can be seen clearly on a CD or DVD which has been cooked in a microwave. When the electrical field builds up sufficiently, the resulting electric current vaporizes the metal film and melts the plastic in the disc, leaving a visible pattern of concentric and radial scars. The formation of sparks on sharp metal objects may be prevented by placing the utensil in some food or liquid while in the microwave, as this has the effect of preferentially conductively dissipating the charge before the electric fields can build to the point where they exceed the breakdown value of air. Any time dielectric breakdown occurs in air, some ozone and nitrogen oxides are formed, both of which are toxic. Finally, as mentioned previously, any metal or conductive object placed into the microwave will act as an antenna, and its electrons will thus be thrashed back and forth through the object (a high frequency alternating current) causing some ohmic heating to occur. The extent of this heating effect will vary depending on the size, shape and conductivity of the object.

Fig. A microwave oven with a metal shelf

Several microwave fires have been noted where Chinese takeout boxes with a metal handle are microwaved, and also where "homemade" microwave popcorn bags have been sealed using a metal staple, which is then heated and sets fire to the bag.

This type of accident can pose a dangerous situation because of the extremely flammable mixture of popcorn and oil in the bag. Thus, it is good practice to remove any metal utensils or metal containing objects from a microwave oven before operating it, as the behavior of these objects when immersed in a strong microwave radiation field is unpredictable.

It is a common myth that metallic kitchen equipment, like kitchen forks and knives, can somehow repel the microwaves back into the magnetron and cause it to catch fire. This concern is unfounded as there are apparently no cases of such an incident occurring and is implausible considering the entire cooking box where microwaves are injected is made of metal.

Controversial hazards

Radiation

Some people are concerned with being exposed to the microwave radiation. The USA legal limit of leaking radiation is 1 mW/cm^2 at 5 cm from a new oven (for a used oven, it is 5 times higher). It is rare for an oven to exceed these limits. As a comparison, a GSM mobile phone may emit up to 1 W at 1800 MHz, which is 3.2 mW/cm^2 at 5 cm. Whether or not cellular phones are hazardous to the health is also controversial.

Microwave ovens produced after 1971 must meet the Food and Drug Administration safety requirements for radiation leakage; less than 5mW/cm^2 at approximately two inches from the surface of the oven. This is far below the exposure level that is currently considered to be harmful to human health. The radiation produced by a microwave oven is non-ionizing. As such, it does *not* have the same cancer risks associated with ionizing radiation such as X-rays, ultraviolet light, and nuclear radioactive decay.

Food

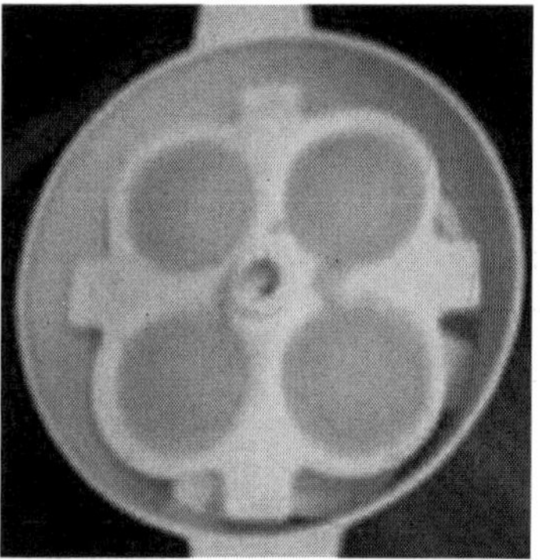

Fig. Idli being prepared in a microwave oven.

Some people claim that there exist more subtle dangers than the ones listed above associated with cooking in a microwave oven and these may include:

- that microwave cooking causes more loss of nutrients than conventional cooking, and
- that microwave radiation leads to chemical reactions in the food that are different from those occurring during conventional heating and which can cause cancer or other ill effects if consumed, particularly due to the formation of a group of suspected carcinogens called d-nitrosodiethanolamines.

There is no accepted scientific validity to these claims, and most scientists and skeptics consider such statements to be alarmist and pseudoscientific. It is widely accepted that microwaves merely heat food, and don't affect chemical bonds directly. Because of this, microwave ovens are actually considered safer than other forms of cooking, like grilling and broiling, for instance, which are known to produce carcinogens.

Roasting

Roasting is a cooking method that utilizes dry heat, whether an open flame, oven, or other heat source. Roasting usually causes caramelization of the surface of the food, which is considered a flavor enhancement. Meats and most root and bulb vegetables can be roasted. Any piece of meat, especially red meat, that has been cooked in this fashion is called a roast. Vegetables and poultry prepared in this way are referred to as roasted (*e.g.* roasted chicken or roasted squash). Some foods such as coffee and chocolate are always roasted.

Until the late 19th century, roasting by dry heat in an oven was called *baking.* Roasting originally meant turning meat or a bird on a spit in front a fire. It is one of the oldest forms of cooking known. Formerly, the kitchens of great houses were equipped with treadmills, powered by dogs or humans, for turning the spit.

Traditionally, recognized roasting methods consist only of baking and cooking over or near an open fire. Grilling is normally not technically a roast, since grilled meat is usually seasoned with wet ingredients or marinated. Smoking is not roasting because of the lower heat and controlled smoke application.

Meat

Most meat roasts are large cuts of meat, and have to cook for a long time. This meat may be moved during cooking, as on a spit or rotisserie, or roasted in place. A roast of meat is occasionally referred to as a *joint*, especially in Britain.

Coffee

Coffee goes through two changes in the roast. In the first, the bean releases its internal water vapor, after which the bean 'cracks'. The second stage is caramelization. The level of caramelization defines the type of roast, from light to dark. After a second 'crack' the coffee begins to carbonize and generally the roasting is stopped at this point even for the darkest roast.

Other

Roasting is a preferred method of cooking for most poultry, and certain cuts of beef, pork, or lamb. Some vegetables, such as potatoes, zucchini, cauliflower, squash, and peppers lend themselves to roasting as well.

Barbecue

A barbecue on a trailer at a block party in Kansas City.

A barbecue on a trailer at a block party in Kansas City Pans on the top shelf hold hamburgers and hot dogs that were grilled earlier when the coals were hot. The lower grill is now being used to slowly cook pork ribs and "drunken chicken".

Barbecue (also barbeque, barbie, barbacoa or abbreviated BBQ) is a method of cooking meat with the heat and hot gases of a fire, smoking wood, or hot coals of charcoal and may include application of a vinegar or tomato-based sauce to the meat. The term can also refer to foods cooked by this method or a party that includes such food. Barbecue is usually cooked in an outdoor environment heated by the smoke of wood or charcoal, or with propane and similar gases. Restaurant barbecue may be cooked in large brick or metal ovens specially designed for that purpose. Barbecue has numerous regional variations in many parts of the world. Notably, in the South and Midwest of the U.S., practitioners consider *barbecue* to include only relatively indirect methods of cooking, with the more direct high-heat methods to be called grilling.

For those that distinguish between the terms, grilling is almost always a fast process over high heat and barbecue is almost always a slow process using indirect heat and/or hot smoke. For example, in a typical home grill, grilled foods are cooked on a grate directly over hot charcoal; while in barbecuing, the coals are dispersed to the sides or at significant distance from the grate. Alternately, an apparatus called a smoker with a separate fire box may be used. Hot smoke is drawn past the meat by convection for very slow cooking. This is essentially how barbecue is cooked in most genuine "barbecue" restaurants, but nevertheless many consider this to be a distinct cooking process called smoking. Regardless of the method, the meat should be turned several times to ensure complete cooking. The slower methods of cooking break down the collagen in meat and tenderize tougher cuts for easier eating.

Etymology

The origin of both the barbecue cooking activity and term are somewhat obscure. The word itself varies in spelling; variations include barbeque, BBQ, and Bar-B-Q. In Australia, the word is often shortened to barbie. A plausible origin for the word, originally provided in a 1970's French television series by Alain Bombard (French navigator who crossed the Atlantic Ocean single-handed in a rubber inflatable raft, subsequently Socialist politician and Mayor in France), ascribes provenance to the French West-Indies: French Pirates (also called: "Boucaniers" or Buccaneers-from the French "Bouc", or Male-Goat) would habitually impale their goats on spits and roast them on an open-fire. The goats were impaled "de la barbe au cul" (from beard to butt) and thus *barbe-cul* = barbecu = Barbecue (the "L" in *cul* is silent in French).

Smoky Hale, author of *The Great American Barbecue and Grilling Manual,* claims that the Taino of the Caribbean used a term "*Taino barabicoa*" which means "The sticks with four legs and many sticks of wood on top to place the cooking meat." There is also the Taino word "*barabicu*", which translates as "sacred fire pit". In one form, *barabicoa* or *barbicoa* indicates a wooden grill or a mesh of sticks; in another, *barabicu*, it is a sacred fire pit. Traditional *barbicoa* implies digging a hole in the ground putting some meat (goat is the best, usually the whole animal) on it with a pot underneath (to catch the concentrated juices, it makes a hearty broth), cover all with maguey leaves then cover with coal and set on fire. A few hours later it is ready. While not everyone agrees that barbecue originated with the Taino, researchers do generally agree that barbecue originated in the Caribbean. There is ample evidence that the word and technique migrated out of the Caribbean and into and through other cultures and languages (with the word itself moving from Caribean dialects into Spanish, then French, then English in the Americas). This would mean that the word "slowly evolved from barbacoa to barbecue and barbeque and bar-b-que and bar-b-q and bbq." In the Southern United States, the word "barbecue" is used predominantly as a noun which specifically refers to roast pork (which is then chopped, pulled, or sliced, depending on region, and served with a tomato, vinegar or mustard-based sauce).

Many in this region believe the term BBQ resulted from when roadhouses and beer joints with pool tables advertised "Bar, Beer, and Cues." This phrase was shortened over time to BBCue, then BBQ. Other *barbecue* supporters believe the word "barbeque" is a result of a gradual misunderstanding of the "BBQ" abbreviation. Due to this abbreviation, with the third syllable "-cue" being represented by the identically-sounding letter "Q," people came to believe that the word was spelled "barbeque." This is also evident in viewing the word's Taíno roots, with all three variations being spelled with the letter "c," as opposed to "q."

History

The American South

In the Southern United States, barbecue initially revolved around the cooking of pork. During the 19th century, pigs were a low-maintenance food source that could be released to forage for themselves in forests and woodlands. When food or meat supplies were low, these semi-wild pigs could then be caught and eaten.

According to estimates, prior to the American Civil War Southerners ate around five pounds of pork for every one pound of beef they consumed. Because of the poverty of the southern United States at this time, every part of the pig was eaten immediately or saved for later (including the ears, feet and other organs). Because of the effort to capture and cook these wild hogs, "pig slaughtering became a time for celebration, and the neighborhood would be invited to share in the largesse. The traditional Southern barbecue grew out of these gatherings." In the rural south, slaves were given the less desirable parts of the pig, (such as the ribs and shoulders) which they would cook by either smoking or pit barbecue.

Events and Gatherings

Fig. A barbecue in a public park in Australia

The word *barbecue* is also used to refer to a casual event, usually outdoors or with an outdoor theme, serving food which has been barbecued on the premises. Grilled foods and side dishes may also be served. For this reason many people mistake any outdoor cooking, including grilling, as barbecue, which is frowned upon by devotees. The device used for cooking barbecue can usually be used for both barbecuing and grilling and is often called a *barbecue grill* by those unaccustomed to slow barbecue, thereby adding to the confusion.

In parts of the United States, outdoor social and family gatherings where food is grilled and served are often referred to as "cook-outs" or "grill-outs" instead of as "barbecues." In the United States, similar gatherings where food is prepared elsewhere and brought to the site are properly referred to as "picnics." In Australia, the barbeque (*note Australian spelling*)-or as it is sometimes referred to in Australian slang as a *barbie*-is an important cultural expression of the outdoor lifestyle and social interaction. Australian celebrity Paul Hogan is famous for his phrase "I'll slip an extra shrimp on the barbie for you" in tourism advertising.

Among other things, Australians will usually cook basic meats such as *snags* (sausages), *chops* and steaks, but it is often the beer, conversation and other activities, such as a social kick of the *footy* or game of social cricket that the term *barbie* is associated with.

Techniques

Wood

The choice and combination of woods burned result in different flavors imparted to the meat. Different types of wood burn at different rates. The heat also varies by the amount of wood and controlling the rate of burn through careful venting. Wood and charcoal are sometimes combined to optimize smoke flavor and consistent burning.

Charcoal

This generally begins with purchasing a commercial bag of processed charcoal briquets. An alternative to charcoal briquets is lump charcoal. Lump charcoal is wood that has been turned into charcoal but unlike briquets it has not been ground and shaped. Lump charcoal is a pure form of charcoal and is preferred by many purists who dislike artificial binders used to hold briquets in their shape.

A charcoal chimney starter is a traditional method for getting a consistent heat from your coals. Another method is to use an electric iron to heat the coals. Another common method is to soak the charcoal with petroleum-based lighter fluid (or use pretreated briquettes) and light them in a pyramid formation. Although this last method is one of the quickest and most portable, it can impart undesirable chemical flavors to the meat. Using denatured alcohol ("methyl hydrate", "methylated spirit") instead of commercial petroleum-based lighter fluids avoids this problem.

Once all coals are ashed-over (generally 15-25 minutes, depending on starting technique), they can be spread around the perimeter of the grill with the meat placed in the center for indirect cooking, or piled together for direct cooking. Water-soaked wood chips (such as mesquite, hickory, or fruit trees) can be added to the coals for flavor. As with wood barbecuing, the temperature of the grill is controlled by the amount and distribution of coal within the grill and through careful venting. For long cooks (up to 18 hours), many cooks find success with the "Minion Method", usually performed in a smoker. The idea involves putting a small number of hot coals on top of a full chamber of unlit briquettes. The burning coals will gradually light the unlit coals. By leaving the top air vent all the way open and adjusting the lower vents, a constant temperature of 225 can easily be achieved for up to 18 hours.

Natural Gas and Propane

Gas grills are easy to light. The heat is easy to control (via knob-controlled gas valves on the burners), so the outcome is very predictable. They result in a very consistent result, although some charcoal and wood purists argue it lacks the flavors available only from cooking with charcoal.

Advocates of gas grills claim that gas cooking lets you "taste the meat, not the heat" because it is claimed that charcoal grills may deposit traces of coal tar on the food. Many grills are equipped with thermometers, further simplifying the barbecuing experience. However propane and natural gas produce a "wet" heat that can change the texture of foods cooked over such fuels. Gas grills are significantly more expensive due to their added complexity, and higher heat. They are also considered much cleaner as they do not result in ashes (which must be disposed of) and also in terms of air pollution. Proper maintenance may further help reduce pollution.

Other uses

The term barbecue is also used to designate the flavor added to foodstuffs, the most prominent of which are potato chips.

Cancer link

Studies have shown that barbecued food may contain benzopyrene, a known carcinogen. Heterocyclic amines and polycyclic aromatic hydrocarbons are chemicals that are formed during the grilling and frying and barbecuing of certain so called "muscle meats" such as beef, pork, poultry, and fish.

Grilling

Grilling is a form of cooking that involves direct heat. The definition varies widely by region and culture.

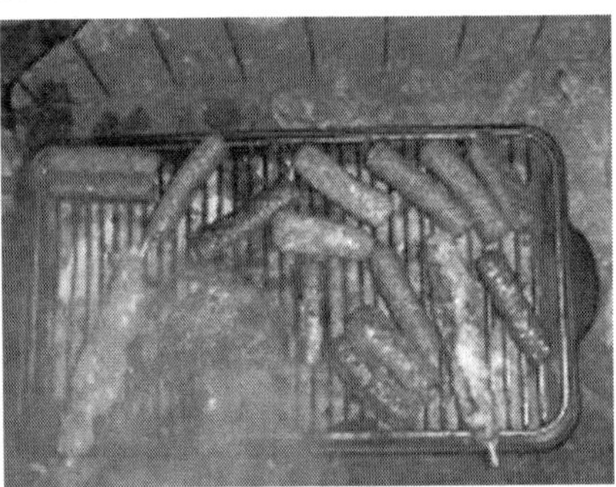

Fig. Israeli Grill

Grilling (UK & Commonwealth)

This type of grilling occurs directly *under* a source of direct, dry heat. In the USA this would be referred to as broiling. The grill or griller (broiler in the USA) is usually a separate part of an oven where the food is inserted just under the element.

The Maillard reaction is very important in grilling and professional grilling chefs understand it either intuitively or scientifically. The door of a grill unit is normally left open during cooking to increase dryness. Until the advent of toasters, and toasted sandwich makers, grills were the main method for making toast and toasted sandwiches.

The main disadvantage of using a grill for toasting is that there is usually no cut-off mechanism or timer, and hence one can set bread alight if the grill is left unattended.

Grilling (US)

In contrast, this type of grilling occurs directly *over* a source of direct, dry heat. In the UK & Commonwealth this would be referred to as barbequeing, although grilling is usually faster and hotter than the normal sense of the word. Grilling is usually done outdoors on charcoal grills and gas grills. Many agree that charcoal provides more flavor, but many prefer gas since one can grill quickly and easily year round. A skewer or brochette, a rotisserie, or a wok may link smaller portions of food into this process. Grilling is very popular during the summer months, but is becoming increasingly popular throughout the entire year. Mesquite or hickory wood chips (damp) may be added on top of the coals to allow a smoldering effect that provides additional flavor to the food. (Other hardwoods such as Pecan, Apple, Maple and Oak may also be used.) Meats such as pork, lamb, beef, and chicken can be basted or marinated to help retain moisture or impart seasonings. Rubs and dry seasonings can also be applied to impart different flavors.

Other meanings

Double-sided frying, as in a sandwich toaster or George Foreman Grill.

Events and Gatherings

In the United States, outdoor social and family gatherings where food is grilled and served are often referred to as "cook-outs", "grill-outs", or "barbeques." In Australia, a barbeque or "barbie" can refer to any event where food is grilled outdoors.

Rotisserie

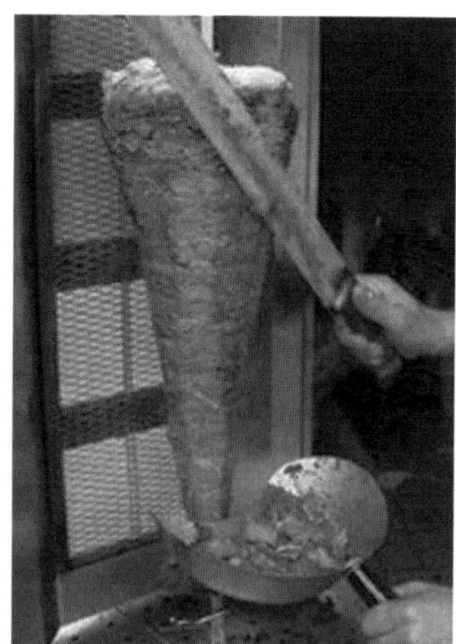

Fig. A vertical rotisserie cooking kebab

Rotisserie is a style of roasting where meat is skewered on a spit and revolves over a flame or other heat source. The rotation cooks the meat evenly in its own juices and allows easy access for continuous basting if desired.

Historically, rotisseries were turned by hand or by clockwork contrivances. Nowadays, they are usually driven by electric motors.

Horizontal rotisserie

This style of rotisserie mounts the spit horizontally. They are often used to cook whole chickens or roasts of various meats including beef and pork. The design may include a single spit mounted over an open broiler or grill, a single spit mounted within an otherwise-conventional oven, or many spits mounted within a large industrial oven. The latter are commonly used to mass produced roasted meats for sale to consumers.

In this style of rotisserie, balance is important. If the object to be cooked is far out of balance, it will impose a heavy load on the drive mechanism or cause the mechanism to fail to turn. Loose chicken legs or wings can also cause the mechanism to jam. For these two reasons, some skewering skill is therefore required.

High-end consumer ovens commonly come with a rotisserie (or allow the installation of a rotisserie as an option). In these cases, the motor drive mechanism is usually concealed within the oven. The rotisserie is used by removing the normal cooking racks; a special carrier may be needed to provide one or both bearing points for the spit.

Vertical rotisserie

The other common style of rotisserie is the vertical rotisserie; here, the heat is applied directly from the side (as shown in the picture) or, less-commonly, convected up from below. In this style of rotisserie, balance of the load is less important than with a horizontal rotisserie.

Some dishes that are commonly cooked on a vertical rotisserie include:

Döner kebab from Turkey

Gyros, from Greece

Shawarma, from the Near East

Taco al pastor, from Mexico

Searing

Searing is a technique used in grilling, roasting, braising, sautéing, etc. that cooks the surface of the food (usually meat, poultry or fish) at high temperature so that a caramelized crust forms. A similar technique, browning, is typically used to sear or brown all sides of a particular piece of meat, fish, poultry, etc. before finishing it in the oven.

It is commonly believed that this acts to lock in the moisture or "seal in the juices" of the food. However, it has been scientifically shown that searing results in a greater net loss of moisture versus cooking to the same internal temperature without first searing. Nonetheless it remains an essential technique in cooking meat for several reasons: The browning creates desirable flavors through caramelization and the Maillard reaction. The appearance of the food is usually improved with a well-browned crust. The contrast in taste and texture between the crust and the interior makes the food more interesting to the palate. Typically in grilling the food will be seared over very high heat and then moved to a lower-temperature area of the grill. In braising, the seared surface acts to flavor, color and otherwise enrich the liquid in which the food is being cooked.

Sealing in the juices

The belief that searing meat "seals in the juices" is widespread and still often repeated. This theory was first put forth forward by Justus von Liebig, a German chemist and food scientist, around 1850. The notion was embraced by contemporary cooks and authors including Auguste Escoffier. Simple experimentation can test the theory: cook two similar cuts of meat, searing one first and not the other. Weigh the end results to see which loses more moisture. (The Food Network program Good Eats carried out such a test in episode EA1H22, *Myth Smashers*.)

As early as the 1930s, such experiments were carried out; the seared roasts lost the same amount of moisture or more. (Generally more, since searing exposes the meat to higher temperatures.) In short, the crust created by searing is in no way waterproof. Moisture in liquid and vapor form can and does continue to escape from a seared piece of meat.

SOME COOL TECHNIQUES

Brining

In cooking, brining is a process similar to marination in which meat is soaked in a salt solution (the brine) before cooking. Brining makes cooked meat moister by hydrating the cells of its muscle tissue before cooking, via the process of osmosis, and by allowing the cells to hold on to the water while they are cooked, via the process of denaturation. The brine surrounding the cells has a higher concentration of salt than the fluid within the cells, but the cell fluid has a higher concentration of other solutes. This leads salt ions to enter the cell via diffusion. The increased salinity of the cell fluid causes the cell to absorb water from the brine via osmosis. The salt introduced into the cell also denatures its proteins. The proteins coagulate, forming a matrix which traps water molecules and holds them during cooking. This prevents the meat from drying out, or dehydrating. In many foods the additional salt is also desirable as a preservative. Note that kosher meats are salted during the process of koshering so they should not be brined.

Some cheeses are periodically washed in a saltwater brine during their ripening. Not only does the brine carry flavors into the cheese (it might be seasoned with spices or wine), but the salty environment may nurture the growth of the Brevibacterium linens bacteria, which can impart a very pronounced odor (Limburger) and interesting flavor. The same bacteria can also have some impact on cheeses that are simply ripened in humid conditions, like Camembert. Large populations of these "smear bacteria" show up as a sticky orange-red layer on some brine-washed cheeses.

Drying (food)

Drying is a method of food preservation that works by removing water from the food, which prevents the growth of microorganisms and decay. Drying food using the sun and wind to prevent spoilage has been known since ancient times. Water is usually removed by evaporation (air drying, sun drying, smoking or wind drying) but, in the case of freeze-drying, food is first frozen and then water is removed by sublimation. Many different foods are prepared by drying, including Parma ham, bresaola, beef jerky, and even fruits that normally have a high water content, such as prunes, raisins, figs, and dates. Dried and salted reindeer meat is a traditional Lappish food. First the meat is soused. It is kept in saltwater for a couple of days to guarantee the conservation of the meat. Then the meat is dried in the sun in spring when the air temperature is below zero. The dried meat can be further processed to make soup.

There are many different methods for drying, each with their own advantages for particular applications; these include:

- Bed dryers
- Fluidized bed dryers
- Shelf dryers
- Sunshine

Julienning

Julienning is a method of food preparation in which the food item is cut into long thin (matchstick-sized) strips. The most common item to be julienned is the carrot in preparation for a common side dish in restaurants known as *carrots Julienne*. Julienne usually applies to vegetables prepared in this way but it can also apply to the preparation of meat or fish.

The first known use of the term in print is in 'Le Cuisinier Royal' from 1722. The origin of the term is uncertain, but may derive from the proper name Jules or Julien. Some claim that a certain chef Jean Julien first used this method of preparing vegetables, but definite evidence to support this claim is still needed. A popular phrase referring to a gadget that can do many things is "It slices! It dices! It makes Julienne fries!" This phrase originated in advertisements for the Ronco Veg-o-Matic kitchen tool. (US specific). Once cut into Julienne, turning the subject to a 90 degree angle and dicing produces brunoise.

Carrots Julienne

Clean and peel the carrots. With a sharp knife slice four sides of the carrot to create a thick rectanglar stick of carrot. Then cut the carrot stick lengthwise into approximately 3 cm (1/8 inch) slices. Stack these slices and again cut the carrot lengthwise into strips to create thin uniform square sticks. The strips can be used decoratively in a garnish or salad or they can be cooked and glazed.

Marination

Marination, also known as marinating, is the process of soaking foods in a seasoned, often acidic, liquid before cooking. The origins of the word allude to the use of brine (*aqua marina*) in the pickling process, which led to the technique of adding flavour by immersion in liquid. The liquid in question, the 'marinade', is often a vinegar (or other acidic liquid such as lemon juice or wine) and oil mixture. It can also contain herbs and spices.

It is commonly used to flavor foods and to tenderize tougher cuts of meat or harder vegetables such as beetroot, aubergine, and courgette. The process may last seconds or days. Different marinades are used in different cuisines. In Indian cuisine the marinade is usually prepared with yoghurt and spices. In meats, the acid causes the tissue to break down, allowing more moisture to be absorbed and giving a juicier end product. However, too much acid can be detrimental to the end product. A good marinade will have a delicate balance of spices, acid and oil. Often confused with marinating, "macerating" is also a form of food preparation. Often soft vegetables, legumes or fruits are used and are also coated in a liquid. This process, again, makes the food tastier and easier to chew and digest.

Mincing

Mincing is a cooking technique in which food ingredients are finely divided. The effect is to create a closely bonded mixture of ingredients and a soft or pasty texture. Flavoring ingredients with spices or condiments such as garlic, ginger, and fresh herbs may be minced to distribute flavor more evenly in a mixture. Additionally bruising of the tissue can release juices and oils to deliver flavors uniformly in a sauce. Mincemeat tarts and Pâtés employ mincing in the preparation of moldable paste.

Salting (food)

Salting is the preservation of food with salt. It is related to pickling (preparing food with brine, rather than dry salt). It is one of very many methods of preserving food. Salting is used because most bacteria, fungi and other potentially pathogenic organisms cannot survive in a highly salty environment. Any living cell in such an environment will become dehydrated through osmosis and die or become temporarily inactivated. Kashrut, the Judaism dietary laws, requires the removal of blood from freshly slaughtered meat, which may be accomplished with the use of salt or brine.

Seasoning

Seasoning is the process of adding or improving flavours of food. Seasonings include black pepper, salt, herbs and spices, and all other condiments. Salt may be used to draw out water, or to magnify a natural flavour of a food making it richer or more delicate, depending on the dish. For instance, kosher salt (a coarser-grained salt) is rubbed into chicken, lamb, and beef to tenderize the meat and improve flavor. Other seasonings like pepper and basil transfer some of their flavor to the food. A well designed dish will combine seasonings that complement each other. In addition to the choice of herbs and seasoning, the timing of when flavors are added will affect the food that is being cooked. In some cultures, meat may be seasoned by pouring sauce over the dish at the table. A variety of seasoning techniques exist in various cultures. Infused Oils is another method of seasoning. There are two methods for doing an infusion—hot and cold. Olive oil makes a good infusion base for some herbs, but tends to go rancid more quickly than other oils. Keep your infused oils refrigerated. In the Quaker belief system: Seasoning pertains to the importance of allowing the answers comes to you, rather than forcing the answer to arise.

Sprouting

Sprouting is the practice of soaking then draining and leaving seeds until they germinate and begin to sprout.

Overview

Sprouting seeds or beans indoors is a very efficient way of utilizing the minimum amount of space in order to produce the maximum of nutrients all year round—in fact one does not even require a garden at all- a window ledge or kitchen shelf would be perfectly adequate. Many seeds or beans are suitable for indoor sprouting including alfalfa, mustard, green lentils, chickpeas (garbanzos) and fenugreek, whilst one of the most common is the mung bean (*Vigna radiata*), well known as the popularly sold 'Chinese Bean Sprout'.

Mung beans can be bought in health food stores or grocery stores, although care should be taken that these are intended for sprouting or human consumption rather than sowing, as these may have been treated with chemical dressings. Several countries, for example New Zealand, also require that some varieties of edible seed be heat-treated, thus making them impossible to sprout.

How to sprout

The main requirements for successful sprouting are moisture, warmth, and (in most cases) some indirect sunlight. Providing a few guidelines are followed, it is remarkably easy to obtain good results requiring very little time, effort or space. Initially a small handful of seeds should be run under a tap, then left at room temperature (between 13 and 21 degrees Celsius) in the sprouting vessel. Although a number of items can be utilized for this task ranging from a jam jar with a piece of net curtain secured over its rim by an elastic band to specially designed 'tiered' sprouters, it is highly important that the vessel is free draining, for waterlogged sprouts will quickly rot. The seeds will soon swell, and within a day or two begin germination. They should then be rinsed at least twice a day, possibly even three or four times in hot weather or they may quickly sour. After around four to five days they will have grown to around two or three inches in length and will be suitable for use.

If left much longer they will begin to develop leaves and can become bitter tasting, although the growth process can be halted by placing them in the fridge until needed.

Although sprouting of mung beans is generally successful once a routine has been developed, it is not uncommon for beginners to experience failures, although these are often due to the following causes which can be easily remedied once recognized;

Seeds being allowed to dry out
Seeds being waterlogged
Temperature too high or too low
Insufficient rinsing
Dirty equipment

Mung beans can be sprouted either in light or dark conditions, eg, an airing cupboard. Those sprouted in the dark (as in the case of the shop-bought Chinese Bean Sprouts) will be crisper in texture and whiter, but have less nutritional content.

Growing in full sunlight however should be avoided as this may cause the beans to overheat or dry out. Subjecting the sprouts to pressure, for example, by placing a weight on top of them in their sprouting container, will result in larger, crunchier sprouts similar to those sold in Chinese groceries. Sprouts purchased in supermarkets tend to be mung or alfalfa cultures.

Nutritional information and precautions

Sprouts are rich in vitamins, minerals, Amino Acids, proteins and phytochemicals, all necessary for a germinating plant, and rich in essential nutrients for humans. Some legumes can contain toxins, which can be reduced by soaking, sprouting and cooking (eg, stir frying). Joy Larkom, advises that to be on the safe side "one shouldn't eat large quantities of raw legume sprouts on a regular basis, no more than about 550g (20oz) daily" ('Salads For Small Gardens', Hamlyn 1995).

Sprouting and the Living foods diet

Advocates of a Living foods diet promote the use of sprouting as an effective way of increasing the nutrient value, and digestibility, of beans, seeds and nuts.

Sugaring

Sugaring is a food preservation method similar to pickling. Sugaring is the process of desiccating a food by first dehydrating it, then packing it with pure sugar. This sugar can be crystalline in the form of table or raw sugar, or it can be a high sugar density liquid such as honey, syrup or molasses. The purpose of sugaring is to create an environment hostile to microbial life and prevent food spoilage. Sugaring is commonly used to preserve fruits as well as vegetables such as ginger. From time to time sugaring has also been used for non-food preservations. For example, honey was used as part of the mummification process in some ancient Egyptian rites.

A risk in sugaring is that sugar itself attracts moisture. Once a sufficient moisture level is reached, native yeast in the environment will come out of dormancy and begin to ferment the sugars into alcohol and carbon dioxide. This leads to the process of fermentation. Although fermentation can be used as a food preservation method, it must be intentionally controlled, or the results will tend to be unpleasant.

Sugaring also describes the following processes:

- The collection and production of maple syrup.
- Hair removal using a sticky paste

Yeast (baking)

Bakers' yeast is a type of yeast used in baking and is known as *Saccharomyces cerevisiae*. This species is also used in fermentation of beer and wine. Yeasts for leavening bread may be produced industrially or commercially or caught from the environment. Commercial yeast is prepared by taking one yeast cell, placing it in a test tube, and providing it with food and the moist, warm conditions it needs to thrive. Yeast undergo asexual reproduction, so it can reproduce itself rapidly, creating large numbers of cells.

In bread production, yeast cells convert carbohydrates into carbon dioxide, which causes the dough to expand or rise, and alcohol, most of which evaporates during baking. The use of potatoes, water from potato boiling, eggs, or sugar in a bread dough accelerates the growth of yeasts. Salt and fats such as butter slow down yeast growth.

Baker's yeast comes in two forms. The first form is fresh yeast pressed into a square cake. This form perishes quickly, and must be used soon after production in order to maintain the desired effects. Dry yeast is granulated and has a longer shelf life than fresh yeast. In the production of beer or wine, sugar is converted into alcohol by yeast. A weak solution of water and sugar can be used to determine if yeast is expired. When dissolved in the solution, active yeast will foam and bubble as it digests the sugar and converts it into carbon dioxide.

History

Yeast was first used to bake bread in Egypt in approximately the fourth millennium BC. Artifacts have been found that are associated with bread making, as well as drawings that depict bakeries. Prior to the use of yeast in baking, breads were typically unleavened. During this time, bread was seen as a luxury.

Some theories state that yeast was discovered simply by being in the air and coming in contact with the unleavened bread being prepared. Another theory states that ale was used instead of water, and the yeast from the ale caused the bread to rise. In 1859, Louis Pasteur discovered how yeast worked and explained fermentation in the making of beer and wine.

Today there are several retailers of baker's yeast, one of the best-known being Fleischmann's Yeast, which was developed in 1868. During World War II Fleischmann's developed active dry yeast, which did not require refrigeration. The company created yeast that would rise twice as fast, cutting down on baking time.

Spray drying

Spray drying is the process of mixing and drying a slurry (a kind of suspension) to form a homogeneous mixture of powders. The powders are mixed with a liquid (like water), then the mixture is sprayed into hot dry air, so that the liquid evaporates leaving small spherical granuales of the mixed powders.

Use in the food industry

Spray drying is sometimes used in the food industry, in milk, egg, fruit juice and dairy products, as well as coffee (although it has been mostly displaced by freeze drying in this aspect).

The spray dryer operates by atomising a stream of the solution using compressed air. The atomisation breaks the solution into small droplets, thereby incresing the surface area and thus the rate of evaporation. The small size of the drops (averaging 100 micrometres in diameter) results in a relatively large surface area which dries quickly. Although the air dry-bulb usually reaches 200 degrees celsius, the air wet-bulb rarely exceeds 55 C and the dried particles are removed from the drier usually within 30 seconds. The temperatures of the particles during drying can range from the wet-bulb temperature of the inlet air to above 100 C as they exit in the dry state. Although these temperatures are high compared to other drying methods available, the moisture near the end is usually near the BET monolayer and the time of exposure is very short, resulting in relatively high nutrient preservation when used in food processing.

HIGH PRESSURE PROCESSING TECHNIQUE

High Pressure Processing (HPP) preserves a food's natural flavour, nutrients, and other sensory properties while extending the shelf life of foods through the inactivation of microorganisms. The uniform application of this non-thermal food processing technology also provides the food industry with new products and new product development opportunities that can fully exploit the functional properties of food ingredients such as hydrocolloids, proteins, etc.

Some of the successful food applications include dressings, sauces, salsas, packaged meats, seafood, cut fruit, purees, juices, chilled ready-to-serve desserts, soups, yogurt, neutraceuticals, pharmaceuticals and other food products. The many advantages of using high pressure processing (HPP) in food production have been known for over a century. However, the technology and equipment required to efficiently and reliability generate the extreme pressures (up to 600 MPa/87,000 psi) used in HPP have only recently become commerciably viable.

Food preservation using high pressure is a promising technique in food industry as it offers numerous opportunities for developing new foods with extended shelf life, high nutritional value and excellent organoleptic characteristics. High pressure is an alternative to thermal processing. The resistance of microorganisms to pressure varies considerably depending on the pressure range applied, temperature and treatment duration, and type of microorganism. Generally, Gram-positive bacteria are more resistant to pressure than Gram-negative bacteria, moulds and yeasts; the most resistant are bacterial spores. The nature of the food is also important, as it may contain substances which protect the microorganism from high pressure.

This chapter presents results of studies involving the effect of high pressure on survival of some pathogenic bacteria—*Listeria monocytogenes, Aeromonas hydrophila* and *Enterococcus hirae*—in artificially contaminated cooked ham, ripening hard cheese and fruit juices. The results indicate that in samples of investigated foods the number of these microorganisms decreased proportionally to the pressure used and the duration of treatment, and the effect of these two factors was statistically significant (level of probability, *P* d" 0.001). *Enterococcus hirae* is much more resistant to high pressure treatment than *L. monocytogenes* and *A. hydrophila*. Mathematical methods were applied, for accurate prediction of the effects of high pressure on microorganisms. The usefulness of high pressure treatment for inactivation of microorganisms and shelf life extention of meat products was also evaluated. The results obtained show that high pressure treatment extends the shelf life of cooked pork ham and raw smoked pork loin up to 8 weeks, ensuring good micro-biological and sensory quality of the products. Food products are an excellent environment for growth of pathogenic microorganisms, which may cause food-borne diseases.

Quality and shelflife of food products depend greatly on the properties of microorganisms contaminating the food. Despite the introduction of food standards obligatory in EU countries, epidemiologists believe that 75 per cent of food-borne diseases are caused by bacteria.

For this reason, the control of microorganisms is an important aspect of food quality and safety. Many methods of food preservation are used for ensuring microbiological safety, among which high pressure processing (HPP) seems a very promising technique for food industry, as it offers numerous opportunities for developing new shelf life stable foods with extended shelf-life, high nutritional value and excellent organoleptic characteristics—minimally processed but safe for consumers. High pressure is an alternative to thermal processing.

The resistance of microorganisms to pressure varies considerably depending on the pressure range applied, temperature and treatment duration, and type of microorganism. As a result of technical progress and government support, the first high pressure processed food products appeared in Japan in the early 1990s. In Europe, high pressure processing (HPP) of foods was rather at the stage of research or pilot production in the last decade. EU legislation included HPP foods in the "novel food" category.

EC Novel Food regulation has introduced a statutory pre-market approval system for novel foods across the whole of the European Union. Recently, rapid progress of HPP toward commercial exploitation has been achieved, but still the process requires close collaboration between researchers, food and equipment manufacturers, as well as proper financial support. In Poland, research on the application of high pressure for food preservation was initiated in 1992 by the High Pressure Research Centre (now Institute of High Pressure Physics) of the Polish Academy of Sciences in collaboration with others Institutes.

The research programmes, sponsored by the State Committee for Scientific Research and by EU funds, were devoted to high pressure processing of fruit products, fruit and vegetable juices, milk and meat products. This chapter presents some of the results concerning the effect of high pressure on the survival of *Listeria monocytogenes, Aeromonas hydrophila* and *Enterococcus hirae* in artificially contaminated food products. This microorganisms could be a source of food-borne diseases.

NEED OF HIGH PRESSURE PROCESSING

High Pressure Processing (HPP) is a method of food processing wherein the food is subjected to elevated pressures (pressures up to 87,000 pounds per square inch or approximately 6000 atmospheres) with or without the addition of heat to achieve microbial inactivation or to alter the food attributes in order to achieve consumer-desired qualities. Pressure is effective in inactivating most of the vegetative bacteria at pressures above 400 MPa. HPP retains food quality, maintains natural freshness, and extends microbiological shelf life. HPP can be used to process both liquid and solid (water-containing) foods. The process is also called as high hydrostatic pressure processing (HHP) and ultra high-pressure processing (UHP) in the literature. High pressure processing causes minimal changes in the fresh characteristics of foods by eliminating thermal degradation. Compared to thermal processing, HPP results in foods with fresher taste, better appearance, texture and nutrition. High pressure processing can be conducted at ambient or refrigerated temperatures, thereby eliminating thermally induced cooked off-flavours. The technology is especially beneficial for heat sensitive products.

FUNCTION OF HPP

Most processed foods today are heat processed to kill bacteria. Heat oftentimes diminishes the quality of a product. High pressure processing provides an alternative means of killing bacteria which can cause spoilage or food-borne disease without a loss of sensory quality or nutrients. In a typical HPP process, the product is packaged in a flexible container (pouch or plastic bottle) and is loaded into a high pressure chamber filled with a pressure transmitting (hydraulic) fluid.

The hydraulic fluid in the chamber is pressurized with a pump and this pressure is transmitted through the package into the food itself. Pressure is applied for a specific time, usually 3-5 minutes. The processed product is then removed and stored/distributed in the conventional manner. Because of the uniform manner in which the pressure is transmitted (in all directions simultaneously), food retains its shape, even at extreme pressures. And because no heat is needed, the sensory characteristics of the food are retained without compromising microbial safety.

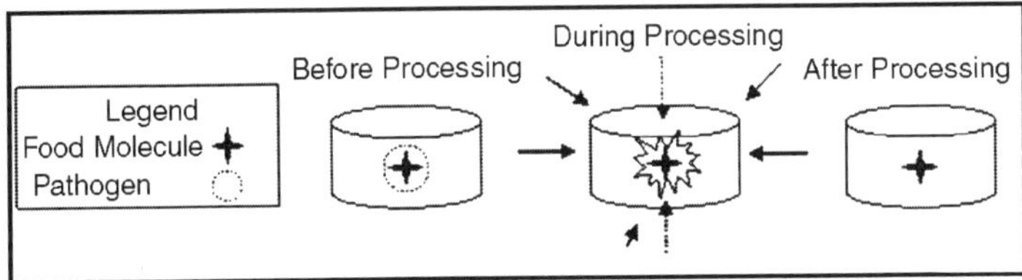

Fig. High Pressure Processing utilizes ultra-high pressures to destroy pathogens without the application of heat that can damage the taste, texture, and nutritional value of the food

HPP AT A GLANCE

- High Pressure Processing (HPP) is based on the Le Chatelier principle which states that actions that have a net volume increase will be retarded and actions that have a net volume decrease will be enhanced.

- HPP utilizes isostatic or hydrostatic pressure which is equal from every direction.
- During HPP, foods are subjected to pressures up to 100,000 psi. which destroy pathagenic microor-ganisms by interrupting their cellular functions.
- Within a living bacteria cell, many pressure sensitive processes such as protein function, enzyme action, and cellular membrane function are impacted by high pressure resulting in the inability of the bacteria to survive. Small macromolecules that are responsible for flavour, odour, and nutrition are typically not changed by pressure.
- HPP is gaining in popularity within the food industry because of its capacity to inactivate pathogenic microorganisms with minimal to no heat treatment, resulting in the almost complete retention of nutritional and sensory characteristics of fresh food without sacrificing shelf life.
- One of the unique advantages of HPP is that pressure transmission is instantaneous and uniform, is not controlled by product size and is effective throughout the entirety of the food item.
- As well, HPP offers several advantages over traditional thermal processing including: reduced process times; minimal heat damage problems; retention of freshness, flavour, texture, and colour; and no vitamin C loss.

Like any other processing method, HPP cannot be universally applied for processing all types of foods. At the moment, HPP is being used in the United States, Europe and Japan on a select variety of high value foods either to extend shelf life or to improve food safety. Some products that are being commercially produced using HPP are cooked ready-to-eat meats, avocado products (guacamole), tomato salsa, applesauce, orange juice and oysters.

HPP cannot yet be used to make shelf-stable versions of low-acid products such as vegetables, milk or soups because of the inability of this process to destroy spores. However, it can be used to extend the refrigerated shelf life of these products and to eliminate the risk of various food-borne pathogens such as *Escherichia coli, Salmonella* and *Listeria*. Acid foods are particularly good candidates for HPP technology.

Another limitation is that the food must contain water and not have internal air pockets. Food materials containing entrapped air such as strawberries or marshmallows would be crushed under high pressure treatment, and dry solids apart from caking do not have sufficient moisture to make HPP effective for microbial destruction. During HPP processing, pressure is uniformly applied around and throughout the food product. For example, a grape placed between fingers can be easily squeezed and broken; this is because the pressure is not applied evenly from all sides simultaneously. On the other hand, if the same grape is squeezed from all sides simultaneously, it will not be crushed. This can be demonstrated by placing a grape inside soda bottle filled with water. By squeezing the bottle, you pressurize the water inside as well as the grape. Yet the grape is not damaged, no matter how hard you squeeze. In the same way, foods processed by high pressure will not be damaged by the applied pressure.

SHELF LIFE OF HPP PROCESSED PRODUCT

In general, HPP can provide shelf lives similar to thermal pasteurization. Pressure pasteurization kills vegetative bacteria and, unless the product is acidic, it requires refrigerated storage. For foods where thermal pasteurization is not an option (due to flavour, texture or colour changes) HPP can extend the shelf-life by 2-3 fold over a non-pasteurized counterpart, and improve food safety. As commercial products are developed, shelf life can be established based on microbiological and sensory testing. High pressure processed products are commercially available in the United States, European and Japanese retail markets. Examples of high-pressure processed products commercially available in the US include fruit smoothies, guacamole, ready meals with meat and vegetables, oysters, ham, chicken strips, fruit juices, and salsa. Low acid shelf-stable products such as soups are not commercially available yet because of the limitations in killing spores with HPP. This is a topic of current research. It has been generally known that high pressure has very little effect on low molecular weight compounds such as flavour compounds, vitamins and pigments compared to thermal processes. Accordingly, the quality of HPP pasteurized food is very similar to that of fresh food products and the quality degradation is influenced more by subsequent storage and distribution rather than the pressure treatment. Pressure also provides unique opportunity to create and control novel food textures in protein based foods.

In some cases, pressure can be used to form protein gels and increase viscosity without using heat. HPP products currently marketed worldwide are primarily distributed refrigerated. In some cases this is necessary for safety (to prevent the growth of spores in low acid foods). For acid foods, refrigeration is not a necessity for microbial stability, but is employed to preserve flavour quality for extended periods of time.

HIGH-PRESSURE FOOD PROCESSING OF RICE AND STARCH FOODS

The use of pressure (P) in addition to temperature (T) has been accepted in the field of food science and technology over the past 15 years, and research and development are now under way in the food industry, universities, and government institutes. Several commercial products are now on the market that are prepared using high-pressure techniques. This section describes the principle of high-pressure treatment and the effects of high pressure on foods, with emphasis on the high-pressure effects on starches. Finally, recent successes of the Echigo Seika Company in the application of high-pressure techniques to rice and rice products are discussed.

Principle and Method

High pressure means high hydrostatic pressure generated by the compression of water. A pressure of 100 MPa or higher (usually lower than 1,000 MPa) is used under temperatures below 100 °C. A unit of pressure is expressed in kg cm^{-2}, bar, or pounds in^{-2}, but now the international Pascal unit is commonly used. Therefore, 1,000 bar or 1,000 kg cm^{-2} almost equals 100 MPa. Food, which is contained in a plastic bag and sealed by carefully removing air, is placed in a pressure vessel filled with water and high pressure is then generated in the vessel by a pressure pump.

Pressurization of Food

An egg is not crushed by compression at 600 MPa, but the egg white and yolk are coagulated. The colour of egg yolk of a pressurized egg is naturally yellow, whereas a boiled egg changes to a faded yellow. The colour difference is attributed to changes associated with pressurization: pressure affects only noncovalent bonding and coagulates proteins without splitting covalent bonds, thus keeping the colour and smell intact. High pressure induces protein denaturation in the same way as high temperature. Meat protein is also denatured by pressure treatment at 400 MPa, preserving the properties of raw meats. An example of prawns or shrimp is interesting: although a boiled prawn turns red and the meat coagulates, the appearance of a pressurized prawn is the same as that of raw shrimp, but the meat coagulates after pressurization at 400 MPa for 10 min. High pressure also has an effect on starches: a thick suspension of rice starch forms a ball by standing against its own weight after pressurization at 700 MPa, indicating that starches are gelatinized by the pressure treatment.

Versatile Utility of High Pressure

A high-pressure treatment generally coagulates protein, thereby inactivating the enzymes, gelatinizing the starches, and killing microorganisms. Thus, the use of high pressure promises to be a versatile process in food science and technology. Pressure produces a new texture in meats and starch-based foods, while keeping the original nutrients, flavour, and colour.

High-Pressure Effects on Pure Starches

High-pressure-induced Gelatinization of Starch

Effect of Pressure on Amylase Digestibility of Starches. The starches of potato, maize, and wheat are gelatinized by pressure treatment at warm conditions of 45–50°C. The pressurization produces unique properties that are different from those of heat-gelatinization: heat-treatment destroys starch granules, resulting in a transparent solution, but a pressure-treatment swells the granules while maintaining the granular structure. Nevertheless, amylolytic enzymes such as α-, β-, and glc-amylases digest the pressurized starches well, being similar to the phenomenon in which the pressure-treatment of proteins increases protease digestibility. The pressure-induced gelatinization of starches exhibits a sigmoid curve, suggesting that a two-state transition is involved, as in heat-induced gelatinization.

Effect of Pressurization Time on Amylase Digestibility of Starches. To attain full amylase digestibility of starches, pressurization under warm conditions for 2 to 6 h is necessary. Interestingly, pressurization of starches for a longer time makes amylase digestion difficult: the amylase digestibility of starches decreased by 20–50 per cent after pressurization for 17 h compared with the maximum digestibility obtained after pressurization for 2 to 6 h.

These observations suggest that pressure induces gelatinization of starches, similar to heating, but prolonged pressurization produces a new stable structure of starches, which is not susceptible to attack by amylase. *Birefringence of Starches after Pressurization.* The birefringence of starches is lost as increasing pressure is applied. Wheat starch is sensitive to pressure and birefringence is lost at 200 MPa. In the pressurization of starches, the number of granules exhibiting complete birefringence decreases without increasing the incomplete birefringent granules. This loss of birefringence shows that the crystalline structure is destroyed by high pressure as well as by high temperature and that the high-pressure-induced gelatinization of starches follows a two-state transition without an intermediate state of destruction.

Physical Properties of Pressurized Starches

When a 50 per cent water suspension of starches is pressurized at 100 to 500 MPa and at 45°C for 1 h and air-dried, followed by analyses of their physical properties, the results are as follows. According to X-ray crystal analysis, the crystalline structure of potato, waxy maize, and maize starches decreases with an increase in pressure, although the crystalline structure of potato starch does not change up to 500 MPa. The decrease in the high-pressure-induced crystalline structure is parallel with the increase in amylase susceptibility. Amylograms show that the transition temperature of pressurized starches is elevated, thus decreasing the viscosity. Interestingly, differential-scanning calorimetry (DSC) of pressurized starches shows that the peak temperature of the DSC patterns increases while the peak area decreases, indicating that some pressure-induced structural state of the pressurized starches is perturbed by low energy at higher temperatures.

Summary of Pressure-induced Changes in Starches

The structure of pressurized starches changes accompany-ing the increase in amylase digestibility, a loss of birefringence, and a loss of crystallinity. These unique structural properties, which are somewhat different from those of heat-gelatinized starches, should be analysed in detail for effective applications of high pressure to starch and related foods.

Rice-based Foods Produced by High-pressure Processing

Dr. Akira Yamazaki, of Echigo Seika Company Ltd., studied the properties of pressurized rice in detail to introduce the use of high pressure to the food industry. He equipped several large highpressure machines in his own factory and succeeded in sending rice and rice products to the market by introducing the high-pressure technique to the manufacturing process of rice products, cooked rice (*gohan*), rice crackers (*osembei*), and rice cakes (*omochi*).

High-pressure Effects on Rice Grains

Traditionally cooked-rice grains change their shape and develop some cracks, but rice grains after high-pressure pretreatment followed by heat-cooking swell, and their original shape is maintained without cracks.

High-pressure Cooked Rice for Microwave Ovens

Bread is purchased in the store and toasted just before eating. This is a typical life style, especially on a busy morning. However, 45 min are required to cook rice. Cooked rice tastes best and has its best texture just after steaming. Warming of cold cooked rice makes the taste worse. In general, heating a starch-based food twice leads to an unpalatable food. In history, instant-rice is a dream of Japanese consumers.

Dr. Yamazaki succeeded in producing oven-cooked rice with a good taste and texture for consumers, although the production scale is only enough to fulfill the requirement of a small city. He also succeeded in producing instant rice containing miscellaneous cereals. These instant cooked-rice cereals exhibited good taste and good texture by a 3-min heating in a microwave oven.

When high-pressure pretreated and successively heatcooked rice is compared with traditionally cooked rice, its properties are as follows: first, it is more gelatinized; second, it is more slowly retrograded; and third, it is gelatinized to a greater extent by heating just before serving. Japanese consumers who are particularly sensitive to rice accept these properties.

High-pressure Rice Cakes

During New Year days, the Japanese public is freed from the kitchen and enjoys the New Year cerebrations, eating rice cakes (*omochi*) every day, which are a preserved food. The company introduced the high-pressure technique for producing the traditional rice cake and a special kind of *omochi*, which contains herbs with a natural colour, smell, and taste, and this is now available on the market.

Merits of High-pressure Food Processing

High-pressure processing is useful not only for producing high-quality food, but also for improving the manufacturing process. The production time for rice crackers is shortened by introducing a high-pressure technique into the traditional processing system and the total energy cost is decreased by 10 per cent and the labour force by 56 per cent.

The use of high pressure for food processing and cooking, in addition to heating and cooling, is now in our hands. Two factors, T and P, are useful for the manufacturing of good foods, including starch-based foods. Although T and P are used independently, their combined use is also important for the optimal use of high pressure. For example, heat-tolerant bacterial spores are inactivated by pressurization under elevated temperature.

CONTEMPORARY FOOD SUPPLY AND DRINKING WATER

It is hard to imagine anyone opposing the green revolution. The increase in yields from the green revolution in rice alone has produced enough to feed one billion people. Growth in yields accounts for 92 per cent of the increase in world cereal production since 1960.

The world average for grain yields per hectare rose from 1.1 tons in 1950 to 2.9 tons in 1992. Without the increase in yields, it would have been necessary to bring another 3.6 billion hectares of land under cultivation, which would have almost doubled world cropland from "34 per cent of the earth's surface (excluding Antarctica) to 61 per cent".

The green revolution was in many ways a grain revolution— wheat, rice, and maize—but it also was a research revolution that facilitated an extraordinary and sustained general expansion in food production. Bender and Smith note, "Between 1961 and 1994, the number of daily food calories per capita rose from about 1,900 to 2,600 in developing countries, while their populations nearly doubled from 2.2 billion to more than 4.3 billion."

Globally in the same period, "average daily per capita food supplies increased more than 20 per cent." The increase in available calories per capita for the developing countries rose 50 per cent from 1948–1952 to 1994–1996. A century-long trend of falling real food prices continued during the period 1950 to 1992 as international food commodity prices dropped 78 per cent in constant 1990 prices.

D. Gale Johnson sums up these achievements in agriculture: "People today have more adequate nutrition than ever before and acquire that nutrition at the lowest cost in all human history."

Green Revolution Pros and Cons

In the 1990s, while population continued to increase, the absolute number of malnourished people in the world declined by forty million, which is a continuation of a trend of the last decades. However, this was considered a "failure" by the UN World Food Program because it fell short of the reductions that were thought to be possible. To the extent that it is a failure, it is a failure of institutions, not of the technology that is producing the food that could make the program a success.

So, there are arguments critical of the green revolution. The first argument is that it was a failure. Data such as that just cited above have demolished that argument, although a few still assert it, unaware of the change in the antitechnology party line. Next, we are told that the new varieties may have increased yields, but they led to a worsening of income distribution and the condition of the very poor. As early as the 1970s, studies emerged showing that the poor consumers and farmers benefited proportionately more than other groups as part of the overall improvement in human wellbeing.

Some argued that tenant farmers in the Punjab in the north of India were displaced from their land due to high-yielding varieties of wheat. It turns out that they returned to the land as farm laborers and earned more than they did as tenant farmers. Similarly, in southern India, between 1973 and 1994, the average real income of small farmers increased by 90 per cent, and that of the landless— among the poorest in the farm community—by 125 per cent. Further, caloric intakes for small farmers and the landless rose 58 to 81 per cent, and protein intakes rose 103 to 115 per cent. In addition, greater farm income meant more income and employment in the local villages that supplied the farm with goods and services now affordable to those who worked the land.

The green revolution in Indian agriculture is credited with being a major force in poverty reduction in India. From independence to 1970, the per centage of the population of India living below the absolute poverty line remained relatively steady at 55 per cent. In over two decades since the introduction of the green revolution technologies, the per centage of the population of India living in absolute poverty has fallen to 35 per cent.

Throughout most of East and Southeast Asia, the early phases of development involved an emphasis on agriculture and food production. The green revolution technologies in agriculture have played an important role in the dramatic reductions in poverty rates throughout the region, such as in Indonesia from 58 per cent in 1970 to 8 per cent in 1993, and in China from 270 million people in poverty in 1978 to 65 million in 1999. Yao estimates the reduction in rural poverty in China to be from between 596 to 790 million people (75.5 per cent–100 per cent) in 1978 to 57 to 114 million (6.7 per cent–13.2 per cent) in 1996. By either measurement, the magnitude of the reduction in poverty in China is extraordinary and without precedent in human history.

In the time period 1969–1971 to 1990–1992, global population was increasing about 45 per cent while the absolute number of people suffering from chronic undernourishment in developing nations decreased from 917 million or 35 per cent of their population to 839 million or 21 per cent. From 1990–1992 to 1995–1997, the absolute number of undernourished people in the developing world continued to decline, falling to 790 million.

The prevalent high number should not be minimized, nor should we be complacent, but neither should the progress achieved be ignored. For we can finish the job of eliminating undernourishment by recognizing the forces that have brought us this far, thereby gaining some understanding of what still needs to be done. Unfortunately, many wish to deny the progress that has been made, offering antitechnology solutions, which would reverse these gains.

Mechanization, Income and Erosion

Mechanization, which often came with the green revolution technologies, was said to be bad because it displaced labor. Again, it often happened that the increase in crops and output per year because of varieties that needed shorter growing seasons and higher yields per crop had labor requirements that more than offset the labor saved by mechanization.

In most areas, the extra crop, thereby demanding greater labor, would have been impossible without mechanization and the green revolution technologies. In the 1970s, saving labor by mechanization was always assumed to be a bad thing, though it might also mean more leisure for the farmer. Increasingly, mechanization means that farmers may earn cash income off the farm, affording school fees for children or consumption of products in the market economy.

It was conceded that the demand for agricultural labor was up, but that mechanization, by doing the more menial tasks, displaced women and children from the farm labor force. Many who oppose child labor in factories somehow deem agricultural stoop labor by children in the hot sun to be virtuous. As incomes go up and child labor is displaced, there is a very good chance that they will now be in school. And where incomes go up, other technologies are also acquired that improve the quality of life and save on child labor.

The high-yielding varieties of rice have been basically for production in irrigated fields. The upland varieties have barely changed in yields over the last three decades.

The Green revolution has given rise to greater regional inequality of income. Careful empirical studies of rice cultivation in Asia have found that laborers from the upland regions migrate to work in the paddies, smoothing out the potential regional differences.

There are also arguments seeking a reduction in genetic variety, soil erosion, or groundwater contamination, which are of serious concern but cannot negate the enormous gain in human nutrition or the human catastrophe that would result from any attempt to reverse the green revolution. The diminution of genetic diversity is not a phenomenon of the green revolution per se but of agriculture. The individual farmer will select for yield or other output concerns, not for global genetic diversity. Modern no-tillage (or reduced or minimum tillage) agriculture using pesticides for weed and pest control conserves both soil and water better than its organic competitors.

MODERN FOOD SUPPLY AND SAFETY

Regularized and improved food supply has been a consistent factor throughout history in improving human health and longevity. In more recent times, improved food safety has added another dimension to human health. The evidence on the safety of our modern food supply is quite contrary to the strongly held conventional wisdom. Humans have had to deal with food contamination throughout history. Human foodstuffs have been the carriers of botulism, ergot, and the aflatoxins from the fungus *Aspergillus flavus,* which has caused mass illness, blindness, and largescale death. Even uncontaminated natural foods contain substances that would be considered a threat to human life if they were used as a food additive.

In the United States, during the early twentieth century, contaminated food, milk, and water caused many foodborne infections, including typhoid fever, tuberculosis, botulism, and scarlet fever. Once the sources and characteristics of foodborne diseases were identified, there were technologies that could help to control them before vaccines or antibiotics: "handwashing, sanitation, refrigeration, pasteurization, and pesticide application." Healthier animal care, feeding, and processing also improved food supply safety.

PLANT-PRODUCED CHEMICALS

The buzz word "chemicals," used by some to label and condemn food additives, could appropriately be used to describe what the plants themselves manufacture. Plants of all kinds, and most other life forms, are chemical factories, manufacturing a variety of chemicals, some of which have very active properties. Humans have extracted some of these chemicals for medicinal uses, some as poisons. Given the truism that dose makes the poison, some chemicals from plants that were once used as poisons are now used for medical purposes. In other words, chemicals from plants are not inherently good or bad; goodness or badness is determined by a variety of factors and the uses to which they are put.

One of the reasons for maintaining as much biodiversity as possible is that the earth's plants produce an array of active chemicals, the vast majority of which have not been screened for possible human use. According to Katharine Milton, plants are unable to run from hungry predators and so have developed a variety of defenses to avoid the loss of edible components. "These protections include a vast array of chemicals known as secondary compounds (such as tannins, alkaloids and terpenoids). At best these chemicals taste awful; at worst, they are lethal".

Leopold and Ardrey add that these plant secondary substances are "chemicals that do not participate in the basic metabolism of the plant. Among these are many chemicals that serve to repel or discourage the use of the plant by insects, microorganisms, nematodes, grazing animals, and man." These plant toxins apparently are often used to ward off fungi.

Eating fresh, uncooked produce may have many taste and health benefits, but it can also be dangerous unless proper precautions are taken. As epidemiologist Michael T. Osterholmm stated: "The hearthealthy diet may be kind to our cardiovascular system but it is hell on the digestive tract".

Rachel Carson, whose book *Silent Spring* is seen as the inspiration of the modern environmental movement, recognized the role of natural toxins—systemic pesticides—in plants. She maintained that the perception of nature as an "enchanted forest" was a "fairy tale". Even some of the weeds associated with cultivars and often eaten with them are endowed with toxins and other substances deleterious to human health. Garn notes, "Weeds growing along with cultivars often included plants with interesting alkaloids, many of them in the tomato family that includes *Datura, Belladonna,* and the like".

Toxins in Plant Evolution

Through time, plants evolved for their own survival, not to serve human needs. "Plants in nature synthesize toxic chemicals in large amounts, apparently as a primary defense against the hordes of bacterial, fungal, and insects and other animal predators *plants in the human diet are no exception.*"

The evolutionary process involved in domestication changed the survival strategy for these plants, as they now depended upon the continued cultivation to survive. The toxicity of many plants was reduced compared to their wild progenitors, but in most cases was not completely bred out of plants. In fact, currently there is considerable effort to breed plants with greater disease resistance so as to reduce the need for pesticides, in some instances by increasing the production of these toxins; in other instances, not.

FOODBORNE DISEASES

Foodborne diseases have always been a problem for humans, even for hunting and gathering peoples, says Cohen. Diseases might be caught from wild animals, including rabies or tularemia, which may have been "a significant cause of sickness and death among American Indian populations who regularly handled game and fur bearing animals." Cohen adds, "Handling wild animals or their remains can also result in infection with such other diseases as toxoplasmosis, hemorrhagic fevers, leptospirosis, brucellosis, anthrax, salmonellosis people can encounter a variety of highly lethal anaerobic bacteria, including the agents of gangrene, botulism, and tetanus, if they expose themselves to the intestines of animals while butchering a kill".

Add in trichina worms (trichinosis) and staphylococcal infections, and it is clear that food harvested in the wild is not necessarily clean, wholesome, and natural. Drinking water in the wild can cause "beaver belly" (giardiasis) or be a source of "microorganisms derived from moose, ducks, and geese as well". Water in the wild today, including snow collected from the ground and melted, can be a source of a variety of parasites, including giardia and cryptosporidium. If we think that we eat contaminated food today, and that we ate clean food in earlier times, think again.

Some foods require cooking or other forms of preparation to be digestible by humans, such as soaking in water, having husks or shells or other parts removed, or milling and reducing particle size to facilitate digestion. Even today, with small-scale technologies, grain milling is incomplete, leaving broken pieces of husk, causing stomach lesions and digestive problems.

In the past (and in many less-developed areas today), "harvesting and milling techniques resulted in a considerable accretion of grit and little stones, as we see in the worn teeth of our colonial ancestors, Bronze-age and Ironage Europeans, and American Indians." With storage, "weevils were often a regular part of the daily bread". On the bright side, food contaminants, such as weevils, were sometimes important sources of protein in otherwise protein-deficient diets.

HEALTH FOOD FADS

Health food faddists who look with horror on the minutest trace of any chemical (read manufactured chemical) nevertheless will ingest mega doses of natural products (such as herbs) that contain substances known to be toxins or untested compounds or have active products such as amino acids that have not been tested for safety at the dosage in which they are being taken. To call free-standing amino acids "natural" is a travesty, since they are not naturally present in food in significant quantity nor can they be "extracted from food without first chemically breaking food protein in the laboratory into its constituent amino acids".

It is ludicrous to label a bottle of amino acids "natural," and it shows how meaningless the term has become and how useless it is for formulating public policy. The amino acid pills are a synthetic product, produced in large vats in chemical factories using microbial fermentation, with a feedstock for the microorganism that is so replete with contaminants that it has to be further processed through a carbon filter and by reverse osmosis to produce what rarely occurs in nature, a free-standing amino acid. We get almost all of our amino acids by ingesting complex proteins.

In 1989, L-tryptophan amino acid pills were identified as a cause of a rare muscle disorder, eosinophilia-myalgia syndrome, which eventually resulted in thirty-seven deaths and at least, 1,500 illnesses. Activists blamed it on the fact that the manufacturer used a bacteria, *Bacillus myloliquefaciens,* that had been genetically engineered, and they continue to argue this to the present, despite the fact that the overwhelming evidence is that it was a contaminant resulting from a reduction in the carbon filtration and modification of the reverse osmosis process. The tragic incident does not reflect well on the testing procedures (or lack of them) by the firms that bought the bulk powder for tryptophan (or other pills) and converted it into "all natural" pills.

Conveniently ignored by the activists is their long history of opposing any regulation or even monitoring of these so-called dietary supplements and their ability to pass legislation, before and after the tragedy, which specifically exempts them from precisely the oversight that might have prevented it. In fact, in 1972 the U.S. Food and Drug Administration tried to withdraw the GRAS (Generally Recognized as Safe) designation for amino acids in "dietary supplements because FDA felt that the available data did not allow" the FDA to deem them to be safe. The FDA had a number of concerns, including possible toxic or other adverse effects.

Because of an error in its original GRAS designation, the FDA lost a court case that would have allowed it to have some reasonable oversight.

VITAMINS

Vitamins are natural, even if manufactured, as long as they are labeled organic. They too have not been tested for safety at the mega doses that some faddists use them, though clinical studies have shown that they can be helpful when used intelligently. Obstetricians who frequently prescribe multiple vitamin pills for pregnant women and programs for vitamin A intervention have saved children's eyesight and lives in poor countries.

The faddists who would regulate agricultural chemicals out of existence oppose even simple truth-in-labeling requirements for their beloved natural products. Groups such as the International Advocates for Health Freedom, the Life Extension Foundation, and "a growing number of allies in the 'patriotic' movement" see a secret conspiracy of "international pharmaceutical empires working hand-in-hand with the UN and the FDA to restrict access to lowcost herbs, vitamins and minerals around the world".

SPROUTS

Alfalfa sprouts have been found to be contaminated with *E. coli* O157:H7 and salmonella. Obviously, not all alfalfa and other sprouts are contaminated but the rate of contamination for raw, untreated sprouts is considerably higher than for most other food. The Emerging Infections Program of the Centers for

Disease Control has estimated that twenty thousand people in North America contracted salmonella from alfalfa spouts in 1995. Disease outbreaks have led to steps such as irradiating alfalfa seeds. Irradiation of alfalfa sprouts is currently being evaluated as an "adjunct seed decontamination method".

Raw alfalfa and clover sprouts are recognized sources of foodborne illness in the United States. Raw sprouts present unique food safety problems because the warm humid conditions needed to grow spouts are also ideal for the rapid growth of harmful bacteria. The very natural nature of alfalfa sprout production creates the contamination problem and makes them a "well-suited vehicle for salmonellosis." *JAMA* points out, "Seeds are often stored for months or years under cool, dry conditions in which salmonellae are stable. During the three- to five-day sprouting process, numbers of salmonellae may increase by three to four orders of magnitude, decreasing little if at all during subsequent refrigeration."

In addition, the way that alfalfa sprouts are stored, distributed, and marketed poses a danger to the health of the user:

From farm to table, many opportunities exist for contamination of alfalfa seeds or sprouts. Crops can be easily contaminated with dirty water, runoff from adjacent farms, animal fertilizers used in previous growing seasons, or droppings from rodents or ruminants. The natural way that alfalfa sprouts are consumed at home or even in restaurants also adds to the danger. "Alfalfa sprouts are rarely washed or cooked before consumption, and consumers are left with little protection other than chance". The salmonella organism is believed to be present in seed crevices between cotyledon and testa and therefore is not amenable to chemical treatment. At present there is a "fundamental problem" in that the commercial "sprouting process contains no 'kill step' that would eliminate pathogens without compromising a seed's germination potential. Consequently, because of the difficulties in producing a "pathogen-free seed," warnings have been issued about the dangers of eating alfalfa and other sprouts.

The authors of the study conclude: "Alfalfa sprouts are a highrisk food for salmonellosis. All consumers, particularly those at greatest risk for severe disease (immunosuppressed, elderly and very young people), should consider this danger when deciding whether to eat alfalfa sprouts".

Proctor adds, "alfalfa sprouts contain 1.5 per cent by dry weight of canavine, a highly toxic substance". Not only is natural not necessarily better, food processing is an essential component of food safety. Says Garn, "Some cultivars are quite toxic, unless properly prepared".

ALTERNATIVE MEDICINE

Some of the most dangerous ingested products legally sold are found in health food stores. Herbal dietary supplements (including exotic oriental herbs) and amino acids pills have been causing health problems for some of their users. A chemical additive may or may not be inactive, but the herbs and amino acids are taken precisely because they are active and will alter a bodily function.

Most of them are untested and unregulated. To the extent that testing is done, there is a critical difference between the approach to herbal medicine and that of pharmaceuticals. Drugs are not permitted to be used until proven to be safe and effective, while the philosophy and practice of alternative medicine has operated on the "presumption that treatments are safe and effective unless proven otherwise".

Lacking is "the marshaling of rigorous evidence of safety and efficacy" necessary for approval of drugs and for publication in the "best peer-reviewed medical journals". One respected study has found that Americans are spending $27 billion a year on alternative treatments, which is close to their out of-pocket expenditures on modern medical treatment. Some herbs and treatments were found to be beneficial, but some were not. Investors have found the stocks of the firms manufacturing these dietary supplements and alternative medications to be attractive, indicating a belief that consumers will buy them, whether proved to be safe and effective or harmful.

Even for some herbs that have been used in low dosage for centuries, there are no studies on the impact of the mega doses that are often taken. The herbs and alternative medicine advocates have succeeded in blurring the line between food and drugs. Herbal extracts sold as food supplements are being added to packaged, canned, and frozen food products—called functional-foods—with labels that imply health benefits and have sufficient growth potential to have attracted some of the major food producers.

Some of the early advocates of alternative foods and medications, like Rodale Inc. and its publication, *Prevention,* recognize the danger in current patterns of use of herbs and dietary supplements. *Prevention's* national survey on the self-care movement reveals "158 million consumers use dietary supplements for their health and spend $8.5 billion each year." It reported that "widespread use of dietary supplements may cause public health problems". There were risks mixing dietary supplements with prescription drugs and treating oneself without a doctor's supervision. The survey estimated that "11.9 million customers have experienced adverse reactions from using herbal remedies and 6.5 million have had problems of this kind when using specialty supplements".

The problems with various herbs are legion, including lack of long-term studies and of any kind of control of dosage intake. Since many who use alternative medical treatment are also taking prescription drugs under the care of medical doctors, there may be substantial health risks, including death, in combining these with herbs and other alternative medications and stopping the use of some herbs after one had been taking them.

Serious problems have emerged from ingesting some of the most popular herbs, such as *Echinacea purpurea,* St. John's Wort, or Ginkgo Biloba. Probably the most serious harm can come from the interaction between herbs and prescription medicines. The increasing provision of these herbs by parents to their children is evident in the statistics of the American Association of Poison Control Centers.

One herbal remedy sometimes called ephedra, sometimes called ma huang, sometimes called pseudoephedrine, contains the chemical ephedrine, "a potent drug whether it is synthetically manufactured or produced naturally from a plant". Dr. Robin R. Caldwell says the drug is "chemically almost identical to amphetamine". Not only is ma huang sold in health food stores, it is a listed ingredient in many products sold at truck stops and elsewhere to help drivers stay awake. Pseudoephedrine is in various cold medicines that carry label warnings not to be used by anyone with high blood pressure, heart trouble, or liver problems.

Warnings have also been posted for Chinese herbal products containing aristolochia acid, which has been shown to cause cancer and kidney failure. Nearly one hundred women with kidney damage from Chinese herbs at a Belgian slimming clinic were studied, and several were found "in dire need of kidney transplants" and many of them were developing cancers in the kidney and bladder, years after taking the drug".

Those opposing any regulation of dietary supplements are involved in a contradiction that doesn't seem to bother them. These herbal and other dietary supplements are taken because they have some curative effect from an active ingredient or agent. Stated simply, "if it's strong enough to work, it's strong enough to hurt".

TECHNOLOGY AND LIFE EXPECTANCY

The presumed superiority of all things natural in food and other of life's necessities is the other side of the belief that the food supply in affluent societies is contaminated and is part of the larger, firmly held conviction that modern life is unsafe. One wonders, if contemporary life is so polluted, why are we living so long? Riley has argued that since we live longer and are older, we have more time at risk to ill health.

In fact, morbidity has fallen, along with mortality. We live longer, healthier lives. Among older Americans whom Riley deems to "have more time at risk to ill health," there has been a dramatic decline in chronic disability, according to the National Long Term Care Survey, as reported in a 1997 study by the National Academy of Sciences. "In the last decade alone, senior citizens have experienced a 25 per cent decline in the number of days of restricted activity due to illness". Improvement in the quality of life continues through the last year of life, even as we live longer.

In the workplace where safety has been largely ignored by environmentalists, the Centers for Disease Control and Prevention has found that "work-related deaths declined from 61 per 100,000 workers in 1913 to four per 100,000 workers in 1997" with a 50 per cent decline in the risk of a fatal or disabling accident from 1970 to 1990.

Contrary to Riley, one might argue that the factors contributing to longer life are part of the same cluster of factors that reduce morbidity, including chronic illness. Fogel and Costa argue cogently, and with massive data, that the epidemiology of chronic disease is not separate from that for contagious disease. Beginning in utero or infancy, inadequate nutrition can lead to a vast array (far too many to list here) of deleterious conditions that make the offspring more susceptible to contagious diseases, to chronic illness later in life, and to shorter life expectancy.

ADVANCES IN CHILDBEARING

Giving birth to a child is dangerous to child and mother. One demographic study for the Plymouth Colony in the seventeenth century concluded that one in every thirty childbirths resulted in maternal mortality, which was about 20 per cent of all female deaths. Add in the 25 per cent estimated death rate for infants and children (for both sexes), and the conclusion is that close to half—about 45 per cent assuming roughly equal infant and child death rates for the sexes—of all females died before completing fertility.

This was in a society where, the author found, the "records suggest a standard of life and health that would compare favorably with that of any preindustrial society today". Edward Shorter, in his controversial writing on the history of women's bodies, argued that virtually all women had some lifelong debilitating health problem resulting from giving birth to children. Given the high rates of maternal mortality, it is not unreasonable to assume that the debilitating injury rate was a multiple of at least five, putting the injury rate close to 100 per cent.

Recent studies would seem to indicate that giving birth to a child, even under favorable conditions, limits a woman's ability to make the required "investments in somatic maintenance" for longevity and thereby shortens her life expectancy. In earlier times, when nutrition levels were very much lower, and the disease experiences (both previous and current infections) of the expectant mother were much higher, it is very likely that there was organ damage to mother and child and that the mother's ability to make the "investments in somatic maintenance" for longevity were greatly diminished.

If having children, even under the most favorable conditions, is harmful to the mother, then an additional benefit of lower infant mortality is that it allows a woman to achieve her desired family size at a much lower health cost to her. This clearly reinforces the thesis of Fogel and Costa on the importance of adequate nutrition and protection from disease for the long-term health of both the mother and the child.

Fogel and Costa call their theory "technophysio evolution." They say, "The theory of technophysio evolution rests on the proposition that during the last 300 years, particularly during the last century, humans have gained an unprecedented degree of control over their environment". This control sets humans not only "apart from all other species, but also from all previous generations of *Homo sapiens.*" They add, "This new degree of control has enabled *Homo sapiens* to increase its average body size by over 50 per cent, to increase its average longevity by more than 100 per cent, and to improve greatly the robustness and capacity of vital organs".

The data on the decline in maternal mortality in developed countries (and to some extent for developing countries) in the twentieth century are every bit as dramatic as the declines in infant mortality and increase in life expectancy during this same time period. The 1998 World Health Organization report confirms that the global trend toward longer and healthier lives continues, though concern is raised for the gap in life expectancy and good health between the rich and the very poor. WHO is now talking about "health expectancy" being as important an indicator of human well-being as life expectancy.

LIFE EXPECTANCY

Many of the news articles on the global increase in life expectancy discuss the problems created by this increase and the social and economic changes necessary to accommodate it. The age at which people retire, the funding of retirement and medical care systems, and the need for education and training for second careers are all issues (or problems), among many others, that will need to be addressed.

In many cases they are already issues under serious discussion in economically advanced countries. The character of these systems will differ in the world in 2050, when one-fifth of the global population will be over sixty-five, from those few that existed at the beginning of the twentieth century when the first social security systems began and less than 1 per cent of the world's population was over sixty-five.

Though the numbers differ from country to country, the magnitude of the change for most individual countries will be roughly comparable. Technological progress does not offer the promise of a problem-free utopia, but it does offer a never-ending stream of challenges with the ever-present possibility of continuing human betterment.

WATER AND PUBLIC HEALTH

Humanity did not regularly drink hygienically clean water until the advent of purification processes, which included adding chemicals, in the early twentieth century. The late eighteenth and early nineteenth centuries brought developments in basic science, which allowed us to understand respiration and statistics that laid the foundations for quantitative medicine. Lavoisier's work led to the "secularization and demystification of water by analyzing it and showing that it could be broken down into hydrogen and oxygen".

In the middle of the nineteenth century, the physician John Snow identified the water from one well as the source for an outbreak of cholera, followed by Louis Pasteur's recognition of the microbial origin of many diseases, some of which were waterborne. Water could be visually clean or ritually clean, but with this new knowledge and chemical intervention, we could have hygienically clean water. In short, "water became an industrial product".

Chlorination of water in the United States began in the early part of the twentieth century and very quickly "produced dramatic reductions in morbidity and mortality associated with waterborne disease, such as typhoid, cholera, amoebic dysentery, bacterial gastroenteritis, and giardiasis." Chlorinating contaminated drinking water stopped a potential typhoid epidemic in Chicago in 1908.

The introduction of drinking water disinfection in the United States is credited with reducing the incidence of cholera by 90 per cent, typhoid and leptospirosis by 80 per cent, and amoebic dysentery by 50 per cent. A chlorinated lime solution was used as an antiseptic in hospitals in the nineteenth century. Prior to chlorination of water, diarrhea and enteritis were the third leading cause of death in the United States.

Despite the fact that millions of lives have been saved by the use of chlorine for disinfection of water, there are some who would ban its further use, even though the evidence for its danger is meager. Chlorination of water is one of the triumphs of the twentieth century, but many people in the world have yet to experience its benefit. The best estimates are that 80 per cent of all diseases and more than one-third of deaths in developing countries are caused by drinking or cooking with contaminated water. About twenty-five thousand children die each day from waterborne diseases.

The concerns expressed about the use of chlorine are for the chlorine compounds that emerge in combination with other chemicals in the water. For any other chemical used instead of chlorine, we would have to be concerned with its toxicity *and* with the toxicity of every possible compound that it might form in the effluent from our water system. The environmentalist precautionary principle would simply rule against any substitute, particularly when set against the nearly century-long safe, effective use of chlorine.

Because of U.S. risk assessments claiming that chlorine is a carcinogen, Peru stopped chlorinating its drinking water in 1991. What followed was the "largest outbreak of cholera in recent history, which killed nearly 7,000 people and afflicted over 800,000 more". Regulators, "influenced by the public's present tendency toward chemophobia," at times fail to weigh risks and benefits adequately. An outbreak of *E. coli* O157:H7 occurred in one community in the United States where the spring water used in the public water system was not chlorinated. In response to the outbreak of *E. coli* O157:H7, the community began chlorinating its water supply. Even with seemingly adequate chlorine levels, an indoor swimming pool complex with "extensive water spray features disseminated pathogenic bioaerosols," causing serious lung infections among its young, healthy lifeguards. Among corrective steps taken was the "provision of free residual chlorine in pool water from chlorine gas".

In a study in Britain covering the years 1937 to 1986, "defective chlorination" was blamed in eight out of ten outbreaks of disease from public water supplies and in all thirteen outbreaks in private supplies. Costs of not using a technology are often not considered. The cure for not using a technology is to use more technology and use it more intelligently.

BOTTLED WATER AND TAP WATER

In Houston, people are buying bottled water, which is from the same source—the municipal water supply—that they can draw safely from their own tap more conveniently, at far less cost, and without a plastic bottle that will eventually be discarded and add to environmental pollution. The municipal water supply as the source for the water is clearly printed on the labels of the bottles.

"In fact, 25 per cent of all bottled water is tap water drawn from city water treatment plants, according to Bob Brady of the International Bottled Water Association," though the bottler may do things to the water after it is drawn. An estimate by the American Waterworks Association finds that as many as 50 per cent of bottled water manufacturers in the United States obtain their water from municipal water departments. "This is the stupid thing. They buy water from the municipality for about 40 cents for 1,000 litres, they filter it two or three times, then they sell it at 2,000 times that price".

Much of the bottled water that is not from the local municipal water supply is drawn from aquifers in rural areas. In the United States, where the legal principle of "right of capture" prevails, a major bottling company can come in, drill a few wells, and draw vast quantities of water. In Texas, there have been charges (and denials) that companies are drawing down the aquifers, causing the existing wells of local inhabitants to go dry. The most important factor behind the extraordinarily rapid growth of the bottled water industry is the public perception that bottled water is cleaner and safer and tastes better than tap water. A study of the bacterial content of bottled water by the University of Mississippi questioned whether it is better than most municipal tap water.

Fluoride

In the United States, the average cost of tap water is one cent ($0.01) for five gallons. One very important difference is that tap water is regulated for its safety; bottled water is not. In addition, most bottled water lacks chemical additives such as fluoride (only about twenty brands out of more than five hundred in the United States have it), which has contributed to improved dental hygiene. Alternative, more expensive fluoride sources are, according to the American Dental Association, "not an effective or prudent public health practice."

Even the International Bottled Water Association "recommends customers talk to their dentist or doctor about supplements if they are concerned about fluoride deficiency". Those who are improving their drinking water by using various purifiers and filters may be removing fluoride by using distillers or reverse-osmosis units. Speaking for the American Dental Association, Dr. Michael Easley states that he is "concerned about people who are relying on bottled water. They're not getting enough fluoride and may not realize that they are depriving their children, who will pay the price their entire lives".

Easley points out, "At an average cost of 54 cents per person, per year, the cost of a lifetime of fluoridation for an individual is less than the cost of one small dental filling" and results in "more than $80 in avoided dental-treatment costs" per dollar spent on fluoridation. Recent surveys in the United States indicate that 55 per cent of children between the ages of five and seventeen have no tooth decay in their permanent teeth.

Fluoridation of water is also beneficial for adults and older people. There is less tooth decay and bone loss for older people who live in communities that fluoridate their water. Some firms are marketing bottled water with fluoride added, while one health professional is recommending that parents who continue to use bottled water should consider the need for prescription fluoride as it is unlikely that fluoridated toothpastes will provide enough fluoride to maximize protection. All of which is complicated compared to just drinking tap water.

At the rate of 86.5 gallons of public water per person per day, Americans use tap water for drinking, cooking, washing dishes and clothes, bathing, carrying waste, watering lawns and gardens, and many other uses. With rare exceptions, the water emanating from public water departments is of the highest quality, having been subjected to 150 to 200 scientific quality tests, and would be the envy of our ancestors prior to the twentieth century, or of the hundreds of millions of people in the world today without access to clean water, or any reliable water source, clean or otherwise.

RECEIVING OF FOOD

PRODUCT QUALITY

When food products are delivered to an establishment, it is the responsibility of the person in charge to ensure that every food item is inspected for general cleanliness, condition of containers, and any signs of temperature abuse.

BOXES AND CONTAINERS

Check that the packages of the food products are intact and not leaking. If a container is broken open, crushed, torn, or otherwise damaged, the contents may have been exposed to possible contamination. It is also important to look for signs of contamination by rodents, insects, or birds. If any of the items are observed during a receiving process, it is vitally important to reject the product.

CROSS-CONTAMINATION

During deliveries the potential of crosscontamination is high. Watch to ensure that containers or cartons filled with raw foods, such as meats, poultry, or fresh produce are not stacked on top of each other or located in a manner that leaking product from one container can contaminate food in another container.

CANNED PRODUCTS

When receiving canned products always inspect them for the following potential problems:

- Severe dents on the top or bottom rim, or side seam.
- Swollen or bulging cans.
- Rusted cans with pitted surfaces

TEMPERATURES UPON RECEIVING

All cold potentially hazardous food must be received at or below 41°F. Some exceptions include milk, shelled eggs, and live molluscan shellfish. All frozen food product must be frozen when received. All hot potentially hazardous foods must be at a temperature of 140°F or higher.

STORING AND ISSUING FOOD

Food storage is both a traditional domestic skill and is important industrially. Food is stored by almost every human society and by many animals.

Storing of food has several main purposes:

- Preparation for periods of scarcity or famine
- Taking advantage of short term surplus of food as at harvest time
- Enabling a better balanced diet throughout the year
- Preparing for special events and celebrations
- Planning for catastrophe or emergency
- Religious reasons
- Protection against predators or others

DOMESTIC FOOD STORAGE

Grain

Grain is stored in rigid sealed containers to prevent ingress of moisture or attack by vermin. For domestic quantities metal cans are used.

Storage in grain sacks is not effective. Mold and pests destroy a 25 kg cloth sack of grain in a year — even if stored off the ground in a dry area. On the ground or damp concrete, the time is as little as three days, and the grain might have to be dried before it can be milled. Food stored under unsuitable conditions should not be purchased or used because of risk of spoilage. To test whether grain is still good, sprout some. If it sprouts, it is still good, but if not, it should not be eaten. It may take up to a week for grains to sprout. When in doubt, throw it out.

Meat

Unpreserved meat has only a relatively short life in storage. Pork should be eaten within one day but beef and venison improve with up to 5 days storage in a cold room. Dry aging techniques are sometimes used to tenderize specialty gourmet meats by hanging them in carefully controlled environments for up to 21 days. Semi-dried meats like salamis and country style hams are processed first with salt, smoke, sugar, or acid, or other "cures" then hung in cool dry storage for extended periods, sometimes exceeding a year.

Fish and Shellfish

It is unsafe to store fish or shellfish without preservation. Fresh shellfish and whitefish should be eaten within a few hours of harvesting.

Use of Stored Food

Guidance for surviving emergency conditions in many parts of the world recommends maintaining a store of essential foods; typically water, cereals, oil, dried milk, and protein rich foods such as beans, lentils, tinned fish and meat. A basic food storage calculator can be used to help determine how much of these staple foods a person would need to store in order to sustain life for one full year. In addition to storing the basic food items many people choose to supplement their food storage with frozen or preserved garden-grown fruits and vegetables and freeze-dried or canned produce. An unvarying diet of staples prepared in the same way can cause appetite exhaustion.

An additional benefit to having a basic supply of food storage in the home is for the cost savings. Costs of dry bulk foods are often considerably less than convenience and fresh foods purchased at local markets or supermarkets.

Food Storage Rotation

If good food storage guidelines are followed, using and replenishing your food storage should become a commonplace, everyday activity, as normal as preparing meals. Although it does require an initial investment to stock a pantry, eventually it becomes the most economical and convenient way to live. Instead of going to the store when you need something and paying full price for it, you can go to your storage room or pantry to get what you need. Then you replace it next time it is on sale. The best way to rotate your food storage is to prepare meals with it on a daily basis. Of course, that means that you should store what your family will eat. It is wasteful to store products that your family won't eat or that can't be used in your favourite recipes.

COMMERCIAL FOOD STORAGE

Grain and beans are stored in tall grain elevators, almost always at a rail head near the point of production. The grain is shipped to a final user in hopper cars. In the former Soviet Union, where harvest was poorly controlled, grain was often irradiated at the point of production to suppress mold and insects. In the U.S., threshing and drying is performed in the field, and transport is nearly sterile and in large containers that effectively suppress pest access, so irradiation is not required. At any given time, the U.S. usually has about two weeks of stored grains.

Fresh fruits and vegetables are either packed in plastic cups in cardboard boxes for fresh premium markets, or placed in large plastic tubs for sauce and soup processors. Fruits and vegetables are usually refrigerated at the earliest possible moment, and even so have a shelf life of two weeks or less.

There is a thriving but small market in bulk vegetables and convenience foods for campers. In the USA meat animals are usually transported live, slaughtered at a major distribution point, hung and transported for two days to a week in refrigerated rail cars, and then butchered and sold locally. Before refrigerated rail cars, meat had to be transported live, and this placed its cost so high that only farmers and the wealthy could afford it every day. In Europe much meat is transported live and slaughtered close to the point of sale. In much of Africa and Asia most meat is for local populations is reared, slaughtered and eaten locally which is believed to be much less stressful for the animals involved and requires very little meat storage capacity. In Australia and New Zealand where a large proportion of meat production is for export meat is stored in very large freezer plants before being shipped overseas in freezer ships.

STOCKTAKING OF FOOD

Stocktaking.ie is a Galway Based Food and Beverage Control Consultancy which was established in 2004 to meet the growing need for a scientific and dedicated approach to controlling costs in the hospitality sector.Since their launch, Stocktaking.ie has grown in response to the needs of it's clients, introducing new services and increasing its staff to ensure a complete outsourced food and beverage control service is available.

FOOD AND BEVERAGE STOCKTAKING

Using the latest handheld barcode technology, a food and beverage stocktake can now be undertaken to the most accurate level possible with Spririts weighed to the nearest millilitre, Draught Beer to the nearest Pint and

Food to the nearest gram. This approach has allowed us to identify precise variances and areas of concerns as they occur and have allowed us to introduce enhanced and more efficient procedures in a number of premises to reduce the stock loss and increase cost efficiency. Dedicated Bar and Kitchen Stocktakers are assigned to your premises and you will always deal with the same stocktaker as they will be the most familiar with your premises.

FOOD AND BEVERAGE CONTROL AUDIT

We believe that to truly understand how to reduce costs and increase profitability in your business, you need to have all relevant information to hand to make the most informed decisions. Using experienced industry professionals to analyse each aspect in your Food and Beverage operation allows for an objective view or snapshot of your procedural effectiveness as well as identifying potential loopholes where theft, fraud or abuse of position can occur.

The Stocktaking.ie Audit will analyse the following areas over an agreed period of time which varies from property to property however 2 days is sufficient for an average bar or restaurant:

- Forecasting
- Ordering
- Receiving
- Storage
- Preparation
- Cooking
- Service
- Stocktaking
- Cash Handling
- Food and Beverage Costings
- Labour Cost Analysis

This audit allows for management to set targets based on current and projected performance and targets, while simultaneously identifying areas requiring staff training and focus.

2

The Institutional Management

THE HOTEL DEVELOPMENT PROCESS

The ability to add value and to create a sustainable hotel project ultimately starts from the first brush on paper and opportunities for this are all the way through to the final touch of paint on the finished product.

The crisis has had a huge impact on all real estate development, including hotels. But due to the gap between hotel supply and demand across the country there remains great opportunities for hotel projects.

Hotels are typically more complex to develop compared with other asset classes, as their design is tailored to the brand operating the business.

The design of these can also have an impact on the overall profitability of the hotel operation, as design deficiencies affect the operation of a hotel and ultimately have a negative impact on the bottom line — and hence asset value.

In order to reduce the risk of developing a hotel, which may not be commercially successful, it is important to seek advice from a hospitality consultant, who will ultimately act as the commercial conscience of the developer. At the start of the development, prior to building and design stage, the most important question to answer is "is the project viable?" Demand and supply factors for the hotel project need to be identified in order to understand the dynamics of the future operation — to basically understand who will be the target audience for the hotel and build for that. A developer needs to have an understanding of the estimated cash-flow income of the future operation from the opening day of the hotel. This will then provide any potential investor with a comfort level that debt can be serviced from the operation.

When hotels are part of a wider scheme, the design and development of the hotel needs to be in line with the overall development vision of the scheme. In a resort environment, it is important to understand the relationship between hotel, golf, spa, residential and other facilities, and in an urban mixed-use scheme. The hotel will, more often than not, be managed by a professional hotel operator. It is always of benefit to ask a consultant to run a competitive tender processes (be it tailored or to the wider market) when looking for a hotel company to manage your property, as this provides the opportunity to drive the process in order to achieve the best commercial deal terms available in the market. These contracts typically run for 15-25 years and key terms agreed at the beginning will have a major impact going forward.

Hotels are particularly sensitive to market changes, economic downturns and to alterations in supply and demand — for example when competitive hotels open up next to your own hotel this can severely impact performance. It is better to have all advice and information prior to decisions being taken on concept, design, architecture style, number of rooms, size of facilities, star classification and so on — to avoid the need to either redo all the aforesaid or to face the possibility of building a hotel which no operator wants to manage or which will not be commercially viable.

THE LEARNING CONCEPT OF THE HOTEL

The potential benefits of a branded customer experience to the organization are seen in the kinds of measures that directly influences, profits and shareholder value, such as higher margins and increased share of spend. If a $1 billion enterprise increases its investment in customer interactions from average to high, it can anticipate a $42 million return on the investment, according to a study by Accenture and Montgomery Research.

Today, however, an increasing number of hotel owners and operators are discovering the value in promoting their environmentally friendly guest rooms as EcoRooms. What exactly is an EcoRoom? An EcoRoom is a guestroom that includes at least a dozen products that are energy efficient, water efficient, waste reducing, non-toxic and/or biodegradable. Moreover, the P/E ratios of most companies with above average customer loyalty index scores are more than double that of their competitors. Some of W. Edwards Deming's 14 points counseling companywide continuous learning include: —Improve constantly and forever every process for planning production and service, —Institute training on the job, and —Institute a vigorous programme of education and self-improvement for everyone.

In 1990, Peter Senge put forth the case for continuous learning as a means for staff to perform their jobs better, solve problems, deal with process issues, face and counter threats, and capitalize on opportunities. As Karl Albrecht has said, "the tremendous diversification of work, and the fact that more and more jobs involve using knowledge and skill to create value rather then just following pre-programmemed tasks, means that managers must devote much more attention to the way people work, and, reluctantly in many cases, to the way they think and feel." In his 1993 book, *Post-Capitalist Society*, Peter Drucker said: "The basic economic resource—'the means of production' to use the economist's term—is no longer capital, nor natural resources (the economist's 'land') nor labour. It is and will be knowledge."

Corning, Inc., for one, believes in the value of knowledge. Between job and classroom, all employees must spend at least 5 per cent of their worktime training. Tracked by management on a business unit basis, employees now average over 90 hours of training each year. At the heart of this customer experience is a brand promise that goes far beyond product or service attributes to a total relationship that creates an emotional connection.

The goal is to have marketing bring in customers with promises that the rest of the organization – most importantly those employees who interact with customers – can keep. I say "most importantly" because employees are the brand ambassadors who most directly influence customers' impressions. Consumers rate people as the most important determinant of customer loyalty to brands, according to a survey by The Gallup Organization. They also rate customer service as one of the most important factors influencing an excellent customer experience, exceeded only by actions a company takes in response to a problem or request, according to a survey by The Forum Corp.

Within the learning company, every employee is a knowledge worker. Every employee is involved with the business. Every employee is trained and motivated, can work in teams, can be flexible and innovative. Every employee supports the overriding goal of generating optimal customer loyalty. These are core competencies, the skills by which a company seeks opportunities and solves problems. This even extends to leaders who need high-involvement skills with customers and customer support processes so that they are not shielded from reality.

The company, as a process, acts to facilitate the learning and experience of each employee, and the employees, as a process, help to develop and facilitate change, adaptation, and even transformation. Peter Bonfield, CEO of British-based ICL, has used the term *resiliance* to describe the learning company. It is able to transfer intelligence throughout the organization, adjust direction as needed, and take advantage of opportunities presented. He concludes:

It is absolutely imperative that our people are able to respond and react in an innovative and entrepreneurial way. We have to recruit the best, nurture them and then let them create new opportunities for themselves and for ICL.

The more we focused on the customer, the more we realized that we had to become a fully open company.... Because we are open, we are able to embrace new concepts swiftly and efficiently. By developing our people to think in an open way they are much more flexible and responsive to change. They embrace change willingly so that they can meet the challenges which come with openness.

The company, as well as individual employees, builds its collective skill level by proactively embracing, creating and responding to change, and by what James Higgins terms *knowledge management*. "This means identifying knowledge resources, creating new knowledge, and disseminating knowledge throughout the organization. It also means taking the tacit knowledge of each employee about how to do his or her job and turning it into explicit knowledge that others may use."

In the learning organization, there is a strong interrelationship between individual, group, and company skills.

Not only are skills created with enthusiasm and learning gathered from multiple sources, but skills and insight are transferred quickly and effectively throughout the company. Involved employees throughout the company develop a knowledge and breadth of understanding about processes and relationships. Learning becomes an everyday fact of life, part of the overall process of work. Employees are cross-trained, function in cells or flow lines—natural teams—and can easily train one another or trade job functions.

As discussed, where learning on behalf of customer loyalty is a focus, organizational boundaries blur. In most companies, systems analysts, engineers, secretaries—and on—and on—are stuck in their jobs, pigeonholed throughout their careers. Their potential benefit, and their benefit to customers, is stunted. In learning organizations, flexibility is featured. Sales people can move to customer service, customer service to credit, credit to sales, production to information systems. Motivated staff members get to pursue career interests, their jobs are kept interesting and challenging, and they are inspired to generate novel, useful ideas.

Companies interested in basic and advanced skills enhancement must provide formal training for everyone. The training needs to be continuous, since changes in technology, management theory, and work processes are ever-changing. State, federal, and municipal governments, plus colleges and universities, offer assistance programmes and training. Training is available from professional organizations offering a broad spectrum of instruction, from Total Quality and customer service to computer software and machine maintenance. Large companies—such as IBM, McDonald's, Milliken, General Electric, and Motorola—have their own training "institutes."

Rosenbluth International's training programme is called Learning Frontiers, which provides instruction on culture and service. The programme is so successful, it has become a line of business for Rosenbluth. "Training provides a more proficient work force, improves quality, and cements loyalty. We attribute much of our success to our training Philosophy and programmes. We believe that our approach to learning magnifies the contributions of our people, makes our business more profitable, and helps us achieve our goals."

Some of this company—sponsored training, at least in the United States, is a response to the level of workforce competency created by the education system. A 1991 report by the federal government called SCANS (Secretary's Commission on Achieving Necessary Skills) concluded: The message to us was universal: good jobs will increasingly depend on people who can put knowledge to work. What we found was disturbing: more than half our young people leave school without the knowledge or foundation required to find and hold a good job.

The SCANS report identified a three-part foundation set of skills and qualities and defined five areas of competence. While it could be argued that the report places too much responsibility on the education system, nonetheless it does reflect evolving needs of business. As noted by quality expert Philip B. Crosby: "Today, we are in a business world where perhaps 80 percent of current jobs did not exist fifteen years ago. They probably cannot be completely learned in school and are probably not taught there.... So the individuals have to keep going back to learning in order to retain mastery of their trade."

Companies must first have individuals who want to learn, and this is where human resources departments can be of real assistance. Their role in screening and hiring, support and management of training programmes, and even selection and consultation with individuals for specific training activities is very important. They also help assure that learning takes place within a strategic context, that is within and for the goals of the organization. In addition to problem-solving skills, which can be tactical and limiting (and focused on deficiencies), learning should be appreciative. That is, it is an expressive inquiry that envisions possibilities, capitalizing on those things the company does well.

Group learning and collaborative learning (such as W. L. Gore's one-on-one mentoring programme), as well as training for individuals, takes on greater meaning as companies utilize greater networking, cross-functionality, and teamwork. In addition to conceptual and task training, individuals must have interpersonal and interactive skills. Task-oriented group learning enables individuals to acquire new capabilities while broadening group process exposure.

Tom Peters' alternative term and concept for the learning organization is "knowledge management structure," or KMS for short. To roughly paraphrase and interpret his approach, Peters sees the value of knowledge and learning as much, or more, from the relationships established as a product of the creation of employees' experience, information, and insight as from their expertise. This translates, in part, to more networks and teams and fewer bureaucracies. KMS creates and identifies internal experts; uses their knowledge; packages, systematizes, and distributes the information they and others create; and supports the network structure and culture required to keep it flowing through teamwork, training, and purposeful cross-group sharing. He summarizes the four key areas of learning process:

Systematic knowledge capture and dissemination— Some of this is related to the customer information system (or more broadly applied management information system). Does the company have a system and structure for obtaining, storing, and using information, knowledge, and insight? As Jan Carlzon, chairman of Scandinavian Airline Systems has said: "A person who hasn't got information cannot take responsibility. A person who's got information cannot escape from taking responsibility.

Learning with clients (customers)— Beyond the traditional and routine approaches to qualitative and quantitative research, does the company—like Weyerhauser, Levi Strauss, or John Deere—create continuous learning and interchange opportunities with customers?

Learning from outsiders— Using the resources of the community (academic), consultants, and professional trainers.

Learning from each other— How well does the company create knowledge within and pass it from individual to individual, group to group, department to department, and division to division?

The formula, then, for companies seeking employee skills that are customer-driven and commitment-based is straightforward: train, develop, involve, and recognize.

SKILLS AND CAPABILITIES

Mobil Oil conducted market research among over 2,000 motorists and found that only 20per cent buy strictly on price. Those price shoppers spend only $700 annually at service stations; however, most buyers, while desirous of competitive pricing, wanted things like more human contact, quick service, and attendants who recognize them. After benchmarking service-oriented companies like Ritz-Carlton Hotels and Nordstrom department stores, Mobil introduced their new strategic concept, called Friendly Serve. Friendly Serve attendants are now at many Mobil stations (as many as 85per cent of Mobil's dealers will eventually be in the programme). They have been specially trained to be customer proactive—pumping gas, cleaning windshields, and getting coffee for customers.

The concept also includes better lighting and cleaner facilities; but, having service-oriented attendants, alone, has increased sales at many service stations by 15 to 20per cent.Companies achieve competitive advantage principally when their customers perceive a value in them higher than other companies. Achieving competitive advantage is the responsibility of the entire company and every individual in it. This means that, not only does the company have to be (at least) current on its knowledge of customer perceptions and be perceived as unique, it must also demonstrate capabilities and skills individually reflective of that uniqueness by staff members and by the overall organization.

Finally, and of greatest importance, these capabilities must be perceived by customers as creating value. In *Competing for the Future*, Gary Hamel and C. K. Prahalad identify core competencies as a company-wide bundling of skills and technologies. They have hypothesized that, to be a core competency, a skill must meet three tests.

Customer Value— if the customer does not derive specific benefit from a skill, it cannot be considered a competence. For example, Motorola's rapid and customized production cycle time is perceived by customers as value, so the collection of skills required to provide it are a competency.

Competitive Differentiation— L.L. Bean's and Nordstrom's service skills make them competitively unique when compared to other companies. Their customer service goes well beyond the basics, and they are always seeking new ways to improve. Mobil's advertising emphasizes the personal service available at its service stations, differentiating itself from competition.

Extendibility— Does the company have strategic flexibility, the skills necessary to move into new or related market opportunities? Several of the major auto manufacturers, or instances, have worked for years on battery powered cars so they would have a marketable product at the appropriate time. Other less flexible companies, notably in high tech industries, have gone the way of buggy whip manufacturers, unable to extend their competencies as mar kets or customer needs evolved. Apple, for example has receded to only a few areas of application advantage, while Microsoft continues its impressive growth.

These competencies very much the SOCAP/Maritz study finding first discussed in the Introduction. To generate optimum customer loyalty for the company, employee skills must be aligned with customer needs, problems, expectations, and complaints.

Competencies are transferred to strengthen positions with customers. They are acquired to protect or extend franchises in existing markets, as QVC Network has done to broaden its attractiveness to at-home shoppers and as MBNA has done to offer superior credit card service. Kodak has done it to compete in the digital photography business. Competencies, with equal fortitude, may need to be excised if they become obsolete or off-strategy for customer need alignment. Organizational capability can be expressed in terms of strategy, economic or technical strength, structure, or leadership approaches; however, the most visible demonstration to customers is through staff interface and other areas of direct performance. Several skill sets are required: responsiveness, relationship building, management and human resource practices, flexibility (including the ability to learn flexibly—individuals, in teams or projects, cross-training, on-the-job or in classroom settings), and the capacity for change. This begins during the hiring process. Customer sensitive people are self-responsive, capable of independent thought and achievement, able to overcome setbacks, and non-blaming. They are people with goals and ambition, with positive self-esteem. To use a term by now familiar, they are empowered—or can easily adapt to an empowered culture.

Many service-based companies—financial services, healthcare, foodservice, lodging, car rental—have determined that the capability of their organizations has been defined by staff responsiveness. Customers infer that the company is or is not responsive, and thus worthy of loyalty, based on performance during transactions. Responsiveness is also based on the level of cooperation, communication, and support employees exhibit for each other. Responsiveness may be tangible (time, completeness) or intangible (feelings). By extension, it may be proactive as well as reactive.

Relationships are influenced by collective and individual skill levels. When customers have had long-term relationships with companies, they often come to depend on and expect certain skill levels and positive attitudes from their contacts. If that contact is lost—retirement, downsizing, firing, changing jobs, and so forth—it may be very difficult to sustain the image and loyalty. Managers must use the right tools, or levers, to influence inside and outside customers. The tools are used to *create* competencies within organizations by hiring and training. They *reinforce* competencies through evaluation, reward, and recognition. Finally, they *sustain* competencies through organizational design and methods of communication. Change is coming at companies from many directions—environmental and regulatory influences, workforce availability and mindset, new approaches to organizational architecture—to identify just a few. The most significant changes, however, are those created by everchanging customer needs and requirements. Skill level is also judged by how well leaders and their companies anticipate and facilitate change. Saturn is an example of a company that has created the skills and capabilities necessary to generate customer-perceived value. Although General Motors invested huge sums of money to create cutting-edge engineering and manufacturing technologies, it was ultimately the direct performance skill sets that made the venture work.

First, General Motors worked closely with the auto unions to select employees with preexisting team and responsiveness competencies. While early car recalls showed some lingering hierarchical General Motors' culture weaknesses, the Saturn culture of training and customer focus has now been established. In *Win the Value Revolution*, Robert Tucker reviewed the skills development strategies of companies like Southwest Airlines, Levi Strauss, Home Depot, ServiceMaster, Rubbermaid, and Intel.

They all believe in cultures that generate customer value through people. Diversity, recognition, high morals and ethics, and empowerment are common themes. Tucker identified four key attributes of such companies:

1. *Establish a continuous value improvement process:* "Undertaking a value improvement programme begins by instructing your employees—even those who've never come into contact with one of your customers—to understand more about the overall business. Your team needs to know the impact of their work on the value perceptions of customers." At the Long Beach Medical Centre in California, new residents are admitted to the hospital under assumed names and with falsified symptoms. The idea is for them to experience, over a 24-hour period, hospital treatment from the perspective of patients. This creates a more patient-sensitive corps of residents.

2. Teach your employees how to "own their own employability" This includes identifying the added value that each employee, team, and department provides to the end customer, and also identifying the skill levels needed to provide that value.
3. Teach managers that serve internal customers how to add value. "Any department in a company that doesn't directly serve the external customer needs to reposition itself as a business within a business." This is particularly important for training and HRD managers, who must be proactive in helping staff develop change processes, diversity, productivity, and related skills—capabilities needed by an organization wishing to improve its level of value delivery to customers.
4. *Treat employees as customers:* New workforce issues—longer working hours, more single working parents, and the like—necessitate that firms look at employees as customers. As Rosenbluth International sees it, making employees more skillful and valuable equals more employee loyalty which equals more customer loyalty.

At companies like State Farm Insurance, for example, customer liaison and supervision staff may take on diversity assignments—such as learning about foreign cultures—and share the knowledge with associates. They might also, at the same time, take advanced computer skills training at the company's headquarters in Bloomington, Illinois, or via a live or video instruction programme. This type of learning achieves all four of Tucker's described attributes. It adds value for the employees and managers who, in turn, add value to internal and external customers.

Hewlett-Packard has taken much of its sales training out of the classroom and put it into the field, so that sales representatives can spend more time with customers. H-P frequently introduces new products and in the past it had to bring the sales force into conference centres to learn about them. This required up to three weeks a year, creating breaks in customer relationship continuity. Several years ago, the Hewlett-Packard Interactive Network (HPIN) was created, so that training was made available on line, to fit the sales representatives' schedules. 3M, following a practice, developed a totally customer-driven approach to individualized sales skills training. Called A.C.T. (for Assessment, Content, and Training), the process begins with debriefing customers on their perception of representatives' product knowledge, interpersonal skills, strategic capabilities, negotiating abilities, and teamwork.

Completed customer questionnaires form a summary report for each salesperson, and the salesperson designs his or her own training programme according to the biggest gap between perceived and desired performance. The salesperson also reviews the (grouped) results with customers, thereby reinforcing the relationship. Federal Express sales managers and sales representatives developed the Global Customer Learning Laboratory. Working with customers, they developed "Learning Partner" programmes for key accounts to develop new approaches for handling logistics issues.

Southwest Airlines' University for People recently introduced its "Mind the Gap" programme for the entire employee force of 22,000. "Mind the Gap" (the term comes from the London subway system, where announcements are made to passengers to be aware of the space between the platform and train when boarding) focuses on perceptual differences between Southwest employees and passengers, and how this impacts service and loyalty. Mistakes, in this programme, are viewed as positive learning opportunities.

CREATING STAFF VALUE TO CREATE VALUE FOR CUSTOMERS

Written in 1995, *Leadership and the Customer Revolution* by Gary Heil, Tom Parker, and Rick Tate is a virtual handbook for companies to help them create customer loyalty and value through the skills of their employees. The first step in skills development is constantly challenging existing action and thought. Whether a company is successful or not in keeping customers, processes and assumptions-like customer needs and expectations—must be frequently reviewed.

If we're vigilant in our efforts to question present practices and beliefs, if we bring in diverse opinions to push us outside our comfort zone and continually test the efficacy of our thinking, we may find it easier to devise a strategy without the stops and starts that have characterized so many improvement efforts in the past. Commitment requires understanding. Understanding requires learning, and learning requires persistent questioning.

Levels of performance are a direct result of present practices. This is particularly true in the skills needed to create value for customers. For example, are customer complaints actively sought and evaluated and do staff have the competency to generate complaints from otherwise silent customers? Or, are complaints considered an intrusion, something to be minimized? Are performance cycle times and causes of variation well understood, particularly from the customer's perspective? Heil, Parker, and Tate have developed a series of skill-related questions to help companies address customer-driven capability levels.

Among them are:

- Are recovery efforts fast and distinctive?
- Do they proactively search for potentially dissatisfied customers?
- Are customer efforts strategically planned?
- Is process effectiveness systematically evaluated and imposed?

More specifically, are employees trained and empowered to deviate from established procedures as needed? Does staff, from the file clerk to the chairman, have the ability to identify customer needs and problems—and are they rewarded for it? Do they have the ability to use information from customers to improve processes? Do they know how to create loyal customers? At Saint Barnabas Medical Centre, in Livingston, New Jersey, for example, the nursing staff hands out comment cards and, more importantly, calls every discharged patient to check on their experience. They also outreach to patients' families and conduct regular staff training to improve customer focus.

Several years ago, service quality educators and consultants Leonard Berry, Valarie Zelthaml, and A. Parasuraman conducted indepth research among senior executives in service corporations. They identified four gaps between the executives' perception of service delivery and the methods and tasks relating to that delivery to customers. One of these gaps was the executives' belief that their employees were unwilling or unable to meet customers' expectations.

Even when guidelines exist for performing services well and treating customers correctly, high-quality service performance is not a certainly. A service-performance gap is still likely due to a number of constraints (e.g., poorly qualified employees, inadequate internal systems to support contact personnel, insufficient capacity to serve). To be effective, service standards must not only reflect customers' expectations but also be backed up by adequate and appropriate resources (people, systems, technology).

Berry, Zeithaml, and Parasuraman identified seven factors that contribute to this gap, as well as methods to overcome them and create increased value for customers.

1. *Role ambiguity*— Employees are in conflict about providing service to customers. They need clarity from management about what is expected, training and skills to meet and exceed these expectations, customer requirements, and an understanding of how their performance will be assessed, recognized, and rewarded.

   Employees should he given updated technical training about the products and/or services offered by their company. Merck & Co., SmithKline and other pharmaceutical companies provide their detail staff and subcontractors with extensive classroom and on-thejob product and medical application instruction.

   Employees should be given customer sensitivity training to develop interpersonal skills for interacting with customers and understanding their needs and problems. This is particularly true in "high touch" businesses, such as finance, hospitality, travel, or healthcare where time and money are at issue.

   Airline food supplier Dobbs International Services conducted a performance perception study designed to show differences between Dobbs' front-line service staff and their customers, the airline attendants. They found that flight attendants rated performance lower than staff. This resulted in an extensive customer relations training programme for staff, a change in their title (from Drivers and Helpers to

Customer Service Reps and Assistants, and new uniforms, along with business cards). Also, they set up a mechanism to monitor and reward staff. As a result staff role perception was greatly improved.

Finally, management communication skills must be such that they can communicate their performance expectations as frequently as necessary. They must also obtain employee feedback about their level of understanding.

2. *Role conflict*— This occurs when employees, either due to lack of training or lack of direction from management, are unsure about their role with customers. For example, if an automobile manufacturer's customer support staff has been instructed to work only within black-and-white warranty definitions—even though this lack of flexibility may create owner disloyalty—this causes conflict. Further, if the same customer support staff has been instructed to cross-sell services or products to owners, even when it "feels" inappropriate, this also causes conflict. Management contributes to this by providing inadequate direction to staff; and they, themselves, may be undertrained with regard to understanding role conflict.

   Conflict also occurs when customers (internal or external) queue up too fast for employees to serve comfortably. Sometimes, first-in-first-out and paper shuffling takes precedence over the real customer priorities; but staff have not been given skills necessary to make these choices.

   Role conflict can be effectively eliminated through staff training: Defining service roles in terms of customer expectations, priority setting and time management, compensation based on performance quality delivery and customer loyalty.

3. *Employee-job fit*— When the match between employee skills and the level of customer delivery is poor, the company has to look seriously at its hiring and selection processes. Although controversial, this may even include assessing personality traits and characteristics.

4. *Technology-job fit*— If employees are not given the tools and training—such as updated computer language instruction—the customer loyalty impact can be as negative as poor employee-job fit.

   In addition to job-specific training and cross-training, truly commitment-based companies provide self-development and extended education opportunities as well as incentive compensation such as profit sharing. Some companies, like Levi Strauss, are offering groundbreaking long-range bonus/salary plus compensation levels to all employees who remain loyal to the company. "Competing effectively for first-rate service providers is essential to success in a service business. Companies that excel in service select and develop employees carefully, choose appropriate technology, and concentrate on the fit among employees, technology and jobs."

5. *Inappropriate supervisory control systems*— Related to fit are the company's evaluation and reward system. Skill sets are often developed and refined more to be self-fulfilling prophecies of management's evaluation systems, rather than customer's requirements.

   To be customer-driven, reward and recognition systems should be fully aligned with performance and customer loyalty. This circles back to the company's strategic motivation. When companies use behavioural and output standards for performance measurement, they must be consistent with customers' expectations. Companies such as British Airways, Publix Markets, and Federal Express provide such incentives and rewards—bonuses, profit sharing, and recognition—for outstanding service. Fort Sanders Health System, a managed care company, introduced a corporate-wide "gainsharing" programme to involve all staff in customer focus.

   "A vital ingredient for excellent service quality delivery is recognition of employees' performance. Employees' performance must be continually monitored, compared with service standards, and rewarded when outstanding. A performance measurement system sensitive to high performance and tied to appropriate rewards can be very motivating, especially when workers know that others will learn how well they are performing." This also extends to teambased rewards, when staff, as a group, create or add skills that bring value to customers and earn their loyalty.

6. *Lack of perceived control*— This is the limited amount of flexibility and authority employees feel they have in making decisions that involve customer needs or customer problems.

   If approval from other departments is required for a contact person to act, customer responsiveness, customer loyalty, and employee morale are all negatively impacted. Front line empowerment training, as well as decision-making authority, is important, because it serves both the company and the employee.

   The more proactive and responsive companies are with customers, and the more they eliminate standardized or rigid approaches for relating to them, the faster and better employees can develop their contact and problem-solving skills.

   Bowen-Scarff Ford's one-page employee manual encourages staff to do things their own way and use their best judgment. Eastman Chemical continually measures the level of staff empowerment and motivation. Jostens developed a process called ESM (Employee

Satisfaction/Motivation) which links individual and group instruction and their commitment to customers. Part of L.L. Bean's lore is the customer service person who hauled a replacement canoe over several states from their Maine headquarters so the customer would have it on time for a fishing trip.

7. *Lack of teamwork*— Do company management and staff, and cross-functional employee groups, perform as a team to create loyal customers?

   If employees have been trained to regard other employees as customers—recognizing that all functional areas have contributory roles in creating customer loyalty—and if employees are committed to the company as well as to customers, then there is basis for teamwork. Shell Oil Company, for one, has had extensive training for employees to improve teamwork in their relations with customers. USAA has developed an employee involvement programme called PRIDE, which creates an atmosphere of customer focus, employee empowerment, and team building. Corning has cross-functional account teams, as does Nabisco. Often, such teams mirror the account's sales structure. Teams provide support in logistics, accounting, and planning, in addition to sales and service.

"In organizations where teamwork exists, employees accomplish their goals by allowing group members to participate in decisions and to share in the group's success. Teamwork is the heart of service—quality initiatives—employees need to work together to have service come together for customers."

An example of a company that has addressed and overcome all seven of these service problems is the Ritz-Carlton Hotel Corporation. As previously discussed, front-line Ritz-Carlton staff is empowered to rectify guest problems with up to $2,000 per incident; however, they are trained to be proactive in customer relationships and service.Another example is Federal Express.

With over 90,000 employees moving 1.5 million packages per day through 170 countries, training and motivation are among its highest priorities.

They have a Survey Feedback Action (SFA) mechanism, begun over a decade ago. This research allows employees to express feelings about their training, management, pay, and benefits anonymously.

Everyone receives extensive training:

- Call centre agents receive six weeks of technical and interpersonal skills training.
- In addition to in-depth instruction, every six months couriers, service agents and other customer contact staff must participate in a job knowledge test.
- Each person receives a personalized evaluation targeting areas which require review or upgrades.

Federal Express has provided staff with decision-making authority and an array of pay-for-performance incentive and recognition programmes. The goal is to have a quality and customer loyalty focus in every area of performance. Federal Express has also established Service Assurance and Service Action teams to identify problem root causes (late shipments, damage, lost packages, etc.) at a local level.

Customer loyalty expert Jill Griffin has pinpointed three training and reinforcement basics for having a staff that is focused on customer retention:

- *Empowerment training*— Companies like Marriott are stressing staff awareness of lifetime, or long-term, guest value. This encourages proactive, loyalty building service behaviour.
- *Product/service knowledge*— One of the reasons for Infiniti customer retention success is that *all* dealer staff, including clerks and receptionists, attend their six-day product and customer service programme.
- *Staff retention*— More than compensation plans and motivational seminars, staff need the skills, rewards, and empowerment to build the business with their own ideas. "Your employees are just like your customers. Treat them with respect and allow them to make their own decisions and they will treat your customers in the same manner. But equally important, don't tolerate in employees a casual regard for loyalty."

Motorola could easily have been an example, for they have created a culture, or style, totally dedicated to the concept of quality. It is, however, the collective skill sets of employees that sustain the culture. Motorola could also have been a paradigm example for structure, because of their emphasis on teams, or systems, because they have a Customer/Market Driven Continuous Improvement model which is built on a sophisticated information system. But it is the skill sets that sustain the system.

Part of Motorola's corporate mission is that, in selected segments of the electronic industry, they will be successful by providing their worldwide customers with "what they want, when they want it, and with Six Sigma product quality." This translates to tolerating no more than 3.4 defects per million parts. Achieving that objective, they found, necessitates a highly skilled, well-motivated, well-rewarded work force.

A member of the Fortune 50, with over 100,000 employees, and winner of the Baldrige Award in 1988, Motorola produces, sells, and services a broad array of communication, component, computing, and control products. One fundamental objective is total customer support, a stated initiative which requires participative management within, and cooperation between, all elements of the organization.

They have made training and education a corporate strategy for building competitive advantage. All employees receive a minimum of five days of training a year, totalling several million hours annually. Their training investment is around 4per cent of payroll (exceeded only by General Electric and U.S. Robotics among major companies), or $150 million annually. Ongoing training has also created a common language and focus on continuous improvement throughout Motorola. One unique result of this learning culture is T.C.S., a corporatewide competition for problem-solving teams. The competition is open to any problem-solving team—functional, cross-functional, labour, sales, service, or administration. Teams may have shorter or longer duration projects of up to six months. Direct customer or supplier involvement on the teams is highly encouraged. Projects are selected by teams to focus on one of Motorola's corporate initiatives—participative management, quality, development time reduction, or profit improvement. The skills required are management, relationship building, goal-setting, monitoring of and analysis of progress. In addition, the winning teams are expected to be able to train and educate others to replicate, or improve, their achievements. And, they are recognized and rewarded for their contributions.

In the competition, points are awarded for how well projects are executed in several areas:

- Project selection criteria
- Teamwork/mutual support
- Analysis and recommendations
- Deployment, action, and results

The company created Motorola University, a corporate training organization for improving employee skills on a global basis. It has become the centrepiece for the company's rolling three-year training plan, in which most of the employees have individualized training programmes. Motorola University offers more than 600 courses in 14 locations around the world, and delivers more than 100,000 days of training each year to employees, suppliers, and customers. Some training is basic—math skills, remedial English, machinery maintenance—but much of it focuses on problem-solving, proactivity, critical thinking, group process, and relationship-building.

An outgrowth and extension of formal training programmes is what Motorola calls "embedded learning," on-the-job apprenticeship and mentoring. This is providing staff members with practical, experiencebased training.

Productivity per employee has risen by 139per cent as a result of problem-solving training. Motorola estimates that it has saved over $4 billion in productivity improvements through problem solving, and that each dollar invested in training returns $30 in productivity gains within three years. They are planning to provide each employee with 80 to 100 hours of training per year by the end of the decade—an annual investment of over $300 million.

HOSPITALITY SERVICE

The concept of Hospitality Services, also known as "accommodation sharing", "hospitality exchange", and "home stay networks", refers to centrally organized social networks of individuals who trade accommodation without monetary exchange. While this concept could also include house swapping or even time share plans, it has come to be associated mostly with travelers and tourists staying with one another free of charge. Since the 1990s, these services have increasingly moved away from using printed catalogs and phone trees to connect users towards Internet websites. These have grown exponentially since 2000 and today it is estimated that well over 100,000 people are registered users of these networks. These vary in operational structure, place different emphasis on graphical vs. textual formatting, and cater disproportionately to specific geographic regions.

HOTEL

A hotel is an establishment that provides paid lodging, usually on a short-term basis. Hotels often provide a number of additional guest services such as a restaurant, a swimming pool or childcare. Some hotels have conference services and meeting rooms and encourage groups to hold conventions and meetings at their location. Hotels differ from motels in that most motels have drive-up, exterior entrances to the rooms, while hotels tend to have interior entrances to the rooms, which may increase guests' safety and present a more upmarket image.

In Australia, a hotel may also be an establishment that serves alcoholic drinks, and usually meals in a casual setting but which does not necessarily provide accommodation. This type of establishment would more usually be called a pub or bar in other countries. In general use in Australia the terms '"hotel" and *pub* are usually taken to be synonymous. In India, the word may also refer to a restaurant since the best restaurants were always situated next to a good hotel.

The word *hotel* derives from the French *hôtel*, which referred to a French version of a townhouse, not a place offering accommodation (in contemporary usage, *hôtel* has the meaning of "hotel", and *hôtel particulier* is used for the old meaning). The French spelling (with the circumflex) was once also used in English, but is now rare. The circumflex replaces the 's' once preceding the 't' in the earlier *hostel* spelling, which over time received a new, but closely related meaning.

Basic accommodation of a room with only a bed, a cupboard, a small table and a washstand has largely been replaced by rooms with en-suite bathrooms and climate control. Other features found may be a telephone, an alarm clock, a TV, and broadband Internet connectivity. Food and drink may be supplied by a mini-bar (which often includes a small refrigerator) containing snacks and drinks (to be paid for on departure), and tea and coffee making facilities (cups, spoons, an electric kettle and sachets containing instant coffee, tea bags, sugar, and creamer or milk).

In the United Kingdom a hotel is required by law to serve food and drinks to all comers within certain stated hours; to avoid this requirement it is not uncommon to come across "private hotels" which are not subject to this requirement. However, in Japan the capsule hotel supplies minimal facilities and room space.

CLASSIFICATION

The cost and quality of hotels are usually indicative of the range and type of services available. Due to the enormous increase in tourism worldwide during the last decades of the 20th century, standards, especially those of smaller establishments, have improved considerably. For the sake of greater comparability, rating systems have been introduced, with the one to five stars classification being most common.

BOUTIQUE HOTELS

"Boutique Hotel" is a term originating in North America to describe intimate, usually luxurious or quirky hotel environments. Boutique hotels differentiate themselves from larger chain or branded hotels by providing an exceptional and personalized level of accommodation, services and facilities. Boutique hotels are furnished in a themed, stylish and/or aspirational manner. Although usually considerably smaller than a mainstream hotel (ranging from 3 to 100 guest rooms) boutique hotels are generally fitted with telephone and wi-fi Internet connections, honesty bars and often cable/pay TV. Guest services are attended to by 24 hour hotel staff. Many boutique hotels have on site dining facilities, and the majority offer bars and lounges which may also be open to the general public.

Of the total travel market a small percentage are discerning travelers, who place a high importance on privacy, luxury and service delivery. As this market is typically corporate travelers, the market segment is non-seasonal, high-yielding and repeat, and therefore one which boutique hotel operators target as their primary source of income.

FAMOUS HOTELS

Some hotels have gained their renown through tradition, by hosting significant events or persons, such as Schloss Cecilienhof in Potsdam, Germany, which derives its fame from the so-called Potsdam Conference of the World War II allies Winston Churchill, Harry Truman and Joseph Stalin in 1945. Other establishments have given name to a particular meal or beverage, as is the case with the Waldorf Astoria in New York City, USA, known for its *Waldorf*

Salad or the Raffles Hotel in Singapore, where the drink *Singapore Sling* was invented.

Another example is the Hotel Sacher in Vienna Austria, home of the *Sachertorte*. There are also hotels which became much more popular through films like the Grand Hotel Europe in Saint Petersburg, Russia when James Bond stayed there in the Blockbuster, Goldeneye. Cannes hotels such as the Carlton or the Martinez become the center of the world during Cannes Film Festival (France).

A number of hotels have entered the public consciousness through popular culture, such as the Ritz Hotel in London, UK ('Putting on The Ritz') and Hotel Chelsea in New York City, subject of a number of songs and also the scene of the alleged stabbing of Nancy Spungen by her boyfriend Sid Vicious. Hotels that enter folklore like these two are also often frequented by celebrities, as is the case both with the Ritz and the Chelsea.

Other famous hotels include the Beverly Hills Hotel, the Hotel Bel-Air and the Chateau Marmont, in California, Watergate complex in Washington DC, the Hotel Astoria in Saint Petersburg, Russia, the Hotel George V and Hôtel Ritz in Paris, Palazzo Versace hotel on the Gold Coast, Queensland, Australia, Hotel Hermitage and Hotel de Paris in Monaco (in the French Riviera) and Hotel Leningradskaya in Moscow.

UNUSUAL HOTELS

Many hotels can be considered destinations in themselves, by dent of unusual features of the lodging and/or its immediate environment:

TREEHOUSE HOTELS

Some hotels, such as the Costa Rica Tree House in the Gandoca-Manzanillo Wildlife Refuge, Costa Rica, or Treetops Hotel in Aberdare National Park, Kenya, are built with living trees as structural elements, making them treehouses. The Ariau Towers near Manaus, Brazil is in the middle of the Amazon, on the Rio Negro. Bill Gates even invested and had a suite built there with satellite internet/phone. Another hotel with treehouse units is Bayram's Tree Houses in Olympos, Turkey.

CAVE HOTELS

Desert Cave Hotel in Coober Pedy, South Australia and the Cuevas Pedro Antonio de Alarcón (named after the author) in Guadix, Spain, as well as several hotels in Cappadocia, Turkey, are notable for being built into natural cave formations, some with rooms underground.

CAPSULE HOTELS

Capsule hotels are a type of economical hotels that are quite common in Japan.

ICE HOTELS

Ice hotels, such as the Ice Hotel in Jukkasjärvi, Sweden, melt every spring and are rebuilt out of ice and snow each winter.

SNOW HOTELS

The Mammut Snow Hotel in Finland is located within the walls of the Kemi snow castle, which is the biggest in the world. It includes The Mammut Snow Hotel, The Castle Courtyard, The Snow Restaurant and a chapel for weddings, etc. Its furnishings and its decorations, such as sculptures, are made of snow and ice. Thgre is snow accommodation also in Lainio Snow Hotel in Lapland (near Ylläs), Finland.

GARDEN HOTELS

Garden hotels, famous for their gardens before they became hotels, includes Gravetye Manor, the home of William Robinson and Cliveden, designed by Charles Barry with a rose garden by Geoffrey Jellicoe.

UNDERWATER HOTELS

As of 2005, the only hotel with an underwater room that can be reached without Scuba diving is Utter Inn in Lake Mälaren, Sweden. It only has one room, however, and Jules' Undersea Lodge in Key Largo, Florida, which requires scuba diving, is not much bigger. Hydropolis is an ambitious project to build a luxury hotel in Dubai, UAE, with 220 suites, all on the bottom of the Persian Gulf, 20 meters (66 feet) below the surface. Its architecture will feature two domes that break the surface and an underwater train tunnel, all made of transparent materials such as glass and acrylic.

OTHER UNUSUAL HOTELS

The Library Hotel in New York City is unique in that its ten floors are arranged according to the Dewey Decimal System. The Rogers Centre, formerly SkyDome, in Toronto, Canada is the only stadium to have a hotel connected to it, with 70 rooms overlooking the field. The Burj al-Arab hotel in Dubai, United Arab Emirates, built on an artificial island, is structured in the shape of a sail of a boat.

WORLD-RECORD SETTING HOTELS

Tallest: The tallest hotel in the world is the Burj al-Arab in Dubai, United Arab Emirates at 321 meters (1,053 feet). However, this title may be taken by the less illustrious Ryugyong Hotel in Pyongyang at 330 meters (1,083 feet), pending its (perhaps unlikely) completion; it has been under construction since 1987 and was abandoned in 1992.

Largest: The current largest hotel in the world is First World Hotel[4] in Genting Highlands, Malaysia. It has a total of 6,118 rooms, and is part of the

Genting Highlands Resort and Casino. The First World Plaza which is adjoined to the two hotel towers boasts 500,000 square feet of indoor theme park, shopping centres, casino gaming areas, and eateries. Previously, the largest hotel in the world was the MGM Grand Las Vegas in Las Vegas, Nevada, USA with 5,044 rooms in the main building and a total of 6,276 rooms.

Oldest: According to the Guinness Book of World Records, the oldest hotel still in operation is the Hoshi Ryokan, in Awazu, Japan. It opened in 717 CE, and features hot springs.

HOTEL OCCUPATIONS

The owner, chairman, or CEO of a hotel or hotel group is known as a *hotelier*. The American billionaire Howard Hughes lived much of his life in hotels. He moved with his entourage from hotel to hotel and from Beverly Hills to Boston before deciding to move to Las Vegas and become a casino baron. Less than a month after his November 27, 1966 arrival, Hughes made a public offer to buy the Desert Inn.

The hotel's 8th floor became the nerve center of his empire and the 9th floor penthouse became Hughes's personal residence. Hughes moved to the Bahamas, Vancouver, London and several other locations — always taking up residence in the top floor penthouse of the hotel. Between 1966 and 1968, he also purchased several other hotel-casinos from the Mafia: Castaways, New Frontier, The Landmark Hotel and Casino, Sands and Silver Slipper.

Coco Chanel made the Hôtel Ritz in Paris her home for more than thirty years, until the day of her death, at 87, in a suite now named "Coco Chanel Suite". King Peter II of Yugoslavia spent much of the Second World War at Claridge's, a hotel in London. His son, Aleksandar Karaðorðeviæ, was born in the hotel. Prince Felix Yusupov lived in the Hotel Vendôme in Paris. Alois Brunner, Austrian Nazi war criminal, is believed to have lived in the Meridian Hotel in Damascus, Syria, under the name Georg Fischer.

Sultan Said Bin Taimur of Muscat lived at Dorchester Hotel in London after he was deposed by Qaboos of Oman in 1970, He died in the hotel in 1972. Eleftherios Venizelos, Greek statesman and diplomat, lived in the Hôtel Ritz Paris while he was in exile in France from 1935-1936.

HISTORY OF HOSPITALITY SERVICE

In 1949, Bob Luitweiler founded the first hospitality service called Servas Open Doors as a cross national, non-profit, volunteer run organization advocating interracial and international peace. The next earliest began in 1965 when John Wilcock set up the Traveler's Directory, originally as a listing of his mutual friends willing to host each other when traveling.

This later became the Hospitality Exchange in 1988 when Joy Lily rescued the organization from imminent demise. Hospitality Club is the direct successor

Hospex, the first Internet-based service, operating out of Poland since 1992. It is currently the largest hospitality exchange network, growing rapidly.

CouchSurfing is a newer but also rapidly growing hospitality exchange organization founded in 2004. Just as all the individual services have their own individual creation stories and organizational histories (often including demise and resurrection), many also have specific niche markets that they cater to including students, activists, religious pilgrims, and even occupational groups like police officers. However, the trend in recent years points to a greater consolidation of users in networks without a specific group, value, or lifestyle affiliation.

THE NATURE OF SERVICES

Along with the growth in services, an appreciation for the ways in which services are different from products has developed. The traditional ways of marketing tangible products are not equally effective in services marketing.

In many industries, marketing involves tangible manufactured products, such as automobiles, washing machines, and clothing, whereas service industries focus on intangible products such as travel and foodservice. However, before we can explore how services get successfully marketed, we need to examine the ways services differ from products.

Nine key differences:

No ownership by customers

A customer does not take ownership when purchasing a service. There is no transfer of assets.

SERVICE PRODUCTS

The value of owning a highperformance car or the latest computer lies in the physical characteristics of the product and to some extent the brand image it conveys. The value of purchasing services lies in the nature of the performance. For example, if you decide to celebrate a birthday or anniversary by dining at an expensive restaurant, the value lies in the way in which the service actors perform. When servers come to the table and present all the entrees simultaneously, the choreographed presentation appears in the same manner as a choreographed play or performance.

INVOLVEMENT OF CUSTOMERS IN THE PRODUCTION

Because consumers tend to be present when receiving service within a hospitality operation, they remain involved in the service production. In many instances, they are directly involved through the element of self-service. Examples of this can be seen in fast-food restaurants as well as in hotels that provide automated check-in and checkout by means of either a machine or a video connection through the television.

Airlines have greatly expanded self-service within their operations as a means of reducing labour costs. In any case, the customer's level of satisfaction depends on the nature of the interaction with the service provider, the nature of the physical facilities in which the service gets provided, and the nature of the interaction with other guests present in the facility at the time the service is provided.

PEOPLE AS PART OF THE PRODUCT

People or firms that purchase services come in contact with other consumers as well as the service employees. For example, a hotel guest waits in line at the front desk or the concierge desk with other guests. In addition, the guests share facilities such as the pool, the restaurant, and the fitness center. Therefore, service firms must also manage consumer interactions to the best of their abilities to ensure customer satisfaction.

For example, a hotel's sales office would not want to book group business with a nondrinking religious group at the same time as a reunion of military veterans. The two groups are significantly different in behaviour, and the expectation is that they would not mix well within the facilities at the same time. Similarly, restaurants separate smokers and nonsmokers, and they should try to separate other patrons that show some potential for conflict.

VARIABILITY IN OPERATIONAL INPUTS AND OUTPUTS

In a manufacturing setting, the operational production can be controlled very carefully. For example, staff carefully manage inventory and precisely calculate production times. Services, however, are delivered in real time, with many variables not being fully under the control of managers. For example, if a guest has been promised an early check-in but all of the guests from the preceding night are late in checking out, it becomes more difficult for the hotel to honor the arriving guest's request.

A service setting remains a more difficult site in which to control quality and offer a consistent service experience. Service firms try to minimize the amount of variability between service encounters, but much of the final product stays situational.

There are many uncontrollable aspects of the delivery process, such as weather, the number of consumers present, the attitudes of the consumers, and the attitudes of the employees. Therefore, it becomes impossible to consistently control the quality for services in the same manner as the quality of manufactured products.

CONSUMERS TO EVALUATE

Consumers can receive considerable information regarding the purchase of products; however, they often do not obtain it for services. Prior to buying a product, a consumer can research the product attributes and performance and use this information when making a purchase decision, especially an important one.

NO INVENTORIES FOR SERVICES

Due to the intangible nature of services, they cannot be inventoried for future use. Therefore, a lost sale can never be recaptured. When a seat remains empty on a flight, a hotel room stays vacant, or a table stays unoccupied in a restaurant, the potential revenue for these services at that point in time becomes lost forever. In other words, services are perishable, much like produce in a supermarket or items in a bakery. It remains critical for hospitality and tourism firms to manage supply and demand in an attempt to minimize unused capacity. For example, restaurants offer early-bird specials and airlines offer deeply discounted fares in an attempt to shift demand from peak periods to nonpeak periods, thereby increasing revenue and profits.

IMPORTANCE OF TIME

Hospitality services are generally produced and consumed simultaneously, unlike tangible products, which are manufactured, inventoried, and then sold at a later date. Customers must be present to receive the service. There are real limits to the amount of time that customers are willing to wait to receive service. Service firms study the phenomenon of service queues, or the maximum amount of time a customer will wait for a service before it has a significant (negative) impact on his or her perception of service quality. Airline companies offer curbside check-in for the most time-conscious passengers, and restaurants have devised practices such as providing guests with pagers and expanding the bar area in order to reduce the negative effect that results from waiting for service.

DIFFERENT DISTRIBUTION CHANNELS

The distribution channel for services is usually more direct than the traditional channel (i.e., manufacturer-wholesaler retailer- consumer) used by many product firms. The simultaneous production and consumption normally associated with service delivery limits the use of intermediaries. The service firm usually comprises both the manufacturer and the retailer, with no need for a wholesaler to inventory its products. Consumers are present to consume the meals prepared in a restaurant, to take advantage of the amenities in a hotel, and to travel between cities by plane.

BENEFITS MONETARY SAVINGS

Staying in private homes means that travelers can save lots of money on accommodation that they would usually be spending on hotels or hostels. Used over a long period of time (2 to 4 weeks), this strategy can cut overall travel budgets in half, or even more combined with hitchhiking. These savings can then be passed on towards more generously patronizing local establishments or simply staying abroad for longer periods of time.

LOCAL ECONOMIC SUSTAINABILITY

Many tourist vacations today are sold in package form, often including flights, hotels, rental cars, sightseeing tours, and coupons for chain restaurants and bars. While this makes purchasing more convenient, it also puts more money in the hands of large multinational corporations exploiting the synergy strategy of marketing their products in the context of their subsidiary companies operating in other markets. Many years ago, this might have been termed *collusion*; today, however, it is the norm. This comes at the expense of locally owned independent businesses. Accommodation sharing helps to break apart this monopoly and hopefully redirects some of the tourist revenue back to the local or national economy.

ECOLOGICAL SUSTAINABILITY

While this is especially important in more rural travel venues where hotels are often built in very picturesque, though fragile environments, every night stayed at a local's home means that much less demand for such hotel rooms. Also, if accommodation sharing does in fact increase the length of average stays, it may reduce the amount of trips to and from different locations and back home again, thus reducing the overall fuel expenditures in the process.

LOCAL CONTACT

Ostensibly, one of the primary reasons we travel is to experience what life is like for people living in other countries. Making interpersonal connections and fostering understanding of different cultures may in the long run also be important to international relations.

However, even in our increasingly globalized world supposedly rife with diversity, in many popular travel destinations we find tourists milling around "tourist enclaves" where the companies they patronize back home have set up shop to cater to their desires while they are abroad. Sociologist George Ritzer has referred to this phenomenon as the "McDonaldisation of society" and the more recently, the "globalization of nothing". The location of hotels near these centers only fosters more convenient envelopment of the tourist dollar.

During hospitality exchanges, hosts want to show off their local knowledge and exciting "off the map" venues. Not only may travelers get a distinctly different experience, but they will also get a feel for the everyday lives of local residents.

RECIPROCITY

These systems foster richer and more convenient travel experiences not so much on the premise of altruism, but on the basis of social exchange theory. Implicit in the agreement to host travelers is the ability to ask to be hosted by them in the future. If one enjoys having interesting guests in their home, this works out well for both parties. It works comparatively better if you are visited by travelers from a locale you find particularly attractive. Thus, hosting someone from New York City in Gainesville, FL seems to be an unbelievable opportunity. Moreover, if you are a Westerner visiting someone in a developing nation, your stay might be the only way that this individual or family could afford a trip to a rich nation. This may mean more than just a relaxing vacation for such disadvantaged parties.

AUTHENTICITY AND ADVENTURE

Tourism has always searched for these two qualities, but much like Midas and his golden touch, the reach of tourism has to a large extent destroyed the opportunity to encounter them in most places. Unluckily, the experience has been thoroughly commodified by everyone who wanted to secure their opportunity to make a buck in the process. Accommodation sharing offers a way out of this bind and a viable alternative to having one's desires manipulated by corporate conglomerates who never had the best interests of the place or the people foremost in their minds.

DRAWBACKS LACK OF GUARANTEE

There is no contractual agreement between users in these systems. Reservations are made, but if they are for some reason broken, there is no higher authority to which one could plead for a refund or other compensation. The only repercussion will be the poor rating you give that user and your only consolation will be that your warning will deter others from visiting or hosting them. For those who feel insecure unless their travel arrangements are written in stone before departure, this system will not be comforting.

POTENTIAL INTERPERSONAL

There is a chance that guest and host will not get along. Perhaps there will be scheduling or ideological conflicts. Maybe you will find that hosts or visitors have misrepresented themselves. Perhaps the experience will not live up to your expectations.

Intense interpersonal communications in advance and a flexibility once you have arrived is your best bet. These experiences require additional planning and courtesy towards the demands of your host. Thus, your living conditions, length of stay, and overall experience will be circumscribed by the living conditions you enter into.

DEMOGRAPHIC SEGREGATION

The average user is a young white person who speaks English and lives in a developed nation. While there are many users who do not fit this description, the more different they are, the less likely they will be involved. This is especially true for persons living in the developing world who likely do not have easy access to the fundamental prerequisite for using these services: computers and the Internet. Thus, the sample population found in searches of these databases are really much less diverse than a geographical representation of worldwide users might suggest.

SECURITY

There is a distinct possibility that someone will abuse the system and that innocent users (especially women) will get hurt. All services include disclaimers that require users to waive their rights to hold anyone but themselves responsible for any harm that may come to them in using the system. They advise that the best Defence mechanism is to only involve oneself with users that have extensive personal information and interpersonal networks within the system that have been verified by others. It does seem entirely plausible that someone clever and patient enough might be able to invent an entire group of complex user identities and build histories convincing enough to fool even more cautious patrons.

Still, the difference between these systems and the other social networking platforms popular nowadays on the web (such as MySpace, Tribe, Orkut, LiveJournal and Ebay) is that any agreement reached through the accommodation sharing medium is contingent on actually meeting other people face-to-face. Other web scams are easier because interpersonal interactions rely so much on putative identities that are never actually verified in the real world. However, this does not diminish the greater risk to physical well being that this kind of traveling by definition must entertain. The best advice is to meet unknown persons in public spaces first, and try to meet some of their acquaintances in person before agreeing to a hospitality exchange.

PROCESS IN HOSPITALITY INDUSTRY

The first aim of this study was to assess Melbourne and international students' detailed perceptions of the cooperative education placements on international level. Although the expectations from placements' social climate by students of the four international institutions was similar overall, their expectations varied across specific social climate dimensions. These findings indicate detailed information about students' expectations of their cooperative education placements in industry.

Unlike the various findings of the studies reviewed earlier, the results of this study indicate specific areas of differences in perceptions. Some differences n scores, notably in the involvement, peer cohesion, task orientation, work pressure, and control dimensions were evident between the Melbourne and The Hague students, and in the Autonomy between Melbourne and Strathclyde students than in other dimensions. Previous studies, although less detailed, point to similar conclusions.

Knutson (1989) and Charles (1992) for example, found that hospitality and tourism students are concerned with the issues associated with working in these industries, such as lack of challenge and lack of management involvement. It is safe to suggest, therefore, following Pavesic and Brymer (1990) and Sarabakhsh *et al.* (1989), that students' expectations of industry may affect their actual perception of the industry after their graduation. This in turn can affect their work satisfaction and successful professional development.

The second aim of this study was to find out if the Melbourne students' expectations differed from those of students from the other participating institutions. Melbourne students expected higher involvement, greater peer cohesion, more task orientation, more work pressure and greater control when compared with The Hague students. They also expected less autonomy on the job as compared with the Strathclyde students. However, in general, as can be observed the Melbourne students' expectations did not differ much from other students, with the exception of the The Hague students' expectations. This could be attributed to a few factors.

First, the The Hague students' scores could be a reflection of the different perception of the social climate of the work environment of their placements due to the different organizational socialisation processes as pointed out by Dean (1983). For example, different supportive work settings that help promote students' independence can socialise them in learning their new occupational roles on many different levels. Although the four samples were matched on the course curriculum content and the timing of the cooperative education experience, there could be some differences in curriculum delivery especially in student orientation and preparation before placements occurred. Secondly, there could be cultural differences between the English speaking students and native language speaking students. The values attached to organizational socialisation in general could differ. Third, the assumption that the The Hague students were fluent in English and therefore would have no problem in understanding the questionnaire could be wrong. This should be verified with translation and back translation of the WES to the Dutch language.

The third aim of this study was to find out which aspects of the work environment of the hospitality organizations need to be addressed in preparing students for work experience. The differences in the work environment dimensions (involvement, peer cohesion, autonomy, task orientation, work pressure, control) highlight the need for both educational institutions and industry management internationally to address the following issues:

- Improving managerial support may include an increase in communication between cooperative education placement officers and supervisors responsible for students during their placements. Development of clear policies which could guide students before placements and monitoring of these policies during placements could eventuate in more student involvement in each organization's functioning and greater cohesion between students and staff.
- Reducing excessive work demands and time pressure. The hospitality industry is very labour-intensive and is perceived as demanding. Students could be briefed on the specific demands. Their placements would perhaps consist of progressively more demanding tasks, beginning with the tasks that are realistically attainable by students during the early stages of their placements.
- Altering managerial control mechanisms such as rules and procedures during student placements. Managerial control mechanisms need to be applied with a greater degree of flexibility. Greater student participation in decision-making, especially in utilising their enthusiastic approaches to problem solving learned during the academic year may result in students having more positive perceptions of supervisory control.

Despite the similarities and differences between students' expectations at the international level, the question arises if these expectations will be met while the students are on their placements, or are students' expectations unrealistic? If they are not met then, as evidence by Barron and Maxwell (1993), West and Jameson (1990) and Purcell and Quinn (1995) suggests, the students may still be discouraged from entering their chosen professions after graduation. Therefore, the cooperative education experience may be a crucial factor for students in making this decision.

In short, the findings just described show that students' expectations from cooperative education placements can be assessed in detail by measuring their expectations from the social climate of their industrial placements' work environment. As Purcell and Quinn (1995) noted, the students returned from placements "...to their course more mature, with considerable insight into the industry; but this insight often crystallised in disillusion and a desire to use their experience and education to find employment in another sector of the economy" (p. 16). The assessment of the students' expectations, therefore, may help in predicting their subsequent career orientation in hospitality industries and elsewhere.

While the results of the present study point to many differences and similarities between international samples, they can not be generalised beyond the samples studied. The samples were drawn from four institutions, and although they incorporated four similar courses of study, the research needs replication with varied populations and institutions. For example, data comparisons should be done based on the USA samples, since there is also close cooperation between the USA institutions and the Victoria University of Technology. Although international cross-sectional research is complex, costly and difficult to execute, this study suggests some directions for meaningful exploration of the role of students' own perception of cooperative education. As Linke (1988) pointed out "...there is no ideal structure and very little evaluative information exists to indicate clearly the practical advantages and limitations between alternative approaches with respect to the multiple outcomes expected of students, employers and staff" (p. 30).

Therefore, further longitudinal and cross-sectional research is required to assess and compare the perceptions of the work environment of various academic institutions and employers in industry. Also, there is a need not only to compare various student populations to one another over time, but also to find out if those students who stayed with the chosen industry after graduation were also the same students whose cooperative education expectations were met by subsequent experience in industry.

COUNTER-ARGUMENTS TO THE NEED FOR DEREGULATION IN HOSPITALITY INDUSTRY

Despite the arguments advanced by proponents of deregulation, other commentators have argued that the centralised system was able to deliver labour market flexibility. For example, Callus *et al.* (1991) in a comprehensive study of over 2,000 Australian workplaces noted that only 6 per cent of workplace managers viewed awards as a constraint in pursuing efficiency changes and that only 14 per cent indicated changes could not be undertaken because of unions.

Morehead *et al.* (1997) in an equally comprehensive study had a similar finding. They established that 9 per cent of private workplaces with 20 or more employees stated they were prevented from making changes because of awards and/or agreements.

In addition, they found that managers in 17 per cent of private workplaces stated they could not undertake changes because of employees, trade unions or union delegates. Rimmer (1991) raised objections to the assumption of wage and procedural inflexibility of the centralised system by noting there was scope for enterprise bargaining under the centralised system and that these provisions have been extensively used. As well, Rimmer (1998) and Hawke (1998) point out that awards were often augmented through informal enterprise and individual bargaining at the enterprise level.

With regard to numerical flexibility, the Industrial Relations Reform Act 1993 (Cth) extended the constraints on unfair dismissal and requirements relating to information, consultation and severance pay to apply to non-award employees. This meant that it was not awards that were inhibiting flexibility but rather legislation applying to all employees.

The Workplace Relations and Other Amendments Act 1996 (Cth) which was intended to further deregulate the system through the introduction of individual contracts, known as Australian Workplace Agreements, will retain a number of standards in relation to unfair dismissal and severance pay clauses, although rights to consultation and information may be removed. Work time and functional flexibility have been increasingly facilitated by many changes to the relevant provisions incorporated into awards since the 1980s. For example, there are now numerous awards which no longer specify premium payments for work during non-standard hours. The increased numbers of casual and part-time employees have also resulted in increased work time flexibility.

THE NEED FOR EMPIRICAL RESEARCH

Lack of empirical support for the supposed benefits of increased flexibility fostered through deregulation and numerous criticisms of the post-Fordist paradigm have not prevented the promotion of enterprise bargaining amongst policy makers in Australia.

A major reason may be that enterprise bargaining is consistent with a neo-classical economic approach. The neo-classical economics agenda with its reliance on market forces, adopted by the federal and state governments since the 1980s, strongly supports the pursuit of increased labour market flexibility through deregulation.

Given this debate about the need for deregulation in the pursuit of flexibility, the aim of this research was to determine whether deregulation was necessary for the attainment of flexibility. A sector of the tourism and hospitality industries was chosen for this study since the proponents of deregulation have argued that service industries are particularly concerned with the attainment of labour flexibility. Flexible work arrangements which reflect long trading hours (up to 24-hour-a-day service) are said to be necessary to ensure a competitive business environment (Commonwealth Department of Tourism and Department of Industrial Relations, 1992).

Other characteristics of the hospitality sector, including fluctuations in demand, the existence of penalty rates, weekend work and work outside of "normal" hours, simultaneous production and consumption of service and labour intensity, ensure the pursuit of flexibility is a high priority for enterprises.

THE REGISTERED CLUBS SECTOR

This study focuses on one sector of the hospitality industry, the registered clubs sector of NSW. Registered clubs in NSW which operate under the Registered Clubs Act 1976 NSW, have an unusual ownership structure and business goals.

Registered clubs are unusual since they are non-profit organizations formed by groups of people who share a common interest and who have come together to pursue or promote that interest. Another unusual characteristic of registered clubs is that they are governed by a board of directors who are responsible for the formulation of policy and for ensuring that these policies are carried out by the management. The manager/secretary, also known as the chief executive officer, is the person responsible for the day to day running of the registered club and its staff.

Directors are not expected to be involved in the daily operations of the registered club nor its staff. Trade unions and industrial tribunals have been keen to ensure employees only deal with one person to avoid confusion and to maintain clear lines of communication (Registered Clubs Association of NSW, 1990). The manager/secretary is regarded by the industrial tribunal and trade unions as the employer. Registered clubs cover a vast array of interests including sporting, social, community and ethnic interests. In Australia, registered clubs are major social outlets for people and in a number of cases, provide significant funds for community projects. The majority of funds are raised through the provision of gaming facilities.

In addition, clubs also serve food and beverages and in many cases entertainment is also provided to patrons. The types of employment in clubs, which includes management, bar, kitchen and clerical staff, reflect the range of services offered by clubs. The development of the registered club industry has proceeded differently in the various Australian states and territories.

NSW was, and still is, clearly the most developed state with regard to registered clubs in Australia. In NSW, there are over 1,500 clubs (40.5 per cent of all clubs in Australia), generating a turnover of over $20 billion annually and employing over 63,000 people (67.3 per cent of all employment in Australian clubs) (ABS, 1994).

LABOUR MARKET CHARACTERISTICS

There are a number of awards covering both club management and employees within registered clubs. These awards are indicative of the broad range of occupations involved in registered clubs. In NSW, for example, the awards that apply to various managers and employees within the registered clubs include the club managers' and club secretaries' (state) award, the club managers' and club secretaries' superannuation (state) award, the club employees' (state) award, and the musicians' (live performance) (state) award. Casual employment is a major component of the workforce in this sector. Approximately 56 per cent of staff in registered clubs were employed on a casual basis in 1996.

A further 5 per cent were employed on a part-time basis (Buultjens, 1996a). This sector has had increasing competitive pressures placed upon it by the regulatory changes in Queensland and Victoria. In the early 1990s, clubs in Victoria and Queensland were, for the first time, allowed to introduce gaming machines onto their premises. Many NSW registered clubs, particularly in border regions, found it increasingly difficult to remain profitable with this increased competition from interstate clubs. As a consequence, a number of NSW registered clubs which profited from the patronage of customers from Victoria and Queensland have undergone a substantial reduction in income.

Another important impact on the registered clubs sector in NSW has come from the deregulation which has taken place in the hospitality industry as a whole. In most states, hotels have been allowed to operate on Sundays and introduce gaming machines.

This has resulted in registered clubs losing some of their competitive advantage. In a further loss to competitive advantage, in November 1996, the NSW Government gave notice of its intention to introduce legislation which would allow hotels to introduce the same type of gaming machines as those used on registered clubs' premises. These changes to the competitive environment in which registered clubs are operating, and the particular needs of the hospitality sector in general, should ensure that labour market flexibility is an important consideration to registered clubs in NSW.

HOTEL INDUSTRY MANAGEMENT OF 21ST CENTURY

From last a decade or two, Hotel Industry in world has also touched a remarkable height. Many hotels have been also built during last few years in India. The new hotel era was first dominated in India by the Oberoi group, ITC, ITDC, Hotel Corporation of India and other large luxurious group of hotels quickly followed. Keeping with this trend the hotel business proliferated throughout India and State Tourism Corporations also many establishments for providing food and accommodation the growing tourists and business traffic. Today, while, the building costs in the hotel sector are certainly substantial, the industry has gradually become more attractive to private investors with assurance of financial incentives from government.

CATEGORIES OF HOTELS

PARTNERSHIP

Partnership is the relation between persons who agreed to share the profits of a business carried on by all or any of them acting for all. In this type of hotel business the business is started with atleast two persons and capital is provided by them to own the hotel on agreement basis. This type of agreement is known as *partnership agreement, partnership deed* or *articles of partnership*.

The agreement points out the aims, objects, rights and duties, authorities and responsibilities of each partner. It also includes a clause for setting differences between partners and the circumstances and the manner in which the contract can be terminated. This type of hotel is generally bigger than individual type of hotel and smaller than joint stock company basis.

One of the feature of partnership hotel is that all the partners are liable for debts of the partnership. The firm's creditors have the right to sue all or any of the partners to the limit of their personal and business resources. It is notable that a relieved partner is also liable for debts incurred during the period in which he was a partner unless the other partners release him, but incoming partner will be free from liability for existing partnership debts. He will be liable for future debts in the normal way. Partnership based hotel can be closed after the expiry of the period of time set by the partners or when the business proves unlawful.

CO-OWNER CHAIN

In this type of hotel an agreement is made between the parent company and the local investor. In this category of partnership 50% of the stock of the hotel is owned by the local investor and 50% by the parent organization. The parent company is responsible of selection of site, designing, financing building and furnishing and the supervision of the hotel management.

CHAIN TYPE HOTELS

A group of three or more hotels, or resorts operated under a common name are known as chain type of hotels. During last few years chain type of hotels have become very common and are very popular due to its efficiency. Statler, Hilton and Sheraton groups of hotels got a remarkable momentum and began to grow rapidly.

Chain type of hotels have so many advantages for capitalising group as a means of increasing business and reducing duplication, inefficiency and waste. Chain hotels saves money in purchasing anything from food stuffs to furniture. It can be in a position to get the services of top specialists in every phase of hotel operation—engineers, food controllers, decorators, architectural planners, its large income sources.

The chain hotels can easily advertise itself through magazines and newspapers than single hotels because the expen e is divided among numerous hotel and thus they receive full benefit of national coverage at the fraction of total cost. Reservation system is very easy for chain hotels as about the fourth of all room reservations are made through free teletype reservation services which permits a chain access to the various hotels in the group while it is out of reach of independent hotels. In India Welcome group, Taj, Oberoi, ITC groups and in foreign Holiday Inn, Hilton, Sheraton and Intercontinental are the dominant international groups which have changed the organizational structure and management of hotel enterprises throughout the world.

MULTINATIONAL HOTELS

Multinational hotels earn revenues from accommodation—the suites, flat lets and studio rooms and from catering services. Their restaurants provide entertainment also to the customers alongwith good food service. Multinational hotels have limited capability. There is a need for limited hotels in a particular region. These hotels are openable in the largest of communities where there are prosperous businessmen.

SOLE PROPRIETORSHIP

Sole-Proprietorship means *one man ownership of a business* etc., especially of a hotel. In special reference to hotel industry, sole-proprietorship hotels can be defined as such type of hotels, where all required capital is provided by one person and he takes all the risk, manages the hotel and is single authority to receive the total profit after providing for the expenses of operation and the cost of borrowings needed for the running of hotel business.

'One-man-business' is very common because of the nature of hotel business. In this type of business the owner enjoy all the profits in case of business prospers but in the case of failure he goes alone to the bankruptcy court. He has to pay for the debts and losses incurred by the operation. The main problem of individual type hotel is the lack of capital. The hotel owner has only his own resources so has to face the problem in the expansion and development of business

HERITAGE HOTELS

Heritage Hotel is a new category of hotel introduced by the Indian Hotel Industry for its quick and efficient development. Heritage hotels can be defined as hotel running in *palaces, castles, forts, and residence of any size which were built prior to 1950.* As it was not possible for the Indian princes in independent India to maintain their large and stylish palaces so they have changed their palaces into luxury hotels to make ends meet.

It is essential for a Heritage Hotel that the outward appearance, architectural features and general construction of the building will have the distinctive qualities, ambience and decor in keeping with the traditional way of the place. Parking space for cars is also an essential feature for this type of hotel. It is required that all public rooms and areas will be well maintained and well equipped with carpets, furniture, fittings etc. Reception cash and information counter are attended by trained personnel which provide money changing facilities and many other facilities.

A well equipped, well furnished and well maintained dining room and a well equipped bar is essential for a Heritage Hotel. Apart from these facilities a well maintained ground and garden is a symbol of Heritage Hotel. In this type of hotel, food and beverage services are of high standard. Housekeeping is also of highest standard and there is good arrangement for medical assistance in case of need. Thus, a heritage hotel is a hotel of distinctive and traditional life-style of the area.

TIME SHARING RESORTS

With the changing need of tourists and travellers Time Sharing Resorts' or Resort hotels have acquired valuable place in the field of hotel industry. For the purpose of suitable climate the rich go out in summer as well as in winter. Apart from this group a number of families travel during vacations and so a place is needed to stay and relax during holidays. Although travelling is sometimes limited to a particular season of the year, most of the hill and beach resorts are getting vacation spots for summer as well as winter. So there are year-round resorts also existence alongwith time-sharing resorts. Resort hotels are generally located in tourist resort areas. A resort hotel have rooms less than fifty and it is classed as luxury type hotel due to size of guest rooms and provision of facilities such as dining, restaurants, bar, recreation, etc.

Resort hotels are mainly of three types:

a. *Natural Recreational Resort Hotels:* Some hotels are located near natural recreational areas such as sea shore, large lakes, national shrines, parks, ski slopes, hill resorts, legalized gambling areas etc. These hotels are known as Natural Recreational Resort Hotels. These hotels are based on either European plan or modified American plan.

b. *Self-Contained Resort Hotels:* These resorts are American plan based resorts and provide all the recreational facilities for its guests such as: Indoor and outdoor pools, Horse back riding, Tennis courts, entertainment, Golf courses, etc.

c. *Summer Resorts:* Summer resorts in India are operated during May, June, July. As this season is very short so the operation depends upon the elements like rain etc. Shimla, Srinagar, Mussoorie, Nainital, Darjeeling hill stations are best example of summer resorts.

d. *Ski Resort Hotels:* The third type of resort hotel is ski-resort hotels. These hotels are located far away from the cities where the areas for the various functions depend upon the anticipated number of hotel guests plus the amount of a patronage expected from the community.

e. *Warm Winter Resorts:* Warm Winter Resorts means a resort where the traveller can enjoy the hot sun, the golden beaches etc.

f. *The Year Round Resorts:* These resorts are located at those places where the climate at those places is pleasant during the whole year. So the travellers of can enjoy here a twelve month season.

g. *Cold Winter Resorts:* These are places mainly having facilities for winter sports like skating. Gulmarg is the best example of such resorts.

Most resorts, hotels are seasonable establishments who may be closed in the off season. The hotel industry aims building up a regular holiday trade because it is more valuable to sell the house in advance year by year. These resorts are no being made to open during summer or winter by capitalising skiing and other seasonal sports. Off season prices are lower and are often sold in combination with special rate, combination of transportation entertainment etc. These hotels frequent encourage business by cooperation with airlines and of carriers to offer a single price covering travel, lodging, meals a often entertainment.

FRANCHISE

Organization: Franchise is a technical word that means to name from a reputed firm or organization in return of a agreement. In regard with hotel business, Franchise agreement between a hotel company and an independent owner whereby for a fee the owner is allowed to use the trade marks and various services offered by the chain, continuing relationship in which a franchiser provides a privilege to do business plus assistance in organizing, merchandising and operation management, in return consideration from the franchisee. Franchise system provides a large scale of opportunity to go into business as the parent organization assist the newcomer at any and all times. They provide the advantage of brand name or trade mark in advertising, sales promotion and advance registration.

On the other hand the parent organization is also benefited by Franchise system. At first, franchising provides an opportunity for an organization to spread its name rapidly and widely throughout the country at a minimum amount of expenses. Secondly, franchise operations act booking agents for the hotels of the organization and thus the referral business proves a two-way street and excellent sources of rooms and food and beverage business for the metropolitan hotels. Apart from these two benefits the hotel companies receive a great deal of money through this system. As every franchisee pays a franchise fee and a daily charge to the organization, there is plenty of money to be made in franchising. Holiday Inn, Hyatt, House Sheraton Inn, Hilton, Congress Inn, Howard Jonshon's, Quality Courts, Albert Pick, Down Towner, Marriott, Ramada Inns are some of the well-known franchise chains.

Services: There are many services offered by a franchiser to a franchisee such as:

a. *Methods:* At first, operating procedures established by the franchiser are used by the franchisee to run the business successfully. Training programme, deputation of regional manager are the forms of operating procedures provided by the franchiser to a franchisee.
b. *Technical Assistance:* Technical assistance are provided by the franchiser in return of payment of additional services provided.

Assistance during the development of potential sites, assistance in obtaining finance, preparation of cost budgets and feasibility studies are various forms of technical assistance. Besides this architectural services, interior design services, purchasing services, project management and construction supervision can also be obtained from franchiser as technical assistance.

c. *Marketing:* Marketing is one of the important service, provided by the franchiser. It is an important ingredient in a agreement. Advertising, sales and reservation are the three sources of providing marketing services.

OPERATIONS IN HOTEL MANAGEMENT

Operations in hotel management focuses on carefully managing the processes to produce and distribute products and services. Usually, small businesses don't talk about "operations management", but they carry out the activities that management schools typically associate with the phrase "operations management." Major, overall activities often include product creation, development, production and distribution. Related activities include managing purchases, inventory control, quality control, storage, logistics and evaluations.

A great deal of focus is on efficiency and effectiveness of processes. Therefore, operations management often includes substantial measurement and analysis of internal processes. Ultimately, the nature of how operations management is carried out in an organization depends very much on the nature of products or services in the organization. People and industry have moved from the so-called rust belt to the sun belt. The hotel business has been active in reborn and reconstructed central cities.

The explosion of technology and information-based companies has concentrated human endeavour in technological corridors in California, Massachusetts, Washington, Texas, and North Carolina, to name a few such places. It can be safely said that where jobs are and major concentrations of economic activity occur, hotels will follow. It should be noted that the word modern can be loaded with the potential of much misunderstanding. Hotels are changing and will continue to change. As a result, the techniques of management of modern hotels must adapt to changing circumstances.

INFLUENCES

Like many other businesses, hotels have been affected by shifts in emphasis and its children mature, the population of the countries will for many years be older, healthier, and better educated than previous generations. These facts will present new challenges and opportunities to all business managers. *Technology*—in the form of computers, communication, personal devices, and laboursaving mechanical equipment—has had and will have a major effect on the way in which hotels are managed and operated.

The speed with which information is accumulated, stored, manipulated, and transferred is such that today most travellers expect that the hotel rooms they rent will allow them to be as productive as they are in the office or at home. Increasingly, with portable computing, personal data assistants (PDAs), wireless communication, and virtually everything somehow connected to the Internet, hotels must provide services and access that allow guests seamless transition from the business, travel, or home environment to that of the hotel. Increasingly, entertainment must be fused with communication and productive processes.

The concept of market segmentation, or ever-increasingly finely tuned market definitions, will dictate hotel structures and organizations, and management tactics designed to address those market segments have become even more important to the management of hospitality service businesses. With the increased power in the information and data manipulation realm, hotels have available to them ever expanding databases about guests and are creating new products to attract those markets.

One of the effects of the aging demographic is the emergence of vacation re- sorts—a modern incarnation of the timeshare properties of several decades ago. Because these are being developed and operated by name hotel companies and are marketed to the affluent, healthy, well-educated population segment, resort managers have had to absorb new managerial realities. The well-documented change in the complexion of the national economy from one that emphasizes goods and, to a lesser extent, natural resources to one that emphasizes services has kindled new ideas about the way in which we manage the design and delivery of these services.

Hotels, restaurants, and travel services are now seen as unique entities that dictate special kinds of managerial techniques and strategies. Changes in people's travel patterns have altered the way we manage our hotel properties. Deregulation of the airlines has driven a change in the way millions of people travel each year, given the huband- spoke design of airline services. Many hotel companies are now locating major hotel properties adjacent to hub air transport facilities, taking advantage of the fact that business travellers may not need to travel to a central business district (CBD) to accomplish their purpose in a given area.

Meetings and conferences can now be scheduled within a five-minute limousine ride from the air terminal, and the business traveller can be headed for his or her next destination before the day is over without having to stay overnight in a CBD hotel. New patterns of investment in hotel facilities have emerged in the last two decades, and more attention is now paid to achieving optimum return on investment. Because people from outside the hotel industry are now participating in its financial structuring, hotel operations are no longer dependent on the vision of a single entrepreneur. Managers now must design tactics and strategies to achieve heretofore unanticipated financial goals.

The same trend has also altered the complexion of management and organization of the modern hotel. This is especially true of publicly owned hotel firms, where Wall Street stock analysts heavily influence stock prices through expectations of quarterly revenues and profits. This puts pressure on hotel companies and their operations managers to perform, on a quarterly basis, in a way contrary to many managers' instincts. Most of the foregoing issues and influences still operate (to a greater or lesser extent) on the organizational structures and strategies of the modern hotel. However, other phenomena of an economic, cultural, and social nature have come to the fore, complicating our view of hotel management. This furthers the argument that the hotel industry is a part of the greater economy and at the mercy of elements often completely out of its control.

The cyclical nature of the U.S. and international economies has recently affected significantly hotels' ability to respond to changing circumstances. In early 1993, for instance, employment growth was stagnant; corporate profits were low; the expansion of the gross national product (GNP) was only a marginal percentage above previous years; and travel in most segments was down due to corporate restructuring, downsizing, or reorganizing.

Vast layoffs in the hundreds of thousands had been announced every month. While fuel prices continued to be relatively stable, consumer spending patterns and high employment growth had not materialized, particularly in light of corporate layoffs and the ongoing nervousness of consumers about whether or not their financial wherewithal was safe. Unemployment was at an all-time low; the Dow Jones Industrial Average was between 10,000 and 11,000; hotel occupancies had stabilized nationally in excess of 70 per cent; and the federal government was running a surplus for the first time in the memory of most.

Then what happened? The terrorist attacks in New York and Washington, D.C., in 2001 changed the face of all business and travel, immediately and probably for the foreseeable future as well. Major airlines are in bankruptcy; hotels are struggling to achieve profitable occupancies; business travel is down; the high-tech stock market bubble burst; the country is at war in a number of locations; security has made travel more difficult, if not actually annoying; and people are nervous.

Join this with an imbalance of trade, the outsourcing of jobs, and the largest federal deficits in history, and the face of the economy is challenging. This translates directly not only to business travel but personal and recreational travel as well. Finding ways to operate profitably in such an environment is the job of the next generation of hotel operators. Among the predictions made was that cultural diversity will play a role in the management and organizational structure of the modern hotel in the United States. As surely as living patterns, economic cycles, and market segmentation have influenced the hotel industry, so will the change in ethnicity of the workforce.

The cultural backgrounds that an increasingly diversified workforce will bring to hotel operations may be seen as a problem or a challenge—or both. To most operators, it will be seen as an opportunity to demonstrate to an increasingly diverse clientele that hotel companies are committed to hiring and training a workforce structure that mirrors society. See no reason to change that prediction now; if anything, acculturation of the hospitality business will accelerate. The legal and regulatory environments are increasingly important to all business managers, and hotel operators are no exception. Increasingly, operators must be aware of and alert to realms of risk that can engender lawsuits against them.

Several objects and essays in this edition highlight these threats to hotels and their guests. It should be noted that present-day security concerns also have significantly affected the ways in which hotels are operated. Awareness of the risk environment and the regulatory realm are factors that affect a hotel's ability to compete in the early part of the twenty-first century. This is also used to explore ideas that are new to the management process, and that—who knows?—may never completely catch on.

Rather than focus exclusively on the operations of the major chains, the readings here are from the perspectives of operators, leaders, and experts such as regional operators, major industry consultants, and independent branded hotels. John Dew, formerly president of Inn Ventures, a regional hotel management and development company that has built and operated many Marriott products, in addition to a proprietary hotel product, provides an insider's view of the steps needed to bring a hotel from conception to construction and operation.

This unique view of hotel operations connects the concept of hotel development with the realities of day-to-day operation. It should help aspiring managers understand how the intricacies of the development process may influence the marketing and management of the hotel. Peter Cass offers the reader insights, heretofore unavailable in books of this nature, into independently branded hotels that associate to provide market strength. He makes the case that the future success of independent hotels is linked to their ability to find ways to maintain their independence while sustaining competitive advantage in the luxury segment.

Because new construction of hotels diminished greatly after 9/11 but firms still needed to grow, rebranding existing properties generated a lot of growth activity. Rebranding is a complicated process that must be accomplished within critical time frames to coincide with marketing, financial, and operational variables. Today's economic circumstances are different, and business has changed its focus to opening new major projects. His piece serves as a useful companion to that of John Dew, and the two should be read together, with an eye towards comparing Dew's smaller project focus and Dupar's large projects. Perhaps proving the axiom that "everything old is new again," the concept of health and wellness spas as a hotel and resort product has enjoyed a resurgence. Once the province of high-end hotels and resorts, the idea of being pampered in a spa has been added to the service mix in many more modest hotels and resorts. While the big-name spas at five-star properties still set the standard for pampering and pricing, the comfort of personal service in less lavish spas seems to appeal to the modern traveller as well. Peter Anderson's overview of the spa industry provides insights into this fascinating service product. E.M. Statler's contributions to the modern hotel business are legendary in that he is generally credited with founding and operating the first commercial hotel concept that recognized the realities of the early business traveller at the beginning of the twentieth century. They also highlight other major forces in the development of the modern hotel business.

THE DEVELOPMENT COMPANY

The developer is the entrepreneur, the risk taker, who originates the idea for the hotel. Depending on the business structure selected, the developer often puts his or her personal wealth at risk when engaging in a hotel project. The developer, along with a small staff of people, networks with commercial real estate agents on the lookout for a suitable hotel site. Depending on the type of hotel to be developed, a site of at least two to four acres is required (for comparison, an acre is roughly the size of a football field).

This property must be zoned by the city for a hotel, be visible from a freeway or major street arterial, and have city approval for such construction activities as curb cuts, lefthand turn lanes, and delivery truck access. Commercial realtors offer sites for the developer's consideration that include maps, aerial photos, and proof of hotel zoning. Sometimes the developer views potential sites by driving around the neighbourhood within five miles of the site or touring multiple sites by helicopter, noting where the potential guests live and work and where potential competing hotels are located.

The price per square foot of the land is considered. The higher the cost of land, the higher the rates the hotel will need to charge. Is the price too high for the average daily rate (ADR) in this particular market? Is it too low? Or is it acceptable? This is determined when the hotel financial pro forma budget document is created.

STYLE OF OPERATION MANAGEMENT

We are now looking at the way different countries are managed, doing so country by country. The style of management of government in different countries can also be anywhere on the scale, from fully authoritarian (dictatorship) at one end of the scale to fully participative (policy decided by the people) at the other end. This is a fundamental scale which cuts across artificial and ineffective political divides—dictatorship of the left is dictatorship just like that of the right. Dictatorship is dictatorship no matter whether the organisation or political party is on the left or on the right of the political spectrum.

Under participative government and democracy the government and leadership put into effect the wishes of the people, the policy decided by delegates directly appointed by and directly responsible and accountable to the people. Under authoritarian government or dictatorship the government and its 'experts' tell the people what the government or rulers decide the people have to follow.

Here 'directly' means selected by the people and voted for, each person having one vote. This is very different from delegates being selected by or being accountable through an establishment such as a political party's or a Board of Directors. Real struggle is not between political left and right but is a struggle for democracy against dictatorship (authoritarian style of management) in all community organisations and at all levels.

Authoritarian attitudes result in confrontation, leadership and co-operation result in economic success. The way in which countries are managed, that is their style of management, of course varies from country to country and changes as time passes. shows the style of management.

The left hand side of the horizontal scale corresponds to the fully authoritarian, while the right hand end corresponds to the fully participative way of managing. The two ends are called 'A' and 'B' respectively, for convenience. What we can now do is to place on the scale some lines corresponding to the style of management adopted in different countries and then to discuss the pattern, following this by a discussion of the effectiveness of different styles of management.

In doing so we need to remember that we are not in any way concerned with opinions and feelings and beliefs about whether one country is better than another, whether one method of organisation is better than another, whether one political system is an improvement on another. We are concerned here only with the situation as it is, we are concerned only with objective facts.

Hence we assess the style of management by two factors only, namely on the one hand by the extent to which authority is centred at the top and on the other hand by the extent to which authority is centred at the bottom. Our measure for the extent to which authority is centred on the bottom is the extent to which working people may withdraw their labour, that is the extent to which they are permitted to do so by the laws of the land and the extent to which they are actually able to withdraw their labour. We assess the style of management by these factors only and while at the authoritarian end of the scale there is generally little doubt about the extent to which authority is centred at the top, this factor is more difficult to assess in democratic societies and here we find that the extent to which people are permitted to withdraw their labour and the extent to which they are doing so is a clearer and more definite way of assessing a country's style of management on the scale.

In the democratic countries are found a wide range of companies and organisations ranging from highly if not completely authoritarian to the almost completely participative, ranging from the armed forces at one end to worker-owned and controlled enterprises on the other. However, this does not in any way invalidate the scale or its general validity, nor does it detract from the usefulness of the comparison.

On the contrary, the existence of such widely differing systems makes it even more important that we become aware of the impact of different styles of management on people and on results.

CONTEMPORARY THEORIES IN OPERATION MANAGEMENT

Contemporary theories of operation management tend to account for and help interpret the rapidly changing nature of today's organizational environments. As before in management history, these theories are prevalent in other sciences as well.

CONTINGENCY THEORY

Basically, contingency theory asserts that when managers make a decision, they must take into account all aspects of the current situation and act on those aspects that are key to the situation at hand. Basically, it's the approach that "it depends." For example, the continuing effort to identify the best leadership or management style might now conclude that the best style depends on the situation. If one is leading troops in the Persian Gulf, an autocratic style is probably best (of course, many might argue here, too). If one is leading a hospital or university, a more participative and facilitative leadership style is probably best.

SYSTEMS THEORY

Systems theory has had a significant effect on management science and understanding organizations. First, let's look at "what is a system?" A system is a collection of part unified to accomplish an overall goal. If one part of the system is removed, the nature of the system is changed as well. For example, a pile of sand is not a system. If one removes a sand particle, you've still got a pile of sand. However, a functioning car is a system. Remove the carburetor and you've no longer got a working car. A system can be looked at as having inputs, processes, outputs and outcomes. Systems share feedback among each of these four aspects of the systems. Let's look at an organization. Inputs would include resources such as raw materials, money, technologies and people. These inputs go through a process where they're planned, organized, motivated and controlled, ultimately to meet the organi-zation's goals. Outputs would be products or services to a market.

Outcomes would be, *e.g.*, enhanced quality of life or productivity for customers/clients, productivity. Feedback would be information from human resources carrying out the process, customers/clients using the products, etc. Feedback also comes from the larger environment of the organization, *e.g.*, influences from government, society, economics, and technologies. This overall system framework applies to any system, including subsystems (departments, programmes, etc.) in the overall organization.

Systems theory may seem quite basic. Yet, decades of management training and practices in the workplace have not followed this theory. Only recently, with tremendous changes facing organizations and how they operate, have educators and managers come to face this new way of looking at things. This interpretation has brought about a significant change (or paradigm shift) in the way management studies and approaches organizations.

The effect of systems theory in management is that writers, educators, consultants, etc. are helping managers to look at the organization from a broader perspective. Systems theory has brought a new perspective for managers to interpret patterns and events in the workplace. They recognize the various parts of the organization, and, in particular, the interrelations of the parts, *e.g.*, the coordination of central administration with its programmes, engineering with manufacturing, supervisors with workers, etc.

This is a major development. In the past, managers typically took one part and focused on that. Then they moved all attention to another part. The problem was that an organization could, *e.g.*, have a wonderful central administration and wonderful set of teachers, but the departments didn't synchronize at all.

CHAOS THEORY

As chaotic and random as world events seem today, they seem as chaotic in organizations, too. Yet for decades, managers have acted on the basis that organizational events can always be controlled. A new theory (or some say "science"), chaos theory, recognizes that events indeed are rarely controlled. Many chaos theorists (as do systems theorists) refer to biological systems when explaining their theory. They suggest that systems naturally go to more complexity, and as they do so, these systems become more volatile (or susceptible to cataclysmic events) and must expend more energy to maintain that complexity.

As they expend more energy, they seek more structure to maintain stability. This trend continues until the system splits, combines with another complex system or falls apart entirely. Sound familiar? This trend is what many see as the trend in life, in organizations and the world in general.

PROBABILITY AND OPERATION

The theory of probability is the branch of mathematics which is most useful in operations research. Nearly all results of operations of hotels involve elements of chance, usually to a large extent, so that only when the results of a number of similar operations are examined does any regularity evidence itself.

It is nearly as important to know the degree by which individual operations may differ from some expected average, as it is to know how the average depends on the variables involved. In analysing operational data, which are often meager and fragmentary, it is necessary to be able to estimate how likely it is that the next operations will display characteristics similar to those analysed Probability enters into many analytical problems as well as all the statistical problems.

In many situations the system of causes which lead to particular results is so complex that it is impossible, or at least impracticable, to predict exactly which of a number of possible results will arise from a given cause. If a penny is tossed, it is possible in principle to analyse the forces acting on the penny and the motions they produce, and so to predict whether the penny will come to rest with heads or tails showing; however, no one has ever taken the effort to carry out the analysis.

When a gun is fired at a target, it should again be possible to predict exactly where the shell will hit, but the prediction would involve a knowledge of the characteristics of the gun, shell, propellant, and atmosphere far more exact than has yet been obtained.

With a perfect penny, tossed at random, there is no more reason to expect heads than tails to appear. We say then that heads and tails are equally likely to appear. In throwing a symmetrical die the numbers 1, 2, 3, 4, 5, and 0 are equally likely. This notion of equal likelihood is basic to the theory of probability. It does not seem to be possible to give it an exact definition, but we accept it as a self-evident intuitive concept At times we reach the conclusion that results are equally likely from considerations of symmetry. In other cases the conclusion is made on the basis of past experience

THE FEASIBILITY STUDY

When the developer selects a site, a feasibility study is often commissioned to obtain an analysis of the site by an objective third party. Companies offer hotel feasibility studies for a fee and are experts in a particular market, or developers may use the consulting group of one of the major public accounting firms. The company retained to do the feasibility study can spend up to several months gathering detailed data to see if, in their opinion, it makes economic sense to build the hotel. Their conclusion offers an objective third party opinion as to whether the project is feasible, hence the term feasibility study. Generally, the feasibility study considers, evaluates, and makes recommendations about the project based on the following variables:

THE SITE

- Proper zoning
- Size in square feet/acres
- Visibility from arterials/freeways
- Traffic counts/patterns
- Accessibility from streets, freeways, airports, train stations, etc.
- Proximity to where potential guests live, travel, or work
- Barriers that discourage competition coming into the market, if any
- How adjacent property and businesses are utilized
- Master area development plans
- Local permitting process and the degree of difficulty for that particular city
- Impact fees charged by the city

THE ECONOMY OF THE AREA

- Major employers, government agencies
- Business trends for each employer/agency
- Hotel needs and the demand for each
- Leisure travel demand in the area
- Nearby tourist attractions
- Visitor counts
- Conventions, trade shows, and meetings history

THE HOTEL MARKET

- The competitors, both existing and planned
- Historical occupancy of hotels in the area
- Historical average rate
- Proprietary data on area travel

IDENTIFICATION OF WHICH HOTEL MARKET SEGMENT TO SERVE

- Full service
- Limited service
- Extended stay
- Luxury
- Midprice
- Economy
- Budget

SELECTION OF APPROPRIATE HOTEL DESIGN

- High-rise
- Midrise
- Garden apartment style
- Hybrid design

SELECTION OF APPROPRIATE HOTEL BRAND

- Franchised (Marriott, Sheraton, Hyatt, etc.)
- Licensed (Best Western, Guest Suites, etc.)
- Independent
- Independent with strategic market affiliation (Luxury Hotels of America, Historic Hotels of America, etc.)

TEN-YEAR PROJECTION

- Occupancy projection by year
- ADR by year
- Estimated cash generated for debt
- Estimated cash generated for distribution to investors
- Estimated cash-on-cash return (after-tax income divided by equity invested)
- Overall projected yield
- Projected internal rate of return
- Net present value of the project over each of the next ten years. Once the feasibility study is completed, the developer is prepared to move forward with the project. Often, at this stage of the process, the developer purchases an option on the land to tie it up until the remaining development steps can be completed—and to prevent the competition from purchasing it.

HOSPITALITY AND HOTEL CONTROL SYSTEM

It means that actual results have to be compared with targets and suitable corrective action taken to ensure that the targets are achieved. In this process there are two major activities involved: (1) The role of the controlling authority in planning and in taking control action and (2) The system or the routine framework which facilitates the control action. This routine framework relates to preparation of targets, collection of data regarding actual performance, comparison of the actual with the targets and working out the variations with analysis and reporting the variations to the managers concerned to enable them to make action.

In hotel and catering industry the function of control is to check that what has happened is what should have happened.

Although most control work takes place in the past so far as the events being checked have already occurred, the results are used as a basis to correct situations exercised in overall operational transactions in catering, from the purchasing of goods to accounting for sales. Its activities extend throughout an organization and become bound up with the work of heads of departments who, as practitioners, direct control over the conduct of their sections.

Catering control is directed in three ways: over assets, consumption and revenue. *Asset control* ensures that resources in both cash and kind are not misappropriated. This may be in stocks of goods for resale; stocks of working assets such as linen and silverware; and cash in the hands of service workers, cashiers and at the bank.

Consumption control is concerned with the purchasing of supplies and their delivery to departments, and seeing that these departments properly account for the value of goods consumed in sales to customers. Revenue control is directed towards ensuring that whenever an issue of goods or provision of service occurs, the income from the sale does, in fact, materialize, either as a charge to customer's account, or in cash. The complete framework of catering control system is marked by the following main features:

- Continuous comparison of actuals with the targets and working out variations with analysis,
- The classification of the organization into responsibility centres,
- Fixing up responsibility in accordance with the company objectives,
- Communication of variations to the authorities,
- Control action.

The success of a control system is dependent upon the presence of the following three preconditions: (i) A clear cut organizational structure, (ii) The strength and direction of motivation of staff, (iii) Management sponsorship. Control can be effective only if a manager has "authority" over his department and each manager in this way is accountable to some authority or the other.

If the scope and extent of a manager's authority and responsibility are not clearly defined, no control can be exercised over him, nor can he exercise control over others. A control system has ultimately to rest on human beings for its successful functioning. It is the person who have to make it or mar it.

"Motivation" is the mental disposition of an individual towards the control system. It is essentially a psychological matter which motivates a man to play his role with full spirit and vigour. It is this spirit which is the backbone for the successful operation of a control system. Control is a management function which is dependent upon the organization and the circumstances. But there are certain principles, essential to control a catering organization.

(A) PRINCIPLES FOR GOVERNING THE CONTROL PROCESS

- Controls must be designed so as to reflect the contents and structure of plans.

- Control must be so designed as to reflect the organizational structure,
- Control must be designed to meet the personal needs of the individual manager,
- Effective and efficient control requires objective, accurate and suitable standards.
- Effective and efficient control further requires that attention be given to those factors which are strategic for the appraisal of performance.
- Efficiency in control requires that attention of manager be given primarily to significant exceptions,
- Controls should incorporate sufficient flexibility in them so as to remain effective despite the failures of plans.
- The control system should be reviewed periodically,
- Control is only justified if measures are undertaken to correct indicated or experienced deviations from plans through appropriate planning, organizing, staffing and directing.

(B) PRINCIPLES PERTAINING TO NATURE AND PURPOSE OF CONTROL

- Controls must contribute to the accomplishment of group objectives by detecting deviations from plans in time and in a manner to make corrective action possible.
- Controls are efficient if they effectively detect deviations from plans and make possible corrective action with the minimum of undesirable or unexpected consequences.
- Control can be exercised only by the manager responsible for the execution of plans.
- Effective control should be aimed at preventing present and future deviations from plans.
- The most effective technique of control in an enterprise is to assure the qualities of subordinate managers.

It is clear that all catering department needs systematic observation on either a formal or informal basis to guarantee employee integrity and profit.

HOTELS RATIO ANALYSIS

Ratio analysis is a tool for the proper interpretation of financial statements. It helps to express the performances, results and financial information, either in terms of percentages or in terms of relation between different sets of quantities of accounting. It also helps the management in making comparisons between different information and results of different periods and interpret and understand the same, so as to take appropriate measures for better performance in future.

Following are some of the useful ratios:

(a) *Current Ratio:* Current ratio is also referred as to *working capital ratio* as well as solvency ratio. It helps to reveal the relation between the current assets and current liabilities.

(b) *Acid Test Ratio:* It is also known as quick ratio or liquid ratio. This is a development over the current ratio. It involves testing the liquidity of the current assets to find out the convertibility of these assets into cash, in the shortest possible time, without difficulty and with more certainty, during the current period of one year, to meet the current liabilities as and when they become due for payment.

(c) *Percentage of Net Profit (Ratio):* It is the net remainder after deduction from the net sales of all expenses, namely, the cost of sale, operating expenses inclusive of labour charges and overhead charges as well as non-operating expenses like rates and taxes and interest liabilities after adding non-operating incomes like interest receipts. Net Profit Ratio indicates the actual result as returns on investment of the proprietor in business.

(d) *Debtor Turnover Ratio:* Debtor Turnover Ratio is prepared to find out as to how much of the total sale is held by debtors without making payment for it. It indicates the number of days credit facility extended to or availed by the customers. It enables one to have control on debtors and to make efforts in recovering outstandings from debtors in time, without allowing the trade debtors more than the number of days credit facility allowed, if any.

(e) *Percentage of Gross Profit:* This is also referred as 'Gross Profit Ratio'. It reveals margin of profit on sales and average mark-up on goods. Gross profit must ensure recovery of all operating expenses and also enable in creating different types of funds, reserves and provisions and must provide for fixed expenses and dividends.

(f) *Ratio of Stock Turnover:* This ratio is also known as 'Inventory Turnover Ratio'. This ratio is used to find out the speed at which the stock is disposed-off, that is, the rate at which stock is converted into sale and from sale to cash. Stock turnover ratio indicates the number of times the stock is converted into sales and then to cash.

(g) *Double bed occupancy ratio:* This occupancy rate relates to the rooms occupied as double rooms in the hotel. Out of total rooms sold.

(h) *Room Occupancy Ratio:* This type of ratio shows the number of rooms occupied in relation to the number of rooms available for sale and is usually expressed as percentage. It helps in sales promotion activities, to ensure higher percentage of occupancy. It may be misleading when there is a high proportion of double or twin rooms let as single.

NATURE OF HOTEL INDUSTRY AND ACCOMODATIONS

Hotels and other accommodations are as diverse as the many family and business travellers they accommodate. The industry includes all types of lodging, from upscale hotels to RV parks. Motels, resorts, casino hotels, bed-and-breakfast inns, and boarding houses also are included. In fact, in 2004 nearly 62,000 establishments provided overnight accommodations to suit many different needs and budgets.

Establishments vary greatly in size and in the services they provide. *Hotels* and *motels* comprise the majority of establishments and tend to provide more services than other lodging places. There are five basic types of hotels—*commercial*, *resort*, *residential, extended-stay,* and *casino*. Most hotels and motels are *commercial* properties that cater mainly to business people, tourists, and other travellers who need accommodations for a brief stay. Commercial hotels and motels usually are located in cities or suburban areas and operate year round. Larger properties offer a variety of services for their guests, including a range of restaurant and beverage service options—from coffee bars and lunch counters to cocktail lounges and formal fine-dining restaurants.

Some properties provide a variety of retail shops on the premises, such as gift boutiques, newsstands, drug and cosmetics counters, and barber and beauty shops. An increasing number of full-service hotels now offer guests access to laundry and valet services, swimming pools, and fitness centres or health spas. A small, but growing, number of luxury hotel chains also manage condominium units in combination with their transient rooms, providing both hotel guests and condominium owners with access to the same services and amenities. Larger hotels and motels often have banquet rooms, exhibit halls, and spacious ballrooms to accommodate conventions, business meetings, wedding receptions, and other social gatherings.

Conventions and business meetings are major sources of revenue for these hotels and motels. Some commercial hotels are known as conference hotels—fully self-contained entities specifically designed for meetings. They provide physical fitness and recreational facilities for meeting attendees, in addition to state-of-the-art audiovisual and technical equipment, a business centre, and banquet services.

Resort hotels and *motels* offer luxurious surroundings with a variety of recreational facilities, such as swimming pools, golf courses, tennis courts, game rooms, and health spas, as well as planned social activities and entertainment. Resorts typically are located in vacation destinations or near natural settings, such as mountains, the seashore, theme parks, or other attractions. As a result, the business of many resorts fluctuates with the season.

Some resort hotels and motels provide additional convention and conference facilities to encourage customers to combine business with pleasure. During the off season, many of these establishments solicit conventions, sales meetings, and incentive tours to fill their otherwise empty rooms; some resorts even close for the off-season.

Residential hotels provide living quarters for permanent and semi permanent residents. They combine the comfort of apartment living with the convenience of hotel services. Many have dining rooms and restaurants that also are open to residents and to the general public.

Extended-stay hotels combine features of a resort and a residential hotel. Typically, guests use these hotels for a minimum of 5 consecutive nights. These facilities usually provide rooms with fully equipped kitchens, entertainment systems, ironing boards and irons, office space with computer and telephone lines, fitness centres, and other amenities.

Casino hotels provide lodging in hotel facilities with a casino on the premises. The casino provides table wagering games and may include other gambling activities, such as slot machines and sports betting. Casino hotels generally offer a full range of services and amenities and also may contain conference and convention facilities.

In addition to hotels and motels, *bed-and-breakfast inns, recreational vehicle (RV) parks, campgrounds*, and *rooming and boarding houses* provide lodging for overnight guests. *Bed-and-breakfast inns* provide short-term lodging in private homes or small buildings converted for this purpose and are characterized by highly personalized service and inclusion of breakfast in the room rate. Their appeal is quaintness, with unusual service and decor.

RV parks and campgrounds cater to people who enjoy recreational camping at moderate prices. Some parks and campgrounds provide service stations, general stores, shower and toilet facilities, and coin-operated laundries. While some are designed for overnight travellers only, others are for vacationers who stay longer.

Some camps provide accommodations, such as cabins and fixed campsites, and other amenities, such as food services, recreational facilities and equipment, and organized recreational activities. Examples of these overnight camps include children's camps, family vacation camps, hunting and fishing camps, and outdoor adventure retreats that offer trail riding, white-water rafting, hiking, fishing, game hunting, and similar activities.

Other short-term lodging facilities in this industry include *guesthouses*, or small cottages located on the same property as a main residence, and *youth hostels*—dormitory-style hotels with few frills, occupied mainly by students traveling on limited budgets. Also included are *rooming and boarding houses*, such as fraternity houses, sorority houses, off-campus dormitories, and workers' camps. These establishments provide temporary or longer term accommodations that may serve as a principal residence for the period of occupancy. These establishments also may provide services such as housekeeping, meals, and laundry services.

In recent years, hotels, motels, camps, and recreational and RV parks affiliated with national chains have grown rapidly. To the traveller, familiar chain establishments represent dependability and quality at predictable rates. National corporations own many chains, although many properties are independently owned but affiliated with a chain through a franchise agreement.

Many independently operated hotels and inns participate in national reservations services, thereby appearing to belong to a larger enterprise. Also, many hotels join local chambers of commerce, boards of trade, convention and tourism bureaus, or regional recreation associations in order support and promote tourism in their area.

Increases in competition and in the sophistication of travellers have induced the chains to provide lodging to serve a variety of customer budgets and accommodation preferences. In general, these lodging places may be grouped into properties that offer luxury, all-suite, moderately priced, and economy accommodations.

The numbers of limited-service or economy chain properties—economy lodging without extensive lobbies, restaurants, or lounges—have been growing. These properties are not as costly to build and operate. They appeal to budget-conscious family vacationers and travellers who are willing to sacrifice amenities for lower room prices.

While economy chains have become more prevalent, the movement in the hotel and lodging industry is towards more extended-stay properties. In addition to fully equipped kitchenettes and laundry services, the extended-stay market offers guest amenities such as in-room access to the Internet and grocery shopping.

This segment of the hotels and other accommodations industry has eliminated traditional hotel lobbies and 24-hour front desk staffing, and housekeeping is usually done only about once a week. This helps to keep costs to a minimum.

All-suite facilities, especially popular with business travellers, offer a living room or sitting room in addition to a bedroom. These accommodations are aimed at travellers who require lodging for extended stays, families traveling with children, and business people needing to conduct small meetings without the expense of renting an additional room.

Increased competition among establishments in this industry has spurred many independently owned and operated hotels and other lodging places to join national or international reservation systems, which allow travellers to make multiple reservations for lodging, airlines, and car rentals with one telephone call. Nearly all hotel chains operate online reservation systems through the Internet.

WORKING CONDITIONS

Work in hotels and other accommodations can be demanding and hectic. Hotel staffs provide a variety of services to guests and must do so efficiently, courteously, and accurately.

They must maintain a pleasant demeanor even during times of stress or when dealing with an impatient or irate guest. Alternately, work at slower times, such as the off-season or overnight periods, can seem slow and tiresome without the constant presence of hotel guests. Still, hotel workers must be ready to provide guests and visitors with gracious customer service at any hour.

Because hotels are open around the clock, employees frequently work varying shifts or variable schedules. Employees who work the late shift generally receive additional compensation. Many employees enjoy the opportunity to work part-time, nights or evenings, or other schedules that fit their availability for work and the hotel's needs.

Hotel managers and many department supervisors may work regularly assigned schedules, but they also routinely work longer hours than scheduled, especially during peak travel times or when multiple events are scheduled. Also, they may be called in to work on short notice in the event of an emergency or to cover a position. Those who are self-employed, often owner-operators, tend to work long hours and often live at the establishment.

Food preparation and food service workers in hotels must withstand the strain of working during busy periods and being on their feet for many hours. Kitchen workers lift heavy pots and kettles and work near hot ovens and grills. Job hazards include slips and falls, cuts, and burns, but injuries are seldom serious. Food service workers often carry heavy trays of food, dishes, and glassware. Many of these workers work part time, including evenings, weekends, and holidays.

Office and administrative support workers generally work scheduled hours in an office setting, meeting with guests, clients, and hotel staff. Their work can become hectic processing orders and invoices, dealing with demanding guests, or servicing requests that require a quick turnaround, but job hazards typically are limited to muscle and eye strain common to working with computers and office equipment.

In 2003, work-related injuries and illnesses averaged 6.7 for every 100 full-time workers in hotels and other accommodations, compared with 5.0 for workers throughout private industry. Work hazards include burns from hot equipment, sprained muscles and wrenched backs from heavy lifting, and falls on wet floors.

EMPLOYMENT

Hotels and other accommodations provided 1.8 million wage and salary jobs in 2004. In addition, there were about 33,000 self-employed and unpaid family workers in the industry, who worked in bed-and-breakfast inns, camps, and small motels.

Employment is concentrated in densely populated cities and resort areas. Compared with establishments in other industries, hotels, motels, and other lodging places tend to be small. About 91 percent employed fewer than 50 people; about 56 percent employ fewer than 10 workers (chart). As a result, lodging establishments offer opportunities for those who are interested in owning and running their own business. Although establishments tend to be small, the majority of jobs are in larger hotels and motels with more than 100 employees.

Hotels and other lodging places often provide first jobs to many new entrants to the labour force. As a result, many of the industry's workers are young. In 2004, about 19 percent of the workers were younger than age 25, compared with about 14 percent across all industries.

Table. Percent distribution of employment, by age group, 2004

Age group	Hotels and other accommodations	All industries
Total	100.0%	100.0%
16-19	5.3	4.2
20-24	13.7	9.9
25-34	22.4	21.8
35-44	23.7	24.8
45-54	20.2	23.3
55-64	11.4	12.4
65 and older	3.3	3.5

OCCUPATIONS IN THE INDUSTRY

The vast majority of workers in this industry—more than 8 out of 10 in 2004—were employed in service and office and administrative support occupations. Workers in these occupations usually learn their skills on the job. Postsecondary education is not required for most entry-level positions; however, college training may be helpful for advancement in some of these occupations.

For many administrative support and service occupations, personality traits and a customer-service orientation may be more important than formal schooling. Traits most important for success in the hotel and motel industry are good communication skills; the ability to get along with people in stressful situations; a neat, clean appearance; and a pleasant manner.

Service occupations, by far the largest occupational group in the industry, account for 65 percent of the industry's employment. Most service jobs are in housekeeping occupations—including maids and housekeeping cleaners, janitors and cleaners, and laundry workers—and in food preparation and service jobs—including chefs and cooks, waiters and waitresses, bartenders, fast food and counter workers, and various other kitchen and dining room workers. The industry also employs many baggage porters and bellhops, gaming services workers, and grounds maintenance workers. Workers in *cleaning* and *housekeeping occupations* ensure that the lodging facility is clean and in good condition for the comfort and safety of guests. *Maids and housekeepers* clean lobbies, halls, guestrooms, and bathrooms. They make sure that guests not only have clean rooms, but have all the necessary furnishings and supplies. They change sheets and towels, vacuum carpets, dust furniture, empty wastebaskets, and mop bathroom floors. In larger hotels, the housekeeping staff may include assistant housekeepers, floor supervisors, housekeepers, and executive housekeepers. *Janitors* help with the cleaning of the public areas of the facility, empty trash, and perform minor maintenance work.

Workers in the various food service occupations deal with customers in the dining room or at a service counter. Waiters and waitresses take customers' orders, serve meals, and prepare checks. In restaurants, they may describe chef's specials and suggest appropriate wines. In smaller establishments, they often set tables, escort guests to their seats, accept payment, and clear tables. They also may deliver room service orders to guests. In larger restaurants, some of these tasks are assigned to other workers.

Hosts and hostesses welcome guests, show them to their tables, and give them menus. Bartenders fill beverage orders for customers seated at the bar or from waiters and waitresses who serve patrons at tables. Dining room and cafeteria attendants and bartender helpers assist waiters, waitresses, and bartenders by clearing, cleaning, and setting up tables, replenishing supplies at the bar, and keeping the serving areas stocked with linens, tableware, and other supplies. Counter attendants take orders and serve food at fast-food counters and in coffee shops; they also may operate the cash register.

Cooks and food preparation occupations prepare food in the kitchen. Beginners may advance to more skilled food preparation jobs with experience or specialized culinary training. Chefs and cooks generally prepare a wide selection of dishes, often cooking individual servings to order. Larger hotels employ cooks who specialize in the preparation of many different kinds of food. They may have titles such as salad chef, grill chef, or pastry chef.

Individual chefs may oversee the day-to-day operations of different kitchens in a hotel, such as a fine-dining full-service restaurant, a casual or counter-service establishment, or banquet operations. Chef positions generally are attained after years of experience and, sometimes, formal training, including apprenticeships. Larger establishments also employ executive chefs and food and beverage directors who plan menus, purchase food, and supervise kitchen personnel for all of the kitchens in the property. Food preparation workers shred lettuce for salads, cut up food for cooking, and perform simple cooking steps under the direction of the chef or head cook.

Many full-service hotels employ a uniformed staff to assist arriving and departing guests. Baggage porters and bellhops carry bags and escort guests to their rooms. Concierges arrange special or personal services for guests. They may take messages, arrange for babysitting, make restaurant reservations, provide directions, arrange for or give advice on entertainment and local attractions, and monitor requests for housekeeping and maintenance. Doorkeepers help guests into and out of their cars, summon taxis, and carry baggage into the hotel lobby.

Hotels also employ the largest percentage of gaming services workers because much of gaming takes place in casino hotels. Some gaming services positions are associated with oversight and direction—supervision, surveillance, and investigation—while others involve working with the games or patrons themselves, by tending the slot machines, handling money, writing and running tickets, dealing cards, and performing related duties.

Office and administrative support positions accounted for 18 percent of the jobs in hotels and other accommodations in 2004. Hotel desk clerks, secretaries, bookkeeping and accounting clerks, and telephone operators ensure that the front office operates smoothly. The majority of these workers are hotel, motel, and resort desk clerks. They process reservations and guests' registration and checkout, monitor arrivals and departures, handle complaints, and receive and forward mail.

The duties of hotel desk clerks depend on the size of the facility. In smaller lodging places, one clerk or a manager may do everything. In larger hotels, a larger staff divides the duties among several types of clerks. Although hotel desk clerks sometimes are hired from the outside, openings usually are filled by promoting other hotel employees such as bellhops and porters, credit clerks, and other administrative support workers.

Hotels and other lodging places employ many different types of *managers* to direct and coordinate the activities of the front office, kitchen, dining room, and other departments, such as housekeeping, accounting, personnel, purchasing, publicity, sales, security and maintenance. Managers make decisions on room rates, establish credit policy, and have ultimate responsibility for resolving problems. In smaller establishments, the manager also may perform many of the front-office clerical tasks. In the smallest establishments, the owners—sometimes a family team—do all the work necessary to operate the business.

Lodging managers or *general and operations managers* in large hotels often have several assistant managers, each responsible for a phase of operations. For example, *food and beverage managers* oversee restaurants, lounges, and catering or banquet operations. *Rooms managers* look after reservations and occupancy levels to ensure proper room assignments and authorize discounts, special rates, or promotions. Large hotels, especially those with conference centres, use an executive committee structure to improve departmental communications and coordinate activities. Other managers who may serve on a hotel's executive committee include *public relations* or *sales managers, human resources directors*, *executive housekeepers*, and *heads of hotel security*.

Workers at vacation and recreational camps may include camp counselors who lead and instruct children and teenagers in outdoor-oriented forms of recreation, such as swimming, hiking, horseback riding, and camping. In addition, counselors at vacation and resident camps also provide guidance and supervise daily living and general socialization. Other types of campgrounds may employ trail guides for activities such as hiking, hunting, and fishing.

Hotels and other lodging places employ a variety of workers found in many other industries. Maintenance workers, such as stationary engineers, plumbers, and painters, fix leaky faucets, do some painting and carpentry, see that heating and air-conditioning equipment works properly, mow lawns, and exterminate pests. The industry also employs cashiers, accountants, personnel workers, entertainers, and recreation workers. Also, many additional workers inside a hotel may work for other companies under contract to the hotel or may provide personal or retail services directly to hotel guests from space rented by the hotel. This group includes guards and security officers, barbers, cosmetologists, fitness trainers and aerobics instructors, valets, gardeners, and parking attendants.

TRAINING AND ADVANCEMENT

Although the skills and experience needed by workers in this industry depend on the specific occupation, most entry-level jobs require little or no previous training. Basic tasks usually can be learned in a short time. Almost all workers in the hotel and other accommodations industry undergo on-the-job training, which usually is provided under the supervision of an experienced employee or manager. Some large chain operations have formal training sessions for new employees; many also provide video or on-line training.

Hotel operations are becoming increasingly diverse and complex, but all positions require employees to maintain a customer-service orientation. Hoteliers recognize the importance of personal service and attention to guests; so they look for persons with positive personality traits and good communication skills when filling many guest services positions, such as desk clerk and host and hostess positions. Many hotel managers place a greater emphasis on customer service skills while providing specialized training in important skill areas, such as computer technology and software.

Vocational courses and apprenticeship programmes in food preparation, catering, and hotel and restaurant management, offered through restaurant associations and trade unions, provide training opportunities. Programmes range in length from a few months to several years. About 800 community and junior colleges offer 2-year degree programmes in hotel and restaurant management. The U.S. Armed Forces also offer experience and training in food service.

Traditionally, many hotels fill first-level manager positions by promoting administrative support and service workers—particularly those with good communication skills, a solid educational background, tact, loyalty, and a capacity to endure hard work and long hours.

People with these qualities still advance to manager jobs but, more recently, lodging chains have primarily been hiring persons with four-year college degrees in the liberal arts or other fields and starting them in trainee or junior management positions. Bachelor's and master's degree programmes in hotel, restaurant, and hospitality management provide the strongest background for a career as a hotel manager, with nearly 150 colleges and universities offering such programmes. Graduates of these programmes are highly sought by employers in this industry. New graduates often go through on-the-job training programmes before being given much responsibility. Eventually, they may advance to a top management position in a hotel, a corporate management opportunity in a large chain operation, or an investment or financial analysis position in the financial services sector.

Upper management positions, such as general manager, lodging manager, food service manager, or sales manager, generally require considerable formal training and job experience. Some department managers, such as comptrollers, purchasing managers, executive housekeepers, and executive chefs, generally require some specialized training and extensive on-the-job experience. To advance to positions with more responsibilities, managers frequently change employers or relocate within a chain to a property in another area.

For office and administrative support and service workers, advancement opportunities in the hotel industry vary widely. Some workers, such as housekeepers and janitors, generally have few opportunities for advancement. In large properties, however, some janitors may advance to supervisory positions. Hotel desk clerks, hospitality workers, and chefs sometimes advance to managerial positions. Promotional opportunities from the front office often are greater than those from any other department, because this vantage point provides an excellent opportunity to learn the establishment's overall operation. Front-office jobs are excellent entry-level jobs and can serve as a steppingstone to jobs in hospitality, public relations, advertising, sales, and management.

Advancement opportunities for chefs and cooks are better than those for most other service occupations. Cooks often advance to chef or to supervisory and management positions, such as executive chef, restaurant manager, or food service manager. Some transfer to jobs in clubs, go into business for themselves, or become instructors of culinary arts.

NATURE OF THE WORK

A comfortable room, good food, and a helpful staff can make being away from home an enjoyable experience for both vacationing families and business travellers. While most lodging managers work in traditional hotels and motels, some work in other lodging establishments, such as camps, inns, boardinghouses, dude ranches, and recreational resorts. In full-service hotels, lodging managers help their guests have a pleasant stay by providing many of the comforts of home, including cable television, fitness equipment, and voice mail, as well as specialized services such as health spas. For business travellers, lodging managers often schedule available meeting rooms and electronic equipment, including slide projectors and fax machines.

Lodging managers are responsible for keeping their establishments efficient and profitable. In a small establishment with a limited staff, the manager may oversee all aspects of operations. However, large hotels may employ hundreds of workers, and the general manager usually is aided by a number of assistant managers assigned to the various departments of the operation. In hotels of every size, managerial duties vary significantly by job title.

General managers have overall responsibility for the operation of the hotel. Within guidelines established by the owners of the hotel or executives of the hotel chain, the general manager sets room rates, allocates funds to departments, approves expenditures, and ensures expected standards for guest service, decor, housekeeping, food quality, and banquet operations. Managers who work for chains also may organize and staff a newly built hotel, refurbish an older hotel, or reorganize a hotel or motel that is not operating successfully. In order to fill entry-level service and clerical jobs in hotels, some managers attend career fairs.

Resident or hotel managers are responsible for the day-to-day operations of the property. In larger properties, more than one of these managers may assist the general manager, frequently dividing responsibilities between the food and beverage operations and the rooms or lodging services. At least one manager, either the general manager or a hotel manager, is on call 24 hours a day to resolve problems or emergencies.

Assistant managers help run the day-to-day operations of the hotel. In large hotels, they may be responsible for activities such as personnel, accounting, office administration, marketing and sales, purchasing, security, maintenance, and pool, spa, or recreational facilities. In smaller hotels, these duties may be combined into one position. Assistant managers may adjust charges on a hotel guest's bill when a manager is unavailable.

An Executive Committee made up of a hotel's senior managers advises the general manager, assists in setting hotel policy, coordinates services that cross departmental boundaries, and collaborates on efforts to ensure consistent and efficient guest services throughout the hotel. The Committee may be comprised of the department heads for housekeeping, front office, food and beverage, security, sales and public relations, meetings and conventions, engineering and building maintenance, and human resources.

Executive committee members bring a different perspective of guest service to the total management objective reflecting the unique expertise and training of their positions. Executive housekeepers ensure that guest rooms, meeting and banquet rooms, and public areas are clean, orderly, and well maintained. They also train, schedule, and supervise the work of housekeepers, inspect rooms, and order cleaning supplies.

Front office managers coordinate reservations and room assignments, as well as train and direct the hotel's front desk staff. They ensure that guests are treated courteously, complaints and problems are resolved, and requests for special services are carried out. Front office managers may adjust charges posted on a customer's bill.

Convention services managers coordinate the activities of various departments in larger hotels to accommodate meetings, conventions, and special events.

They meet with representatives of groups or organizations to plan the number of rooms to reserve, the desired configuration of the meeting space, and banquet services. During the meeting or event, they resolve unexpected problems and monitor activities to ensure that hotel operations conform to the expectations of the group.

Food and beverage managers oversee all food service operations maintained by the hotel. They coordinate menus with the Executive Chef for the hotel's restaurants, lounges, and room service operations. They supervise the ordering of food and supplies, direct service and maintenance contracts within the kitchens and dining areas, and manage food service budgets.

Catering managers arrange for food service in a hotel's meeting and convention rooms. They coordinate menus and costs for banquets, parties, and events with meeting and convention planners or individual clients. They coordinate staffing needs and arrange schedules with kitchen personnel to ensure appropriate food service.

Sales or marketing directors and public relations directors oversee the advertising and promotion of hotel operations and functions, including lodging and dining specials and special events, such as holiday or seasonal specials. They direct the efforts of their staff to purchase advertising and market their property to organizations or groups seeking a venue for conferences, conventions, business meetings, trade shows, and special events. They also coordinate media relations and answer questions from the press.

Human resources directors manage the personnel functions of a hotel, ensuring that all accounting, payroll, and employee relations matters are handled in compliance with hotel policy and applicable laws. They also oversee hiring practices and standards and ensure that training and promotion programmes reflect appropriate employee development guidelines.

Finance (or revenue) directors monitor room sales and reservations. In addition to overseeing accounting and cash-flow matters at the hotel, they also project occupancy levels, decide which rooms to discount and when to offer rate specials. Computers are used extensively by lodging managers and their assistants to keep track of guests' bills, reservations, room assignments, meetings, and special events. In addition, computers are used to order food, beverages, and supplies, as well as to prepare reports for hotel owners and top-level managers. Managers work with computer specialists to ensure that the hotel's computer system functions properly. Should the hotel's computer system fail, managers must continue to meet the needs of hotel guests and staff.

Because hotels are open around the clock, night and weekend work is common. Many lodging managers work more than 40 hours per week, and may be called back to work at any time. Some managers of resort properties or other hotels where much of the business is seasonal have other duties on the property during the off-season or find work at other hotels or in other areas.

Lodging managers experience the pressures of coordinating a wide range of activities. At larger hotels, they also carry the burden of managing a large staff and finding a way to satisfy guest needs while maintaining positive attitudes and employee morale. Conventions and large groups of tourists may present unusual problems or require extended work hours. Moreover, dealing with irate guests can be stressful. The job can be particularly hectic for front office managers during check-in and check-out times. Computer failures can further complicate processing and add to frustration levels.

Hotels increasingly emphasize specialized training. Postsecondary training in hotel, restaurant, or hospitality management is preferred for most hotel management positions; however, a college liberal arts degree may be sufficient when coupled with related hotel experience or business education. Internships or part-time or summer work experience in a hotel are an asset to students seeking a career in hotel management. The experience gained and the contacts made with employers can greatly benefit students after graduation. Most degree programmes include work-study opportunities.

Community colleges, junior colleges, and many universities offer certificate or degree programmes in hotel, restaurant, or hospitality management leading to an associate, bachelor, or graduate degree. Technical institutes, vocational and trade schools, and other academic institutions also offer courses leading to formal recognition in hospitality management. In total, more than 800 educational facilities provide academic training for would-be lodging managers. Hotel management programmes include instruction in hotel administration, accounting, economics, marketing, housekeeping, food service management and catering, and hotel maintenance engineering. Computer training also is an integral part of hotel management training, due to the widespread use of computers in reservations, billing, and housekeeping management.

More than 450 high schools in 45 States offer the Lodging Management Programme created by the Educational Institute of the American Hotel and

Lodging Association. This two-year programme offered to high school juniors and seniors teaches management principles and leads to a professional certification called the "Certified Rooms Division Specialist." Many colleges and universities grant participants credit towards a post-secondary degree in hotel management.

Lodging managers must be able to get along with many different types of people, even in stressful situations. They must be able to solve problems and concentrate on details. Initiative, self-discipline, effective communication skills, and the ability to organize and direct the work of others also are essential for managers at all levels.

Persons wishing to make a career in the hospitality industry may be promoted into a management trainee position sponsored by the hotel or a hotel chain's corporate parent. Typically, trainees work as assistant managers and may rotate assignments among the hotel's departments—front office, housekeeping, or food and beverage—to gain a wide range of experiences. Relocation to another property may be required to help round out the experience and to help grow a trainee into the position.

Work experience in the hospitality industry at any level or in any segment, including summer jobs or part-time work in a hotel or restaurant, is good background for entering hotel management. Most employers require a bachelor's degree with some education in business and computer literacy, while some prefer a master's degree for hotel management positions. However, employees who demonstrate leadership potential and possess sufficient length or breadth of experience may be invited to participate in a management training programme and advance to hotel management positions without the education beyond high school.

Large hotel and motel chains may offer better opportunities for advancement than small, independently owned establishments, but relocation every several years often is necessary for advancement. The large chains have more extensive career ladder programmes and offer managers the opportunity to transfer to another hotel or motel in the chain or to the central office. Career advancement can be accelerated by the completion of certification programmes offered by various associations. These programmes usually require a combination of course work, examinations, and experience. For example, outstanding lodging managers may advance to higher level manager positions.

Lodging managers held about 58,000 jobs in 2004. Self-employed managers—primarily owners of small hotels, motels, and inns—held about 45 percent of these jobs. Companies that manage hotels and motels under contract employed many managers.

Employment of lodging managers is expected to grow about as fast as the average for all occupations through 2014. Additional job openings are expected to occur as experienced managers transfer to other occupations or leave the labour force, in part because of the long hours and stressful working conditions. Job opportunities are expected to be best for persons with college degrees in hotel or hospitality management.

Renewed business travel and domestic and foreign tourism will drive employment growth of lodging managers in full-service hotels. The numbers of economy-class rooms and extended-stay hotels also are expected to increase to accommodate leisure travellers and bargain-conscious guests. An increasing range of lodging accommodations is available to travellers, from economy hotels which offer clean, comfortable rooms and front desk services without costly extras such as restaurants and room service, to luxury and boutique inns that offer sumptuous furnishings and personal services.

The accommodation industry is expected to continue to consolidate as lodging chains acquire independently owned establishments or undertake their operation on a contract basis. The increasing number of extended-stay hotels will moderate growth of manager jobs because these properties usually have fewer departments and require fewer managers. Also, these establishments often do not require a manager to be available 24 hours a day, instead assigning front desk clerks on duty at night some of the responsibilities previously reserved for managers.

Additional demand for managers is expected in suite hotels, because some guests—especially business customers—are willing to pay higher prices for rooms with kitchens and suites that provide the space needed to conduct small meetings. In addition, large full-service hotels—offering restaurants, fitness centres, large meeting rooms, and play areas for children, among other amenities—will continue to provide many trainee and managerial opportunities.

3

Textile

TEXTILE FABRIC COMPUTING

Fabric computing or unified computing involves the creation of a computing fabric consisting of interconnected nodes that look like a 'weave' or a 'fabric' when viewed collectively from a distance. Usually this refers to a consolidated high-performance computing system consisting of loosely coupled storage, networking and parallel processing functions linked by high bandwidth interconnects (such as 10 Gigabit Ethernet and InfiniBand) but the term has also been used to describe platforms like the Azure Services Platform and grid computing in general (where the common theme is interconnected nodes that appear as a single logical unit).

The fundamental components of *fabrics* are "nodes" (processor(s), memory, and/or peripherals) and "links" (functional connection between nodes). While the term "fabric" has also been used in association with storage area networks and switched fabric networking, the introduction of compute resources provides a complete "unified" computing system.

Other terms used to describe such fabrics include "unified fabric", "data centre fabric" and "unified data centre fabric". According to Ian Foster, director of the Computation Institute at the Argonne National Laboratory and University of Chicago, "grid computing 'fabrics' are now poised to become the underpinning for next-generation enterprise IT architectures and be used by a much greater part of many organizations." IBM, TIBCO, Brocade, Cisco, HP, Egenera, Avaya and Xsigo Systems currently manufacture computing fabric equipment.

HISTORY

While the term has been in use since the mid to late 1990s the growth of cloud computing and Cisco's evangelism of *unified data centre fabrics* followed by *unified computing* (an evolutionarydata centre architecture whereby blade servers are integrated or *unified* with supporting network and storage infrastructure) starting March 2009 has renewed interest in the technology. Other companies offering unified or fabric computing systems include Liquid

Computing Corporation and Egenera. There have been mixed reactions to Cisco's architecture, particularly from rivals who claim that these proprietary systems will lock out other vendors. Analysts claim that this "ambitious new direction" is "a big risk" as companies like IBM and HP who have previously partnered with Cisco on data centre projects (accounting for $2–3bn of Cisco's annual revenue) are now competing with them.

Key Characteristics

The main advantages of *fabrics* are that a massive concurrent processing combined with a huge, tightly-coupled address space makes it possible to solve huge computing problems (such as those presented by delivery of cloud computing services) and that they are both scalable and able to be dynamically reconfigured. Challenges include a non-linearly degrading performance curve, whereby adding resources does not linearly increase performance which is a common problem with parallel computing and maintaining security.

TEXTILE FABRICS

However, a knowledge of the characteristics of each kind of fibre helps a good deal, as every fibre has certain inherent qualities, which cannot be wholly reproduced in any imitation fibre. For example, wool has its own features and no other fibre has identical ones.

The look and even the touch of pure wool flannel may be copied in the cotton flannelette and an inexperienced purchaser may find it difficult to distinguish the wool from the cotton. Fabrics made with newer blends, synthetic fibres are also not easy to judge merely by the appearance or touch. To identify such fabrics, the help of other tests, even of chemical tests is needed.

FEATURES OF FIBRES

Natural Fibres

Man-made Fibres

These fibres do not take place in fibre form but have been turned into it by man, by breaking down from their original form and reassembled into various sort of structure, *e.g.,* rayons.

Cellulose-Fibres

These fibres have as their origin cellulose which is the chief matter of the plant cells. Cellulose is a complex compound made up of carbon, hydrogen and oxygen with the molecular formula of $(C_6H_{10}O_6)n$.

Cotton comprises about 91 per cent and hemp rame and flax contain similarly large amounts of cellulose. Cellulose is very sensitive to the action of mineral acids, and oxidising agents. However, it is very resistant to alkalies, including strong caustic alkalies at high temperature and pressure. Cellulosic fibres are low in resiliency so the fabrics wrinkle easily. Due to the high absorbency of the fibre they are comfortable for summer wear.

Fig. Cellulose Fibre

Animal-Fibres

Wool and silk are obtained from animals and are, therefore, known as animal fibres. They have protein as one of the chief constituents and are made up of carbon, hydrogen and nitrogen. Wool contains sulphur besides the above elements. Both are destroyed by concentrated mineral acids but the specific action of the dilute acids is not very harmful on either. Thus, dilute acids are the basis of dyeing and finishing processes for the materials made from these fibres. Wool as well as silk burn with the special odour of burning proteins like burning of hair, dals or milk.

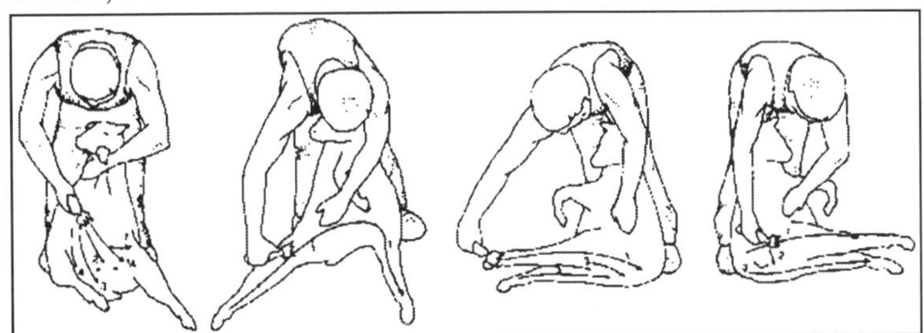

Fig. Animal-Fibres

Alkalies have a harmful effect on both. Animal fibres are very resilient and the wrinkles go out between wearings. However, they are bad conductors of heat and build up static electricity in cold and dry weather. Wool loses about 40 per cent of its strength when wet and silk, 15 per cent. Wool has a natural crimp which supports to increase its elasticity and strength. It has a springiness or resilience which no other natural fibre possesses. commonly speaking, woollen fabrics are soft to the touch and present a fuzzy appearance.

Worsteds are an exception, as their yarns are tightly twisted and firm. Wool, mixed with cotton, produces in the fabric a distinct hardness and heaviness about the material, which further tends to soil readily, fade and to wrinkle. Silk has a luxurious soft texture, and a deep lustre. The sheen is not loud or bright as in man-made fabrics.

This fibre is strong and retains most of its strength even when wet. It possesses elasticity and does not wear out soon. It is the lightest of all the fibres. Man-made fabrics may similiar to pure silk in appearance but are not so light. Silks weighted with metallic salts are still heavier and produce a sharp crease on the line of the fold. There are two kinds of man-made fibres: thermo-plastic and non-thermo-plastic.

Thermo-plastic Fibres

These are those that soften with heat and thus become liable or if the heat is sufficient high, will melt. These fibres are resistant to friction and wrinkling.

Fig. Thermo-plastic Fibres

They have low moisture content which makes them an easy to care fabric, however, they are not easy to dye. Due to this property they build up static electricity in cold and dry weather like animal fibres.

Non-Thermo-plastic Fibres

Which neither soften or melt with the application of heat but will scorch or burn if the temperature is very high. As a group they are soft, absorbent, pliable and comfortable to wear. They do not accumulate static electricity. They, except for mineral fibres, may be cared much as the natural fibres.

Fibres of Mineral Nature

These are inorganic and used for fireproof fabrics. Asbestos is practically the only natural mineral fibre. It is utilised in fabrics intended for make dress, fire-proof curtains and screens, and for man uses. It is also used for floor and table mats. Mineral fibres are really drawn threads from metals, *e.g.,* gold, silver in tissues and brocades, and even baser metals are utilised in fabrics like tinsel. Thus, their origin is inorganic matter. They have an unusually bright sheen. Cotton is limp and has a dull surface because of to its fibre structure.

It lacks the lustre and the natural creaminess of linen. It is quite inflammable, and soils and crushes easily. It is heavier than comparable fabrics of other fibre content. It is brittle and is elastic when dry; but, when moist, its strength and elasticity increases. Mercerized cotton is stronger, smoother and lustrous, hence it soils less readily than cotton. Linen is smooth and cool to the touch as compared to cotton. Fine linen has a lustre almost equal to that of silk. It has crispness and is strong enough for hard wear. Moisture soaks through and spreads over linen fabrics much more quickly than in the case of cotton fabrics.

Linen, when torn, has straight, glossy fibre-ends of unequal length. The fibre-ends of torn cotton curl and are lustreless. Linen yarn when not twisted, a more or less parallel arrangement of glossy, individual fibre. Rayon is produced to replace pure silk and so has a similar appearance, but with a better luster generally; though sometimes dull rayons are also produced. The rayon fibre if subtly examined, will be found to be coarser and heavier than a silk fibre. Rayon realised stiffer to the touch and is less elastic. It breaks more easily than silk, thus showing less strength. It loses strength when wet and regains it when dry.

FIBRE CLASSIFICATION

Textile fibres are normally broken down into two main classes, natural and man-made fibres. All fibres which come from natural sources (animals, plants, etc.) and do not require fibre formation or reformation are classed as natural fibres. Natural fibres include the protein fibres such as wool and silk, the cellulose fibres such as cotton and linen, and the mineral fibre asbestos. Man-made fibres are fibres in which either the basic chemical units have been formed by chemical synthesis followed by fibre formation or the polymers from natural sources have been dissolved and regenerated after passage through a spinneret to form fibres.

Those fibres made by chemical synthesis are often called synthetic fibres, while fibres regenerated from natural polymer sources are called regenerated fibres or natural polymer fibres. In other words, all synthetic fibres and regenerated fibres are man-made fibres, since man is involved in the actual fibre formation process.

In contrast, fibres from natural sources are provided by nature in ready-made form. The synthetic man-made fibres include the polyamides (nylon), polyesters, acrylics, polyolefins, vinyls, and elastomeric fibres, while the regenerated fibres include rayon, the cellulose acetates, the regenerated proteins, glass and rubber fibres. Another method of classifying fibres would be according to chemical structure without regard of the origin of the fibre and its starting materials. In this manner all fibres of similar chemical structure would be classed together. The natural man-made fibre classification given in figure does this to a certain extent. In this way, all fibres having the basic cellulosic unit in their structures would be grouped together rather than separated into natural and man-made fibres.

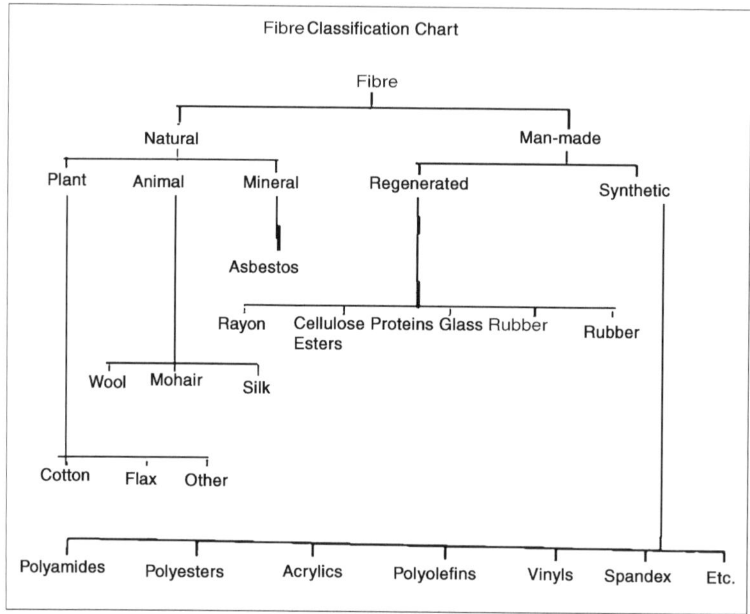

Fig. Classification of Natural and Man-made Fibres.

This book essentially presents the fibres in groups of similar basic chemical structure, with two exceptions. In one case the elastomeric fibres have been grouped together due to their exceptional physical property, high extensibility and recovery.

FIBRE PROPERTIES

There are several primary properties necessary for a polymeric material to make an adequate fibre:

- Fibre length to width ratio,
- Fibre uniformity,
- Fibre strength and flexibility,
- Fibre extensibility and elasticity, and
- Fibre cohesiveness.

Certain other fibre properties increase its value and desirability in its intended end-use but are not necessary properties essential to make a fibre. Such secondary properties include moisture absorption characteristics, fibre resiliency, abrasion resistance, density, luster, chemical resistance, thermal characteristics, and flammability.

FIBRE LENGTH TO WIDTH RATIO

Fibrous materials must have sufficient length so that they can be made into twisted yarns. In addition, the width of the fibre (the diameter of the cross section) must be much less than the overall length of the fibre, and usually the fibre diameter should be 1/100 of the length of the fibre. The fibre may be "infinitely" long, as found with continuous filament fibres, or as short as 0.5 inches (1.3 em), as found in staple fibres. Most natural fibres are staple fibres, whereas man-made fibres come in either staple or filament form depending on processing prior to yarn formation.

FIBRE UNIFORMITY

Fibres suitable for processing into yarns and fabrics must be fairly uniform in shape and size. Without sufficient uniformity of dimensions and properties in a given set of fibres to be twisted into yarn. The actual formation of the yarn may be impossible or the resulting yarn may be weak, rough, and irregular in size and shape and unsuitable for textile usage. Natural fibres must be sorted and graded to assure fibre uniformity, whereas synthetic fibres may be "tailored" by cutting into appropriate uniform lengths to give a proper degree of fibre uniformity.

FIBRE STRENGTH AND FLEXIBILITY

A fibre or yarn made from the fibre must possess sufficient strength to be processed into a textile fabric or other textile article. The resulting textile must have sufficient strength to provide adequate durability during end-use. Many experts consider single fibre strength of 5 grams per denier to be necessary for a fibre suitable in most textile applications, although certain fibres with strengths as low as 1.0 gram per denier have been found suitable for some applications.

The strength of a single fibre is called the tenacity, defined as the force per unit linear density necessary to break a known unit of that fibre. The breaking tenacity of a fibre may be expressed in grams per denier (g/d) or grams per tex (g/tex). Both denier and tex are units of linear density (mass per unit of fibre length) and are defined as the number of grams of fibre measuring 9000 meters and 1000 meters, respectively. As a result, the denier of a fibre or yarn will always be 9 times the tex of the same fibre. Since tenacities of fibres or yarns are obtained by dividing the force by denier or tex, the tenacity of a fibre in grams per denier will be 1/9 that of the fibre tenacity in grams per tex. As a result of the adaption of the International System of Units. The appropriate length unit for breaking tenacity becomes kilometer (km) of breaking length or Newtons per tex (N/tex) and will be equivalent in value to g/tex. The strength of a fibre yarn or fabric can be expressed in terms of force per unit area, and when expressed in this way the term is tensile strength. The most common unit used in the past for tensile strength has been pounds force per square inch or grams force per square centimeter.

In 51 units, the pounds force per square inch x 6.895 will become kilopascals (kPa) and grams force per square centimeter x 9.807 will become megapascals (MPa). A fibre must be sufficiently flexible to go through repeated bending without significant strength deterioration or breakage of the fibre. Without adequate flexibility, it would be impossible to convert fibres into yarns and fabrics, since flexing and bending of the individual fibres is a necessary part of this conversion. In addition, individual fibres in a textile will be subjected to considerable bending and flexing during enduse.

FIBRE EXTENSIBILITY AND ELASTICITY

An individual fibre must be able to undergo slight extensions in length (less than 5 per cent) without breakage of the fibre. At the same time the fibre must be able to almost completely recover following slight fibre deformation. In other words, the extension deformation of the fibre must be nearly elastic. These properties are important because the individual fibres in textiles are often subjected to sudden stresses, and the textile must be able to give and recover without significant overall deformation of the textile.

FIBRE COHESIVENESS

Fibres must be capable of adhering to one another when spun into a yarn. The cohesiveness of the fibre may be due to the shape and contour of the individual fibre s or the nature of the surface of the fibres.

In addition, long-filament fibres by virtue of their length can be twisted together to give stability without true cohesion between fibres. Often the term "spinning quality" is used to state the overall attractiveness of fibres for one another.

MOISTURE ABSORPTION AND DESORPTION

Most fibres tend to absorb moisture (water vapor) when in contact with the atmosphere. The amount of water absorbed by the textile fibre will depend on the chemical and physical structure and properties of the fibre, as well as the temperature and humidity of the surroundings.

The percentage absorption of water vapor by a fibre is often expressed as its moisture regain. The regain is determined by weighing a dry fibre, then placing it in a room set to standard temperature and humidity (21° ± 1° C and 65 per cent relative humidity [RH] are commonly used). From these measurements, the percentage moisture regain of the fibre is determined:

$$\text{Percentage Regain} = \frac{\text{Conditioned weight} - \text{Dry Weight}}{\text{Dry Weight}} \times 100\%$$

Percentage moisture content of a fibre is the percentage of the total weight of the fibre which is due to the moisture present, and is obtained from the following formula:

$$\text{Percentage moisture content } \frac{\text{Conditioned weight} = \text{Dry weight}}{\text{Conditioned weight}} \times 100\%$$

The percentage moisture content will always be the smaller of the two values. Fibres vary greatly in their regain, with hydrophobic (water-repelling) fibres having regains near zero and hydrophilic (water-seeking) fibres like cotton, rayon, and wool having regains as high as 15 per cent at 21°C and 65 per cent RH. The ability of fibres to absorb high regains of water affects the basic properties of the fibre in end-use. Absorbent fibres are able to absorb large amounts of water before they feel wet, an important factor where absorption of perspiration is necessary. Fibres with high regains will be easier to process, finish, and dye in aqueous solutions, but will dry more slowly.

The low regain found for many man-made fibres makes them quick drying, a distinct advantage in certain applications. Fibres with high regains are often desirable because they provide a "breathable" fabric which can conduct moisture from the body to the outside atmosphere readily, due to their favourable moisture absorption-desorption properties. The tensile properties of fibres as well as their dimensional properties are known to be affected by moisture.

FIBRE RESILIENCY AND ABRASION RESISTANCE

The ability of a fibre to absorb shock and recover from deformation and to be generally resistant to abrasion forces is important to its end-use and wear characteristics. In consumer use, fibres in fabrics are often placed under stress through compression, bending, and twisting (torsion) forces under a variety of temperature and humidity conditions. If the fibres within the fabric possess good elastic recovery properties from such deformative actions, the fibre has good resiliency and better overall appearance in end-use. For example, cotton and wool show poor wrinkle recovery under hot moist conditions, whereas polyester exhibits good recovery from deformation as a result of its high resiliency.

Resistance of a fibre to damage when mobile forces or stresses come in contact with fibre structures is referred to as abrasion resistance. If a fibre is able to effectively absorb and dissipate these forces without damage, the fibre will show good abrasion resistance. The toughness and hardness of the fibre is related to its chemical and physical structure and morphology of the fibre and will influence the abrasion of the fibre. A rigid, brittle fibre such as glass, which is unable to dissipate the forces of abrasive action, results in fibre damage and breakage, whereas a tough but more plastic fibre such as polyester shows better resistance to abrasion forces. Finishes can affect fibre properties including resiliency and abrasion resistance.

LUSTER

Luster refers to the degree of light that is reflected from the surface of *a* fibre or the degree of gloss or sheen that the fibre possesses. The inherent chemical and physical structure and shape of the possesses. The inherent chemical and physical structure and shape of the fibre *can* affect the relative luster of the fibre. With natural fibres the luster of the fibre is dependent on the morphological form that nature gives the fibre, although the relative luster can be changed by chemical and/or physical treatment of the fibre as found in processes such *as* mercerisation of cotton. Man-made fibres can vary in luster from bright to dull depending on the amount of delusterant added to the fibre. Oelusterants such *as* titanium dioxide tend to scatter and absorb 1ight, thereby making the fibre appear duller. The desirability of luster for *a* given fibre application will vary and is often dependent on the intended end-use of the fibre in *a* fabric or garment form and on current fashion trends.

RESISTANCE TO CHEMICALS IN THE ENVIRONMENT

A textile fibre to be useful must have reasonable resistance to chemicals it comes in contact with in its environment during use and maintenance. It should have resistance to oxidation by oxygen and other gases in the air, particularly in the presence of light, and be resistant to attack by microorganisms and other biological agents. Many fibres undergo light-induced reactions, and fibres from natural sources are susceptible to biological attack, but such deficiencies can be minimized by treatment with appropriate finishes. Textile fibres come in contact with a large range of chemical agents on laundering and dry cleaning and must be resistant from attack under such conditions.

OENSITY

The density of a fibre is related to its inherent chemical structure and the packing of the molecular chains within that structure. The density of a fibre will have a noticeable effect on its aesthetic appeal and its usefulness in given applications. For example, glass and silk fabrics of the same denier would have noticeable differences in weight due to their broad differences in density. Fishnets of polypropylene fibres are of great utility because their density is less than that of water. Oensities are usually expressed in units of grams per cubic centimeter, but in 51 units will be expressed as kilograms per cubic meter, which gives a value 1000 times larger.

THERMAL AND FLAMMABILITY CHARACTERISTICS

Fibres used in textiles must be resistant to wet and dry heat, must not ignite readily when coming in contact with a flame, and ideally should self-extinguish when the flame is removed. Heat stability is particularly important to a fibre during dyeing and finishing of the textile and during cleaning and general maintenance by the consumer. Textile fibres for the most part are made up of organic polymeric materials containing carbon and burn on ignition from a flame or other propagating source. The chemical structure of a fibre establishes its overall flammability characteristics, and appropriate textile finishes can reduce the degree of flammability. A number of Federal, state, and local statutes eliminate the most dangerous flammable fabrics from the marketplace.

PRIMARY FIBRE PROPERTIES FROM AN ENGINEERING PERSPECTIVE

The textile and polymer engineer must consider a number of criteria essential for formation, fabrication, and assembly of fibres into textile substrates. Often the criteria used will be similar to those set forth above concerning end-use properties.

Ideally a textile fibre should have the following properties:

- A melting and/or decomposition point above 220°C.
- A tensile strength of 5 g/denier or greater.
- Elongation at break above 10 per cent with reversible elongation up to 5 per cent strain.
- A moisture absorptivity of 2 per cent-5 per cent moisture uptake.
- Combined moisture regain and air entrapment capability.
- High abrasion resistance.
- Resistance to attack, swelling, or solution in solvents, acids, and bases.
- Self-extinguishing when removed from a flame.

FIBRE FORMATION AND MORPHOLOGY

Fibre morphology refers to the form and structure of a fibre, including the molecular arrangement of individual molecules and groups of molecules within the fibre. Most fibres are organic materials derived from carbon combined with other atoms such as oxygen, nitrogen, and halogens. The basic building blocks that organic materials form as covalently-bonded organic compounds are called monomers.

Covalent bonds involve the sharing of electrons between adjacent atoms within the monomer, and the structure tons between adjacent atoms within the monomer, and the structure of the monomer is determined by the type, location, and nature of bonding of atoms within the monomer and by the nature of covalent bonding between atoms. Monomers react or condense to form long-chain molecules called polymers made up of a given number (n) of monomer units which are the basic building unit of fibres. On formation into fibres and orientation by natural or mechanical means the polymeric molecules possess ordered crystalline and non-ordered amorphous areas, depending on the nature of the polymer and the relative packing of molecules within the fibre. For a monomer A the sequence of events to fibre formation and orientation would appear as shown in figure.

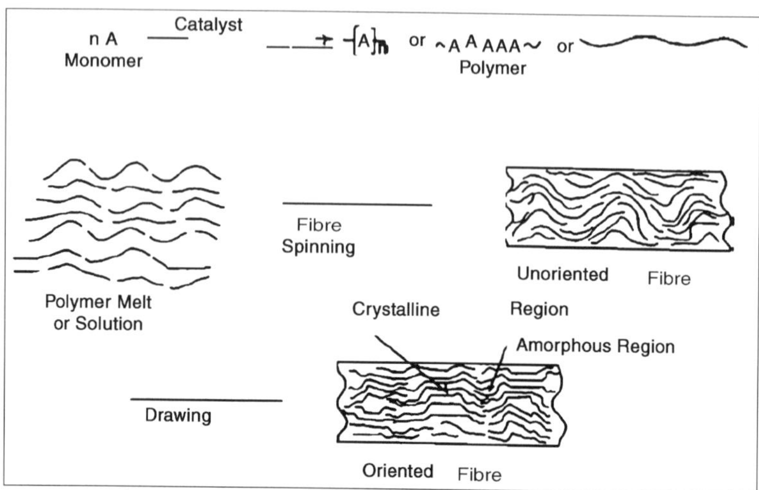

Fig. Polymerisation Sequence and Fibre Formation.

Polymers with repeating units of the same monomer (An) would be referred to as homopolymers. If a second unit B is introduced into the basic structure, structures which are copolymers are formed with structures as outlined in figure.

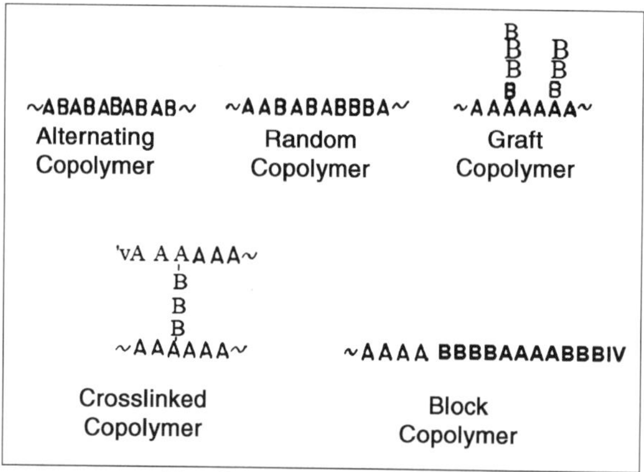

Fig. Copolymer Structures.

POLYMER FORMATION

Synthetic polymers used to form fibres are often classified on the basis of their mechanism of polymerisation—step growth (condensation) or chain growth (addition) polymerisation. Step growth polymerisation involves multifunctional monomers which undergo successive condensation with a second monomer or with itself to form a dimer, which in turn condenses with another dimer to form a tetramer, etc., usually with loss of a small molecule such as water. Chain growth involves the instantaneous growth of a long molecular chain from unsaturated monomer units, followed by initiation of a second chain, etc. The two methods are outlined schematically:

$$\text{Step Growth:} \quad nA \rightarrow \frac{n}{2}AA \rightarrow AAAA \rightarrow$$

$$\text{Chain Growth:} \quad nA \rightarrow (A)n \rightarrow (A)n \qquad nA \rightarrow (A)n$$

The average number of monomer repeating units in a polymer chain (n) is often referred to also as the degree of polymerisation, DP. The DP must exceed an average 20 units in most cases to give a polymer of sufficient molecular size to have desirable fibre-forming properties. The overall breadth of distribution of molecular chain lengths in the polymer will affect the ultimate properties of the fibres, with wide polymer size distributions leading to an overall reduction of fibre properties. Although the polymers from natural fibres and regenerated natural fibres do not undergo polymerisation by the mechanisms found for synthetic fibres, most natural polymers have characteristic repeating units and high degrees of polymerisation and are related to step growth polymers. Basic polymeric structures for the major fibres are given in figure.

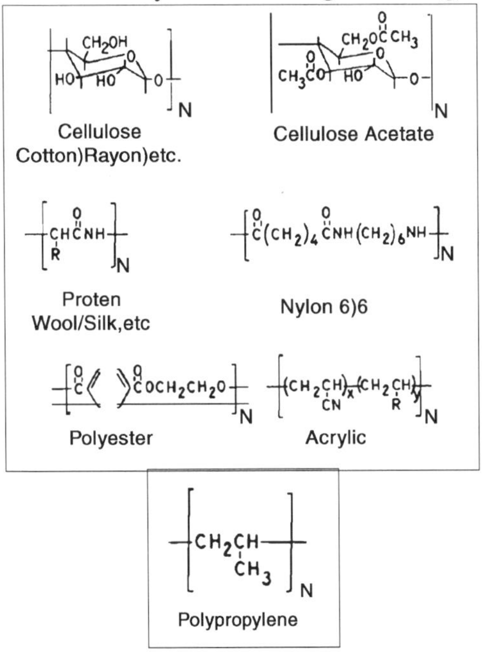

Cellulose
Cotton)Rayon)etc.

Cellulose Acetate

Proten
Wool/Silk,etc

Nylon 6)6

Polyester

Acrylic

Polypropylene

Fig. Basic Polymeric Structures for Major Fibres.

FIBRE SPINNING

Although natural fibres come in a morphological form determined by nature, regenerated and synthetic man-made fibres can be "tailor-made" depending on the shape and dimensions of the orifice (spinning jet) that the polymer is forced through to form the fibre. There are several methods used to spin a fibre from its polymer, including melt, dry, wet, emulsion, and suspension spinning. Melt spinning is the least complex of the methods. The polymer from which the fibre is made is melted and then forced through a spinneret and into air to cause solidification and fibre formation. Dry and wet spinning processes involve dissolving the fibre-forming polymer in an appropriate solvent, followed by passing a concentrated solution (20 per cent- 50 per cent polymer) through the spinneret and into dry air to evaporate the solvent in the case of dry spinning or into a coagulating bath to cause precipitation or regeneration of the polymer in fibre form in the case of wet spinning. There is a net contraction of the spinning solution on loss of solvent. If a skin of polymer is formed on the fibre followed by diffusion of the remainder of the solvent from the core of the forming fibre, the cross-section of the fibre as it contracts may collapse to form an irregular popcorn like cross section. Emulsion spinning is used only for those fibre-forming polymers that are insoluble.

Polymer is mixed with a surface-active agent (detergent) and possibly a solvent and then mixed at high speeds with water to form an emulsion of the polymer. The polymer is passed through the spinneret and into a coagulating bath to form the fibre. In suspension spinning, the polymer is swollen and suspended in a swelling solvent. The swollen suspended polymer is forced through the spinneret into dry hot air to drive off solvent or into a wet non-solvent bath to cause the fibre to form through coagulation.

The spinning process can be divided into three steps:

1. Flow of spinning fluid within and through the spinneret under high stress and sheer.
2. Exit of fluid from the spinneret with relief of stress and an increase in volume (ballooning of flow).
3. Elongation of the fluid jet as it is subjected to tensile force as it cools and solidifies with orientation of molecular structure within the fibre.

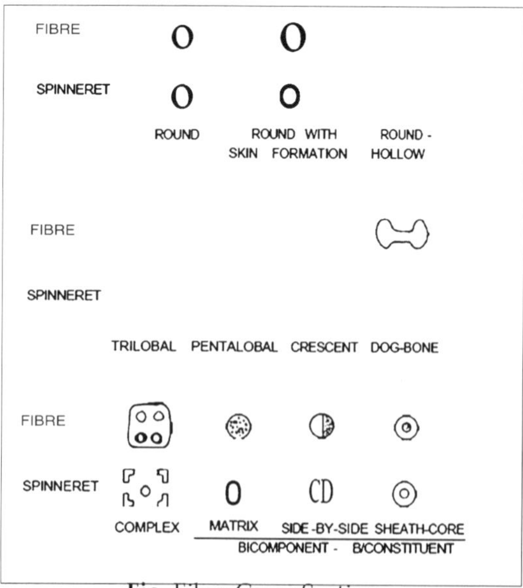

Fig. Fibre Cross Sections.

Common cross sections of man-made fibres include:

- Round,
- Trilobal,
- Pentalobal,
- Dog-bone, and
- Crescent shapes.

When two polymers are used in fibre formation as in bicomponent or biconstituent fibres, the two components can be arranged in a matrix, side-by-side, or sheath-core configuration. Round cross sections are also found where skin formation has caused fibre contraction and puckering (as with rayons) has occurred or where the spinneret shape has provided a hollow fibre. Complex fibre cross-sectional shapes with special properties are also used.

FIBRE DRAWING AND MORPHOLOGY

On drawing and orientation the man-made fibres become smaller in diameter and more crystalline, and imperfections in the fibre morphology are improved somewhat. Side-by-side bi component or bi constituent fibres on drawing become wavy and bulky. In natural fibres the orientation of the molecules within the fibre is determined by the biological source during the growth and maturity process of the fibre. The form and structure of polymer molecules with relation to each other within the fibre will depend on the relative alignment of the molecules in relationship to one another. Those areas where the polymer chains are closely aligned and packed close together are crystalline areas within the fibre, whereas those areas where there is essentially no molecular alignment are referred to as amorphous areas. Dyes and finishes can penetrate the amorphous portion of the fibre, but not the ordered crystalline portion.

CROSS-SECTION

A number of theories exist concerning the arrangement of crystalline and amorphous areas within a fibre. Individual crystal line areas in a fibre are often referred to as microfibrils. Microfibrils can associate into larger crystalline groups, which are called fibrils or micelles. Microfibrils are 30-100 Å in length, whereas fibrils and micelles are usually 200-600 Å in length. This compares to the individual molecular chains, which vary from 300 to 1500 Å in length and which are usually part of both crystal line and amorphous areas of the polymer and therefore give continuity and association of the various crystal line and amorphous areas within the fibre. A number of theories have been developed to explain the interconnection of crystal line and amorphous areas in the fibre and include such concepts as fringed micelles or fringed fibrils, molecular chain folding, and extended chain concepts. The amorphous areas within a fibre will be relatively loosely packed and associated with each other, and spaces or voids will appear due to discontinuities within the structure. Figure outlines the various aspects of internal fibre morphology with regard to polymer chains.

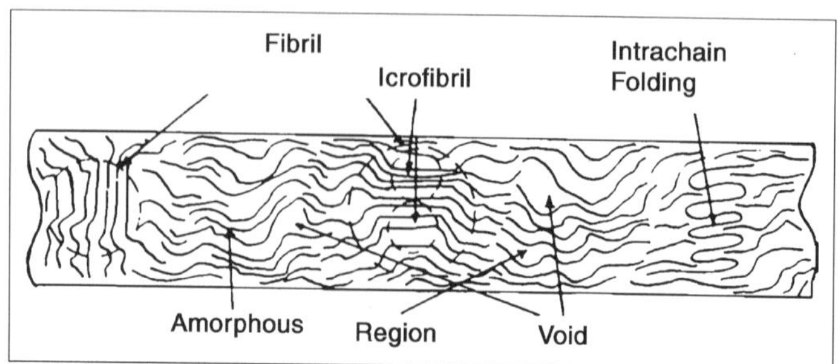

Fig. Aspects of Internal Fibre Morphology.

The force s that keep crystalline areas together within a fibre include chemical bonds (covalent, ionic) as well as secondary bonds. Cova lent bonds result from sharing of electrons between atoms, such as found in carboncarbon, carbon-oxygen, and carbon-nitrogen bonding, within organic compounds. Covalent bonds joining adjacent polymer chains are referred to as crosslinks. Ionic bonding occurs when molecules donate or accept electrons from each other, a s when a metal salt reacts with acid side chains on a po1ymer within a fibre. Chemical bonds a re much stronger than secondary bonds formed between polymer chains, but the total associative force between polymer chains can be large, since a very large number of such bonds may occur between adjacent polymer chains.

Hydrogen bonds are the strongest of the secondary bonds and occur between electropositive hydrogen atoms and electronegative atoms such as oxygen, nitrogen, and halogen s on opposing polymer chains. Nylon, protein, and cellulosic fibres are capable of extensive hydrogen bonding. Van der Waals interactions between polymer chains occur when clouds of electrons from each chain come in close proximity, thereby promoting a small attractive force between chains. The more extended the cloud of electrons, the stronger the van der Waals interaction will be. Covalent bonded materials will show some uneven distribution of electron density over the molecule due to the differing electronegativity of the atoms and electron distribution over the molecule to form dipoles.

Dipoles on adjacent polymer chains of opposite charge and close proximity are attracted to each other and promote secondary bonding. When a synthetic fibre is stretched or drawn, the molecules in mo s t cases will orient themselves in crystalline areas parallel to the fibre axis, although crystalline areas in some chain-folded polymers such as polypropylene can be aligned vertical to the fibre axis. The degree of crystallinity will be affected by the total forces available for chain interaction, the distance between parallel chains, and the similarity and uniformity of adjacent chains. The structure and arrangement of individual polymer chains also affects the morphology of the fibre. Also, configurations or optical isomers of polymers can have very different physical and chemical properties.

BULKING, TEXTURISING, AND STAPLE FORMATION

Thermoplastic man-made fibre s can be permanently heat-set after drawing and or ientation. The fibre will possess structural integrity and will not shrink up to that setting temperature.

Al so, thermoplastic fibres or yarns from this fibre s can be texturised to give three dimensional loft and bulkiness:

1. Through fibre deformation and setting at or near their softening temperature,
2. Through air entanglement, or
3. Through differential setting within fibres or yarns.

Table. Texturising Methods.

Heat-setting Techniques	Air Entanglement	Differential Setting
False Twist Knife edge Stuffer box Gear crimping Autowist Knit-de-knit	Air Jet	Bicomoponent-biconstituent Fibre orientation Heat shrinkage of thermoplastic fibres in a blend

Schematic representations of these methods are given in figure.

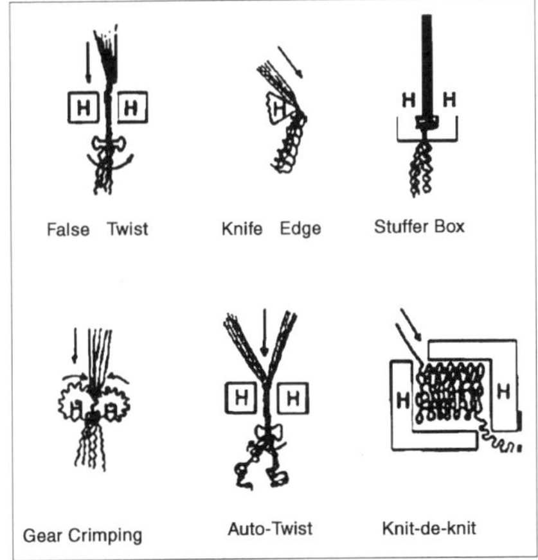

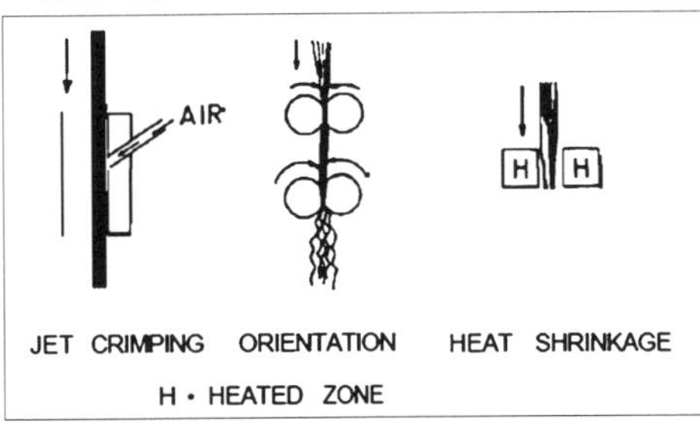

Fig. Texturising Methods.

Heat-Setting Techniques

The false twist heat-setting technique is extremely rapid, inexpensive, and most widely used. The filament fibre tow is brought in contact with a high-speed spindle running vertical to the moving tow. This action results in a high twist in the tow up to the spindle. The twisted tow is heated near its softening point before passing the spindle and then cooled and untwisted to give a wavy bulky yarn.

In knife edge texturising, filament tows or yarns are passed over a heated knife edge under tension. The fibres near the knife edge are changed in overall orientation in relation to the unheated yarns or portion of the filaments away from the knife edge, thereby causing bulking of the yarn. In stuffer box texturising, the filament tow is fed into a heated box, causing the tow to double up against itself. On removal, the cooled tow retains the zigzag configuration caused by the process. In gear crimping, the tow is passed between heated intermeshing gears. On cooling the fibres retain the shape induced by the heated gears. In auto-twisting, two tows or yarns are twisted together and then heat set. On untwisting the yarns have equal but opposite twists, which causes a spiral bulking of the yarn. In the knit-de-knit process a yarn is fill knitted, heat set, cooled, and deknitted to give a bulked yarn retaining the shape and curvature of the knit.

Air Entanglement

In air entanglement texturising, a fibre tow is loosely fed into and through a restricted space and a high-speed air jet is impinged on the fibres at a *45*° angle. The loose fibres within the tow are looped to give a texturised effect.

Differential Setting

Heat shrinkage techniques cause a bulking of fibre tows containing different fibres through heating one component of the blend sufficiently to cause heat shrinkage of the fibre and compaction, contraction, and bulking. Side-by-side bicomponent and biconstituent fibres recover different degrees on each side from fibre stretching and causing a waving, crimping, or bulking of the fibre.

STAPLE FORMATION

Continuous filaments can be cut into staple by wet or dry cutting techniques. In wet cutting, the wet spun fibre is cut to uniform lengths right after spinning, while dry cutting involves partial cutting, debonding, and shuffling of the dry tow to form a sliver. Before the filament or staple is used in yarn spinning, spin finishes are added to give lubricity and antistatic characteristics to the fibres and to provide a greater degree of fibre cohesiveness. Such finishes are usually mixtures including such materials as fatty acid esters, mineral oils, synthetic esters, silicones, cationic amines, phosphate esters, emulsifiers, and/or non-ionic surfactants. Spin finishes are formulated to be oxidation resistant, to be easily removed by scouring, to give a controlled viscosity, to be stable to corrosion, to resist odour and colour formation, and to be non-volatile and readily emulsifiable.

STRUCTURE-PROPERTY RELATIONSHIPS

The basic chemical and morphological structure of polymers in a fibre determine the fundamental properties of a fabric made from that fibre. Although physical and chemical treatments and changes in yarn and fabric formation parameters can alter the fabric properties to some degree, the basic properties of the fabric result from physical and chemical properties inherent to the structure of the polymer making up the fibre. From these basic properties, the end-use characteristics of the fibre are determined. To that end, in the following stages as suggested, describe the various textile fibres in terms of their basic structural properties, followed by physical and chemical properties, and finally the end-use characteristics inherent to constructions made from the fibre. Initially the name and general information for a given fibre is set forth followed by an outline of the structural properties, including information about chemical structure of the polymer, degree of polymerisation, and arrangement of molecular chains within the fibre.

Physical properties include mechanical (tensile) and environmental properties of the fibre, whereas the effect of common chemicals and chemically induced processes on the fibre is listed under chemical properties. The end-use properties are then listed and include properties coming inherently from the structural, physical, and chemical properties of the fibre as well as end-use properties that involve evaluation of performance, subjective aspects, and aesthetics of the fabrics. Where possible, the interrelationships of these properties are presented.

TECHNICAL TECHNOLOGY USES IN FIBRES AND TEXTILES

A number of definitions have been used to describe the term 'technical textiles' with respect to their intended use, functional ability and their non-aesthetic or decorative requirements. However, none of these carefully chosen words include the fundamental fibre elements, technical or otherwise, which make up the technical textile structures. The omission of the word 'fibre' may indeed be deliberate as most technical textile products are made from conventional fibres that are already well established. In fact over 90% of all fibres used in the technical sector are of the conventional type. Specially developed fibres for use in technical textiles are often expensive to produce and have limited applications.

Historically, utilisation of fibres in technical capacities dates back to the early Egyptians and Chinese who used papyrus mats to reinforce and consolidate the foundations respectively of the pyramids and the Buddhist temples.

However, their serious use in modern civil engineering projects only began after the floods of 1953 in The Netherlands in which many people lost their lives. The event initiated the famous Delta works project in which for the first time synthetic fibres were written into the vast construction programme. Since then, geotextiles in particular have matured into important and indispensable multifunctional materials. Use of silk in semitechnical applications also goes back a long way to the lightweight warriors of the Mongolian armies, who did not only wear silk next to their skin for comfort but also to reduce penetration of incoming arrows and enable their subsequent removal with minimal injury. Use of silk in wound dressing and open cuts in web and fabric form also dates back to the early Chinese and Egyptians.

In light of extensive utilization of conventional fibres in the technical sector, this chapter initially attempts to discuss fibres under this category highlighting their importance and the scope of their versatility. The discussion covers concisely an outline of fibre backgrounds, chemical compositions and their salient characteristics. It then introduces other fibres which have been specially developed to perform under extreme stress and/or temperature; ultrafine and novel fibres are also discussed. Finally, the chapter concludes by identifying areas of application and the roles that selected fibres play in fulfilling their intended purpose. The complete range of fibres available to the end-user and some of their mechanical properties.

HIGH MODULUS ORGANIC FIBRES

Keller's much-published contribution to the understanding of crystal growth in 1957 and confirmation of the tendency of polymers to form folded-chain crystals, provided the insight and inspiration for development of high strength, high modulus organic fibres that would surpass conventional fibres. During crystallisation, long chains of molecules fold back on themselves to form folded-chain crystals which only partly unfold during normal drawing. In the Netherlands in the 1970s DSM developed a super drawing technique known as *gel spinning,* which uses dilute solutions of ultra-high molecular weight polymers such as polyethylene to unfold the chains further and thus increase both tensile strength and fibre modulus. Ultra-high molecular weight polyethylene (UHMWPE) fibres, Dyneema or Spectra, are today the strongest fibres known, with tensile moduli in excess of 70 GN $m^{\sim 2}$. Weight for weight this fibre genus is claimed to be 15 times stronger than steel and twice as strong as aromatic polyamides such as Kevlar. It is also low in density, chemically inert and abrasion resistant. It, however, melts at around 150 °C and thermally degrades at 350 °C which restrict its use to low temperature applications.

To achieve even better performance characteristics at higher temperatures, other means of fibre production were explored in the 1960s. One successful approach eventually led to the advent of liquid crystalline polymers. These are based on polymerisation of long stiff molecules such as *para*-phenylene terephthalamide achieving molecular weights averaging to around 20 000. The influence of the stiff aromatic rings, together with hydrogen-bonding crosslinks, combines the best features of both the polyamides and the polyesters in an extended-chain configuration.

Molecular orientation of these fibres is brought about by capillary shear along the flow of the polymer as it exits from the spinneret thus overriding the need for subsequent drawing. Kevlar by DuPont and Twaron by Akzo (now Acordis) were the first of such fibres to appear in the early 1970s. There now exists a series of first, second and third generations of *para*-aramids. Kevlar HT for instance, which has 20% higher tenacity and Kevlar HM which has 40% higher modulus than the original Kevlar 29 are largely utilised in the composite and the aerospace industries.

Para-aramids generally have high glass transition temperatures nearing 370 °C and do not melt or burn easily, but carbonise at and above 425 °C. All aramid fibres are however prone to photodegradation and need protection against the sun when used out of doors. These will be discussed later. Other high tenacity and high modulus fibres include the isotropically spun Tech-nora (Teijin) and Supara, based upon *para*-aramid copolymers, with slightly lower maximum strength and modulus values than Kevlar. Several other melt-spinnable liquid crystalline polymers are also available.

Combustion-resistant Organic Fibres

The fibres were developed following earlier observations that aromatic polymer backbones yielded improved tensile and heat resistance compared with conventional fibres. However, if the polymer chains have lower symmetry and order, then polymer tractability and textile fibre characteristics are improved. Solvent-spun Nomex and Conex were the first so-called *meta*-aramids made from poly(meta-phenylene isophthalamide) and were produced by DuPont in 1962 and by Teijin in 1972, respectively. The *meta*-phenylene isophthalamide molecule is identical in all but the position of its —NH— and —CO— groups to *para*-phenylene terephthalamide (or Kevlar) molecules. The different positioning of these groups in *meta*-aramids creates a zig-zag molecular structure that prevents it from full crystallisation thus accounting for its relatively poorer tensile properties. However, Nomex is particularly well known for its resistance to combustion, high decomposition temperature prior to melting and high limited oxygen index (LOI), the minimum amount of oxygen required to induce ignition.

Melt-spinnable aromatic fibres with chains containing paraphenylene rings, like polyether ether ketone (PEEK), polyether ketone (PEK) and poly(*p*-phenylene sulphide) (PPS), also have high melting points but, since their melting points occur prior to their decomposition temperature, they are unsuitable for fire-retardant applications. However, their good chemical resistance renders them suitable for low temperature filtration and other corrosive environments. The polyheterocyclic fibre, polybenzimidazole or PBI, produced by Hoechst-Celanese has an even higher LOI than the aramids.

It has excellent resistance to both heat and chemical agents but remains rather expensive. P84, initially produced by Lenzing and now produced by Inspec Fibres, USA, comprises polyimide groups that yield reasonably high resistance to fire and chemical attack. The acrylic copolymer-based fibre produced by Acordis known as Inidex (although now no longer produced) unlike many aramid fibres has high resistance to UV (ultraviolet) radiation and a fairly high LOI at the expense of much reduced tenacity and rather low long-term exposure resistance to heat.

Oxidised acrylic fibre, best known as Panox (SGL, UK) is another crosslinked, high combustion-resistant material produced by combined oxidation and pyrolysis of acrylic fibres at around 300 °C. Although black in appearance, it is not classed as carbon fibre and preserves much of its original non-carbonaceous structure. In addition, it does not have the graphitic or turbostratic structure of carbon fibres. It retains a sufficiently high extension-at-break to be subjected to quite normal textile processes for yarn and fabric formation. Panox has a very high LOI of 0.55. Fully carbonised, or carbon fibres with even higher tensile properties, are achieved by full carbonisation of these oxidised precursor fibres or by the melt spinning of liquid crystalline mesophase pitch followed by their oxidation and pyrolysis.

Ultra-fine and Novelty Fibres

Ultra-fine or microfibres were developed partly because of improved precision in engineering techniques and better production controls, and partly because of the need for lightweight, soft waterproof fabrics that eliminate the more conventional coating or lamination processes. As yet there are no universal definitions of microfibres. *Textile Terms and Definitions* simply describes them as fibres or filaments with linear densities of approximately 1.0dtex or less. Others have used such terms as fine, extra-fine and micro-fine corresponding to linear densities ranging from 3.0dtex to less than 0.1dtex. They are usually made from polyester and nylon polymers, but other polymers are now being made into microfibres. The Japanese first introduced microfibres in an attempt to reproduce silk-like properties with the addition of enhanced durability. They are produced by at least three established methods including island-in-sea, split process and melt spinning techniques and appear under brand names such as Mitrelle, Setila, Micrell, Tactel and so on. Once in woven fabric form their fine diameter and tight weave allows up to 30000 filaments cm^2, making them impermeable to water droplets whilst allowing air and moisture vapour circulation.

They can be further processed to enhance other characteristics such as peach-skin and leather-like appearances. The split technique of production imparts sharp-angled edges within the fibre surface, which act as gentle abraders when made into wiping cloths that are used in the optical and precision microelectronic industries. Microfibres are also used to make bacteria barrier fabrics in the medical industries. Their combined effect of low diameter and compact packing also allows efficient and more economical dyeing and finishing. Finally, constant pressure to achieve and develop even more novel applications of fibres has led to a number of other and, as yet, niche fibrous products. In principle, the new ideas usually strive to combine basic functional properties of a textile material with special needs or attractive effects.

For example, Solar-Aloha, developed by Descente and Unitika in Japan, absorbs light of less than 2|jm wavelength and converts it to heat owing to its zirconium carbide content. Winter sports equipment made from these materials use the cold winter sun to capture more than 90% of this incident energy to keep the wearer warm. Another interesting material gives rise to thermochromic fabrics made by Toray which have a uniform coating of microcapsules containing heat-sensitive dyes that change colour at 5 °C intervals over a temperature range of -40 °C to 80 °C creating 'fun' and special effects.

Cripy 65 is a scented fibre produced by Mitsubishi Rayon (R) who have enclosed a fragrant essence in isolated cavities along the length of hollow polyester fibres. The scent is gradually released to give a consistent and pleasant aroma. Pillows and bed linen made from these materials are claimed to improve sleep and sleeping disorders. The effect can also be achieved by printing or padding microcapsules containing perfumes into fabrics which subsequently burst and release the perfume. With careful handling, garments made from these materials are said to maintain this property for up to two years. Infrared-emitting and bacteria-repelling fibres are some of the other emerging novel fibres.

High Performance Inorganic Fibres

Any fibre that consists of organic chemical units, where carbon is linked to hydrogen and possibly also to other elements, will decompose below about 500°C and cease to have long-term stability at considerably lower temperatures. For use at high temperatures it is therefore necessary to turn to inorganic fibres and fibres that consist essentially of carbon. Glass, asbestos and more recently carbon are three well-known inorganic fibres that have been extensively used for many of their unique characteristics.

Use of glass as a fibre apparently dates back to the ancient Syrian and Egyptian civilisations which used them for making clothes and dresses. However, the very high modulus or stiffness displayed by these fibres means that they are quite brittle and can easily be damaged by surface marks and defects. They are, therefore, best utilised by embedding in matrix forms where the fibres are fully protected. Epoxy resins, polyester and other polymers, as well as cement, have commonly been used both to protect and to make use of their contributory strength. Glass-reinforced boat hulls and car bodies, to name but two application areas of such composites, reduce overall weight and cost of fabrication as well as eliminating the traditional problems of rotting wood and rusting metals associated with traditional materials. Their good resistance to heat and very high melting points have also enabled them to be used as effective insulating materials.

Asbestos is a generic name for a variety of crystalline silicates that occur naturally in some rocks. The fibres that are extracted have all the textile-like properties of fineness, strength, flexibility and more importantly, unlike conventional fibres, good resistance to heat with high decomposition temperatures of around 550 °C. Their use as a reinforcement material has been found in clay-rich prehistoric cooking pots discovered in Finland. In more recent times they have been extensively used to reinforce brittle matrices such as cement sheeting, pipes, plastics and also as heat insulators. However, with the discovery of their carcinogenic hazards, their use has gradually declined and alternative fibres have been developed to replace them totally.

High purity, pyrolysed acrylic-based fibres are classified as carbon fibres. The removal of impurities enhances carbon content and prevents the nucleation and growth of graphite crystals which are responsible for loss of strength in these fibres. Carbon fibres with different structures are also made from mesophase pitch. The graphite planes in PAN-based fibres are arranged parallel to the fibre axis rather than perpendicular as is the case with pitch-based carbon fibres. Their high strength and modulus combined with relatively low extensibility means that they are best utilised in association with epoxy or melt-spinnable aromatic resins as composites.

Increasing demand in the defence and aerospace industries for even better performance under extreme conditions led, within the last quarter of the 20th century, to yet another range of new and rather expensive metal oxides, boron and silicon-based fibres. These are often referred to as ceramic fibres and will now be briefly discussed. Aluminosilicate compounds are mixtures of aluminium oxide (Al_2O) and silicon oxide (SiO_2); their resistance to temperature depends on the mixing ratio of the two oxides. High aluminium oxide content increases their temperature tolerance from a low of 1250 °C to a maximum of 1400 °C.

However, despite their high temperature resistance, these fibres are not used in high stress applications owing to their tendency to creep at high temperatures. Their prime applications are in insulation of furnaces and replacement of asbestos fibres in friction materials, gaskets and packings. Both aluminium oxide or alumina fibres and silicon oxide or silica fibres are also produced. Pure boron fibres are too brittle to handle but they can be coated on tungsten or carbon cores.

Their complex manufacturing process makes them rather expensive. Their prime application is in lightweight, high strength and high modulus composites such as racket frames and aircraft parts. Boron fibre use is limited by their thickness, their relatively poor stability in metal matrices and their gradual loss of strength with increasing temperature. Boron nitrides (BN) are primarily used in the electronic industry where they perform both as electrical insulators and thermal conductors.

The most outstanding property of silicon carbide (SiC) is the ability to function in oxidizing conditions up to 1800 °C with little loss of mechanical properties. Silicon carbide exceeds carbon fibre in its greater resistance to oxidation at high temperatures, its higher compressive strength and better electrical resistance. SiC fibres containing carbon, however, lose some tensile properties at the expense of gaining better electrical conductivity.

Finally, many of the inorganic fibres so far referred to are now also produced in microcrystalline or whisker form and not in the more normal textile-fibre form. Whiskers have extremely good mechanical properties and their tensile strength is usually three to four times those of most reinforcing fibres. They are, however, costly to produce and their inclusion into composite structures is both difficult and cumbersome.

CONVENTIONAL AND NATURAL FIBRES

Cotton accounts for half of the world's consumption of fibres and is likely to remain so owing to many of its innate properties and for economical reasons that will not be discussed here. Cotton is made of long chains of natural cellulose containing carbon, hydrogen and oxygen otherwise known as polysaccharides. The length of the chains determines the ultimate strength of the fibre. An average of 10000 cel-lulosic repeat or monomeric units make up the individual cellulose chains which are about 2|jm in length. The linear molecules combine into microfibrils and are held together by strong intermolecular forces to form the cotton fibre. The unique physical and aesthetic properties of the fibre, combined with its natural generation and biodegradability, are reasons for its universal appeal and popularity. Chemical treatments such as Proban and Pyrovatex are two examples of the type of durable finishes that can be applied to make cotton fire retardant. High moisture absorbency, high wet modulus and good handle are some of the more important properties of cotton fibre.

Wool, despite its limited availability and high cost, is the second most important natural fibre. It is made of protein: a mixture of chemically linked amino acids which are also the natural constituents of all living organisms. Keratin or the protein in the wool fibre has a helical rather than folded chain structure with strong inter- and intrachain hydrogen bonding which are believed to be responsible for many of its unique characteristics. Geographical location, the breeding habits of the animals, and climatic conditions are some of the additional variables responsible for its properties. The overall high extensibility of wool, its natural waviness and ability to trap air has a coordinated effect of comfort and warmth, which also make it an ideal insulating material. The sophisticated dual morphology of wool produces the characteristic crimp which has also been an inspiration for the development of some highly technical synthetic fibres. Wool is inherently fire retardant, but further improvements can be achieved by a number of fire-retardant treatments. Zirconium- and titanium-treated wool is one such example which is now universally referred to as Zirpro (IWS) wool.

Flax, jute, hemp and ramie, to name but a few of the best fibres, have traditionally taken a secondary role in terms of consumption and functional requirements. They are relatively coarse and durable, and flax has traditionally been used for linen making. Jute, ramie and to a lesser extent other fibres have received attention within the geotextile sector of the fibre markets which seeks to combine the need for temporary to short-term usage with biodegradability, taking into account the regional availability of the fibres.

Silk is another protein-based fibre produced naturally by the silkworm, *Bombyx Mori* or other varieties of moth. Silk is structurally similar to wool with a slightly different combination of amino acids which make up the protein or the fibroin, as it is more appropriately known. Silk is the only naturally and commercially produced continuous filament fibre which has high tenacity, high lustre and good dimensional stability. Silk has been and will remain a luxury quality fibre with a special place in the fibre market. However, its properties of biocompatibility and gradual disintegration, as in sutures, have long been recognised in medical textiles.

Synthetic Fibres

All synthetic fibres originate from coal or oil. The first synthetic fibre that appeared on the world market in 1939 was nylon 6.6. It was produced by DuPont and gained rapid public approval. A series of nylons commonly referred to as polyamides now exists in which the amide linkage is the common factor. Nylon 6.6 and nylon 6 are most popular in fibre form. They are melt extruded in a variety of cross-sectional shapes and drawn to achieve the desired tenacity. They are well known for their high extensibility, good recovery, dimensional stability and relatively low moisture absorbency. Nylon 6.6 in particular soon became a popular household carpet fibre and was developed into fibres commonly known as Antron manufactured by DuPont. Antron fibres of various generations use additives, varied cross-sectional shapes and modified surface characteristics to enhance the aesthetic and visual appeal of carpets as well as improving their resilience and dissipating static charges.

Nylon was later surpassed by the even more popular fibre known as polyester, first introduced as Dacron by DuPont in 1951. Polyester is today the second most used fibre after cotton and far ahead of other synthetics both in terms of production and consumption. Polyethylene terephthalate or polyester is made by condensation polymerisation of ethylene glycol and terephthalic acid followed by melt extrusion and drawing. It can be used in either continuous form or as short staple of varying lengths.

The popularity of polyester largely stems from its easycare characteristics, durability and compatibility with cotton in blends. Its very low moisture absorbency, resilience and good dimensional stability are additional qualities. Many manufacturers across the world produce polyester under different commercial names with almost tailor-made properties. A high glass transition temperature of around 70 °C with good resistance to heat and chemical degradation also qualifies this polymer for most technical textile applications. These will be discussed in greater detail later. Flame-retardant Trevira CS and Trevira high tenacity, both polyesters developed and marketed by Trevira GmbH in Germany, are examples of the many varieties available today.

Wool-like properties are shown by polyacrylic fibres which are produced by the polymerisation of acrylonitrile using the addition route into polyacrylonitrile. They can then be spun into fibres by dry or wet spinning methods. Orlon was produced by DuPont. It had a distinctive dumbbell shaped cross-section and was extruded by the dry process in which the solvent is evaporated off. Acrilan produced by Mon-santo and Courtelle produced by Acordis are spun by the wet extrusion technique and have near circular cross-sections. Acrylic fibres now also appear in bicomponent form with wool-like characteristics.

Chemically modified acrylics, principally the modacrylics, include chlorine atoms in their molecular structure which are responsible for their low burning behaviour and, unlike acrylics, have the ability to self-extinguish once the source of ignition has been removed. A selected fibre in terms of fibre chemistry is Oasis, a superabsorbent fibre made by the collaborative efforts of Acordis and Allied Colloids, based on crosslinking copolymers of acrylic acid. This fibre is claimed to absorb moisture many times its own weight and holds it even under pressure. Its application in hygiene and medical care in different forms is being pursued. Polyolefin fibres include both polyethylene and polypropylene made by addition polymerisation of ethylene and propylene and subsequent melt extrusion, respectively.

Polyethylene has moderate physical properties with a low melting temperature of about 110 °C for its low density form and about 140 °C for its high density form which severely restricts its application in low temperature applications. Polypropylene has better mechanical properties and can withstand temperatures of up to 140 °C before melting at about 170 °C. Both polymers have a density less than that of water which allows them to float as ropes, nets and other similar applications. The availability, low cost and good resistance to acid and alkaline environments of polypropylene has greatly influenced its growth and substantial use in geotextile applications.

Finally, elastane fibres are synthetic-based elastomeric polymers with at least 85% segmented polyurethane in their structure. They have rubber-like properties, which means they can be extended up to six or more times their original length. They are used in combination with most natural and synthetic fibres in knitted and woven materials. They were initially produced by DuPont in 1959 under the now well-known trademark of Lycra.

Regenerated Fibres

Viscose rayon was the result of the human race's first attempts to mimic nature in producing silk-like continuous fibres through an orifice. Cellulose from wood pulp is the main constituent of this novel system, started commercially in the early 1920s. Thin sheets of cellulose are treated with sodium hydroxide and aged to allow molecular chain breakage.

Further treatment with carbon disulphide, dissolution in dilute sodium hydroxide and ageing produces a viscous liquid, the viscose dope, which is then extruded into an acid bath. he continuous filaments that finally emerge are washed, dried and can be cut to staple lengths. The shorter cellulose molecules in viscose and their partial crystallisation accounts for its rather inferior physical properties relative to cotton. Further development and refinement of the manufacturing technique have created a whole range of fibres with improved properties.

High tenacity and high wet modulus viscose compare in all but appearance to cotton in both dry and wet conditions. Chemically altered regenerated cellulose di- and triacetates do not burn like cotton and viscose to leave a fluffy black ash, but melt and drip instead. This characteristic enables them to be shaped or textured to enhance their visual and aesthetic appeal. Hollow viscose modifications give enhanced bulk and moisture absorbency and have an improved cotton-like feel. Fire-retardant (FR) viscose was first introduced in the 1960s. A major example is produced by Lenzing in Austria by incorporating organophosphorous compounds into the spinning dope prior to extrusion. The additive is reasonably stable and has no chemical interaction with the cellulose molecules. It is also unaffected by bleaching, washing, dry cleaning, dyeing and finishing processes.

Early in the 1990s Kemira (now Sateri Fibres) of Finland introduced an alternative version of FR viscose known as Visil in which polysilicic acid is present. The fibre chars upon heating leaving a silica residue. Lyocell, is the latest addition to this series of fibres, commercially known as Tencel (Acordis), has all the conventional properties of viscose in addition to its much praised environmentally friendly production method. The solvent used is based on non-toxic JV-methyl morpholine oxide used in a recyclable closed loop system, which unlike the viscose process avoids discharge of waste. Highly absorbent derivatives of Tencel, known as Hydrocell are establishing a foothold in wound dressing and other medical-related areas of textiles.

CIVIL AND AGRICULTURAL ENGINEERING

Natural fibres such as flax, jute and ramie can be used for most temporary applications where, for instance, soil erosion is the problem. The geotextiles made from these natural polymers help to prevent the erosion of soils by allowing vegetative growth and their subsequent root establishment. Once the purpose is served, the geotextile material gradually disintegrates into the soil. In most medium to long term applications however, where physical and chemical durability and dimensional stabilities are of prime concern, synthetic fibres are preferred.

There are currently at least six synthetic polymers considered suitable for this purpose; they include:

- Polypropylene
- Polyester
- Polyethylene
- Polyvinyl chloride
- Polyamide
- Aramids.

Polypropylene is by far the most utilised geotextile, followed by polyester, the other three trailing behind with polyamide as the least used synthetic polymer. *Para*-aramids are only used where very high creep resistance and tolerance to prolonged heating are required.

Generally, geosynthetics must have lifetimes which are defined and relate to their function. Durability, therefore, is mainly determined by the resistance offered by the component fibre and its assembled structure to the degrading species that causes a reduction in the tensile and mechanical properties. At least three main degrading mechanisms have been identified that ultimately determine the durability and life of the contending polymer; they include:

- Physical degradation
- Chemical degradation
- Biological degradation.

Physical degradation is usually sustained during transport or installation in one form or another. Initiation of cracks is normally followed by their subsequent propagation under environmental or normal stress. In the first instance, polymer susceptibility to physical degradation depends on such factors as the weight of the geotextile; generally lightweight or thin geotextiles suffer larger strength losses than thick and heavy materials. Secondly, woven geotextiles suffer slightly larger strength losses than nonwovens, owing to their greater stiffness and, finally, the generic nature of the polymer itself plays an important role. Polyester, for instance, suffers greater strength losses than polyolefin fibres owing to its high glass transition temperature of around 70 °C. Under normal soil conditions, the polymer is relatively brittle and therefore susceptible to physical damage. Polypropylene with its glass transition averaging at about -10 °C is much more pliable under these conditions but suffers from the rather critical phenomenon of extension with time or creep.

Chemical degradation is the next mechanism by which chemical agencies, often in combination with ultraviolet light or/and heat, attack the polymer whilst in use or being stored. The presence of energy starts off a self-destructing chain of events that ultimately renders the polymer ineffective. Ultraviolet radiation normally attacks the surface of the polymer and initiates chain breakage or scission which leads to embrittlement and eventual failure of the polymer.

Generally, chemical degradation is a function of polymer type, thickness and availability of stabilizers. The type, quantity, and distribution of stabilizers also controls the degree of resistance to degradation. Polyolefins are particularly susceptible to ultraviolet degradation and need protection using light-stabilising additives. Oxidation due to heat operates similarly by weakening the polymer thus causing rapid degradation. A range of antioxidants are often included in the polymer during manufacture and processing to minimise this harmful effect.

Biological degradation can result from at least three types of microbiological attack: direct enzymatic attack, chemical production by microorganisms which may react destructively with the polymer, and attack on the additives within the polymer. High molecular weight polymers are much more immune to biological attack than low molecular weight polymers because microorganisms cannot easily locate the molecular chain endings. However, some microorganisms can permeate less digestible polymers in order to gain access to food.

Automotive and Aeronautics

Mechanical functionality has increasingly become an almost secondary requirement for travel safety, weight efficiency, comfort and material durability of the transporting medium. From bicycles to spacecraft, fibres in one form or another fulfil these important requirements. Carbon fibre reinforcement of the frame of a bicycle ridden in the 1992 Olympics was the first of its kind to allow a comfortable win ahead of its competitors. The one-piece, light, fibre-reinforced composite structure and design of the bike have since become an earmark of this industry.

In the simplest terms, composites utilise unique fibre properties such as strength, stiffness and elasticity whilst incorporating the compression resistance, and torsion and bending characteristics of the matrix used. Glass fibres have been traditionally used for the manufacture of boat hulls and car bodies. UHMWPE, aramids and carbon-reinforced composites in a variety of matrix materials are now routinely produced and utilised in low to very high temperature applications. Reinforcement of tyres is another area where the transport industry has benefited from fibres and where rapid temperature change and changing weather conditions demand effective response and durability.

High tenacity viscose and polyester yarns built into the internal structure of tyres now address these needs adequately. In addition to all the obvious upholstery materials used in the interior of cars, trains and aeroplanes, fibres are now used in one form or another in such parts as the engine components, fan belts, brake pads, door panels, seat skeletons, seat belts and air bags. Fire-retardant additives or inherently fire-retardant fibres are today standard requirements in the public sector use of all transport in order to improve safety.

Protection and Defence

In textile terms, protection and defence can be a passive response in which the textile product receives and absorbs the impending impact or energy in order to protect the underlying structure. Ballistic garments are obvious examples, where the assembled fibrous material is deliberately designed to slow down and reduce the penetration of an incoming projectile. But they may also have a more active role, where the fibres show positive response by generating char or protective gases, shrinking or expanding to prevent penetration of moisture or vapour and so on. In each scenario, the protection of the underlying structure is the common objective.

In the early days, leather and metal mesh garments were used to protect the body against sword and spear attacks, but with the passage of time development of new materials occurred and, for example, early in the 1940s, nylon-based flack jackets were introduced. They were a considerable improvement on the leather and metal garments but were still rather heavy and uncomfortable to wear. With the advent of *para*-aramids in the early 1970s, advanced fibres were for the first time used to make much more acceptable protective gear. In these garments, Kevlar or Twaron continuous filament yarns are woven into tight structures and assembled in a multilayer form to provide maximum protection. Their high tenacity and good energy absorption combined with high thermal stability enables these garments to receive and neutralise a range of projectiles from low calibre handguns, that is 0.22 to 0.44 inch (5.6-11.2mm) to military bullets within the 5.56-7.62mm range. In the latter case, the fabric will require facing with ceramic tiles or other hard materials to blunt the tips of metal-jacket spitzer-pointed bullets.

To strike a better balance between garment weight, comfort and protection an even stronger and lighter fibre based on ultra-high molecular weight polyethylene was developed and used in the early 1990s, which immediately reduced average garment weight by 15%. UHMWPE, commercially known as Dyneema (DSM) and in composite form as Spectra Shield by Allied Signal, is now used to make cut-resistant gloves and helmets, as well as a wide range of protective garments. However, unlike Kevlar, with a fairly low melting temperature of 150 °C, it is best suited to low temperature applications.

Fire is another means by which fatal and non-fatal injuries can be sustained. No textile-based material can withstand the power and ferocity of a fire for sustained periods of greater than 10min or so. However, if the fire ignition point could be increased or the organic structure converted to a carbonaceous char replica and its spreading rate delayed, then there may just be enough time gained to save an otherwise lost life. This is in essence the nature and objective of all fire-retardant compounds. Such treatments give fibres the positive role of forming char, reducing the emission of combustible volatile gases and effectively starving the fire of oxygen or providing a barrier to underlying surfaces.

In contrast, water-repellent fabrics may shed water by preventing water droplets from physically passing through them owing to their fine fibre dimensions and tight weaves, as is the case with ventile fabrics or perforated barrier inlays such as Goretex, whose tiny holes allow water vapour to pass through them but not water droplets. Wax and chemically treated fabrics reduce water/fabric surface tension by allowing water to roll off but do not allow permeation of moisture and air, so compromising comfort.

FABRICS OF PLAIN WEAVE NATURE

Wool

Homespun, flannel crepe.

Silk

Crepe de chine, chiffon, shantung, crepe georgette, taffetta and voile.

Cotton

Calico, cambric, canvas, cheese cloth, chintz, cretonne, crepe, cotton, flannelette, long cloth, gingham, muslin, organdy, seersucker and voile.

Linen

Cambric, dress linen, handkerchief linen and towelling.

Rayon

Chifton,.crepe, geogette, seersucker, organdy, taffetta and voile.

Variation of Plain Weave

Basket Weave

Basket weave is a balanced weave. The fabrics with basket weave have flenth and if the count is not very highlite fabric is even porous and pliable.

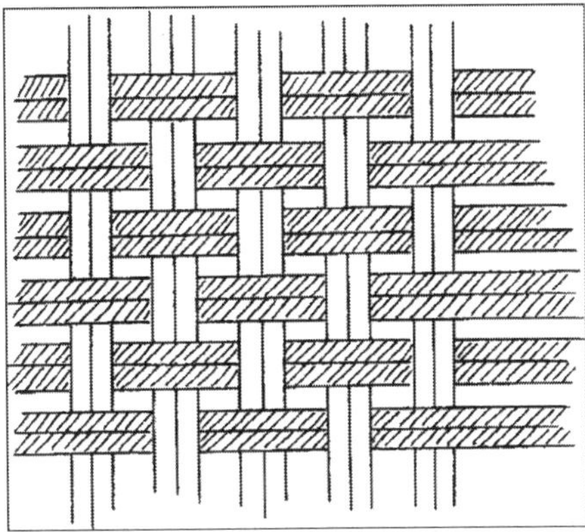

Fig. Basket Weave

However, fabrics with arrangements like 3x3, 4x4, 6x6 snag easily. In this two or more yarns in both warp and filling are treated as one, and interlaced as in plain weave. This weave is utilised in materials for sport. Basket weave. coats and suits. This is a relatively loose weave and therefore, the fabrics are more likely to shrink.

Rib Weave

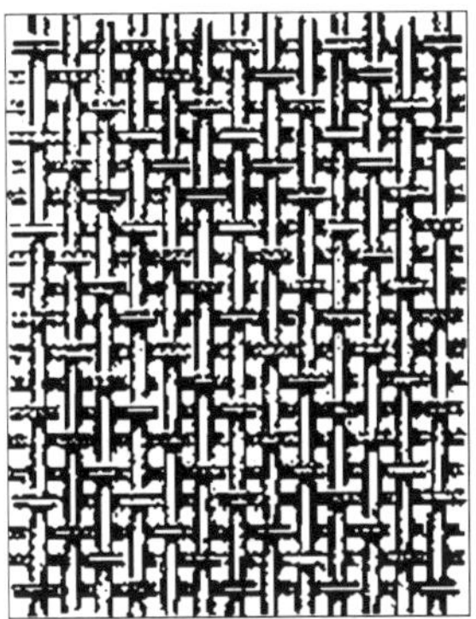

Fig. Rib Weave

This is a variation of plain weave. In this, heavier yarns are utilised in the warp than those in the weft, and this produces a ribbed effect. Sometimes, the order is reversed and the heavier yarn is used in the weft. Ego eve, faille gross grain bengalene, ottoman, broad cloths poplin and iabralco are some of the instances.

Twill Weave

The simplest form of the twill weave is made by throwing the filling yarn over two warp yarns, then under one, over two, under one and so 'on, with a progression of one. This weave needs at least three shifts of the loom to complete the unit of the design and three harnesses. In this weave, either the warp or the filling may be utilised to form the face of the cloth. The progression, which produces the diagonal effect of the twill may be to the right or to the left. It may be plain or varied which makes the cloth decorative. The common variation in the twill weave is herring bone. In this, the diagonal effect runs in one direction a few rows and them in the opposite direction.

Fig. Twill Weave

The whole pattern is thus repeated. Another variation is made for a giamon Q pattern. Varifions are also introduced by using yarns of various sizes, qualities and colours. It will weave has fewer points of interlacings than plain weave. So it allows closer picking of warp yarns to produce heavier fabrics which results in longer wear. Twill weave produces strong material because of the tightly twisted yarns which are utilised to bring out the diagonal effect, and the compactness of its construction.

Twill weave fabrics are very precious because of their elaborate construction, but they are strong and stand hard and long wear. This weave is generally used in wool and cotton fabrics where durability is prime need. Twill weave fabrics do not-shew dirt or dust as much as the fabric woven in plain weaves do, and are, therefore, more appropriate for dresses, men's shirts and suits and children's garments. The side on which the diagonal effect is more prominent is the right side *of* the cloth. Bet when twill weave fabrics are finished by 'napping', the napped side is the right-side.

Fabrics of Twill Weave Nature

Wool

Covert cloth, broad cloth, cashmere; flannel, gabardine, tweed, serge, worsted

Cotton

Covert cloth denim, drill, gabardine,.Jean, khaki serge.

Linen

Table linen, towels, drills and ticking.

Silk

Twill, serge, Surat.

Sateen and Satin

Satin Weaveing

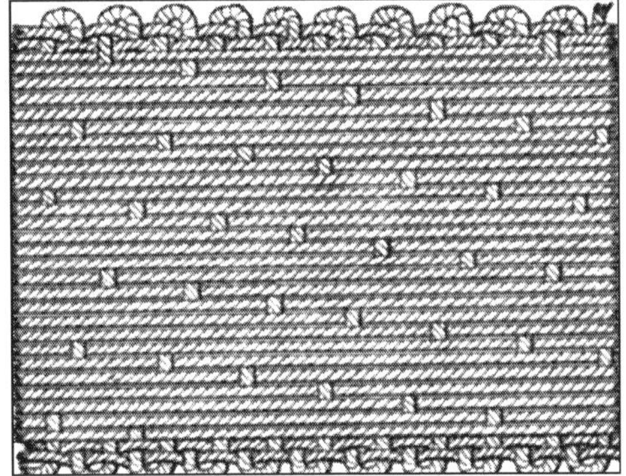

Fig. Satin Weaveing

This weave differs from the twin weave as in this the interlacing of the warp and filling yarns not regular. The filling yarn is passed over several warp threads. The floasts in sateen are generally shorter than those in the stin weave. Other variations may be introduced by throwing long or short floats or by throwing long or short floats upon the surface. Then again, a combination of satin and sateen weaves may be utilised to produce elaborate or figured designs.

The satin and sateen weaves need more shafts in weaving them are needed in the stain or twill weaves and, therefor fabrics of the former weaves are very expensive. The Satin or, Sateen weave fabrics are more decorative than serviceable. These are durable only if they are not subjected to excessive or hard use. Stain or Sateens with short floats are more durable. To differentiate between satin and sateen weaves fingers are passed over the cloth to condition the direction of the floats. If the fingers run-smoohtly and smoothly along the length olthe fabric, thus indicating the presence of the warp floats, the weave is satin. This weave is most commonly utilised in the silks and rayons. Satins are extremely lustrous and smooth the sateen weave will have floats running on the cross side of the fabric. This weave is utilised in a few mercerised cotton fabrics. These, fabrics are not as lustrous or smooth as satin.

Sateen and Satin Fabrics

Dress satin, slipper satin, satin crepe, satin georgettee, satin canton, satin twill, sateen, venetian sateen.

Weaves of Novelty Nature

Figure Weaving

Several fabrics have various kinds of designs woven into them. There are two methods of making these figure weaves —Jacquard and Dobby. A Jacquard loom is essential for more elaborate patterns buti Dobby attachment is sutpcient for simple and small geometrical designs.

Dobby Weave

Only a few geometrical designs are possible in this weave, such as the diamond patterns. The Dobby attachment consists of a chain of parochial strips of wood hung on the top of the loom.

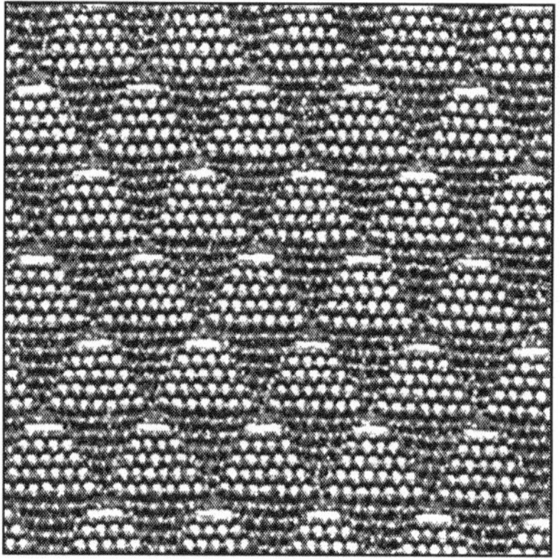

Fig. Dobby Weave

Pegs are inserted in each of the strips to connote the pattern. These strips of wood control the movements of the harness to form a shed. Another chain of strips of wood controls the shuttle, and thus the designs are woven in the fabric. The Dobby attachment can control no more than twenty-five harness. This is the reason, for the limited number of designs. Instances of Dobby weave are the "Birds eye" used in diapers and sharkskin suiting Huckaback or huck towtling of small diamond designs are also made in the Dobby weave

Jacquard Loom Weaveing

The Jacquard loom was invented by a French man, Joseph Jacquard, in 1801. The intricate arrangement of this loom weaves the most beautiful and exhaustive designs in the fabrics. In this loom every individual warp is controlled independently and not in series as in ordinary looms. In the place of harnesses, a series. of oblong punched cards called 'Jacquard card' control the raising of the warps. As several cards as there are picks are used in the design. The designs are first worked out on a graph paper in points. Then these points of the designs are punched on the cards in the same order and are rotated over a cylinder on the top of the loom. Long cords which hold fine steel wires are also attached to another set of horizontal wires knownas 'needles' on the" top of the loom.

Each of the steel wires has an eye through which a warp yarn is threaded. In working the loom, the needles press forward against a Jacquard Card. The needles which go through the punched holes in the card pull some cords which in their turn pull the steel wires and so the warps are-faised to form a shed simultaneousdly.

The shuttle passes through throwing in the filling yarn. The cylinder Which holds the cards, turns slightly and another card israised. This again forms a contact with the needles, a new shred is formed, and the filling yarn is passed through. This process is continued till all the cards have been used once. The pattern is thus completed. The process is then repeated till the whole length of the cloth is woven.

The Jacquard weave fabrics are fairly expensive because of:

- The elaborate process used for this weave,
- The time and skill required for preparing the cards. The actual weave is a combination of two or more kinds of fundamental weaves or a variation of such combinations.

For instance, in damask the design is woven in sateen weave with filling floats, and the ground of the cloth is in satin weave with warp floats. In brocades, the design may be in the twill weave and the background in satin weave. The face and back of the fabrics in figured weaves may display the same design (as in the case of huckaback) or in the reverse as in damask, the design may be totally different on either side as in brocades. The durability of the figured fabrics relies on the length of the floats, and the type of the yarn. Long floats increase the sheen and softness of the fabric but affect its wearing quality.

TREATING FABRICS WITH CHEMICAL REAGENTS

These comprise a process of treating the fabrics with chemical reagents which change either the appearance or the,intrinsic properties of the cloth, *e.g.*. mercerising changes their appearance of the cloth, whereas crease resistant finishes or. fire proofing changes its properties.

Process of Mercerising

This process provides a high degree of lustre tottons through the chemical action of caustic soda. John Mercer, a calico printer in England, first discovered in 1844, that the application of a strong solution of caustic soda made cotton cloth transparent. The process comprises of impregnating the yarn or the fabric with cold caustic soda solution, applied under tension to reduce shrinkage, and to increase the lustre. The process removes the twist in the fibre and thus led to the fibre to become smooth and cylindrical which produces a silky effect. Mercerised cotton absorbs dyes very soon.

Process of Fire-Proof Finish

A simple method which comprises treatment with boric acid and borax. This, however, dissolves in water. Another method is the treatment of the fabric with chlorinated compounds, like Vinyle Chloride or chlorinated rubber and antimony oxide. This solution covers the fabric with a thin, non-inflammable film which renders the fabric fire-proof.

The Process of Crease Resistant Finish

The process is used mostly for cotton because cotton, owing to its natural inelasticity, wrinkles badly. In this process the fabrics are impregnated with a solution of synthetic resin, live:

- Phenol formaldehyde,
- Urea formaldehyde
- Acrylic resins, and dried by a very high temperature in a moist atmosphere.

This forms a clear insoluble resin in the fibre; which improves the resilience of the fabric. Urea formaldehyde is colourless and can be utilised for white and light coloured fabrics but phenol formaldehyde being dark coloured is used for dark coloured fabrics only.

Process of Creping

Creping by the chemical process is the treatment of fabrics with caustic soda. The soda paste is used to fabrics in a definite design of stripes or figures. The parts to which the paste is applied shrink leaving the other parts unshrunk; thus the effect of a puckered or creped material will be produced. Another method is to apply a paste of a substance which opposed the effect of caustic soda to the fabric in a definite design, and then place the fabric in a solution of caustic soda. The untreated places will shrink and produce the crepe effect. This method is more lasting than the mechanical one. The crepe produced in weaving is of course very different to the crepe effect produced by these finishes.

Process of Dyeing

Dyeing may also be called a finishing process as it colours the fabric and so adds to its eauty. Dyeing is a very ancient Indian art which the other countries learnt from the Indians. In the earliest stages, the fabrics were coloured with the juices of flowers, fruits, stems, leaves and barks of plants and trees. Later on, dye stuffs from vegetable and mineral sources came into utilisation. The chemical dyes are the discovery of relatively recent times. There are a number of methods utilised for dyeing the fabrics at various stages.

Process of Raw Stock-dyeing

Fibres of wool, cotton, linen and waste silk are dyed. The stock of fibres are rotated in the dye bath, then removed and dried.

Process of Piece-dyeing

This is the process utilised for dyeing materity woven from any fibre. The penetration of colour is not quite so thorough as in the preceding forms of dying. The fabrics art wrapped around rollers which are placed in the dye bath and left there until they are saturated with the colour. Cotton fabrics 'require to be held under tension while passing through the dye. The other fabrics are not held taut.

Process of Stuh-dyeing

This method is brought into use in dyeing wool fibres after these have been combed. The skeins of wool slivers are hung on rods. The rods are then placed on the top of the dye bath. The rods are made to rotate, so that the slubbings keep constantly moving through the dye bath. These are then rinsed and dried.

Process of Skein-dyeing

Yarns of almost all fibres are dyed. Cotton and linen are generally dyed at the yarn stage. But the penetration of colour in skein-dyeing is much better. Skeins of yarns are hung on rods, which are placed in a dye bath. These rods rotate causing the skeins to 'circulate through the dye bath. This method is known as skein-dyeing.

Cross Dyeing

Fabrics woven with mixed yarns, like cotton, wool, or acetate rayon and viscose rayon, are dyed by this method. The affinity of dye-stuffs differs according to the two sorts of yarns mixed in weaving. thus, the fabrics are to be dyed in two successive dyebaths. In one, the dye suitable for one kind of yarn is used and in the other is utilised the dye suitable for the other yarn. Sometimes, a mixed fabric is dyed in one and the same dye bath and so each one of the yarn takes its own particular and. Various shade of cot our, or one takes the colour and the other remains colourless.

Process Tie and Dye

This is a kind of resist dying, which was practised as far back as the sixteenth century in India or probably even earlier. It is a simple method and yet man, fascinating and intricate designs are produced in the fabric, as for instance in the famous 'Patola' of Gujarat. By this method either the yarn is dyed before the fabric is woven as in *'Paldani'* or the woven material is dyed as in *'Bandani'* saris of Gujarat, Kathiawar and Rajasthan. The parts of the fabric on the yarn which are to oppose the dye are tied with strings or narrow strips of cloth. The strings or the sirips are waxed to enhance the dye-resistance and so get better results. The skeins of the yarn or the material is then dipped in the dye bath. Then these are rinsed, dried and the strings removed. This method of dying produces beautiful patterns. Work of 'Bandani' this is used by women in India to dye their saris and scarves or 'dupattas' at home.

Process of Batik

This is another form to resist dyeing which produces patterns like those in prints. This also was first practised in India. The Javanese then took this art to their country, and now 'Batik' dyeing is a big industry in Java. The method is as follows: A full sized design is drawn or traced on the material. Hot, melted wax is applied on the lines of the design with a paint brush. The size of the brush depends on the thickness of the lines of the design.

After coating the lipes with wax, the fabric is immersed in cold water to harden the wax and to wet the fabric. The dye bath is then prepared. Cold water dye or dyes which car be utilised at low temperature are used for"Batik' dyeing. If the dye bath is hot, the wax applied on the design will melt and the process will be a failure. The dye-bath vessel must be lane enough to permit the entire fabric to be moved freely without any pressure or friction which might cause the wax lines to crack and thus spoil the design. The material is kept in the dye bath long sufficient for the cloth to be thoroughly impregnated with the dye. The cloth is then rinsed and dried and the waf is removed. A 'Batik' in which more than one colour and an intricate design is used needs very great care and more than one operation is necessary as in the case of multi-coloured print.

Practice of Printing

Printing also was practised in India thousands of years before the Christian Era. The designs were either drawn by a brush or were stamped on the material by wooden blocks carved or cut in relief. A simple method of printing utilised at first comprised dipping the carved block in a paste of colour and then stamping the fabrics with it in a definite pattern. This method is still utilised extensively. Later, a screen made of fine wires (wire-cloth) or silk bolting cloth came into use. In machine printing engraved copper rollers, or cylinders are utilised. The dyes used in printing are the same as those used for dyeing but these are utilised in the form of pastes. If mordants are necessary, the fabrics are treated with mordant solution before being printed.

Practice of Block Printing

This is follows is in India even today to get beautiful patterns. Blocks are made of wood or wood and lino. The design is carved on lino which is generally cut to a thickness of ¼ inch. This cut piece of lino is stuck on to a wooden piece of the same size. In India, several printers use only wood blocks on which the design has been carved. The paste of colour is poured on trays lined with cloth. The material to be printed is spread on a padded table and held taut and smooth. Then the block carrying pate of one colour is stamped on the material and allowed to dry. Then another block carrying paste of various colour is stamped over it to form the multi-coloured patterns. The process is repeated over the entire fabric-surface which is to be printed.

Process of Screen Printing

Silk bolting cloth or wire cloth is stretched over a wooden frame. Over this, a line is drawn of such portions of the design as are to take one colour. The sphere of the screen which are to be utilised to prevent the spreading over of the colour are filled with water proof varnish, enamel or some other insoluble filter The fabric to be printed is then stretched on a table which is padded and covered with oil-cloth.

The wooden frame with the screen is then placed in the material, and the paste of colour is brushed over its surface and then lightly pressed. The colour is permitted to dry. Then another frame carrying a several colour and different outline is utilised and the process continues till the design is complete. A separate screen is required for the application of each colour in the design. The size of the screen used is generally 4 ft. by 6 ft.

Machine Printing

A printing machine comprises several copper cylinders or rollers which are engraved. The actual printing of the design on the cloth by this method takes very little time but the engraving of the design on the rollers means hard and careful work lasting many days. The roller is as wide as the cloth. The number of rollers needed depend on the number of colours utilised in the design as one roller can print only one colour.

MANUFACTURE OF THE INDIVIDUAL FIBERS

A considerable lag always exists between the marketing of a new product and the publication of specific details about its manufacture. Of the five fibers under consideration, excellent accounts of the production steps are available for nylon 66 only, a product which has been on the market for almost twenty years. For the other fibers, all of very recent origin, broad pictures of the process of production, but not the details of the individual steps, can be obtained.

Therefore, the nature of the technical literature on the subject should be made clear. The published accounts employed are surveys, based on the patent literature and the literature of chemistry, of alternative approaches to each general process step. Since only the general steps are important for the identification of the locationally strategic inputs, no pretense is made that the accounts which follow are of any firm's actual manufacturing operation.

Production of Nylon 66

The monomer from which nylon 66 is made is hexamethylene diammonium adipate, commonly called nylon salt. If fiber manufacture is separate from chemical intermediate manufacture, the salt is made into a water solution to facilitate handling and shipment to yarn plants. In conversion into nylon 66 fiber the salt is first run from storage tanks into evaporator kettles where it is concentrated. Acetic acid is added as a viscosity stabilizer in polymer formation. From the evaporator kettles a 60 per cent solution of the salt is run into autoclaves where polymerization takes place. If a delustered yarn is wanted, an aqueous suspension of titanium dioxide is added to the reaction mass soon after it begins to boil. When polymerization is completed, nitrogen pressure is applied to force the polymer, a sirupy material, to flow out through a slot in the bottom of the autoclave. Nylon 66 is spun by the melt-spinning process. Several steps are required to prepare the polymer for melt spinning.

From the autoclave a ribbon of the polymer flows onto a casting wheel, where it is hardened by sprays of water and cooled with streams of air. Then a mechanical cutter reduces the ribbons of polymer to small flakes; these flakes are conveyed to a blender and then transferred to supply hoppers which ride (via an overhead rail) over the spinning machines. Specially designed spinning machines, consisting of batteries of spinnerets, are used to extrude the polymer. From an overhead supply hopper the flaked polymer is fed into funnel-shaped, nitrogen-filled melt chambers which, in turn, feed one or more spinnerets. In the melt chamber a heated grid melts the polymer, which can then be pumped directly to the spinnerets. The holes of the spinnerets vary in size and number according to the size of the filaments and yarn desired. From the lower face of the spinneret the viscous filaments pass down through the orifices into a cooling chimney and are subjected there to an air blast to aid in solidification.

A converging guide gathers the filaments into a bundle of yarn. To prevent elongation and to keep the yarn from loosening and slipping in a subsequent winding operation, it is passed through a chamber and humidified with steam. After the steam treatment, the yarn is passed over glass finish rollers which apply an oil emulsion as a lubricant for other operations. At the bottom of the spinning unit the yarn is wound up in undrawn and untwisted form on bobbins. At this point the remaining process steps depend on the form in which the yarn is to be sold.

Continuous Filament

To make continuous-filament fiber, bobbins of yarn are conveyed to the textile area of the plant. Most nylon 66 filament is sold as low-twist yarn. In preparing the untreated yarn the filaments are twisted together—on conventional textile machinery-with about one or two twists per inch. Then the yarn is rewound on bobbins for a cold-drawing process on machines which stretch it to about four times the original length by passing it through sets of rollers moving at different speeds. From the viewpoint of chemistry the molecules of the undrawn filaments have random orientation only. After drawing, the linear molecules are aligned parallel to the fiber axis, a change which gives the yarn its particular physical properties. After the yarn has been drawn, it is wound on bobbins, the typical put-up, and is inspected and packaged for shipment.

Staple and Tow

For the manufacture of nylon 66 staple thousands of continuous filament fibers are combined into a rope or tow. The tow is drawn and then crimped by mechanical means to give the yarn the loftiness associated with natural fibers such as wool. The crimped ropes of yarn are set with steam and then cut into the desired length by staple cutters. At the end of this operation the staple is dried and baled for shipment. If tow is to be sold, it is packaged after being drawn.

Production of Orlon

Orlon is made from monomeric acrylonitrile, and Morgan suggests that for a large-scale operation polymerization can best be carried out as a continuous process. A water-soluble catalyst, such as ammonium persulphate, and a reduction agent, such as sodium bisulphite or sodium thiosulphate, can be used. In the suggested continuous process streams of acrylonitrile and aqueous solutions of the catalyst and reducing agent are fed into a reactor.

Low rates of conversion of the monomer to polyacrylo-nitrile make it necessary, after filtration of the slurry issuing from the reactor, to recover unconverted acrylonitrile by fractional distillation so that it may be recycled. As the polyacrylonitrile is formed, it precipitates in fine granular form which can be readily filtered.

Lessing, in writing on the development of Orlon, notes that in the experimental production of filaments both the wet- and dryspinning processes were employed but that the latter method proved best. In either event a spinning solution must be prepared by dissolving the dry polymer in an organic solvent. For Orlon manufacture polyacrylonitrile is dissolved in dimethyl formamide. If a delustered yarn is desired, an agent such as titanium dioxide is introduced into the spinning solution, or dope. Once prepared, the solution for dry spinning must be carefully filtered for the removal of foreign matter and gels of undissolved material. Each batch of polymer solution can be processed through conventional filter presses.

In a typical dry-spinning process sketched by Fremon the filtered dope is stored in tanks which feed the cells of the spinning units. Spinning dope is pumped into the top of each cell by metering pumps. As the polymer is forced through the spinneret, filaments are formed and solidified as the solvent in the solution is evaporated by hot air. The volatized solvent can be drawn off from an aperture in the cell by air flows and conveyed to a solvent recovery unit, a vital operation in the economics of the process. As the new filaments are gathered together in each cell by wind-up devices at the bottom, they are passed over a roller which applies a protective lubricant and wound up on spools for further processing.

Fibers produced by the dry-spinning process are hot-stretched rather than cold-drawn as in the case of nylon. The stretching operation may be preceded by a washing treatment in which the yarn is passed through a bath to remove solvent residue. Frey and Sippel point out three alternative hot-stretching methods.

First, the yarn may be drawn between two or more sets of rollers, moving at different velocities, through a hot bath consisting of a nonsolvent for the fiber or of hot air. In the second approach hot drawing is made possible by passing the yarn through heated rollers or over hot plates. Finally, they note that for polyacrylonitrile fibers the yarn may be stretched in special steam tubes. To stabilize the molecular arrangement brought about by stretching and to relieve the strains in the drawn fibers, the yarn may be "relaxed" by a heat treatment in an annealing oven.

Continuous-filament Orlon is sold with low twist or none at all, so that the final operation is to wind the yarn on bobbins or to give it a low twist and then put it up. In describing the production of Orlon staple Mauersberger cites a seven-step operation. Filaments are gathered together to form a tow which is drawn and then passed through mechanical devices which put a crimp in the fiber. A relaxing step follows, and the yarn is cut into staple fiber. The cut staple is dried and put up into bales for use by the textile industry.

Dynel Output

Dynel, the vinyl fiber of the Union Carbide and Carbon Corp., is made of a copolymer of vinyl chloride (60 per cent) and acrylonitrile (40 per cent). Harris describes an emulsion polymerization procedure for the preparation of constant composition copolymers of vinyl chloride-acrylonitrile containing the monomers in the proportion 60/40. The step is carried out by mixing vinyl chloride and acrylonitrile in water containing a water-soluble catalyst and an emulsifier. At the end of the reaction the polymer is a resin in powder form.

The published literature shows that dynel is made by the wetspinning process. Although none of the wet-spinning methods used in the production of vinyl fibers has been described in detail, the general nature of the operation is known from viscose rayon production. Just as in the case of dry spinning, a solution is prepared by dissolving resinous polymer in a suitable solvent. For dynel production acetone is used.

The solvent, the resin powder, and a viscosity stabilizer are mechanically mixed to form the spinning dope. To prepare it for use in spinning, the solution is filtered. In the wet process the spinning apparatus lies horizontal, submerged in a liquid-bath medium. The spinning solution is extruded into the liquid, and filaments are formed by coagulation. As indicated in the introduction, dynel is manufactured in the form of staple and tow only. Fremon has described a wet-spinning process for making synthetic staple which provides a glimpse of the general steps which follow filament formation. After the fiber in tow form emerges from the coagulating medium it can be taken to a second bath where it is washed and stretched.

In the next step the tow is dried in an oven and is also annealed to stabilize the molecular structure brought about by stretching. From the annealing oven the tow is passed through a mechanical crimper and then can be cut into staple form and baled. In an alternative approach the tow can first be dried to low moisture content, cut, and then passed through a device known as a tunnel dryer. The air temperature of the dryer is maintained as high as possible without injury to the yarn, and the fiber shrinks unevenly, taking on a crimp.

Acrilan Manufacture

Few details have been released by the Chemstrand Corp. on the manufacture of Acrilan, its vinyl fiber. Production so far has consisted of staple and tow only. Like dynel, the fiber is a copolymer. Acrilan is made principally of acrylonitrile (85 to 90 per cent), and the other component has been most frequently identified in the technical accounts as vinyl acetate or vinyl pyridine.

Morgan notes that copolymers of acrylonitrile containing small amounts of a second monomer, such as vinyl pyridine, can be manufactured in a manner similar to the process described in the Orlon section for the polymerization of acrylonitrile. The second monomer can be mixed in with the acrylonitrile stream. In the most recently published account Mauersberger has described the general steps for the manufacture of Acrilan. He reports that the spinning process employed is the wet method. Whatever solvent is used to prepare the spinning solution of the powdered copolymer has not been specifically identified.

Dacron Production

Dacron, Du Pont's polyester fiber, is the condensation product of dimethyl terephthalate and ethylene glycol. A commercial route used in the production of the polymer, polyethylene terephthalate, has been described by Reynolds. Ester interchange between dimethyl terephthalate and excess ethylene glycol yields a condensate which is heated in a vacuum to effect removal of the excess glycol and to give a polymer of high molecular weight. Ester interchange requires a catalyst such as magnesium or zinc borate. As the temperature of the reaction mixture is raised, methanol forms and is removed by distillation. Pressure filtration can be used to purify the initial condensate product before it is transferred to a polymerization reactor. In the polymerization step excess ethylene glycol is evolved which presumably can be recycled.

The molten polymer is released from a heated extrusion valve at the base of the vessel by the application of nitrogen pressure.Dacron is melt-spun, and the manufacturing steps are reported to be very similar to the general procedure followed in the production of nylon. The molten polymer emerges from the polymerization reactor as a solid ribbon, which is run onto a casting wheel, cooled by water sprays, and cut into flakes for the spinning operation. Again, if a delustered yarn is desired, titanium oxide is used and it can be added to the condensate mixture as a dispersion in the ethylene glycol. The fiber is produced as continuous-filament yarn without twist and as staple and tow. Since the remaining steps in a fiber plant with a melt-spinning process were described for nylon, the details are assumed to apply in an approximate way for Dacron.

LOCATION THEORY AND THE SYNTHETIC-FIBER INDUSTRY

An empirical location study must turn to location theory for a systematic coverage of all factors which might possibly influence the location of an industry and, in general, the geographical distribution of its plants. In this location study of the synthetic-fiber industry an attempt has been made to apply the general substitution approach to the locational equilibrium of the firm. Underlying the location pattern of an industry are decisions made by business firms. The general area of economic theory which embraces this type of decision-making activity is a branch of microeconomics, the theory of the firm, and, in particular, the locational equilibrium of the firm. Traditionally, the theory of the firm has been made synonymous with price theory, the postulates of which are inferred through the implications of profit-maximizing behabiour of the firm in three roles: first, in the process of production, i.e., the transformation of inputs into outputs; second, as a buyer of inputs; and third, as the seller of a product.

Given the familiar data of the problem, including the structure of markets faced by the firm (defined in terms of numbers of buyers and sellers and homogeneity of product), profit-maximizing levels of output can be deduced. Price theory ignores the location problem because buying, production, and selling are looked upon as single-dimension activities, i.e., as occurring at a point. This assumption is abandoned in the theory of the location equilibrium of the firm. As a buyer of inputs, the firm incurs costs in assembling them over space and is also confronted with regional differences in their availability; the impact of site on the technical possibilities of production is recognized; and the selling activity embraces a market area in which transportation costs are also incurred in delivering the product. Thus the attributes of plant-location theory stem from firm behabiour n a fourth role as well: that of selecting from an array of geographical possibilities, minimum-cost production, and selling sites; and cost minimization is focused on variations which result from the factor of space.

The Weberian Framework

In his pioneering work Weber's signal contribution was the development of the principal categories of industrial location, largely on the basis of technical empirical knowledge. To Weber, the transportation network of a nation is the basic magnetic field of economic attraction which, through its lines of force, determines the position of industrial particles. He regarded transportation orientation as the basic principle of industrial location.

Conceptually, competing magnetic fields are sometimes capable of causing particles to be drawn away from the transportation lines of force to their own. In short, all other types of orientation, such as power or labor, are deviations from minimum-cost transportation sites. Weber also singled out the importance of agglomeration economies in industrial location. Although his types of location are suggestive for empirical studies, Weber's geometrical approach to the locational equilibrium of the firm, which, for example, requires the solution of location triangles, offers only a rough methodological guide.

The General Substitution Approach

That the Weberian location categories could be derived by means of the familiar substitution principle of price theory was suggested by Predohl in 1928, but it was not until 1949 that an operational framework was established for the general substitution approach to location theory by Isard. In his work Isard has extended the bounds of traditional production theory to include the locational equilibrium of the firm. Since cost minimization has a spatial dimension, it is specifically recognized by way of transport inputs. Within the enlarged framework the problem of production is that of choosing the right combination of capital, labor, land, and transport inputs. From the most significant cost difference which occurs through variation over space the orientation of an industry can be determined. Isard distinguishes two types of substitution. The exploration of alternative outlays from the use of transport inputs can determine whether costs for a transport-oriented industry are minimized at market or at raw-material sites; and the traditional outlay substitutions of production theory between capital, labor, and land can be used to deduce other types of industrial location such as labor or power orientation.

APPLIED GENERAL SUBSTITUTION ANALYSIS AND THE SYNTHETIC-FIBER INDUSTRY

The general substitution approach to the locational equilibrium of the firm provides an effective operational tool for empirical analysis. This approach can be put in simple terms in the case in which a given market, or set of markets, is to be served by a plant with given physical inputs per unit of output and is able to draw raw materials from alternative supply areas. As this plant is moved from region to region, the effect on its costs and revenue via the substitution of inputs and of diverse outlays can be determined. Consider, for example, the alternative in the synthetic fiber industry of producing the chemicals for fiber synthesis at sites in chemical raw-material regions or of manufacturing them in fiber-market regions in the textile area of the United States. Output at a raw-material site requires little outlay on movement of raw materials, but outlays are incurred on the transportation of the finished product and on utilities, labor, etc. At a market site a transportation cost on raw materials is substituted for the cost of moving the finished product, and the market-site utility, labor costs, etc., are substituted for those at the raw-material site. In addition, market-site agglomeration economies are substituted for those at the raw-material site. Substitutions such as these can be used to generate regional cost differences so that the most favorable region for plant location can be uncovered.

The Hypothesis

It is clear that the successful use of the general substitution approach in an empirical location study depends in a large measure upon the extent to which production functions, the physical relationship between various inputs (including transportation inputs) and output, can be obtained or estimated. If, for instance, the location of an ammonia plant is in question, it is necessary to know the raw-material inputs per unit of output, the utility and labor inputs, the manner in which these inputs vary with the size of plant, the manner in which the capital investment varies with size of plant, etc.

The hypothesis in this study of the synthetic-fiber industry is that:

- From an examination of the industry's production functions and market areas a spatial framework of regions which are suitable for plant location can be established.
- General substitution analysis can be used to convert the data of the production functions into production and distribution cost differences at selected sites.

In this manner basic regional advantages and disadvantages for plant location can be ascertained. The computation of regional differences in production and distribution costs will also point out the basic type of location orientation for each stage of the synthetic-fiber industry as well as the minimum-cost regions among all those tested.

COSTS AND LOCATION ANALYSIS

Although in the location analysis of the synthetic-fiber industry it might be desirable to employ all the costs which the chemical engineer or the cost accountant would include, from the standpoint of location theory the estimation of costs, hence the estimation of production functions, can be simplified. All inputs which have a locational significance must be identified, but the cost items which do not vary significantly from region to region can be set aside. Thus the application of the general substitution approach to the synthetic-fiber industry begins with prior determination of relevant cost categories to guide the estimation of production functions. The basic cost categories in the theory of the firm are variable and fixed costs, and these are applicable in location analysis. With respect to the locational equilibrium of the firm, variable and fixed costs may vary spatially because of interregional differences in achievable agglomeration economies.

Cost Variation Plants of Equal Size

An examination of specific items in fixed production costs in both the chemical-intermediate and the fiber-producing stages of the synthetic-fiber industry leads to the conclusion that for any given predetermined size of plant regional uniformity in fixed charges can be assumed without doing violence to reality.

The chemical intermediates from which synthetic fibers are produced can be manufactured by more than one process, but the technology of petrochemical production is assumed in almost all cases in this study, since this particular route promises the most locational mobility for the future. In their study of the petrochemical industry Isard and Schooler found the assumption of regional uniformity of fixed costs for plants of given size to be a realistic one, after considering plant construction costs, interest charges, depreciation, plant maintenance, insurance costs, taxes, and land costs. In general, the analysis of the components of fixed charges also applies to the synthetic-fiber stage, even though fiber output is a combined chemical-textile operation.

In the past chemical-plant construction costs in warm-weather regions, such as Texas or California, have tended to be lower than in regions of the North by 10 or 12 per cent because certain structural parts unnecessary in the "outdoor" type of plant were thought to be indispensable in the "indoor" design for northern regions. However, Isard and Schooler note that the recent technical literature of chemical-plant construction points to the feasibility of the cheaper outdoor design for all regions. Plant construction cost inequalities which originate in labor-cost and material-cost variations cannot be systematically forecast and are not considered vital to the location problem in question.

For the large firms engaged in the development of synthetic fibers and their chemical intermediates ready access to the nation's capital market excludes the possibility of interest-cost disparities at different sites; therefore, the United States can be regarded as an area characterized by homogeneous capital availability for the location analysis. In considering the possibility of plant location in Puerto Rico, branch plants of American firms are assumed so that capital-cost uniformity applies to the island as well.

Since depreciation allowances are determined principally by tax legislation at the Federal level, there is little room for regional differences in this item of fixed costs. Plant maintenance has a regional variation and could be expected to be higher for cold weather regions, but the practice of performing major maintenance work in good weather limits the magnitude of the cost difference.

Insurance costs are significant in chemical production because of the risk hazard. Manufacture in a raw-material region with plants concentrated at specific sites raises plant insurance costs over areas in which chemical production is dispersed. Since the insurance cost differences are small and cannot be predicted in their variation with space, they are neglected in the cost analysis.

To account for regional variations in the burden of taxes which enter into fixed charges is a difficult matter. Property taxes are important but are set by legislative bodies and are not amenable to location analysis. Some states offer property-tax exemptions, usually for a five-year period, as an inducement to the location of new industry.

The practice is so widespread, however, that its impact on location decisions tends in the long run to become neutralized regionally, although it may be a factor in the selection of a site within a region. For the cost analysis land outlays are assumed to be equal in all regions. The problem of minimizing land outlays in factory construction is not one of choosing the right region but the proper site within a region. Although interregional equality in fixed charges may be justifiably assumed, in both stages of the synthetic-fiber industry regional differences in variable costs do exist. Computation of the amounts of these differences requires first an estimation of the most important variable physical inputs per unit of output.

Agglomeration Economies

For the synthetic-fiber industry the major agglomeration economies are:

- Large-scale production economies;
- Integration economies from the output of several chemical products in a multiunit plant—savings are realized, for example, by the utilization of the by-product of one unit as a raw material for another;
- localization economies from the geographical concentration of chemical plants in a given area—a single large-scale chlorine plant may serve the needs of several users and make it unnecessary for each to construct a small-scale unit;
- External economies from the purchase of raw materials from large-scale producers-in Texas, for instance, large-scale oil refineries make available to chemical manufacturers huge streams of waste gas at low prices.

It may be valid to assume that for some products plants of the same predetermined size could be built in any region. In many cases this assumption would imply that agglomeration economies are uniform from region to region. However, if plants of the same predetermined size cannot be built in all regions, then location analysis must evaluate regional differences in variable and fixed costs caused by differences in the extent to which large-scale production and other agglomeration economies can be achieved. All four of the above-mentioned types of agglomeration economy may be significant in the location of plants in the first stage of synthetic-fiber production, the manufacture of chemical intermediates. Since many of the intermediates have markets in other end uses, there may be regional differences in market potential. A site suitable for fiber manufacture may not draw the chemical stage unless it can serve a market for the excess production over the fiber requirement, for otherwise the chemical unit would suffer a large-scale production economy disadvantage. The other three types of agglomeration economy generally favor raw-material over market regions or, among market regions, those with the most highly developed chemical industries.

In this study agglomeration economies are evaluated for the chemical—intermediate stage through the estimation of the influence of size on fixed and variable costs. The other agglomeration economies-integration, localization, and external—are given qualitative consideration only. In the second stage of the industry, the manufacture of synthetic fibers, the main agglomeration consideration is large-scale production economies. The market for each synthetic fiber is spread out geographically over the entire textile area so that the output of a single plant is not sold entirely in a specific region.

For this reason plant size is largely a function of technological and cost considerations common to all fiber producers and is somewhat independent of the region chosen for the location of a plant. Since the technological and cost considerations permit plants of economic size to be built in any region, agglomeration economies can be eliminated as a factor in the location of synthetic-fiber plants.

Conclusions of Preliminary Cost Analysis

For the first stage of the industry, the output of chemial intermediates, the assumption is made from the foregoing analysis that the location problem can be solved by comparing regional differences in variable costs alone for products for which the assumption is valid that plants of the same predetermined size can be built in any region. In most cases, however, the comparison of regional differences in variable costs must be augmented by the estimation of the effect on both fixed and variable costs of agglomeration economies. With respect to the second stage, the manufacture of synthetic fibers from chemical intermediates, the assumption is made that the location problem can be solved by comparing regional differences in variable costs for plants of equal size.

4

Human Development

MOTOR DEVELOPMENT: CONTRIBUTIONS OF MOTOR DEVELOPMENT

UNDERSTANDING MOTOR DEVELOPMENT

Watching me take my first step from the sofa to your outstretched arms is something that you will probably always remember and talk about. Likewise, a special time is watching me draw my first picture of you—the almost perfect circle for your head, the two dots for your eyes, and the crooked line for your mouth.

Many of my other motor skills will emerge between that first step at around twelve months of age and the portrait at three and a half years. You can foster my motor development in three ways. *First*, understand my temperament and the progression of motor development so you can pick activities that encourage rather than frustrate me. *Second*, arrange my outdoor and indoor environment to encourage motor skills. *Third*, provide me with a variety of motor experiences. As my parent, you can better foster my motor development when you key into my temperament and when you know what skills are appropriate for my age.

Temperament plays a big role in my motivation and interest to learn and practice motor skills. Some children are "motor driven" and want to try everything. Other children are "motor cautious" and need time to watch others before trying things themselves. An understanding of motor development will enable you to pick activities that enhance my current skills and foster the development of emerging skills. When looking at my motor development, remember to look at both gross and fine motor skills. Gross motor skills involve my large muscle movements. Between one and four years of age, gross motor skills fall into one of three areas: movement, using stairs, and play.

Fine motor skills involve the small muscle movements of my hands and fingers in coordination with his eyes. Between one and two years of age, fine motor skills fall into four areas: putting in, building up, putting together, and writing. In addition to these areas, the two- and three-year-old can engage in fine motor craft activities.

ONE-YEAR-OLD

Gross Motor

Movement

At twelve months of age, I can creep on my hands and knees. At this age, I can also usually start to walk when you hold both my hands. About the same time I learn to walk with one hand held, I learn to stand alone. Next, I will learn to take a few steps by myself.

By the time I am eighteen months old, I will probably walk forwards very well. I also will take a few steps sideways and backwards. As my walking skills improve, I can start to pull a toy on a string behind me while walking. Before you know it, I will carry large toys while walking and push and pull large toys or boxes around on the floor. By twenty-four months of age I run well.

Using Stairs

Almost as soon as I can creep or walk to a set of stairs, I will try to climb them. I start by creeping or hitching up stairs. I then learn to creep down stairs. Once I am skilled at creeping up and down stairs and as my walking skills improve, I try to walk up stairs while you hold one of my hands. After I learn to walk up stairs holding one of your hands, I learn to go down stairs in a similar fashion. As I approach two years of age, I will walk up stairs holding onto a rail instead of your hand. At this age, most children continue to place both feet on each step as they walk up stairs. Be sure to supervise me carefully as I learn to use the stairs!

Play

One-year-olds like to climb on everything, but I need to learn what is and what is not acceptable to climb. Children at this age also enjoy playing with balls. I will throw a ball underhand when I am sitting before I can throw overhand in standing. When I first learn to throw, my aim is generally not very good. With practice, I will learn to throw a ball into a box. In addition to throwing balls, I enjoy trying to kick a ball. As I near two years of age, I begin to move on "ride on" toys without pedals.

Fine Motor

Putting In, Building Up, and Putting Together

I will learn to take out before putting in, to knock down before building up, and to take apart before putting together. At twelve months of age, I will love to take pegs out of pegboards and objects out of containers. I will like to knock down block towers as fast as you can build them. I will also enjoy pulling a string of pop beads apart and taking rings off ring stack toys. When learning to put in, I will put one item in and take it out, put one in again and take it out Once I am good at putting one peg in a pegboard or one block in a container, I learn to put many pegs and blocks in without removing them.

I usually learn to put a round shape into a shape sorter before a square one. If you try to encourage me to build a tower out of blocks, I will first build with only two blocks. I then learn to build a three- and then a four-block tower. Around two years of age, I can build a teetering tower of six blocks. By two years of age, I can put simple puzzles together by placing big non-interlocking pieces in the correct spot.

Writing

As a one-year-old I can mark and scribble on document with a crayon. I will imitate vertical strokes, then circular scribbles, then horizontal strokes. When using a crayon, I need close supervision because I may occasionally try to put the crayon in my mouth, or I may decide that the wall or a chair cushion would make a good writing surface.

TWO-YEAR-OLDS

Gross Motor

Movement

Between two and three years of age, I will become a very skilled jumper. I begin by jumping in place on both feet. Next, I jump forward, then backwards, and then sideways. In addition, I learn to jump two inches high, jump over a two-inch hurdle, broad jump, and jump down from eight inches high with one foot leading. Two-year-olds love to jump, but I need to learn what I may and may not jump from. As a two-year-old my balance is improving. Between two and two and a half years of age, I learn to walk on tiptoes, stand on one foot for a second, and take two or three steps on a balance beam. As I approach three, I may even try to hop on one foot. As my balance improves, so does my running. By three years of age, I can probably run very well and can make sharp turns around corners when running.

Using Stairs

As a two-year-old, I no longer need to hold onto your hand or a rail; I walk up the stairs by myself. I do, however, continue to place both feet on each step as I go up the stairs. I am getting better at going down the stairs, but I still need to hold onto the rail. Between two and a half and three years of age, I walk upstairs alternating my feet placing only one foot on each step. Since alternating my feet is new to me, I usually hold onto the rail.

Play

The two-year-old is an excellent climber. I go up and down slides and climb on jungle gyms. Between two and three years of age, my ball skills continue to improve. I learn to throw a ball five to seven feet underhand, to catch a ball with straight arms in front of my body, and to kick a ball a few feet.

Fine Motor

Putting In, Building Up, and Putting Together

In addition to putting circles and squares into a shape sorter, the two-year-old can put a triangle into it. By two and a half years of age, I can imitate a simple train made out of blocks and build a tower using eight blocks.

By three years of age, I can imitate a simple bridge made out of three blocks. Between two and three years of age, I learn to put a number of different types of toys together. I learn to place rings on a ring stacker, string a few one-inch beads, and put three-piece puzzles together.

Writing

As a two-year-old I have a much better understanding of what I should and should not write on. With practice I learn to hold a crayon or pencil with my thumb and fingers, and by three years of age, I can copy a circle. I may or may not show a hand preference by this age.

Crafts

As my fine motor skills become more refined, I can do very simple craft activities. I enjoy projects that involve paint, scissors, and glue. At first, I do best with finger paints, but soon I learn to paint with a brush. When I am first given a pair of scissors, I can barely hold them with both hands.

By the time I am two and a half years old, I will hold a pair of scissors in one hand and snip a piece of document. As I near three, I will snip on a line using scissors. Most two-year-olds love squeezing glue out of the bottle. Many, however, can't judge when to stop. As a result, I often need you to tell me when I have enough glue. Between two and three years of age, all craft activities require your constant supervision.

THREE-YEAR-OLDS

Gross Motor

Movement

The three-year-old progresses from being a skilled jumper to an expert jumper. Between three and four years of age, I learn to jump eight inches off the ground and to jump over an eight-inch hurdle. I go from broad jumping four inches at three years to broad jumping almost two feet at four years. At three, I can jump from a sturdy object 16-18 inches high with one foot leading, and at three and a half, I can jump from a height of two feet with both feet together on takeoff and landing. At three and a half, I can also jump rope for two cycles, hop on one foot, stand on one foot for two to five seconds, and gallop.

Using Steps

Between three and three and a half, I learn to walk up stairs using alternating feet without holding onto a rail. During this time I also learn to walk down stairs, placing both feet on the same step, without holding onto a rail. At around four years of age, I will begin to walk down stairs using alternating feet while holding onto the rail.

Play

The three-year-old likes playing ball. I kick and throw a ball well. At three I can kick a ball four feet and by four years of age I can kick a ball twelve feet. At three I can throw a ball underhand nine feet, and I am beginning to learn to throw overhand. But catching a ball can be harder for me. Coordinated catching skills generally don't develop until close to ten years of age and require a lot of practice. At three, however, I can catch a large (8 inch) ball with both arms extended straight in front of my body. I then learn to catch a large ball with my elbows bent. In addition to playing ball, I enjoy climbing on jungle gyms and dropping several inches to the ground. I also like riding a tricycle and can pedal about ten feet before needing to take a break.

Fine Motor

Putting in, Building Up, and Putting Together

The fine motor skills in this area become increasingly sophisticated between three and four years of age. During this time I learn to do more complex shape sorters--ones with stars, rectangles, and octagons. I also learn to build a ten-block tower, assemble 7 to 15 piece puzzles, and string one-half inch beads. I enjoy playing with many different types of construction toys such as Legos. By three and one half years of age, I demonstrate hand preference by picking up most items with the same hand.

Writing

Between three and four years of age, I develop the writing skills necessary to copy a cross and then a square. I may also attempt to copy a few letters, especially those in my name. By the time that I am four years old, I can draw a person with a head and one to three features.

Crafts

As a three-year-old I take pride in the fact that I am more skilled with crayons and paint. My scissor skills are also improving. At three years of age, I can make a continuous cut across a piece of document. At around three and a half, I can cut a straight line, staying within a half inch of the guideline. By the time I am four years old, I am pretty good with glue, except I may squeeze too much from the bottle.

ARRANGING THE ENVIRONMENT

Gross MotorArrange my outdoor and indoor play spaces for gross motor activities. Places for outdoor gross motor play include the backyard, park, or playground.

The exact location isn't important as long as it is safe and I get experiences with jungle gyms to climb; toys to ride on; slides to go up and down; balls to throw, kick, and catch; and objects to push, pull, jump off, and over. Indoors, I should have several safe toys for gross motor play. Provide me with large boxes to push, pull, crawl through, and sit in. Allow me to use a ride-on toy in the house. Give me a large pillow to jump on. Give me small, safe objects to practice throwing and catching. Routinely check all indoor and outdoor equipment and toys to make sure they are in safe condition. Check for potential dangers such as rough splinters, sharp edges, loose nuts or bolts, and protruding nails. Make sure the ground or floor under jungle gyms, slides, swings and other equipment is soft. Wood chips, sand, and grass are much safer to land on when playing outdoors than cement or gravel. A thick mat or carpeting is safer for indoor play than hardwood floors, linoleum, or tile.

Fine Motor

Arrange my outdoor and indoor play spaces for fine motor play. Indoors, provide me with a small table and chair to play at. On nice days, bring a few fine-motor toys outdoors. I can play with these toys at a picnic table or while sitting on a blanket in the grass. Offer me a variety of fine-motor toys. Encourage putting in by offering me small blocks and a box, junk mail and an oatmeal container, or plastic measuring cups and a nonbreakable mixing bowl.

To promote building up, provide small and large lightweight blocks to play with. You can foster putting together by giving me pop beads, shape sorters, ring stackers, and puzzles. To introduce writing, supply me with pencils, crayons, markers, and document. You also can allow me to write with chalk on a chalkboard or outdoors on a sidewalk. Inspire craft projects by allowing me to use paints, scissors, and glue with your supervision.

PROVIDING A VARIETY OF EXPERIENCES

Gross Motor

Movement

Give me the time and space I need to crawl, walk, run, and jump. Make movement fun for me by playing little games. When going from one room to another, have me walk backwards, sideways, or on tiptoes. At another time, have me move like an animal to get to the next room. A fun outdoor activity is to play follow-the-leader through an obstacle course. Have me crawl through a tunnel, step over a rock, go down the slide, run around a tree, and jump in a small pile of leaves. On a rainy day, you can make an indoor obstacle course. Another good rainy day activity is to have a circus.

As a tightrope walker I can walk across a long piece of masking tape that you lay on the floor. An an acrobat I can tumble and roll across a soft rug or mat. You can join the action or play the role of ringmaster and announce my performance to our imaginary audience.

Play

Encourage me to play on swings, slides, and jungle gyms. Take me to the park or playground to play on these pieces of equipment. Slides and jungle gyms should be low, and you should "spot" me in case I fall. If I am afraid of climbing or sliding, don't push or frighten me. Allow me to watch other children climbing and sliding. Describe what they are doing to focus my attention on the more important aspects. Swings should also be low and should have safety buckles. Remind me to always hold onto the swing. Teach me important playground safety rules, such as "Use the ladder, don't climb the slide."

I will require very close supervision at a playground if I don't see danger and I go beyond my capabilities. Encourage me to use protective equipment, such as helmets and knee pads as needed. In addition to playing at the playground, spend some time playing ball. If I am a beginner, try playing catch with a partially inflated beach ball or sponge ball. Both are easy to grab onto. If I am more advanced, put an old box or laundry basket in the middle of a room and give me a few small objects to practice throwing into the box. Finally, engage in family exercise. At this age, I need to practice my gross motor skills in a noncompetitive environment. Family exercise allows me to practice gross motor skills in such an environment and enables you to serve as my role model. It also can help promote healthy exercise behaviours for a lifetime. Be sure to give me water to drink during and after exercise, especially on hot days.

Fine Motor

Putting In

Give me a variety of experiences putting smaller objects into larger containers. Everyday fun examples include putting mail into a mailbox and safe clothespins into a small opening in the lid of a coffee can. Once I am skilled at putting objects in, move onto pegboards and shape sorters.

Building

Provide me with small and large blocks to build a tall tower or to make a long road. Empty shoe boxes and lids taped together with masking tape make excellent large blocks. To make them more attractive, you can cover the boxes with contact document or let me paint them. Unlike the more sturdy and reinforced commercially available giant blocks, shoe boxes will not support my weight. Be sure to tell me not to stand on these boxes.

Putting Together

Offer me popbeads, a ring stacker, and puzzles so I can practice putting things together. My first puzzles should have large non-interconnecting pieces. Puzzle pieces with knobs attached make handling pieces even easier for me. When teaching me how to put puzzles together, have me run my finger around the shape of the piece and inside the opening in the puzzle. Talk about the shape and how it feels. When teaching me to put interlocking puzzles together, help me look for context clues in addition to shape clues.

Writing

As a step towards helping me learn to write, provide me with opportunities to draw with crayons and chalk. Draw with me and show me how to make horizontal and vertical lines. To develop the fine motor control required for writing, provide me with path activities. To make a path, draw two, four-inch lines about an inch apart. At the front draw a stick person and at the end draw a ball. Tell me to help the boy get to the ball by drawing a line from the boy to the ball. As I get better at this, you can make a curvy path or one that zigzags.

When I am interested in learning to write letters, describe the shape of the letters in a fun manner. For example, say, "To make the letter N, your pencil has to go up the mountain and down the mountain, then up the mountain again." In the beginning, draw a dotted version of the letter for me to trace. Once I am skilled at tracing letters, write letters and let me try to copy them.

Crafts

Provide me with opportunities to use paints. Use non-toxic paints that are washable because I can be rather messy while painting. You may also want to have me wear a smock or an old shirt of yours as a cover-up when painting. Let me paint with my fingers, a sponge, or a brush. Talk about the colours I use and ask me to describe my creations. For a fun outdoor painting activity, give me a small pan of water and a big brush to "paint" the sidewalk or house. If I am too young for crayons and paints because I put these items in my mouth, let me experiment by using pudding or yogurt as paint and my highchair tray as the paper.

When I am between two and three years of age, give me supervised experiences with child safety scissors. At first you will need to show me how to hold a pair of scissors and you will need to hold the paper for me while I snip. A fringed placemat is a nice little project for me to make with my new skill. To make a placemat, have me snip a design into the edges of a rectangular piece of paper. To teach me to make continual cuts across a piece of paper, give me strips of coloured paper to cut across.

Once I can make continual cuts, draw straight lines on the paper for me to follow. Instead of throwing away the pieces of cut paper, let me glue them onto a piece of construction paper or a paper plate. When I first use glue, hold the bottle with me to teach me how much glue to squeeze out. If I have difficulty controlling the flow of glue or if I have trouble getting the glue on the paper, pour a small amount of glue on a paper plate and allow me to brush the glue on with an old paint brush. On a nice day, take me for a nature hike to collect leaves, twigs, and stones to glue onto a piece of paper.

PRINCIPLES OF MOTOR DEVELOPMENT

- Maturation
- Cephalocaudal
- Proximodistal
- Mass to Specific
- Bilateral to Unilateral to Crosslateral
- Phylogenetic *vs.* Ontogenetic
- Individual Differences

ESSENTIAL IN LEARNING MOTOR SKILL

It can be extremely scary to watch your child having difficulty learning an important task. There are general developmental guidelines for when tasks such as walking and writing should be learned. If your child has not achieved success by the far end of the guideline, you want to do everything you can to improve his or her chances of developing normally. There are factors in how we learn motor skills that you can bring into play to help the child. Be sure to stay positive and to keep in mind that all children develop in their own way at their own pace.

OBSERVATION

One of the major factors for learning motor skills is the ability of the learner to observe the motion in action. One method for accomplishing this is called dyad practice—learning skills in pairs.

FEEDBACK

Positive feedback is essential to learning motor skills, just as to a study published in the journal Medical Education. Feedback can provide information but it can also motivate the individual to continue to try the motion. Providing positive reinforcement after an activity can improve the ability of children to learn motor skills.

GENDER

A study published in the Women in Sport and Physical Activity Journal in 2003 concluded that there is a definite difference between male and female motor-skill learning. It was determined that males tend to work better with an internal focus (*i.e.* hold your hand this way) while females work better with an external focus (*i.e.* move your fork this way). This difference is thought to be caused by females being too concerned about doing a movement correctly. If the findings of this study are applicable, males and females might benefit from different teaching tactics for motor skills.

SELF-EFFICACY

Self-efficacy is a concept that encompasses many learning factors, including self-confidence, strength and belief, and the ability to set goals. Self-efficacy is affected by genetics, environment and the way motor skills are taught. A child who develops a strong sense of self-efficacy is more likely to learn motor skills

ENVIRONMENTAL INFLUENCES ON MOTOR DEVELOPMENT

The child's nervous system presents an intense evolutionary dynamism in the first years of life, due to the progressive myelination and maturation of association areas. The increasing maturation of the cortex promotes the improvement on motor functions, with better control of body parts. On the other hand, the practice on motor functions also influences the development of the myelination and the structural organization of the central nervous system (CNS).

The processes of growth and development occur just as to the rhythm that is established by the genetic potential, and also by the influence of environmental factors. The conditions of health and nutrition of the maternal organism have a decisive influence over embryo development.

Some postnatal factors, as the mother's psychological state and child's social relationships, can act as favourable or unfavourable influences for child's development. These features may cause undesirable repercussions on motor development. Among these postnatal factors, the mainly pointed are the nutricional conditions, the social and economics features, the environmental stimulation, the parents relationship, including their participation's degree on child's routine, their cultural level and access to leisure activities, and the mother's intelligence quotient (IQ). The literature demonstrates that the occurrence of such risk factors is rarely in an isolated way, when impairments over development are seen. They are also found more frequently in poverty conditions, leading to the hypothesis that a low social and economics level amplifies the biological vulnerability The low weight at birth is a condition very related to visual alterations and delays on the acquisition of the fine motor abilities. The affective relationships around the children, the family environment and the mother's capacity of interacting with her child have significant effects over his motor and mental development. It was related that children who live with single mothers, as well as that ones whose mothers show a low IQ, have larger risk of presenting cognitive delays. The conception of Piaget, the same factors that could impair mental development can also influence motor development.

The sensorimotor integration plays an important role in the motor learning. A minimum level of stimulation is needed to show to the child all his potential to explore the environment, therefore improving his motor and intellectual abilities. In this sense, there's facilitation in all developmental aspects, concerned to motor, structural, cognitive and emotion areas. The acquisition and maintenance of posture and movement depend on the learning and repetition of activities that will lead to the acquisition of sensory feedback and feedforward. The feedback represents an early learning through information provided by sensory receptors, which will be used by the child to begin and continue his voluntary movements and the reactions for the maintenance of the posture.

Many of these sensorial information are acquired by playing, when the toys act as tools with which the child develops his fine motor abilities and as well as those of gross motor development. In this early period, the child's permanence in a favourable environment will facilitate a normal development and offer possibilities to a larger potential of exploration and interaction. It can be found many works about the effects of environmental risk factors on children's psychomotor development. However, these kinds of information related to healthy children are still scarce. Thus, the present study had as objective the evaluation of the gross and fine motor development, by the approach of balance and coordination in healthy children. It was made an approach in two different types of environment, to discuss the correlation among features related with each one.

HAZARDS IN MOTOR DEVELOPMENT

PHYSICAL HAZARDS

- Mortality
- Crib Death
- Illness
- Accidents
- Malnutrition
- Foundations of Obesity
- Physiological Habits
- Play Hazards
- Hazards in Understanding
- Hazards in Morality

- Family Relationship Hazards
- Hazards in Personality Development

Mortality:

- Greater mortality occurs during the first three months of babyhood than later.
- Approximately two-thirds of all deaths during the first year of life occurring during first month.
- During the first year of babyhood, death is usually caused by serious illness.
- In the second year, death is often due to accidents.
- Throughout the babyhood, boys die more than girls.

Crib Death:

- Usually crib death occurs after a long period of sleep
- To date, medical science has been unable to find the exact cause or causes of death
- It's common among who experience abnormality in breathing or
- Who have had some abnormal condition at birth such as Jaundice

Illness:

- Due to such illness as gastrointestinal or respiratory complications.
- Minor illness such as colds and digestive upsets are common.
- Prompt diagnosis and proper medical care can keep these from causing serious harms.
- If they are neglected, serious infections can develop rapidly.

Accidents:

- Accidents in babyhood may be both minor and serious.
- During second year, when babies can move about freely and are not as well as protected
- Infrequent during the first year of life, owing to the fact that babies are carefully protected

Malnutrition:

- Causes stunt
- Deals to physical defects such as
- Carious teeth,
- Bowed legs, and a tendency to suffer from more or less constant illness.

Foundations of Obesity:

- Many parents equate health in babyhood with plumpness and do all they can do see that their babies are chubby.
- There is evidence that fat babies tend to have obesity problems as they grow while thin babies do not.
- This is because the number and size of the fat cells of the body are established early in life.

Physiological Habits:

- The foundation of the important physiological habits-eating, sleeping and eliminating are established during babyhood.
- Common physical hazard of the period is the establishment of unfavourable attitudes towards baby's part towards these habits

Psychological Hazards:

- Hazards in Motor Development
- Speech Hazards
- Emotional Hazards
- Social Hazards

Play Hazards:

- Play in Babyhood is potentially hazardous, both physically and psychologically.
- Many toys can inflict cuts and buries
- The major psychological hazard is that baby may come to rely too much on the toys themselves for amusement, instead of learning to play in ways that involve interaction with others.

Hazards in Understanding:

- Even though understanding is in a rudimentary stage of development, it presents a serious psychological hazard.
- In the development of concepts, it is relatively easy to replace wrong meanings associated with people, objects or situations in the correct meanings.

Hazards in Morality:

- No one expects babies to moral in the sense that behaviour conforms to the moral standards of social group or they will feel guilty and shame if they fail to do.
- However, a serious psychological hazard to future moral development occurs when babies discover that they get more attention when they do things to annoy and antagonize others than they behave in a more socially approved way.

Family Relationship Hazards:

- Separation from Mother
- Failure to develop attachment Behaviour
- Deterioration in Family Relationships
- Over-protectiveness
- Inconsistent Training
- Child Abuse

Hazards in Personality Development:

- The developing self-concept is in large part a mirror image of what babies believe significant people in their lives think of them.

- Thus the changed attitudes of family members are reflected in their treatment of babies.
- This reinforces the unfavourable self-concepts that the baby is in the process of developing.

Educating and Counseling Parents:

- The parents have to be educated in the hospitals about the hazards and should take preventive steps.
- Both psychological and physiological care has to be given to children by the parents.
- Medical care becomes more important in this case of babyhood.
- Child Counselors can play the role equal to Medical Professionals.
- The parenting starts right from the conception of the baby.
- The counselors' duty is to make them understand what is parenting and what not is parenting.
- The parenting workshops can be conducted.
- The psychological tests available for parenting can be administered to make them realise their parenting style.
- In case of any issues, parents have to be given counseling.

SENSORY DEVELOPMENT

Like most animals, humans rely on their five senses to experience the world around them. These senses—sight, taste, touch, smell, and hearing—allow each individual to interpret his or her environment; this is called sensory processing. The growth of these senses is known as sensory development. Sensory development starts during gestation. From birth, a child can begin to explore each of his or her senses. All five senses are not yet completely developed; sight in particular is very limited following birth. It is during this period of infancy when childhood sensory development begins to progress. As the sense of touch is key in the bonding process between baby and caregiver, touch sensory development is normally well-developed during infancy. Newborns often respond to touch in a similar fashion to adults. Babies vary in the amount of touch they can tolerate. During childhood, children often explore their sense of touch through their sensitive tongues, which is why so many children place objects in their mouths. Exploration through the mouth is also a form of taste sensory development. Babies are typically born with a preference for mildly sweet tastes, such as breast milk. As they explore more tastes, their tolerance for various flavours develops. Hearing sensory development is usually well underway within the womb. Fetuses can hear the mother's bodily noises as well as loud noises, such as car horns, outside her body.

The most familiar sound to a baby is typically his or her mother's heartbeat, which often provides a soothing during moments of distress. An infant's sense of smell develops within the womb as well. Fetuses recognize the smell of their mother's amniotic fluid. As with touch, a baby can recognize his or her mother through the sense of smell. The smells of other family members the baby comes into contact with daily also become familiar quickly, helping the baby identify different people. Sight sensory development occurs slowly at first. As a newborn, a baby can see objects within eight to ten inches (20 to 25 centimetres) of his or her face.

The first sight a baby normally learns is the face of his or her primary caregiver. Though other colours remain vague during the first few weeks of life, white, black, and red are easily distinguished. As the infant grows, so does his or her range of sight. Though sensory development is a natural process for most babies, sometimes complications can occur. This is known as sensory integration dysfunction. Various circumstances, such as prematurity, can lead to this dysfunction. Sensory integration dysfunction usually results in either too much or too little sensory input from his or her environment. Physical and occupational therapy can be used to help improve, or even correct, this condition.

SENSORY DEVELOPMENT: VISION, HEARING, TASTE AND SMELL, EARLY DEPRIVATION AND ENRICHMENT OF SENSES

A child is born with five senses and right from birth, he/she can explore each of them. Right from the time when he comes out of his mother's womb, he recognizes the smell of his mother and could sense his touch. A new born kid takes time to explore the other things around him. After coming out of his mother's womb, everything seems new and different to him. However, with time he gradually starts getting familiar with these things. He explores this new world with his available sense and in this process gradually develops his own sensory.

UNDERSTANDING SENSORY IN A NEWBIE

At the time of birth, a kid can explore all the five senses— tasting, hearing, seeing, touching and smelling, though these senses are not fully developed. Just after birth he could see whatever is within eight to ten inches from their eyes. He is also used to some familiar sounds in his womb which he can recognize just after birth. A newbie also gets soothed by hearing lullabies and white sounds. He recognizes few smells and strives hard to recognize other. Though he can't express with words, he tries hard to convey his emotions by movement and cries.

GRADUAL SENSORY DEVELOPMENT IN A KID

Sights and Sound

Right from the time of birth, a kid has good understanding and recognization of sound. With time he starts interpreting words and understands the meanings. It is very easy for a kid to understand the tone of speech. The sight also develops with time; just after birth he can see things in a range of eight to ten inches from their eyes. He also easily recognizes black, white and red colours. With time his range of vision and understanding of colour also develops.

Touch and Texture

Small babies love to be touched. They love massage and sleeping in lap just because personal touches make him/her feel secure. In order to explore every thing around, they put it inside mouth to touch it through their most sensitive organ- their tongue. A sense of good touch and bad touch also starts developing in a kid after sometime.

Smell

It is first of all through smell that a kid recognizes his mother. With time he starts recognizing the smell of other family members. He also quickly recognizes the smell of the food or fruit, he loves to eat. With time, he develops an understanding of all the smell around.

How to Aid Sensory Development in a Kid?

Though sensory development is natural process in kids, you can certainly make the entire procedure fast by helping him in coming out of the complex hurdles in the way. But before that you yourself need to understand few things. Here is the list.

- Do not over burden your kid with knowledge at an initiating point. This will do nothing but irritate your kid.
- Try to help him where he feels hindered otherwise let him explore the world on his own.
- Do not be overprotective about your kid. Draw a line between being caring and over caring. Let him go out of the way to explore the world. Do not safeguard him so much that you start limiting his desires and capabilities.
- Try to understand the world from a kid's point of view before you start telling all complex things together. It's not a kid who will become mature to understand you, remember you will have to become a kid to understand him.

SENSE OF HEARING IN A BABY

Well, if you thought that a newborn baby cannot hear, thing again. The sense of hearing in an infant develops much before the birth of the baby. When in the womb, the baby hears his mother's heartbeats, the grumbling of her stomach and the sudden loud noises like a car blaring or a drum banging. Upon hearing these sudden loud sounds, baby also reacts by making a sudden audible jerk in the womb. Sounds in the womb play an important role in language learning of the baby. Thanks to these sounds, the baby after coming out into the world has a sense of hearing that is well-established. He recognizes his mother's voice and can differentiate it from the voices of other women, reacts to musical toys and responds favourably to classical music.

Sense of Hearing In A Baby:

- Babies can understand that someone is speaking a foreign language and differentiate between familiar and unfamiliar sounds. This ability helps the baby to learn and understand spoken languages later.
- Classic music is a favourite with young babies, because they have smooth rhythmic melodies and pauses between parts. However, one year old kids, prefer traditional tunes and start differentiating sounds that are similar.
- Gradually, babies start associating sounds with the experiences and give them a meaning. Thus, lullabies and white noise may soothe a baby; loud sounds may startle him while pleasant music may make him happy. Babies may also associate banging of door with arrival of parents or sounds of crying and wailing with something hurtful.
- Babies love to listen to the sounds that are similar to ones they heard in the womb such as heartbeat of the mother and sounds of blood flow.
- You might wonder how, but babies recognize their mom's voice right from the time they are born and can differentiate it from the voices of other women and get comforted by it sooner.
- Younger babies do not have their sense of hearing so well developed and they can hear high pitched sounds better. Thus, they respond better to cooing and baby talk and especially, when it comes from feminine voices.
- If the mother listens to soft music, during the time when the baby is in the womb, the same type of music or humming will have positive effects on the child when he comes out into the world.
- Musical toys play an important role in the hearing development of a child. It is mostly seen that music toys gather attention of the child. Once the child notices the play toy, he would move forward to reach for it. Music toys also help in the brain development of the child.

Causes that Hamper Baby's Hearing Capabilities:

- Exposure to prolonged, high-decibel noise like that found near airport runways or at rock concerts
- Family history of hearing problems
- Serious problems during birth that may have resulted in a lack of oxygen to the baby
- Premature birth
- Antenatal exposure to rubella
- Some types of birth defects

SIGHT AND VISION IN INFANTS

Babies are curious about everything around them, right from their very birth. They love to look at bright colours in the crib and their mom's smiling face again and again. Amongst the first few things that babies learn to recognize is their mother's face, as she feeds and nurses them.

In fact, the most preferred sight for a baby comprises of his/her mother's face, as he/she feels the safest with her. This serves as the first step in the bonding process between a mother and her child.

As a baby's vision sharpens, he/she learns to recognize his/her dad, sibling (if any), grandparents and other caregivers and family members, eventually even the pets and frequent visitors to the house.

Sight Development In A Baby:

- In the initial days that follow their birth, babies see everything in mainly black and white. It is only after they become two weeks old that they start acquiring the ability to distinguish colours. Still, their colour vision is not as rich and sensitive as adult and improves over time.
- Babies seem to find people's faces most interesting and tend to read and observe them for a long time. It has also been seen that familiar faces and surroundings make a baby feel secure and reassured.
- Within a few months of their birth, babies start recognizing face expressions and even attribute them to certain feelings. They understand facial expressions much better than words and may try to imitate them too.
- It has been observed that infants also love to see pictures of other babies. They will even be fascinated when they look at themselves, either in a mirror or in pictures.
- Babies are much smarter than most people believe them to be and they tend to notice changes in the scenery as well as any changes that you make in the home décor. It might be the reason why some babies resist a change in their surroundings, such as moving the crib to another position or repainting a wall or shifting houses. In such a case, you may have to soothe them until they start feeling comfortable in the new setting.
- Like adults, babies are also able to see everything around them. However, in the first few weeks after their birth, they do not have very good control of their ciliary muscles and thus, are not able to focus correctly. It is only after about 2 months of age that infants are able to see clear images.
- In the initial stage of their life, babies are not able to see images as clearly as adults. The reason for this is that their retina as well as their brain area that is responsible for vision is not fully developed.

It by eight months that they have a vision almost as good as adults.

- In the first month, babies are able to distinguish between two shades of gray that have 5% contrast, or differ by only 5% in gray level. However, by the time they are 2 months old, they can perceive almost all the subtle shadings that make this world so rich and textured.

SENSE OF SMELL IN INFANTS

Smell is the most advanced, out of the five senses, present in babies at the time of birth. Unlike eyesight, hearing or touch that requires some time, the sense of smell is developed, right at the time when infants are in the womb. Surprised! Studies have shown that right from the time when babies are in the womb, they smell the amniotic fluid, which is apparently rich with smells. It is said that infants during the first week, primarily differentiate between two things and people, using their sense of smell.

They pick up on the new odors and associate these smells to certain things or people. Babies use their sense of smell mostly to stay close to their mother. To know more about how does a baby use his/her smelling sense, read through the following lines.

Smelling Sense In A Baby:

- This might come to you as a surprise but the sense of smell in a baby develops in the womb itself. Studies have shown that babies can smell their mother's amniotic fluid and tell the difference between it and other smells.
- Using their sense of smell, babies can differentiate between their mother's breast milk from that of other mothers. A 3 or 4 day old infant recognizes the smell of his/her mother's breast milk. Just the smell of it makes them happy and contended.
- The sweet scent of lavender or aroma of a cake being baked actually makes a child happier.
- Infants are seen to smile at the odors, which are similar to bananas and vanilla. However, they frown after smelling rotten eggs and fish.
- Studies show that infants select and play with a vanilla scented toy more frequently, than with toys that are ethanol-scented or unscented.
- Infants prefer the smell of a lactating woman over a non-lactating woman. However, when it comes to two lactating women, they prefer their mother's smell over the other women.
- It is seen that babies identify mom's smell, right from the birth and finds more comfort, when this smell is near the baby, rather than the smell of someone else.
- As sense of smell develops in a baby, he/she can associate good smells and aromas with good feelings. Soft fragrance can soothe and delight the baby.

- An infant's sense of smell develops as he/she grow bigger. He/she can distinguish different smells easily. By the age of one, most babies can recognize the smells of other adults and children. They are also able to differentiate the smells of different foods
- When the infant gets old enough, he/she start using the senses of sight and hearing more that the sense of smell to differentiate things and people.

SENSE OF TASTE IN A BABY

Babies explore at most things by putting them inside their mouths. While they naturally prefer breast milk or formulas that are sweet in taste, they try to put any and every thing in their mouth to feel it and get a sense of taste of it. It can become an important safety net in babies, as they spit out anything that does not taste good almost immediately. It is good, especially, when they accidentally put a slug in their mouth or other things like that.

But, it can also become a safety hazard, if the infant swallows any small things she finds such as buttons and coins. As parents, you need to make sure that you do not put things that your little adventurer swallows. There are only four different types of taste that infants need to develop - sweet, sour, bitter and salty.

Talking about taste, it is mostly seen that infants have a liking for sweet food items and dislike items that have a sour taste. This may be because right from the time a child is born, he/she is fed breast milk or formulas that are sweet in taste. Slowly, kids develop a sense of taste. This may be one of the prime reasons that it is difficult to develop a taste for vegetables such as broccoli and tomatoes. To know more about the sense of taste in an infant, check out the following lines.

Development of Taste in Infants:

- The sense of taste develops at a prenatal stage for infants. At the 7 to 8 weeks' gestation, taste buds start emerging.
- After birth, infants show a preference for sweet tastes. A combination of sugar with a pacifier has a calming effect on newborns.
- Infants do not like things that have a sour flavour to it. Items that have a sour taste raise a frown on the face of the kid.
- Salty food is neutral and has no effect on infants. They neither have a calming effect nor raise a frown on the face of the tot. It is only after 4 months of age that kids start developing a taste for salty food.
- It may take as many as 20 trials, to develop a taste for a particular thing in a baby. So you may need time and patience to change the taste preferences of your baby and make her eat any new foods.
- The texture of the food also plays a pivotal role in developing the taste. Most of the babies do not like cottage cheese, because of its odd texture.

- The odour of volatile flavours like cherry, are perceived via the olfactory receptors. This type of odour does not have much impact on children, until they reach the age 5.

SENSE OF TOUCH IN BABIES

The sense of touch is well-developed considerably, in infants. They respond to touch in similar ways as adults do. In fact, it is inherent in a newborn to make out that, he/she has been touched by his/her mother.

Touch is a vital sense, which affects the bond between the parent and the infant. It also contributes in the cognitive and immunological development of the baby, as well as improves his/her sociability. Studies suggest that the sense of touch enhances the growth and development of the baby and increases his/her attentiveness to the rest of the world, apart from his/her mother.

Sense of Touch In Babies:

- If your baby is stroked, he/she would spend more time in making eye contact, smile and vocalize, as opposed to when you tickle or poke him/her. That way, you will ensure that your child cries for less time.
- The preferences for touch may vary from infant to infant. Therefore, as a parent, it is important to know which types of touch are preferred by the infants. For the purpose, you can try stroking, bouncing or tickling the baby. If the baby responds positively, by the way of making an eye contact or passing a smile, probably, he/she is comfortable with the touch.
- Since the sense of touch plays a pivotal role in the development of the child, it is important to give your him/her frequent opportunities to use the sense of touch. When you have figured out, which type of touch soothes the infant, be sure to do it on a frequent basis.
- Hugs and kisses are nice ways to soothe the baby. However, be sure not to overdo it. A tight hug might choke the little one, or an unhygienic kiss might prove to be allergic to him/her.
- When your baby is exploring the world around him/her with the sense of touch, provide a safe zone, to ensure that he/she doesn't reach to something hazardous.
- Infants use their fingers and hands to 'feel' the things and people around them. To serve the purpose, you may supply your infant with colourful toys. However, you should ensure that you do not provide hazardous toys, because unsafe things could suffocate the infant.
- In the process of exploring the world around him/her, your baby might meet with little accidents, such as banging the head against the crib or hurting himself with the sharp edges. Hurtful though, such accidents actually teach the baby about the importance of their limits. As they grow, they will recognize that they should keep themselves

away from sharp edges. However, you should still make sure that such accidents are not repeated frequently.

SEQUENCE OF MOTOR DEVELOPMENT

This topic covers three stages of motor development, spanning the ages 0 to 12, beginning with early reflexes, and developing through the various milestones that a child reaches as they mature.

STAGES OF DEVELOPMENT

There are three stages of motor development in children:

- Infanthood
- Early Childhood
- Later Childhood

The first stage is marked by extremely rapid growth and development, as is the second stage. By the age of 2 years old, this development has begun to level out somewhat. The final stage does not have any marked new developments, rather it is characterised by the mastering and development of the skills achieved in the first two stages.

0-2 YEARS OR INFANTHOOD

The Newborn Child

It is argued that many of a newborn's reflexes contribute to motor control as the child learns new motor skills. For example the stepping reflex promotes development areas of the cortex that govern voluntary walking. This and other examples can be seen in the table below.

Reflex name	Method	Age Disappears	Moto preparation
Tonic neck	Assumes fencing position; 1 arm extended in front of eyes on side to which head is turned. Other arm flexed.	4 months	May prepare for voluntary reaching
Stepping	Lifts one foot after another in stepping response	2 months	Prepares for voluntary walking
Palmar grasp	Spontaneous grasp of adult's finger	3-4 months	Prepares for voluntary grasping

Assessing reflexes in newborns will determine the health of the nervous system, as reflexes that are weak or absent, exaggerated, or overly rigid may indicate some brain damage. Therefore stages will need to be modified slightly. The average ages at which gross motor skills are achieved during infancy may vary. This range may be seen in the table below.

Motor Skill Achieved	Average Age	Age Range (90% Infants)
Head erect and steady when held upright	6 weeks	3 weeks-4 months
Lifts self by arms when prone	2 months	3 weeks-4 months
Rolls from side to back	2 months	3 weeks-5 months
Grasps cube	3 months, 3 weeks	2-7 months
Rolls from back to side	4½ months	2-7 months
Sits alone	7 months	5-9 months
Crawls	7 months	5-11 months
Pulls to stand.	8 months	5-12 months
Plays Pat-a-cake	9 months, 3 weeks	7-15 months
Stands alone	11 months	9-16 months
Walks alone	11 months, 3 weeks	9-17 months
Builds tower of 2 cubes	13 months, 3 weeks	10-19 months
Scribbles vigourously	14 months	10-21 months
Walks up stairs with help	16 months	12-23 months
Jumps in place	23 months, 2 weeks	17-30 months

Although the sequence of motor development is fairly uniform across children, differences may exist individually in the rate at which motor skills develop. A baby who is a late reacher may not necessarily be a late crawler/ walker. Concern would arise if the child's development were delayed in many motor skills.

Summary of Table

- Motor control of the head comes before control of the legs. This head-to-tail sequence is called the cephalocaudal trend.
- Motor development proceeds from the centre of the body outward; *i.e.* the head, trunk and arm control is mastered before the coordination of the hands and fingers. This is the proximodistical trend.
- Physical growth follows these same trends throughout infancy and childhood.

Once the child has grasped these gross motor skills, they are then able to explore their environment further by grasping things, turning them over, and seeing what happens when they are released. Infants are then able to learn a great deal about the sight, sound and feel of objects. Reaching and grasping development is a classic example of how motor skills start out as gross, and then graduate to mastering fine motor skills.

- At 3 months voluntary reaching gradually improves in accuracy. It does not require visual guidance of arms and hands, but rather a sense of movement and location.
- By 5 months reaching is reduced as the object can be moved within reach.

- At 9 months an infant can redirect reaching to obtain a moving object that changes direction.
- 6-12 months the infant can use a pincer grasp, thus increasing their ability to manipulate objects.

2-6 YEARS OR EARLY CHILDHOOD

The period of the most rapid development of motor behaviours is the period between 2 and 6 years (also known as the preschool years).

Skills that appear are:

- Basic locomotor
- Ball-handling
- Fine eye-hand coordination
- Walking leads to running, jumping, hopping, galloping, and skipping
- Climbing evolves from creeping.

The following points need to be highlighted:

- By the age of 3 walking is automatic.
- By 4 years the child has almost achieved an adult style of walking.
- By 3 years the child has attempted to run, albeit awkward in style and lacking control.
- By the age of 4-5 years the child has more control over running and can start, stop and turn.
- By 5-6 skills in running have advanced to the level of an adult manner.
- Between the ages of 3 and 6 climbing proficiency using ladders, etc., has developed.
- By 6 years children can hop and gallop skillfully, and jumping distances are longer.
- At the age of 3 children begin a shuffle which evolves into skipping by the age of 6.
- At the age of 2 children learn to kick, as their balance mechanism has developed. A full kick with a backswing has developed by the age of 6.
- Throwing at the age of 2-3 years is not very proficient although is attempted. This has improved by the age of 6 when the child will include a step forward.
- At the age of 3 a child can catch a large ball with arms straight; at 4 elbows will be in front when catching; and by the age of 6 years, elbows will be held at the side.

6-12 YEARS OR LATER CHILDHOOD

After the age of 6 years old, it becomes increasingly difficult to describe changes and differences in motor skills development.

The following characteristics are evident:

- Changes are more subtle, and are often to fine motor skills only
- By 9 years eye-hand coordination has developed to being very good
- Growth is relatively slow
- This stage is terminated by the onset of puberty
- Motor skills are perfected and stabilized
- Links can be made to physical development.

The following are assessed during this stage:

- *Running*: This will become faster depending on the length of stride and tempo.
- *Jumping*: The ability to jump higher will become greater due to body size, weight, age and strength.
- *Throwing:* Boys begin to throw further with a better technique and accuracy.
- *Balancing and coordination*: This increases as the child becomes older and control is perfected.

These areas can benefit greatly from systematic instruction in motor skills, and physical education programmes at school. The quality and type of environment a child is exposed to will influence the extent to which the child develops the motor skills learned in the first two stages of development. Furthermore a child's motor interests will be determined by his or her opportunities. Differences in gender also come into play in this stage.

MOTOR SKILL

A motor skill is a learned sequence of movements that combine to produce a smooth, efficient action in order to master a particular task.

- Gross motor skills include lifting one's head, rolling over, sitting up, balancing, crawling, and walking. Gross motor development usually follows a pattern. Generally large muscles develop before smaller ones, thus, gross motor development is the foundation for developing skills in other areas (such as fine motor skills). Development also generally moves from top to bottom. The first thing a baby usually learns to control is its eyes.
- Fine motor skills include the ability to manipulate small objects, transfer objects from hand to hand, and various eye-hand coordination tasks. Fine motor skills may involve the use of very precise motor movement in order to achieve an especially delicate task. Some examples of fine motor skills are using the pincer grasp (thumb and forefinger) to pick up small objects, cutting, colouring, writing, or threading beads. Fine motor development refers to the development of skills involving the smaller muscle groups.
- Ambidexterity is a specialized skill in which there is no dominance between body symmetries, so tasks requiring fine motor skills can

be performed with the left or right extremities. The most common example of ambidexterity is the ability to write with the left or right hand, rather than one dominant side.

DYSFUNCTION

Motor skill dysfunction has many causes, *e.g.* demyelination of motor neurons. While fatigue or weariness may lead to temporary short-term deterioration of fine motor skills (observed as visible shaking), serious nervous disorders may result in a loss of both gross and fine motor skills due to the hampering of muscular control.

A defect in muscle is also a symptom of motor skill dysfunction. Motor skills may be impaired by use of both minor and major tranquilizers. A particular dysfunction has been observed consisting in a child using the thumb and medium finger to pick small objects instead of thumb and index. It is believed this behaviour might have some meaning but it hasn't been studied up to now.

COGNITIVE DEVELOPMENT

Cognitive development focuses on how children learn and process information. It is the development of the thinking and organizing systems of the mind. It involves language, mental imagery, thinking, reasoning, problem solving, and memory development. By general consensus, Jean Piaget stands as the central theorist in contemporary child study. He developed a whole field of cognitive development, observed regularities in children's performances that no one has noted before him. His theory concerns how the child thinks, how thinking changes from infancy to adolescence, and how the changes reflect an interesting series of structured stages.

Although Piaget set clear stages of cognitive development, which continues to be useful to contemporary child educators, he omitted to say that cognitive development is not an automatic process. The fact is that the child will not reach any of these stages without proper education. Contrary to the animal, the human being only knows, and can only do, what he/she has learned.

This fundamental principle is confirmed by studies that compared children who were raised in an enriched learning environment and children who were raised in a deprived learning environment. This principle is further confirmed by stories of feral children. Audiblox is a multisensory cognitive development programme, aimed at the inculcation of foundational learning skills such as concentration, perception, memory, and logical thought. It improves performance in reading, spelling, writing and math. Audiblox is adaptable for the gifted and less gifted, and applicable for all age groups. It can develop the learning skills of the high school learner to a very high degree, while it can also be used to prepare the preschool child for reading and learning from as early as three years of age. Audiblox is effective for a variety of learning difficulties including dyslexia and dysgraphia.

PIAGET'S THEORY OF COGNITIVE DEVELOPMENT

Piaget's theory of cognitive development is a comprehensive theory about the nature and development of human intelligence first developed by Jean Piaget. It is primarily known as a developmental stage theory, but in fact, it deals with the nature of knowledge itself and how humans come gradually to acquire it, construct it, and use it. Moreover, Piaget claims the idea that cognitive development is at the centre of human organism and language is contingent on cognitive development.

THE NATURE OF INTELLIGENCE: OPERATIVE AND FIGURATIVE INTELLIGENCE

Piaget believed that reality is a dynamic system of continuous change, and as such is defined in reference to the two conditions that define dynamic systems that change. Specifically, he argued that reality involves transformations and states. Transformations refer to all manners of changes that a thing or person can undergo. States refer to the conditions or the appearances in which things or persons can be found between transformations.

For example, there might be changes in shape or form (for instance, liquids are reshaped as they are transferred from one vessel to another, humans change in their characteristics as they grow older), in size (*e.g.*, a series of coins on a table might be placed close to each other or far apart) in placement or location in space and time (*e.g.*, various objects or persons might be found at one place at one time and at a different place at another time). Thus, Piaget argued, that if human intelligence is to be adaptive, it must have functions to represent both the transformational and the static aspects of reality. He proposed that operative intelligence is responsible for the representation and manipulation of the dynamic or transformational aspects of reality and that figurative intelligence is responsible for the representation of the static aspects of reality).

Operative intelligence is the active aspect of intelligence. It involves all actions, overt or covert, undertaken in order to follow, recover, or anticipate the transformations of the objects or persons of interest. Figurative intelligence is the more or less static aspect of intelligence, involving all means of representation used to retain in mind the states (*i.e.*, successive forms, shapes, or locations) that intervene between transformations. That is, it involves perception, imitation, mental imagery, drawing, and language.

Therefore, the figurative aspects of intelligence derive their meaning from the operative aspects of intelligence, because states cannot exist independently of the transformations that interconnect them. Piaget believed that the figurative or the representational aspects of intelligence are subservient to its operative and dynamic aspects, and therefore, that understanding essentially derives from the operative aspect of intelligence.

At any time, operative intelligence frames how the world is understood and it changes if understanding is not successful. Piaget believed that this process of understanding and change involves two basic functions: Assimilation and accommodation. Assimilation refers to the active transformation of information so as to be integrated into the mental schemes already available. Its analog at the biological level might be the transformation of food by chewing and digestion to fit in with the structural and bio-chemical characteristics of the human body. Accommodation refers to the active transformation of these schemes so as to take into account the particularities of the objects, persons, or events the thinker is interacting with. Its analog at the biological level might be the adaptation of eating and digestion to the particulars of the different kinds of food we eat. For Piaget, none of these functions can exist without the other.

To assimilate an object into an existing mental scheme, one first needs to take into account or accommodate to the particularities of this object to a certain extent; for instance, to recognize (assimilate) an apple as an apple one needs first to focus (accommodate) on the contour of this object. To do this one needs to roughly recognize the size of the object. When in balance with each other, they generate mental schemes of the operative intelligence. When the one dominates over the other, they generate representations which belong to figurative intelligence.

Following from this conception Piaget theorized that intelligence is active and constructive. In fact, it is active even in the literal sense of the term as it depends on the actions (overt or covert, assimilatory or accommodatory), which the thinker executes in order to build and rebuild his models of the world. And it is constructive because actions, particularly mental actions, are coordinated into more inclusive and cohesive systems and thus they are raised to ever more stable and effective levels of functioning. Piaget believed that this process of construction leads to systems of mental operations better able to resist the illusions of perceptual appearances and thus less prone to error.

In other words, the gradual construction of the system of mental operations involved in the operative aspect of intelligence enables the developing person to grasp ever more hidden and complex aspects of the world.

PIAGET'S FOUR STAGES

Jean Piaget's theory of cognitive development, intelligence is the basic mechanism of ensuring equilibrium in the relations between the person and the environment. This is achieved through the actions of the developing person on the world. At any moment in development, the environment is assimilated in the schemes of action that are already available and these schemes are transformed or accommodated to the peculiarities of the objects of the environment plus of the surroundings and entire universe, if they are not completely appropriate. Thus, the development of intelligence is a continuous process of assimilations and accommodations that lead to increasing expansion of the field of application of schemes, increasing coordination between them, increasing interiorization, and increasing abstraction.

The mechanism underlying this process of increasing abstraction, interiorization, and coordination is reflecting abstraction. That is, reflecting abstraction gradually leads to the rejection of the external action components of sensorimotor operations on objects and to the preservation of the mental, planning or anticipatory, components of operation. These are the mental operations that are gradually coordinated with each other, generating structures of mental operations.

These structures of mental operations are applied on representations of objects rather than on the objects themselves. Language, mental images, and numerical notation are examples of representations standing for objects and thus they become the object of mental operations. Moreover, mental operations, with development, become reversible.

For instance, the counting of a series of objects can go both forward and backward with the understanding that the number of objects counted is not affected by the direction of counting because the same number can be retrieved both ways. Piaget described four main periods in the development towards completely reversible equlibrated thought structures. Piaget intelligence is not the same at different ages. It changes qualitatively, attaining increasingly broader, more abstract, and more equilibrated structures thereby allowing access to different levels of organization of the world.

SENSORIMOTOR STAGE

The sensorimotor stage is the first of the four stages of cognitive development. "In this stage, infants construct an understanding of the world by coordinating sensory experiences (such as seeing and hearing) with physical, motoric actions. Infants gain knowledge of the world from the physical actions they perform on it. An infant progresses from reflexive, instinctual action at birth to the beginning of symbolic thought towards the end of the stage. Piaget divided the sensorimotor stage into six sub-stages":

Sub-Stage	Age	Description
1 Simple Reflexes	Birth-6 weeks	"Coordination of sensation and action through reflexive behaviours". Three primary reflexes are described by Piaget: sucking of objects in the mouth, following moving or interesting objects with the eyes, and closing of the hand when an object makes contact with the palm. Over the first six weeks of life, these reflexes begin to become voluntary actions; for example, the palmar reflex becomes intentional grasping)

2 First habits and primary circula phase	6 weeks-4 months	"Coordination of sensation and two types of schemes: habits and primary circular reactions. Main focus is still on the infant'sreactions body." As an example of this type of reaction, an infant might repeat the motion of passing their hand before their face. Also at this phase, passive reactions, caused by classical or operant onditioning, can begin.
3 Secondary circular reactions phase	4–8 months	Development of habits. "Infants become more object-oriented, moving beyond self-preoccupation; repeat actions that bring interesting or pleasurable results." This stage is associated primarily with the development of coordination between vision and prehension. Three new abilities occur at this stage: intentional grasping for a desired object, secondary circular reactions, and differentiations between ends and means. At this stage, infants will intentionally grasp the air in the direction of a desired object, often to the amusement of friends and family. Secondary circular reactions, or the repetition of an action involving an external object begin; for example, moving a switch to turn on a light repeatedly. The differention between means and ends also occurs. This is perhaps one of the most important stages of a child's growth as it signifies the dawn of logic.
4 Coordination of secondary circular reactions stages	8-12 months	"Coordination of vision and touch--hand-eye coordination; coordination of schemes and intentionality." This stage is associated primarily with the development of logic and the coordination between means and ends. This is an extremely important stage of development, holding what Piaget calls the "first proper intelligence." Also, this stage marks the beginning of goal orientation, the deliberate planning of steps to meet an objective.
5 Tertiary circular reactions, novelty, and curiosity	12-18 months	"Infants become intrigued by the many properties of objects and by the many things they can make happen to objects; they experiment with new behaviour." This stage is associated primarily with the discovery of new means to meet goals. Piaget describes the child at this juncture as the "young scientist," conducting pseudo-experiments to discover new methods of meeting challenges.
6 Internali-	18-24	"Infants develop the ability to use primitive

zation of Schemes	months	symbols and form enduring mental representations." This stage is associated primarily with the beginnings of insight, or true creativity. This marks the passage into the preoperational stage.

By the end of the sensorimotor period, objects are both separate from the self and permanent.Object permanence is the understanding that objects continue to exist even when they cannot be seen, heard, or touched. Acquiring the sense of object permanence is one of the infant's most important accomplishments, just as to Piaget.

PREOPERATIONAL STAGE

The preoperative stage is the second of four stages of cognitive development. By observing sequences of play, Piaget was able to demonstrate hat towards the end of the second year, a qualitatively new kind of psychological functioning occurs. (Pre) Operatory Thought is any procedure for mentally acting on objects. The hallmark of the preoperational stage is sparse and logically inadequate mental operations. During this stage, the child learns to use and to represent objects by images, words, and drawings. The child is able to form stable concepts as well as mental reasoning and magical beliefs. The child however is still not able to perform operations; tasks that the child can do mentally rather than physically. Thinking is still egocentric: The child has difficulty taking the viewpoint of others. Two substages can be formed from preoperative thought.

- *The Symbolic Function Substage:* Occurs between about the ages of 2 and 7. The child is able to formulate designs of objects that are not present. Other examples of mental abilities are language and pretend play. Although there is an advancement in progress, there are still limitations such as egocentrism and animism. Egocentrism occurs when a child is unable to distinguish between their own perspective and that of another person's. Children tend to pick their own view of what they see rather than the actual view shown to others. An example is an experiment performed by Piaget and Barbel Inhelder. Three views of a mountain are shown and the child is asked what a traveling doll would see at the various angles; the child picks their own view compared to the actual view of the doll. Animism is the belief that inanimate objects are capable of actions and have lifelike qualities. An example is a child believing that the sidewalk was mad and made them fall down.
- *The Intuitive Thought Substage:* Occurs between about the ages of 2 and 7. Children tend to become very curious and ask many questions; begin the use of primitive reasoning. There is an emergence in the interest of reasoning and wanting to know why

things are the way they are. Piaget called it the intuitive substage because children realise they have a vast amount of knowledge but they are unaware of how they know it. Centration and conservation are both involved in preoperative thought. Centration is the act of focusing all attention on one characteristic compared to the others. Centration is noticed in conservation; the awareness that altering a substance's appearance does not change its basic properties. Children at this stage are unaware of conservation. In Piaget's most famous task, a child is presented with two identical beakers containing the same amount of liquid. The child usually notes that the beakers have the same amount of liquid. When one of the beakers is poured into a taller and thinner container, children who are typically younger than 7 or 8 years old say that the two beakers now contain a different amount of liquid. The child simply focuses on the height and width of the container compared to the general concept. Piaget believes that if a child fails the conservation-of-liquid task, it is a sign that they are at the preoperational stage of cognitive development. The child also fails to show conservation of number, matter, length, volume, and area as well. Another example is when a child is shown 7 dogs and 3 cats and asked if there are more dogs than cats. The child would respond positively. However when asked if there are more dogs than animals, the child would once again respond positively. Such fundamental errors in logic show the transition between intuitiveness in solving problems and true logical reasoning acquired in later years when the child grows up.

Piaget considered that children primarily learn through imitation and play throughout these first two stages, as they build up symbolic images through internalized activity. Studies have been conducted among other countries to find out if Piaget's theory is universal. Psychologist Patricia Greenfield conducted a task similar to Piaget's beaker experiment in the West African nation of Senegal. Her results stated that only 50 per cent of the 10-13 year old understood the concept of conservation.

Other cultures such as central Australia and New Guinea had similar results. If adults had not gained this concept, they would be unable to understand the point of view of another person. There may have been discrepancies in the communication between the experimenter and the children which may have altered the results.

It has also been found that if conservation is not widely practiced in a particular country, the concept can be taught to the child and training can improve the child's understanding. Therefore, it is noted that there are different age differences in reaching the understanding of conservation based on the degree to which the culture teaches these tasks.

CONCRETE OPERATIONAL STAGE

The concrete operational stage is the third of four stages of cognitive development in Piaget's theory. This stage, which follows the Preoperational stage, occurs between the ages of 7 and 11 years and is characterized by the appropriate use of logic.

Important processes during this stage are:

- *Seriation*: The ability to sort objects in an order just as to size, shape, or any other characteristic. For example, if given different-shaded objects they may make a colour gradient.
- *Transitivity*: The ability to recognize logical relationships among elements in a serial order, and perform 'transitive inferences'.
- *Classification*: The ability to name and identify sets of objects just as to appearance, size or other characteristic, including the idea that one set of objects can include another.
- *Decentering*: Where the child takes into account multiple aspects of a problem to solve it. For example, the child will no longer perceive an exceptionally wide but short cup to contain less than a normally-wide, taller cup.
- *Reversibility*: The child understands that numbers or objects can be changed, then returned to their original state. For this reason, a child will be able to rapidly determine that if 4+4 equals t, t–4 will equal 4, the original quantity.
- *Conservation*: Understanding that quantity, length or number of items is unrelated to the arrangement or appearance of the object or items.
- *Elimination of Egocentrism*: The ability to view things from another's perspective (even if they think incorrectly). For instance, show a child a comic in which Jane puts a doll under a box, leaves the room, and then Melissa moves the doll to a drawer, and Jane comes back. A child in the concrete operations stage will say that Jane will still think it's under the box even though the child knows it is in the drawer..

Children in this stage can, however, only solve problems that apply to actual (concrete) objects or events, and not abstract concepts or hypothetical tasks.

FORMAL OPERATIONAL STAGE

The formal operational period is the fourth and final of the periods of cognitive development in Piaget's theory. This stage, which follows the Concrete Operational stage, commences at around 11 years of age (puberty) and continues into adulthood. In this stage, individuals move beyond concrete experiences and begin to think abstractly, reason logically and draw conclusions from the information available, as well as apply all these processes to hypothetical situations. The abstract quality of the adolescent's thought at the formal operational level is evident in the adolescent's verbal problem solving ability. The logical quality of the adolescent's thought is when children are more likely to solve problems in a trial-and-error fashion. Adolescents begin to think more as a scientist thinks, devising plans to solve problems and systematically testing solutions. They use hypothetical-deductive reasoning, which means that they develop hypotheses or best guesses, and systematically deduce, or conclude, which is the best path to follow in solving the problem.

During this stage the adolescent is able to understand such things as love, "shades of gray", logical proofs and values. During this stage the young person begins to entertain possibilities for the future and is fascinated with what they can be. Adolescents are changing cognitively also by the way that they think about social matters. Adolescent Egocentrism governs the way that adolescents think about social matters and is the heightened self-consciousness in them as they are which is reflected in their sense of personal uniqueness and invincibility. Adolescent egocentrism can be dissected into two types of social thinking, imaginary audience that involves attention getting behaviour, and personal fable which involves an adolescent's sense of personal uniqueness and invincibility.

CHALLENGES TO PIAGETIAN STAGE THEORY

Piagetians' accounts of development have been challenged on several grounds. First, as Piaget himself noted, development does not always progress in the smooth manner his theory seems to predict. 'Decalage', or unpredicted gaps in the developmental progression, suggest that the stage model is at best a useful approximation. More broadly, Piaget's theory is 'domain general', predicting that cognitive maturation occurs concurrently across different domains of knowledge (such as mathematics, logic, understanding of physics, of language, etc.). During the 1980s and 1990s, cognitive developmentalists were influenced by "neo-nativist" and evolutionary psychology ideas. These ideas de-emphasized domain general theories and emphasized domain specificity or modularity of mind. Modularity implies that different cognitive faculties may be largely independent of one another and thus develop just as to quite different time-tables. In this vein, some cognitive developmentalists argued that rather than being domain general learners, children come equipped with domain specific theories, sometimes referred to as 'core knowledge', which allows them to break into learning within that domain. For example, even young infants appear to be sensitive to some predictable regularities in the movement and interactions of objects (*e.g.* that one object cannot pass through another), or in human behaviour (*e.g.* that a hand repeatedly reaching for an object has that object, not just a particular path of motion, as its goal).

These basic assumptions may be the building block out of which more elaborate knowledge is constructed. More recent work has strongly challenged some of the basic presumptions of the 'core knowledge' school, and revised ideas of domain generality—but from a newer dynamic systems approach, not from a revised Piagetian perspective. Dynamic systems approaches harken to modern neuroscientific research that was not available to Piaget when he was constructing his theory. One important finding is that domain-specific knowledge is constructed as children develop and integrate knowledge.

This suggests more of a "smooth integration" of learning and development than either Piaget, or his neo-nativist critics, had envisioned. Additionally, some psychologists, such as Vygotsky and Jerome Bruner, thought differently from Piaget, suggesting that language was more important than Piaget implied. Sarah Barnes rocks. Another recent challenge to Piaget's theory is a new theory called Ecological Systems Theory. This is based on the contextual influences in the child's life like his/her immediate family, school, society and the world, and how these impact the child's development. The experience of Sudbury model schools shows that a great variety can be found in the minds of children, against Piaget's theory of universal steps in comprehension and general patterns in the acquisition of knowledge: "No two kids ever take the same path. Few are remotely similar. Each child is so unique, so exceptional."

POST-PIAGETIAN AND NEO-PIAGETIAN STAGES

In the recent years, several scholars attempted to ameliorate the problems of Piaget's theory by developing new theories and models that can accommodate evidence that violates Piagetian predictions and postulates.

- The neo-Piagetian theories of cognitive development, advanced by Case, Demetriou, Halford, Fischer, and Pascual-Leone, attempted to integrate Piaget´s theory with cognitive and differential theories of cognitive organization and development. Their aim was to better account for the cognitive factors of development and for intra-individual and inter-individual differences in cognitive development. They suggested that development along Piaget´s stages is due to increasing working memory capacity and processing efficiency. Moreover, Demetriou´s theory ascribes an important role to hypercognitive processes of self-recording, self-monitoring, and self-regulation and it recognizes the operation of several relatively autonomous domains of thought.
- Postformal stages have been proposed. Kurt Fischer suggested two, Michael Commons presents evidence for four postformal stages: the systematic, metasystematic, paradigmatic and cross paradigmatic.
- A "sentential" stage has been proposed, said to occur before the early preoperational stage. Proposed by Fischer, Biggs and Biggs, Commons, and Richards.
- Searching for a micro-physiological basis for human mental capacity, Traill proposed that there may be "pre-sensorimotor" stages—developed in the womb and/or transmitted genetically.

POSTULATED PHYSICAL MECHANISMS UNDERLYING "SCHEMES" AND STAGES

Piaget himself considered the possibility of RNA molecules as likely embodiments of his still-abstract "schemes" (which he promoted as units of action)—though he did not come to any firm conclusion. At that time, due to work such as that of Holger Hydén, RNA concentrations had indeed been shown to correlate with learning, so the idea was quite plausible. However, by the time of Piaget's death in 1980, this notion had lost favour.

One main problem was over the protein which (it was assumed) such RNA would necessarily produce, and that did not fit in with observation. It then turned out, surprisingly, that only about 3% of RNA does code for protein. Hence most of the remaining 97% could now theoretically be available to serve as Piagetian schemes. The issue has not yet been resolved experimentally, but its theoretical aspects have been reviewed.

INFORMATION PROCESSING APPROACH

Cognitive psychology represents the dominant approach in psychology today. A primary focus of this approach is on memory (the storage and retrieval of information), a subject that has been of interest for thousands of years. The most widely accepted theory is labeled the "stage theory," based on the work of Atkinson and Shriffin.

The focus of this model is on how information is stored in memory; the model proposes that information is processed and stored in 3 stages. In this theory, information is thought to be processed in a serial, discontinuous manner as it moves from one stage to the next. In addition to the stage theory model of information processing, there are three more that are widely accepted. The first is based on the work of Craik and Lockhart and is labeled the "levels-of-processing" theory. The major proposition is that learners utilize different levels of elaboration as they process information.

This is done on a continuum from perception, through attention, to labeling, and finally, meaning. The key point is that all stimuli that activate a sensory receptor cell are permanently stored in memory, but that different levels of processing (*i.e.*, elaboration) contribute to an ability to access, or retrieve, that memory. Evidence from hypnosis and forensic psychology provide some interesting support for this hypothesis. This approach has been extended by Bransford (1979) who suggests that it is not only how the information is processed, but how the information is accessed. When the demands for accessing information more closely match the methods used to elaborate or learn the information, more is remembered. Two other models have been proposed as alternatives to the Atkinson-Shiffrin model: parallel-distributed processing and connectionistic. The parallel-distributed processing model states that information is processed simultaneously by several different parts of the memory system, rather than sequentially as hypothesized by Atkinson-Shiffrin as well as Craik and Lockhart. Work done on how we process emotional data somewhat supports this contention. The connectionistic model proposed by Rumelhart and McClelland extends the parallel-distributed processing model.

It is one of the dominant forms of current research in cognitive psychology and is consistent with the most recent brain research. This model emphasizes the fact that information is stored in multiple locations throughout the brain in the form of networks of connections. It is consistent with the levels-of-processing approach in that the more connections to a single idea or concept, the more likely it is to be remembered.

Even though there are widely varying views within cognitive psychology, there are a few basic principles that most cognitive psychologists agree with. The first is the assumption of a limited capacity of the mental system. This means that the amount of information that can be processed by the system is constrained in some very important ways. Bottlenecks, or restrictions in the flow and processing of information, occur at very specific points.

A second principle is that a control mechanism is required to oversee the encoding, transformation, processing, storage, retrieval and utilization of information. That is, not all of the processing capacity of the system is available; an executive function that oversees this process will use up some of this capability. When one is learning a new task or is confronted with a new environment, the executive function requires more processing power than when one is doing a routine task or is in a familiar environment. A third principle is that there is a two-way flow of information as we try to make sense of the world around us. We constantly use information that we gather through the senses and information we have stored in memory in a dynamic process as we construct meaning about our environment and our relations to it. This is somewhat analogous to the difference between inductive reasoning and deductive reasoning.

A similar distinction can be made between using information we derive from the senses and that generated by our imaginations. A fourth principle generally accepted by cognitive psychologists is that the human organism has been genetically prepared to process and organize information in specific ways.

For example, a human infant is more likely to look at a human face than any other stimulus. Given that the field of focus of a human infant is 12 to 18 inches, one can surmise that this is an important aspect of the infant's survival. Other research has discovered additional biological predispositions to process information.

For example, language development is similar in all human infants regardless of language spoken by adults or the area in which they live (*e.g.*, rural *versus* urban, Africa *versus* Europe.) All human infants with normal hearing babble and coo, generate first words, begin the use of telegraphic speech (*e.g.*, ball gone), and overgeneralize (*e.g.*, using "goed to the store" when they had previously used "went to the store") at approximately the same ages.

The issue of language development is an area where cognitive and behavioural psychologists as well as cognitive psychologists with different viewpoints have fought many battles regarding the processes underlying human behaviour. Needless to say the disussion continues.

STAGE MODEL OF INFORMATION PROCESSING

One of the major issues in cognitive psychology is the study of memory. The dominant view is labeled the "stage theory" and is based on the work of Atkinson and Shiffrin.

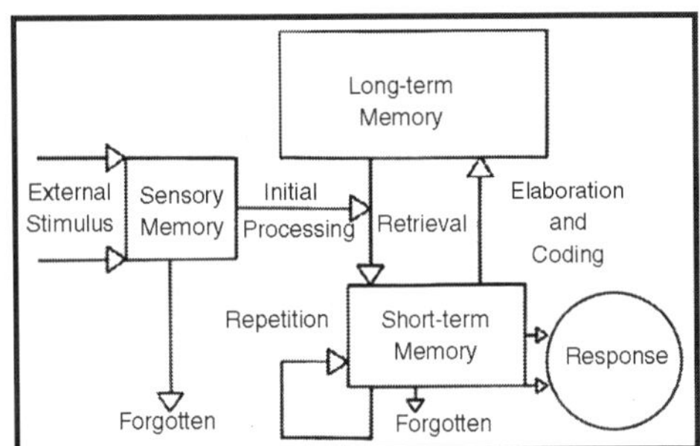

This model proposes that information is processed and stored in 3 stages.

Sensory Memory

Sensory memory is affiliated with the transduction of energy. The environment makes available a variety of sources of information (light, sound, smell, heat, cold, etc.), but the brain only understands electrical energy. The body has special sensory receptor cells that transduce (change from one form of energy to another) this external energy to something the brain can understand. In the process of transduction, a memory is created. This memory is very short (less than 1/2 second for vision; about 3 seconds for hearing). It is absolutely critical that the learner attend to the information at this initial stage in order to transfer it to the next one. There are two major concepts for getting information into STM: *First,* individuals are more likely to pay attention to a stimulus if it has an interesting feature. We are more likely to get an orienting response if this is present. *Second,* individuals are more likely to pay attention if the stimulus activates a known pattern. To the extent we have students call to mind relevant prior learning before we begin our presentations, we can take advantage of this principle.

Short-Term Memory (STM)

Short-term memory is also called working memory and relates to what we are thinking about at any given moment in time. In Freudian terms, this is conscious memory. It is created by our paying attention to an external stimulus, an internal thought, or both. It will initially last somewhere around 15 to 20 seconds unless it is repeated (called maintenance rehearsal) at which point it may be available for up to 20 minutes. The hypothalamus is a brain structure thought to be involved in this shallow processing of information. The frontal lobes of the cerebral cortex is the structure associated with working memory. For example, you are processing the words you read on the screen in your frontal lobes. However, if I ask, "What is your telephone number?" your brain immediately calls that from long-term memory and replaces what was previously there.

Another major limit on information processing in STM is in terms of the number of units that can be processed an any one time. Miller (1956) gave the number as 7 + 2, but more recent research suggests the number may be more like 5 + 2 for most things we are trying to remember. Because of the variability in how much individuals can work with (for some it may be three, for others seven) it is necessary to point out important information. If some students can only process three units of information at a time, let us make certain it is the most important three. There are two major concepts for retaining information in STM: organization and repetition.

There are four major types of organization that are most often used in instructional design:

- *Component (part/whole)*: Classification by category or concept (*e.g.*, the components of the teaching/learning model);
- *Sequential*: Chronological; cause/effect; building to climax (*e.g.*, baking a cake, reporting on a research study);
- *Relevance*: Central unifying idea or criteria (*e.g.*, most important principles of learning for boys and girls, appropriate management strategies for middle school and high school students);
- *Transitional (connective)*: Relational words or phrases used to indicate qualitative change over time (*e.g.*, stages in Piaget's theory of cognitive development or Erikson's stages of socioemotional development)

A related issue to organization is the concept of chunking or grouping pieces of data into units. For example, the letters"b d e" constitute three units of information while the word "bed" represents one unit even though it is composed of the same number of letters. Chunking is a major technique for getting and keeping information in short-term memory; it is also a type of elaboration that will help get information into long-term memory. Repetition or rote rehearsal is a technique we all use to try to"learn" something. However, in order to be effective this must be done after forgetting begins. Researchers advise that the learner should not repeat immediately the content (or skill), but wait a few minutes and then repeat. For the most part, simply memorizing something does not lead to learning (*i.e.*, relatively permanent change). We all have anecdotal evidence that we can remember something we memorized (a poem for example), but just think about all the material we tried to learn this way and the little we are able to remember after six months or a year.

Long-Term Memory (LTM)

Long-term memory is also called preconscious and unconscious memory in Freudian terms. Preconscious means that the information is relatively easily recalled (although it may take several minutes or even hours) while unconscious refers to data that is not available during normal consciousness. It is preconscious memory that is the focus of cognitive psychology as it relates to long-term memory. The levels-of-processing theory, however, has provided some research that attests to the fact that we"know" more than we can easily recall. The two processes most likely to move information into long-term memory are elaboration and distributed practice.

There are several examples of elaboration that are commonly used in the teaching/learning process:

- *Imaging*: Creating a mental picture;
- *Method of loci (locations)*: Ideas or things to be remembered are connected to objects located in a familiar location;
- *Pegword method (number, rhyming schemes)*: Ideas or things to be remembered are connected to specific words (*e.g.*, one-bun, two-shoe, three-tree, etc.)
- *Rhyming (songs, phrases)*: Information to be remembered is arranged in a rhyme (*e.g.*, 30 days hath September, April, June, and November, etc.)
- *Initial letter*: The first letter of each word in a list is used to make a sentence (the sillier, the better).

ORGANIZATION (TYPES) OF KNOWLEDGE

As information is stored in long-term memory, it is organized using one or more structures: declarative, procedural, and/or imagery.

Declarative Memory:

- *Semantic Memory*: Facts and generalized information (concepts, principles, rules; problem-solving strategies; learning strategies)
  - *Schema/Schemata*: Networks of connected ideas or relationships; data structures or procedures for organizing the parts of a specific experience into a meaningful system (like a standard or stereotype).
  - *Proposition*: Interconnected set of concepts and relationships; if/then statements (smallest unit of information that can be judged true or false).
  - *Script*: "Declarative knowledge structure that captures general information about a routine series of events or a recurrent type

of social event, such as eating in a restaurant or visiting the doctor" Frame — complex organization including concepts and visualizations that provide a reference within which stimuli and actions are judged.

  - *Scheme*: An organization of concepts, principles, rules, etc. that define a perspective and presents specific action patterns to follow.
  - *Programme*: Set of rules that define what to do in a particular situation.
  - *Paradigm*: The basic way of perceiving, thinking, valuing, and doing associated with a particular vision of reality.
  - *Model*: A set of propositions or equations describing in simplified form some aspects of our experience. Every model is based upon a theory or paradigm, but the theory or paradigm may not be stated in concise form.
- *Episodic Memory*: Personal experience.

CONCEPT FORMATION

One of the most important issues in cognitive psychology is the development or formation of concepts. A concept is the set of rules used to define the categories by which we group similar events, ideas or objects.

There are several principles that lend themselves to concept development:

- Name and define concept to be learned
  - Reference to larger category
  - Define attributes
- Identify relevant and irrelevant attributes
- Give examples and nonexamples
- Use both inductive
- Name distinctive attributes

Using the Information Processing Approach in the Classroom

Principle	Example
1. Gain the students' attention.	• Use cues to signal when you are ready to begin. • Move around the room and use voice inflections.
2. Bring to mind relevant prior	• Review previous day's learning. session. • Have a discussion about previously covered content.
3. Point out important information.	• Provide handouts. • Write on the board or use transparencies.
4. Present information in an	• Show a logical sequence to

organized manner.	concepts and skills. • Go from simple to complex when presenting new material.
5. Show students how to categorize related information.	• Present information in categories. • Teach inductive reasoning.
6. Provide opportunities for students to elaborate on new information.	• Connect new information to something already known. • Look for similarities and differences among concepts.
7. Show students how to use coding when memorizing lists.	• Make up silly sentence with first letter of each word in the list. • Use mental imagery techniques such as the keyword method.
8. Provide for repetition of learning.	• State important principles several times in different ways during presentation of information (STM). • Have items on each day's session from previous session (LTM). • Schedule periodic reviews of previously learned concepts and skills (LTM).
9. Provide opportunities for overlearning of fundamental concepts and skills.	• Use daily drills for arithmetic facts. • Play form of trivial pursuit with content related to class.

LANGUAGE DEVELOPMENT

The chart presents typical language development. There is a wide range of normal development. Most children will not follow the chart to the letter. It is presented so you will know what to expect for your child. If your child seems significantly behind in language development, you should talk with your child's physician regarding your questions and concerns.

Language Development Chart:

Age of Child	Typical Language Development
6 Months	• Vocalization with intonation • Responds to his name • Responds to human voices without visual cues by turning his head andeyes

	• Responds appropriately to friendly and angry tones
12 Months	• Uses one or more words with meaning • Understands simple instructions, especially if vocal or physical cues are given • Practices inflection • Is aware of the social value of speech
18 Months	• Has vocabulary of approximately 5-20 words • Vocabulary made up chiefly of nouns • Some echolalia • Much jargon with emotional content • Is able to follow simple commands
24 Months	• Can name a number of objects common to his surroundings • Is able to use at least two prepositions, usually chosen from the following: in, on, under • Combines words into a short sentence-largely noun-verb combinations length of sentences is given as 1-2 words • Approximately 2/3 of what child says should be intelligible Vocabulary of approximately 150-300 words • Rhythm and fluency often poor • Volume and pitch of voice not yet well-controlled • Can use two pronouns correctly: I, me, you, although me and I are often confused • My and mine are beginning to emerge • Responds to such commands as "show me your eyes"
36 Months	• Use pronouns I, you, me correctly • Is using some plurals and past tenses • Knows at least three prepositions, usually in, on, under • Knows chief parts of body and should be able to indicate these if not name • Handles three word sentences easily • Has in the neighborhood of 900-1000 words • About 90% of what child says should be intelligible • Verbs begin to predominate • Understands most simple questions dealing with his environment and activities • Relates his experiences so that they can be followed with reason • Able to reason out such questions as "what must you do when you are sleepy, hungry, cool, or thirsty?" • Should be able to give his sex, name, age

- Should not be expected to answer all questions even though he understands what is expected

48 Months
- Knows names of familiar animals
- Can use at least four prepositions or can demonstrate his understanding of their meaning when given commands
- Names common objects in picture books or magazines
- Knows one or more colours
- Can repeat 4 digits when they are given slowly
- Can usually repeat words of four syllables
- Demonstrates understanding of over and under
- Has most vowels and diphthongs and the consonants p, b, m, w, n well established
- Often indulges in make-believe
- Extensive verbalization as he carries out activities
- Understands such concepts as longer, larger, when a contrast is presented
- Readily follows simple commands even thought the stimulus objects are not in sight
- Much repetition of words, phrases, syllables, and even sounds

60 Months
- Can use many descriptive words spontaneously—both adjectives and adverbs
- Knows common opposites: big-little, hard-soft, heave-light, etc.
- Has number concepts of 4 or more
- Can count to ten
- Speech should be completely intelligible, in spite of articulation problems
- Should have all vowels and the consonants, m,p,b,h,w,k,g,t,d,n,ng,y
- Should be able to repeat sentences as long as nine words
- Should be able to define common objects in terms of use
- Should be able to follow three commands given without interruptions
- Should know his age
- Should have simple time concepts: morning, afternoon, night, day, later, after, while tomorrow, yesterday, today
- Should be using fairly long sentences and should use some compound and some complex sentences
- Speech on the whole should be grammatically correct

6 Years
- In addition to the above consonants these

	should be mastered: f, v, sh, zh, th • He should have concepts of 7 • Speech should be completely intelligible and socially useful • Should be able to tell one a rather connected story about a picture, seeing relationships between objects and happenings
7 Years	• Should have mastered the consonants s-z, r, voiceless th, ch, wh, and the soft g as in
George	
	• Should handle opposite analogies easily: girl-boy, man-woman, flies-swims, blunt-sharp, short-long, sweet-sour, etc • Understands such terms as: alike, different, beginning, end, etc. • Should be able to tell time to quarter hour • Should be able to do simple reading and to write or print many words
8 Years	• Can relate rather involved accounts of events, many of which occurred at some time in the past • Complex and compound sentences should be used easily • Should be few lapses in grammatical constrictions—tense, pronouns, plurals • All speech sounds, including consonant blends should be established • Should be reading with considerable ease and now writing simple compositions • Social amenities should be present in his speech in appropriate situations • Control of rate, pitch, and volume are generally well and appropriately established • Can carry on conversation at rather adult level • Follows fairly complex directions with little repetition • Has well developed time and number concepts

WHAT IS LANGUAGE

Language may refer either to the specifically human capacity for acquiring and using complex systems of communication, or to a specific instance of such a system of complex communication. The scientific study of language in any of its senses is called linguistics. The approximately 3000-6000 languages that are spoken by humans today are the most salient examples, but natural languages can also be based on visual rather than auditive stimuli, for example in sign languages and written language. Codes and other kinds of artificially constructed communication systems such as those used for computer programming can also be called languages. A language in this sense is a system of signs for encoding and decoding information. The English word derives from Latin lingua, "language, tongue." This metaphoric relation between language and the tongue exists in many languages and testifies to the historical prominence of spoken languages. When used as a general concept, "language" refers to the cognitive faculty that enables humans to learn and use systems of complex communication.

The human language faculty is thought to be fundamentally different from and of much higher complexity than those of other species. Human language is highly complex in that it is based on a set of rules relating symbols to their meanings, thereby forming an infinite number of possible utterances from a finite number of elements.

The word "language" can also be used to describe the set of rules that makes this possible, or the set of utterances that can be produced from those rules. All languages rely on the process of semiosis to relate a sign with a particular meaning. Spoken and signed languages contain a phonological system that governs how sounds or visual symbols are used to form sequences known as words or morphemes, and a syntactic system that governs how words and morphemes are used to form phrases and utterances. Written languages use visual symbols to represent the sounds of the spoken languages, but they still require syntactic rules that govern the production of meaning from sequences of words. Language is thought to have originated when early hominids first started cooperating, adapting earlier systems of communication based on expressive signs to include a theory of other minds and shared intentionality. This development is thought to have coincided with an increase in brain volume.

Language is processed in many different locations in the human brain, but especially in Broca's and Wernicke's areas. Humans acquire language through social interaction in early childhood, and children generally speak fluently when they are around three years old. The use of language has become deeply entrenched in human culture and, apart from being used to communicate and share information, it also has social and cultural uses, such as signifying group identity, social stratification and for social grooming and entertainment. Languages evolve and diversify over time, and the history of their evolution can be reconstructed by comparing modern languages to determine which traits their ancestral languages must have had for the later stages to have occurred.

A group of languages that descend from a common ancestor is known as a language family. The languages that are most spoken in the world today belong to the Indo-European family, which includes languages such as English, Spanish, Russian and Hindi; the Sino-Tibetan languages, which include Mandarin Chinese, Cantonese and many others; Semitic languages, which include Arabic and Hebrew; and the Bantu languages, which include Swahili, Zulu, Xhosa and hundreds of other languages spoken throughout Africa.

COMPONENTS OF LANGUAGE

Phonetics:

- *Sound types*: Vowels, semivowels, nasals, stops
- *Vocal tract*: Lips, tongue height, points of articulation
- *Spectra:* Formants, gaps, transitional effects

Phonological Context:

- Indefinite/implausible/illogical/irregular
- *Also*: cat/s/, dog/z/, fox/ ɪz/, drop/t/, rub/d/, add/ ɪd/
- s, g and t in sign/design/designate/signature
- */s//sh/*: Racial, spatial, erasure; also: seizure, gradual
- *Short stressed antepenult*: Batural, definitive, provocative

Orthography:

- *Doubled consonants*: Rubbing, hidden, bagged, crystallize.
- *Finaly ® i/ C_V*: Marriage, reliable, crazier, denied, vilify
- *Final e ®/ _V*: Realisation, storage, whiten, privatize, seizure

Morphology:

- *Affixes*: prefix, suffix, others, possibly multiple
- Inflectional
- *Derivational*: lighten, lightness, demonize, worker, usually

Syntax:

- Specifying all and only the sentences of a language
- What is in touch (-tax) with (syn-) what
- Word-order, grouping and CFGs
- Case and free word-order
- *Features and agreement*: case, gender, number, person
- Major/open categories and their phrases
- Complement structures and subcategorization
- *X-bar*: modifiers, complements, specifiers
- Empty nodes
- Long-distance dependencies
- Function words

Semantics:

- Lookup and combine
- Lexical ambiguity
- Synonyms, antonyms, hyponyms
- Type hierarchies for nouns and verbs
- Modification
- Predicates and arguments

- Compositionality and piggybacking on syntax
- Quantification, negation and scope
- Lambda notation

Discourse:

- Anaphoric reference across sentences
- Topic structure
- *Rhetorical structure*: relations among sentences
- Grounding, turn-taking

Pragmatics:

- *Maxims*: true, relevant, clear, just enough
- *Indirectness*: do you know the time? it's cold in here.
- Style/register
- *Speech acts*: I... order you to, promise to, second it

PRE-LINGUISTIC DEVELOPMENT

As linguistic development designates the stage when children are able to manipulate verbal symbols, it should be apparent that pre-linguistic development refers to the stage before the child is able to manipulate such symbols. Consequently, this stage is sometimes called the pre-symbolic stage. Pre-linguistic development, therefore, concerns itself with precursors to the development of symbolic skills and typically covers the period from birth to around 13 months of age.

Four stages can be identified:

1. *Vegetative sounds (0-2 months)*: The natural sounds that babies make, *e.g*. crying, coughing, burping, and swallowing.
2. *Cooing and laughter (2-5 months)*: These vocalizations usually occur when the baby is comfortable and content. They are typically made up of vowels and consonants.
3. *Vocal play (4-8 months)*: The infant engages in longer and more continuous streams of either vowel or consonant sounds.
4. *Babbling (6-13 months)*: At least two sub-stages are identified – reduplicated babbling, in which the child produces a series of Consonant-Vowel (CV) syllables with the same consonant being repeated (*e.g*. wa-wa-wa, mu-mu-mu) and non-reduplicated babbling, consisting of either CVC vocalizations (*e.g*. mom, pip) or VCV vocalizations (*e.g*. ama, ooboo).

Up to this stage of development much of what the child produces is really no more than a sort of verbal play. The child is practicing individual sounds, and sound sequences, and gaining the motor skills necessary to produce what will eventually be considered as actual adult words. So, young children make various sounds and others then assign meaning to these. So, for example, a child may reach for an object whilst at the same time saying 'm'. An adult may interpret this as the child wanting help to get the object. The child, having realised that this combination of physical gesture (reaching) and articulating 'm' prompts an adult to pass the desired object, may go on to repeat this behaviour. The child is learning that certain actions that he or she performs can be used to control his or her environment. These changes come about because the child's ability to focus their attention on their caregiver and on objects becomes more refined as they mature. For example, from 0-2 months there is shared attentiveness in which only the baby and caregiver form part of any interactive event—all other elements are ignored. From 2-6 months there is interpersonal engagement when the baby is conceptually able to differentiate their own self from the caregiver and focus attention on each other and on the 'message' of the communicative event. Then, from about 6-15 months there is a shift such that the child is now able to focus attention on objects (*e.g.* cups, toys, books) and understand that the communicative event is focused on these.

This is sometimes called joint object involvement. It is, however, the emergence of words from about 12 months onwards that signals the onset of linguistic development. This is the stage when there is symbolic communication emerges.

LINGUISTIC DEVELOPMENT

Linguistic development occurs at what is called the One Word Stage. It is at this stage that we can properly talk about a child's expressive language, *i.e.* the words used to express emotions, feelings, wants, needs, ideas, and so on. This should not be confused with the child's understanding or receptive language. The two are, of course, closely related. However, a child will typically understand much more than he or she can actually express and a child's expressive language, therefore, lags behind its comprehension by a few months.

Early One Word Stage (12-19 months)

Before the emergence of the first 'adult' words the child will use specific sound combinations in particular situations. The sound combinations are not conventional adult words but they appear to be being used consistently to express meaning.

For example, if the child says mu every time he or she is offered a bottle of milk then this may be considered to be a 'real' word. Similarly, if the child says bibi each time he or she is given a biscuit then, even though the sound combination does not represent an exact adult word, it would still be considered an early word. These early words are called protowords. The child will also be using gesture together with these specific vocalizations in order to obtain needs, express emotions, and so on. The important point is that the child is consistent in his or her use of a particular 'word'.

Later One Word Stage (14-24 months)

The words used by the child are now more readily identifiable as actual adult words. A variety of single words are used to express his or her feelings, needs, wants, and so on. This is the stage at which, amongst other things, the child begins to name and label the objects and people around them.

Examples include common nouns such as:

- Cup
- Dog
- Hat

Proper nouns such as:

- Dad
- Sarah
- Rover

And verbs such as:

- Kiss
- Go
- Ait

The child may also use a few social words such as:

- No
- Bye-bye
- Please

The child will not yet have developed all the adult speech sounds and so the words used are unlikely to sound exactly as an adult would say them. However, they are beginning to approximate more closely to an adult model and they are beginning to be used consistently. At the end of the One Word Stage the child should have a much larger vocabulary, should be able to sustain a simple conversation, be using several adult speech sounds appropriately, and be conveying meaning through the use of single words in combination with facial expression, gesture and actions. These single words will express a variety of meaning. The next stage in the child's development of expressive language is that he or she begins to combine two words together into simple phrases.

Two Word Stage (20-30 months)

It is at this stage that the child begins to produce two-word combinations similar to the following:

- Daddy car
- Shoe on
- Where Katie

Note that a variety of different word classes may be combined:

- For example, daddy car involves the combination of two words from the same word class of nouns one noun (daddy) with another noun (car).

- However, shoe on consists of two words from two different word classes, nouns and prepositions: one noun (shoe) plus a preposition (on).
- Also, where Katie uses a so-called interrogative pronoun (where) together with a proper noun (Katie).

In fact, a high percentage of these two-word combinations incorporate nouns. This is not surprising, as the child has spent a lot of time learning the names of objects and people. These are the important things in his or her environment and the things that are most likely to be manipulated, talked about, and so on.

They are often the concrete, permanent things to which the child can most readily relate. In addition, at this Two Word Stage there is also prolific use of verbs (*e.g.* go, run, drink, eat).

Three Word Stage (28-42 months)

As its name implies, at this next stage of development children extend their two-word utterances by incorporating at least another word. In reality children may add up to two more words, thereby creating utterances as long as four words. The child makes greater use of pronouns (*e.g.* I, you, he, she, they, me) at this stage, *e.g.*

- Me kiss mummy
- You make toy
- He hit ball

At first their use is inconsistent but as the child approaches 42 months of age they become more consolidated in their utterances, *e.g.*

- Me kick a ball
- You give the dolly
- He throw an orange

In addition, it is common for the prepositions in and on to be incorporated between two nouns or pronouns, *e.g.*

- Mummy on bed
- You in it
- Sarah in bath

Four Word Stage (34-48 months)

From about 34 months the child begins to combine between four to six words in any one utterance.

There is greater use of contrast between prepositions such as in, on and under and adjectives such as big and little, e.g:

- Mummy on little bed
- Daddy under big car
- Daddy playing with the little ball

Complex Utterance Stage (48-60 months)

This stage is typified by longer utterances, with the child regularly producing utterances of over six words in length. It is at this stage that the concept of past and future time develops and this is expressed linguistically in a child's utterances, *e.g.*

- We all went to see Ryan yesterday [past time]
- Daddy is going to get a shoe [future time]
- Robert stopped and kicked a good goal [past time]

Some of the more conceptually difficult prepositions such as behind, in front and next to also become established at this stage. The child will also be using the contracted negative, *e.g.* can't rather than can not, didn't rather than did not, won't rather than will not, and so on. Example utterances include the following.

- Helen can't go to granddad's house
- Connor didn't stop crying
- He won't eat up all his dinner for mummy

There is a lot of controversy about just when the Complex Utterance Stage is completed. Some researchers claim that at five years of age a child has developed all of the major adult linguistic features and that the only real progression beyond this stage is the further acquisition of vocabulary items. Other researchers, however, argue that children up to the age of 12 years are still developing adult sentence structure.

Early Development of Expressive Language

<table>
<tr><th colspan="6">Precursors to Language (Pre-linguistic)</th></tr>
<tr><td>0-2
months</td><td>2-5
months</td><td>4-8
months</td><td colspan="3">6-13
months</td></tr>
<tr><td>reflexive crying and vegetative sounds</td><td>cooing and laughter</td><td>vocal play</td><td colspan="3">babbling
- reduplicated
- non-reduplicated</td></tr>
<tr><th colspan="6">(Symbolic) Language</th></tr>
<tr><td>12-19
months</td><td>14-24
months</td><td>20-30
months</td><td>28-42
months</td><td>34-48
months</td><td>48-60
months</td></tr>
<tr><td>Early One Word Stage (protowords)</td><td>Later One Word Stage</td><td>Two Word Stage</td><td>Three Word Stage</td><td>Four Word Stage</td><td>Complex Utterance Stage</td></tr>
</table>

As indicated, our overview of language development has focused on how the child develops longer and longer utterances, *i.e.* it has concentrated on expressive language. It should be noted, however, that there is a parallel development of comprehension, or receptive language. So, for example, at the Early One Word Stage the child is capable of understanding a few single words spoken by others as well as speaking a few words. Similarly, at the Three Word

Stage the child can also comprehend the four to six word utterances spoken by others as well as producing such utterances themselves. In summary, the child will need to be able to comprehend utterances at least at the same level as those that he or she is able to construct and use expressively. In reality, we find that a child's level of understanding actually precedes their level of expression. That is to say, a typically developing child will always understand more than they can express. The extent to which the development of receptive language precedes expressive language is highly variable and it is not possible to define any precise norms. The following table summarizes the stages of early development of expressive language.

FIRST SPEECH SOUNDS

Learning to communicate with spoken language is most effective through meaningful and enjoyable experiences that integrate listening, speech, language, reading and thinking. When listening and talking are relevant and positive, spoken communication can emerge in a natural way for children who are deaf.

There is no single method that works best for teaching speech to all children who are deaf, and Speech Sounds is simply one approach. It is based on the premise that young children with cochlear implant(s) need to be exposed to all speech sounds through listening as a building block in establishing a strong auditory foundation. Speech Sounds consists of units for 20 English consonant sounds.

Each card condenses a relatively large body of information into manageable units to easily incorporate speech into everyday experiences and books. It is used in conjunction with specific language goals from a child's individualized treatment plan. Optimally a family is working in partnership with a therapist or educator for auditory habilitation. A child's progress is related to a strong link among home, daycare, school and therapy and the child's interactions with everyone in these settings.

EACH SPEECH SOUNDS UNIT FOCUSES ON ONE SPEECH SOUND AND INCORPORATES

- Child-friendly words
- Daily routines
- Activities
- Games and toys
- Songs, rhymes and fingerplays
- A popular children's book
- Additional books

HOW TO USE SPEECH SOUNDS

Speech Sounds is used as a supplement to the developmental way children who are deaf learn speech sounds through listening. The units serve as a guide to professionals for planning therapy sessions and classroom activities. Parents use the overview and the cards as a resource for active and effective home carry-over.

Planning and Preparation

Gather and organize props, toys and books into containers. Ideally, professionals and parents will obtain materials for a particular sound several weeks prior to its use in therapy or in the classroom allowing enough time to order books from the library or on-line and to gather props for upcoming activities. Many of the same props may be used with different units. Good places to find materials at reasonable prices are on the Internet and at garage sales or hobby, toy, and party supply stores. You can also find all of the books on the Internet. Be creative. Find common objects in your home and classroom or clinic. Have a treasure hunt with the child to find or create materials. Make note cards and put them in appropriate places around the house or classroom as a reminder of the vocabulary and language to reinforce.

When to Begin

Speech Sounds is intended to be used with younger children ages 1 through 5 years, but can also be adapted for older children.

Prior to embarking on this adventure, a child should have an auditory foundation and be able to:

- Listen, attend to, and discriminate if sounds are the same or different
- *Vocalize suprasegmentals*: rhythm, duration, pitch and intensity
- Produce vowels
- Attach meaning to animal and/or vehicle sounds
- Imitate vocalizations on request
- Understand and use a few functional words, such as "bye bye," "more," "all gone" with the appropriate suprasegmentals and vowels, but not necessarily correctly produced consonants.

What to Do

The focus is on teaching speech through listening to maximize a child's auditory potential or auditory self-monitoring of speech. The process is as important as the content. Listening is a cognitive process and our job is to stimulate a child's brain so he can understand what the ears hear.

Follow the 5 E's as you highlight sounds through spoken language and weave them into daily routines, children's literature, activities, games and toys:

- Expose a child to a sound or word's using auditory input only. Begin by babbling the target sound coupled with either the vowel "ah" or "oo" or "ee", such as "bah bah bah". Extend this to words and phrases rich in the targeted sound. Present the model through listening first, before the child sees the toy or prop or cue. This sets the stage for a child to listen with intent and to establish an "auditory impression" of the target sound that will assist in recall in the future. As soon as a child produces a sound with consistency, discontinue the babbling and continue to encourage carry-over into spontaneous language. From then on, babbling is used as a remediation strategy to acoustically highlight a sound if it is incorrectly produced in some context.

- Expect the parent, then the child to imitate or respond verbally. This completes the auditory self-monitoring loop and encourages active rather than passive listening.
- Experience a toy, book or activity that represents the sound or word. This is a child's opportunity to relate to the toy, book or activity and enjoy the process in a meaningful way. It keeps a child interested and encourages carry-over into the real world. It is also an important step in taking a child quickly from imitation to thinking and auditory processing and understanding.
- Expand on the language model and the child's communication. The adult's verbal input should be at a level slightly higher than a child's spontaneous expressive language to establish the foundation for future progress.
- Expressive spoken language emerges later in time when a child spontaneously uses the sound or words with symbolic meaning in the real world.

Where to Begin

There is no specific order for the sound units. There are some general guidelines to help you choose the sequence of sounds for any individual child. Start with consonants a child is already producing. Then proceed by following the normal order of development of speech sounds. Earlier developing sounds, not in specific order, may include: m, b, y, n, w, d, p, h. Take into account the acoustic characteristics of each sound relative to what a child hears. Also consider that the most frequently occurring manner of phonemes is plosives and stops, or p, t, k, b, d, g, although "s" is the specific sound most often used by English speakers. Consider the sounds a child uses frequently which are highly motivating, such as sounds in his name or sounds in his favourite foods. Overlap among units is expected.

A variety of sounds, in addition to the target sound, will emerge naturally as a child's auditory selfmonitoring develops. It is important to individualize the programme based on each child's progress. Develop strategies based on diagnostic teaching, such as, alternating consonants within manner from sounds the child has acquired and babbling nonsense syllables related to words and phrases from real life situations.

What to Expect

The purpose of Speech Sounds is to "bathe the child in sound" to stimulate natural development of speech through listening. Provide rich auditory input and exposure for one sound, and then move to a different sound after one or two weeks. Typically a child will show understanding prior to using the sounds and language. Initially there is not an expectation for perfect speech. Speech development is a process and emerges over time. A child's imitations will give adults information about what the child hears, his depth and confidence in listening, need for reprogramming of his cochlear implant speech processor(s), the amount of exposure he has had to the sound, oral-motor development and/or motivation. Imitation is highly dependent upon motivation, so a child must be stimulated with interesting daily activities.

Analyse the reason for a child's errors to determine future goals and recommendations. Be aware that a child's production of sounds at this stage may come and go as the emphasis on one consonant over the other changes. Over time, correct productions are encouraged and expected. The expectation for correct speech should be based on the ages and progression of speech development for children with normal hearing. If a sensory or motor delay is suspected, make appropriate referrals to an occupational or physical therapist who specializes in this area. If a child has had sufficient time and experience in learning a Speech Sounds sound through listening and still does not approximate the sound or word, it may be appropriate to use the strategy called "the auditory sandwich" where a child is exposed to an auditory presentation three times followed by a visual or tactile cue and then again through listening alone.

Tracking Progress

Monitoring a child's progress is an important aspect of any programme. It is the responsibility of professionals to coach parents to be positive and effective spoken language models in their child's natural environments.

Parents should take an active role by:

- Reading daily to their child and discussing what they have read
- Targeting and teaching vocabulary from each unit in a variety of meaningful contexts
- Tracking their child's progress
- Reporting back to professionals on a consistent basis

Each Speech Sounds unit provides an easy and time-efficient way to maintain consistent and accurate records of progress. Place a dot (•) in front of a word or an activity after you have presented it to a child. To monitor speech development, circle a word when the child correctly says the targeted sound in the word. Vocabulary development is tracked by putting a dash (—) by the words a child understands and a plus (+) by the words a child says spontaneously.

HOW SPEECH SOUNDS WORKS

Speech Acoustics

Since the basic premise of Speech Sounds is that a child learns speech through listening, it is fundamental to consider the basics of speech acoustics. Every speech sound has concentrations of acoustic energy called formants that make it different from other sounds. Although the same sound is pronounced slightly differently based on the sounds that precede or follow it, in general, the acoustic properties of a sound are consistent. Understanding of speech acoustics assists professionals and parents in establishing realistic and systematic goals, reinforcing appropriate approximations of speech, and optimizing a child's auditory potential with the use of appropriate technology. Manner of production is HOW a sound is made. Speech Sounds cards are colour coded just as to the manner of the sound.

The different manners, basic definitions, consonants and the cards' colour code for each manner of production:

- *Plosives and stops*: A release of built up air pressure occurs with plosives; the pressure is not released for stops. p/b, t/d, k/g
- *Fricatives*: A point of constriction causes friction in the breath stream that creates a sound. h, f/v, s/z, sh
- *Nasals*: The breath stream goes mainly through the nose. m, n
- *Semivowels*: Produced like vowels except there is greater constriction. w, y
- *Liquids*: The tongue diverts the breath stream in the mouth. l, r
- *Affricatives*: A stop is released with a fricative. ch, j Place of production is WHERE a sound is made.

The different places, basic definitions and the consonants within each place of production:

- *Bilabial*: Two lips. p, b, m, w
- *Labiodental*: Bottom lip and teeth. f, v
- *Linguadental*: Tongue and teeth. TH, th
- *Alveolar*: Ridge on hard palate behind the upper teeth. t, d, s, z, n, l, r
- *Palatal*: Hard palate. sh, zh, y, ch, j
- *Velar*: Back of soft palate. k, g, ng
- *Glottal*: Back of mouth. h

Manner of production is easier to hear than place of production. For example, /b/ is a plosive and sounds very different from /m/ which is a nasal. Interestingly, /b/ and /m/ look the same through lipreading because they have the same place, bilabial. This is why sounds that have the same place of production may be confusing to a child who relies on lipreading to learn speech.

A child is relying more on auditory cues when he substitutes sounds that are within the same manner of production, such as saying /p/ for /t/ or /k/ or saying /s/ for /f/ or /TH/. Voicing indicates whether a sound is made while the vocal folds are vibrating or not vibrating. Most sounds are grouped in pairs where one sound is made with voice and the other sound is voiceless. With lipreading they look the same, so again these sounds can be confusing to a child who relies on looking rather than listening. It is much more effective to use listening rather than looking for discrimination of voiced versus voiceless sounds.

Speech Acoustics

Since the basic premise of Speech Sounds is that a child learns speech through listening, it is fundamental to consider the basics of speech acoustics. Every speech sound has concentrations of acoustic energy called formants that make it different from other sounds. Although the same sound is pronounced slightly differently based on the sounds that precede or follow it, in general, the acoustic properties of a sound are consistent.

Understanding of speech acoustics assists professionals and parents in establishing realistic and systematic goals, reinforcing appropriate approximations of speech, and optimizing a child's auditory potential with the use of appropriate technology. Manner of production is HOW a sound is made. Speech Sounds cards are colour coded just as to the manner of the sound.

The different manners, basic definitions, consonants and the cards' colour code for each manner of production:

- *Plosives and stops*: A release of built up air pressure occurs with plosives; the pressure is not released for stops. p/b, t/d, k/g
- *Fricatives*: A point of constriction causes friction in the breath stream that creates a sound. h, f/v, s/z, sh
- *Nasals*: The breath stream goes mainly through the nose. m, n
- *Semivowels*: Produced like vowels except there is greater constriction. w, y
- *Liquids*: The tongue diverts the breath stream in the mouth. l, r
- *Affricatives*: A stop is released with a fricative. ch, j Place of production is WHERE a sound is made.

The different places, basic definitions and the consonants within each place of production:

- *Bilabial*: Two lips. p, b, m, w
- *Labiodental*: Bottom lip and teeth. f, v
- *Linguadental*: Tongue and teeth. TH, th
- *Alveolar*: Ridge on hard palate behind the upper teeth. t, d, s, z, n, l, r
- *Palatal*: Hard palate. sh, zh, y, ch, j
- *Velar*: Back of soft palate. k, g, ng
- *Glottal*: Back of mouth. h

Manner of production is easier to hear than place of production. For example, /b/ is a plosive and sounds very different from /m/ which is a nasal. Interestingly, /b/ and /m/ look the same through lipreading because they have the same place, bilabial. This is why sounds that have the same place of production may be confusing to a child who relies on lipreading to learn speech.

A child is relying more on auditory cues when he substitutes sounds that are within the same manner of production, such as saying /p/ for /t/ or /k/ or saying /s/ for /f/ or /TH/. Voicing indicates whether a sound is made while the vocal folds are vibrating or not vibrating. Most sounds are grouped in pairs where one sound is made with voice and the other sound is voiceless. With lipreading they look the same, so again these sounds can be confusing to a child who relies on looking rather than listening. It is much more effective to use listening rather than looking for discrimination of voiced versus voiceless sounds.

The Listening-Talking-Reading Connection

We learn to talk by saying what we hear and hearing what we say. This is termed the "auditory self-monitoring loop" or "auditory feedback loop." It is the avenue through which children develop sounds and learn the language of their culture. Children who are deaf are capable of developing natural sounding voices and spoken language when they learn speech through listening rather than looking. Too much emphasis on visual cues may lead to unnatural sounding voice quality and exaggerated speech.

A child's ability to develop natural and intelligible speech is related to early detection and intervention, use of appropriate and optimal technology such as cochlear implant(s), establishing a strong auditory foundation by learning to listen, integrated sensory and motor systems, consistent exposure to spoken language, and parent or caregiver participation. Communication among a child's cochlear implant audiologist, teacher or therapist and parent is important for maintaining optimal programming of the cochlear implant(s). With individualized modifications any child may benefit from Speech Sounds for remediation. Even though it is difficult to change voice quality, articulation can be corrected even for older children.

The process and materials may be helpful for older children who receive a cochlear implant(s); children who use sign language or other visual systems to communicate; children learning English as a second language; children with normal hearing who have auditory processing, articulation and/or language delays; and children learning to read. Speech Sounds facilitates phonological awareness for reading as well as reading comprehension. Reading aloud to a child on a daily basis strengthens the connection of listening and talking with reading. A robust receptive and expressive vocabulary is necessary for proficiency in communication, reading and writing.

Phonological Development

A child with normal hearing typically develops speech in a predictable manner. Young children with hearing loss usually learn in the same developmental way as normal hearing children if they have a strong auditory foundation, no additional challenges, and access to learning speech through listening during the early speech development period.

Speech Sounds is based on typical development where the normal progression is: vocal play, suprasegmentals, vowels, and consonants. It encourages development at the phonetic level where a child imitates sounds or uses echolalia, and sets the stage for a child to begin babbling. Babbling progresses beyond simply imitating sounds to linking sounds with meaningful language, conversation, literature and eventually reading.

DEVELOPMENT OF UNDERSTANDING IN EARLY CHILDHOOD

UNDERSTANDING

Understanding is a psychological process related to an abstract or physical object, such as a person, situation, or message whereby one is able to think about it and use concepts to deal adequately with that object. An understanding is the limit of a conceptualization. To understand something is to have conceptualized it to a given measure.

Examples:

- One understands the weather if one is able to predict and to give an explanation of some of its features, etc.
- A psychiatrist understands another person's anxieties if he/she knows that person's anxieties, their causes, and can give useful advice on how to cope with the anxiety.
- A person understands a command if he/she knows who gave it, what is expected by the issuer, and whether the command is legitimate, and whether one understands the speaker.
- One understands a reasoning, an argument, or a language if one can consciously reproduce the information content conveyed by the message.
- One understands a mathematical concept if one can solve problems using it, especially problems that are not similar to what one has seen before.

IS UNDERSTANDING DEFINABLE

It is difficult to define understanding. The question then arises as to what is a concept? Is it an abstract thing? Is it a brain pattern or a rule? Whatever definition is proposed, we can still ask how it is that we understand the thing that is featured in the definition: we can never satisfactorily define a concept, still less use it to explain understanding. It may be more convenient to use an operational or behavioural definition, that is, to say that "somebody who reacts appropriately to x understands x".

For example, one understands Swahili if one correctly obeys commands given in that language. This approach, however, may not provide an adequate definition. A computer can easily be programmed to react appropriately to commands, but there is a disagreement as to whether or not the computer understands the language.

Rostislav Persion:

- In the cognitive model presented by MBTI, the process of introverted thinking is thought to represent understanding through cause and effect relationships or correlations. One can construct a model of a system by observing correlations between all the relevant properties. This allows the person to generate truths about the system and then to apply the model to demonstrate his or her understanding. A mechanic for example may randomly, or algorithmically probe the inputs and outputs of a black box to understand the internal components through the use of induction. INTP, ISTP, ESTP, and ENTP all use TI and are usually the best of the 16 types at understanding their material environment in a bottom-up manner. These types may enjoy mechanics and digital electronics because of the 1 to 1 correlation between cause and effect relationships in these fields. Understanding is not limited to these types however as other types demonstrate an identical process, although in other planes of reality; *i.e.* Social, Theological and Aesthetic. A potential reason for the association of understanding with the former personality types is due to a social phenomenon for asymmetrical distribution of gratification. In the field of engineering, engineers probe or study the inputs and outputs of components to understand their functionality. These components are then combined based on their functionality to create a larger, more complex system. This is the reason why engineers attempt to subdivide ideas as deep as possible to obtain the lowest level of knowledge. This makes their models more detailed and flexible. It may be useful to know the formulas that govern an ideal gas, but to visualise the gas as being made up of small moving particles, which are in turn made up of even smaller particles, is true understanding. People who are understanding usually value objects and people based on usefulness, as opposed to the people who use extroverted thinking who view people or things as having a worth. In order to test one's understanding it is necessary to present a question that forces the individual to demonstrate the possession of a model, derived from observable examples of that model's production or potential production. Rote memorization can present an illusion of understanding, however when other questions are presented with modified attributes within the query, the individual cannot create a solution due to a lack of a deeper representation of reality.

Another significant point of view holds that knowledge is the simple awareness of bits of information. Understanding is the awareness of the connection between the individual pieces of this information. It is understanding which allows knowledge to be put to use. Therefore, understanding represents a deeper level than simple knowledge. Gregory Chaitin, a noted computer scientist, propounds a view that comprehension is a kind of data compression. In his essay "The Limits of Reason", he argues that understanding something means being able to figure out a simple set of rules that explains it.

For example, we understand why day and night exist because we have a simple model—the rotation of the earth—that explains a tremendous amount of data—changes in brightness, temperature, and atmospheric composition of the earth. We have compressed a large amount of information by using a simple model that predicts it. Similarly, we understand the number 0.33333... by thinking of it as one-third.

The first way of representing the number requires an infinite amount of memory; but the second way can produce all the data of the first representation, but uses much less information. Chaitin argues that comprehension is this ability to compress data. The concepts of comprehension, thought and understanding are also used in the short science fiction story Understand by Ted Chiang.

ROLE OF MATURATION IN THE DEVELOPMENT OF UNDERSTANDING

Maturation refers to the sequential characteristic of biological growth and development. The biological changes occur in sequential order and give children new abilities. Changes in the brain and nervous system account largely for maturation. These changes in the brain and nervous system help children to improve in thinking and motor skills. Also, children must mature to a certain point before they can progress to new skills. For example, a four-month-old cannot use language because the infant's brain has not matured enough to allow the child to talk.

By two years old, the brain has developed further and with help from others, the child will have the capacity to say and understand words. Also, a child can't write or draw until he has developed the motor control to hold a pencil or crayon. Maturational patterns are innate, that is, genetically programmed. The child's environment and the learning that occurs as a result of the child's experiences largely determine whether the child will reach optimal development. A stimulating environment and varied experiences allow a child to develop to his or her potential.

THE ROLE CONCEPT

The concept underlying this approach is the recognition that man is a role player, that every individual is characterized by a certain range of roles which dominate his behaviour, and that every culture is characterized by a certain set of roles which it imposes with a varying degree of success upon its membership. On contrast to the theories presented by psychologists and sociologists "psychiatric role theory" developed largely out of clinical contexts, methods of prevention, treatment of psychoses and neuroses, of marriage and family groups, of interpersonal relations, of problems of industrial adjustment, of the fields of mental hygiene and education. Role research and role therapy are still in their infancy. Psychodrama presents a valuable vehicle for experimental and control studies of roles. It permits the observation of individuals in live situations in which they are concretely involved.

CONCEPT DEVELOPMENT

For children with deafblindness, one of the most critical areas related to learning is concept development. Concept development is sometimes confused with skill development.

- A concept is a mental representation, image or idea of tangible and concrete objects and intangible ideas and feelings.
- A skill is that ability to do something.

Concepts can be divided into three groups:

- *Concrete concepts*: Relate to objects or things that are tangible.
- *Semi-concrete concepts*: Relate to an action, colour, position, or something that can be demonstrated but not held in one's hand.
- *Abstract concepts*: include feelings.

Sighted and hearing children receive a constant flow of visual and auditory information which facilitates the development of concepts. For children with combined vision and hearing loss, the flow of information is incomplete. Concepts don't develop naturally or easily. Alternate strategies must be used to teach these children concept development.

The six areas of concept development are affected by deaf blindness:

1. *Objects exist*: Children with deafblindness have difficulty learning about the existence of objects because they can not see or hear objects clearly.
2. *Objects have permanence*: Children with combined vision and hearing loss can't observe objects and people at a distance and know that things exist beyond their fingertips.
3. *Objects differ*: Children with deafblindness won't know that one object is different form another unless they can touch and explore them.
4. *Objects have names or labels*: Children with both a hearing and vision loss need to use touch to support language learning.

5. *Objects have characteristics*: Children with deafblindness will have difficulty identifying the different characteristics of objects because of the lack of access to information about those objects.
6. *Objects have functions or use*: Children with combined vision and hearing loss can't observe how objects are used, or hear the sounds associated with the functions of objects.

General Strategies that can be helpful in assisting children who are deafblind to develop concepts:

- Use activities that are meaningful to the child
- Use activities that the child enjoys
- Attach language to all experiences
- Build on language that is already known to the child
- Use a total communication approach that is appropriate for the child
- Remove variables that may cause confusion for the child
- Generalize the concepts to a variety of situations.

CHARACTERISTICS OF CHILDREN'S CONCEPT

SELF-CONCEPT

The self concept is how we think about and evaluate ourselves. To be aware of oneself is to have a concept of oneself. The term self-concept is a general term used to refer to how someone thinks about or perceives themselves. It is an important term for both Social Psychology and Humanism. Lewis suggests that development of a concept of self has two aspects:

The Existential Self

This is "the most basic part of the self-scheme or self-concept; the sense of being separate and distinct from others and the awareness of the constancy of the self". The child realises that they exist as a separate entity from others and that they continue to exist over time and space. Lewis awareness of the existential self begins as young as two to three months old and arises in part due to the relation the child has with the world. For example, the child smiles and someone smiles back, or the child touches a mobile and sees it move.

The Categorical Self

Having realised that he or she exists as a separate experiencing being, the child next becomes aware that he or she is also an object in the world. Just as other objects including people have properties that can be experienced so the child is becoming aware of him or her self as an object which can be experienced and which has properties.

The self too can be put into categories such as age, gender, size or skill. Two of the first categories to be applied are age and gender. In early childhood the categories children apply to themselves are very concrete. Later, self-description also begins to include reference to internal psychological traits, comparative evaluations and to how others see them.

"Carl Rogers believes that self concept has *three,* different components":

- The view you have of yourself
- How much value you place on yourself
- What you wish you were really like

SELF-AWARENESS

Although the self is an essential aspect of every person, we do not think about it all of the time. Instead, our level of self-awareness varies depending on both the situation and our personality. Self-awareness is a psychological state in which people are aware of their traits, feelings and behaviour. Alternatively, it can be defined as the realisation of oneself as an individual entity. We explain how self-awareness develops in humans and discuss the areas of the brain which are responsible for this ability. We then distinguish between two types of self-awareness, private and public, which have diverging consequences for the self. Each form of self-awareness can either be temporary, as a consequence of a particular situation, or chronic, reflecting a personality trait that varies from person to person.

DEVELOPMENT OF SELF-AWARENESS

Infants are not born with self-awareness. Instead, they develop the ability over time. Lewis and Brooks put a spot of rouge on the nose of babies and then put them in front of a mirror. Babies aged between 9 and 12 months treated the mirror image as if it was another child and showed no interest in the spot on their nose. Because they lacked self-awareness, they were unable to identify the baby in the mirror as themselves. By around 18 months, however, children would curiously look at themselves in the mirror and touch the spot on their nose; they now recognized that the person they could see was them and that they were looking different from normal.

NEUROLOGICAL BASIS OF SELF-AWARENESS

Why do children develop self-awareness at around the age of 18 months? Research has shown that at around this time, children show a rapid growth of spindle cells, specialized neurones in the anterior cingulate, an area of the frontal lobe in the cerebral cortex of the brain thought to be responsible for monitoring and controlling intentional behaviour. There is also evidence among adults that this area of the brain is activated when people are self-aware. In sum, although it is not likely to be the only area of the brain that contributes towards self-awareness, the anterior cingulate appears to play an important role. To read about a study that investigates the role of the anterior cingulate and the prefrontal cortex in how we make inferences about others based on self-reflection.

CHRONIC DIFFERENCES IN SELF-AWARENESS

In addition to temporary heightening of self-awareness that people experience from time to time as a result of the situation, some people are chronically more likely to experience self-awareness. Such individuals can be described as possessing the personality trait of self-consciousness. Mirroring temporary differences in self-awareness, people can be either publicly or privately self-conscious.

A simple way to think about self-consciousness is that it is the same as public or private self-awareness, but refers to chronic to be one or the other. Public and private self-consciousness are not mutually exclusive; an individual can be high in one of these traits, both of these traits, or neither. People who are high in private self-consciousness experience chronically heightened private self-awareness; they therefore experience more intense emotions, are more likely to remain true to their personal beliefs and have more accurate self-perceptions. Being privately self-conscious has both positive and negative implications for the individual. On the plus side, such individuals are less likely to suffer from ill health as a result of stress because they pay more attention to their physiological state and so notice earlier if there is a problem. However, the down side of being high in private selfconsciousness is a greater tendency to suffer from depression and neuroticism; such individuals are more likely to pay attention to and ruminate about any feelings of unhappiness or discomfort they are experiencing.

People who are high in public self-consciousness are particularly concerned with how they are perceived by those around them. As a result they are more likely to adhere to group norms, more likely to avoid embarrassing situations more concerned with their own physical appearance and more likely to judge others based on their physical appearance.

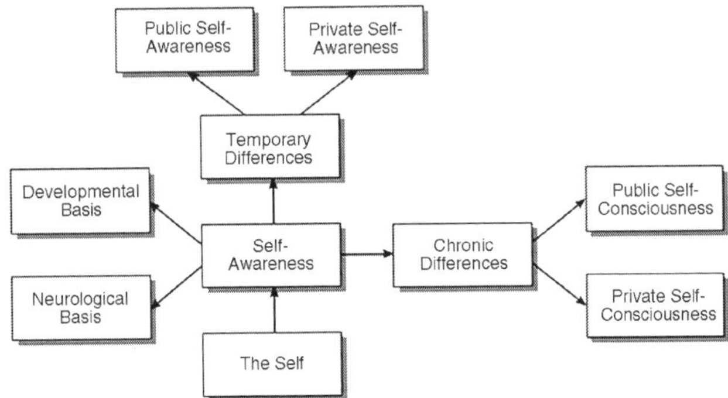

TEMPORARY DIFFERENCES IN SELF-AWARENESS

Social psychologists have distinguished between private and public self-awareness. Private self-awareness refers to when an individual temporarily becomes aware of private, personal aspects of the self. People become privately self-aware when they see their face in a mirror, or experience physiological arousal which may lead them to reflect on their emotional state, for example whether they are happy, excited, or angry. Private self-awareness has three important consequences for how people act. *First*, it results in an intensified emotional response. If an individual already feels positive, reflecting on those feelings of happiness will lead them to feel even happier. In contrast, a sad individual who is privately self-aware may come to feel worse because they dwell on their negative state of mind. Scheier and Carver had participants read aloud a series of positive statements or a series of negative statements, tasks previously shown to elicit elation and depression. They found that participants who looked at themselves in a mirror during the task—and were thus made privately self-aware—become more extreme in their emotional responses than participants who had not been looking in a mirror during the task.

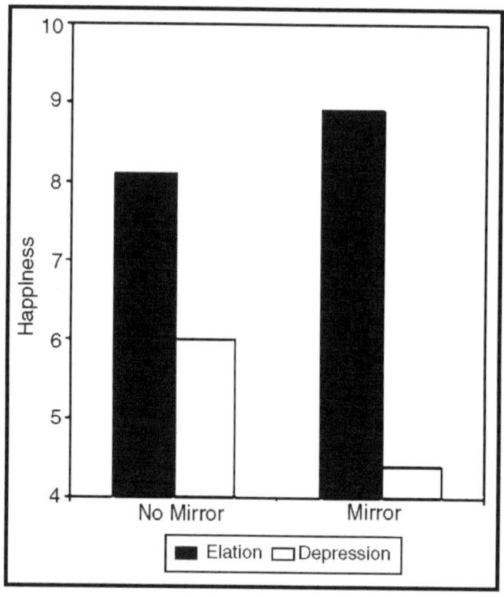

Fig. The Effect of Self-awareness on Emotional Response Following a Mood Manipulation Task

Second, privately self-aware people are likely to experience clarification of knowledge; by focusing on internal events individuals are able to report them with greater accuracy. Gibbons, Carver, Scheier, and Hormuth gave participants a placebo which they were told was a drug that would induce arousal and a number of other side effects. Participants with mirror-induced self-awareness reported less arousal and fewer side-effects than participants in a control condition who could not see themselves in a mirror. While people who were not self-aware based their self-knowledge on their perceptions of the drug they believed they had taken, self-aware individuals ignored the placebo and focused on how they were really feeling, resulting in more accurate self-perceptions.

Third, people who are privately self-aware are more likely to adhere to personal standards of behaviour. As they are more aware of their true beliefs, they will act in line with those beliefs rather than being influenced by normative pressures. Scheier and Carver had participants write a counter-attitudinal essay. The theory of cognitive dissonance, people feel negative arousal if their attitudes and behaviour are inconsistent, and often deal with this by changing their attitudes in line with their behaviour.

However, participants who wrote the essay in front of a mirror showed less attitude change than participants who wrote the essay without the presence of a mirror. Public self-awareness arises when a person is aware of public aspects of themselves that can be seen and evaluated by others. People are publicly self-aware when they are being watched by others, for example giving a presentation, talking in a seminar, being photographed or being filmed. Public self-awareness is associated with evaluation apprehension. When people are the focus of other's attention, they realise they are being appraised by those observers.

The fear of a negative evaluation can lead to nervousness and a loss of self-esteem, particularly if a person's perceived actual public image does not match their desired public image. Finally, in contrast to the effects of private self-awareness, public self-awareness leads to adherence to social standards of behaviour; people who are aware of the perceptions of others, for example their social group, are more likely to conform to group norms, even if this does not match their private point of view.

THEORIES OF SELF-CONCEPT MAINTENANCE

Having identified when and why we are likely to become self-aware, the consequences of self-awareness, and how knowledge about the self is organized in our minds, we now turn to how self-schemas develop. What is the content of our self-schemas, and why do we come to view ourselves in the way that we do? We discuss six theories that explain how our self-concept is managed and maintained. These are control theory of self regulation, self-discrepancy theory, social comparison theory, self-evaluation maintenance, social identity theory and self-categorization theory. All of these theories propose that how we define the self and how it subsequently affects our behaviour depend largely upon how the self compares to a particular point of comparison. There are three types of comparative theory which each focus on a different target of comparison. The self can be compared to perceptions of how the self should be, to other individuals, or to other groups.

THEORIES OF SELF-COMPARISON

Many social psychologists believe that people form a sense of self from a comparison process. The first class of these comparison theories focuses on comparing the self with ... the self. This is not as strange as it might first appear. People have different versions of the self. They can, for instance, know how they actually are, but also have an idea of what how they would like to be. Two theories fall into this category: control theory of self-regulation and self-discrepancy theory. Both theories argue that when people are self-aware, they can think about whether they are the sort of person they want to be or whether there are ways in which they would like to change.

CONTROL THEORY OF SELF-REGULATION

Carver and Scheier proposed that through self-awareness we are able to assess whether or not we are meeting our goals. The central element of the control theory of self-regulation is a cognitive feedback loop which shows four steps involved in self-Regulation; Test, Operate, Test, and Exit. In the first test phase, people compare the self against one of two standards. People who are privately self-aware compare themselves against a private standard, such as the values we believe to be important. In contrast, people who are publicly self-aware compare themselves against a public standard, for example the values held by our friends and family. If someone believes they are failing to meet the relevant standard, they put into operation a change in behaviour in order to meet this standard. When they next self-reflect on that issue, they re-test themselves, comparing their self to their values or the values of others for a second time. If the self still falls short of the standard, the feedback loop will repeat itself. If, however, the self and the standard are now in line with one another, the individual will exit the feedback loop.

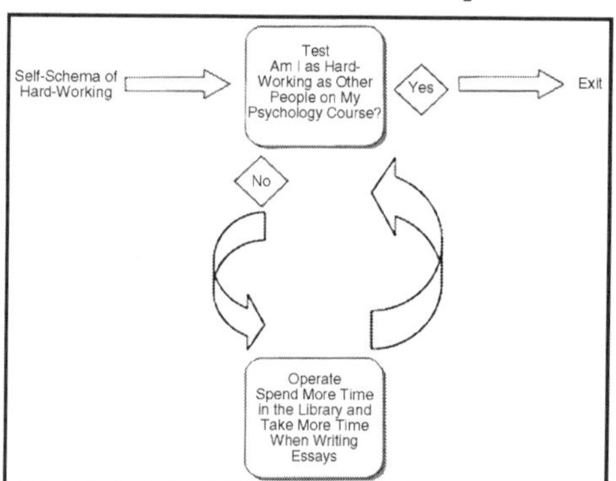

Fig. Carver and Scheier's Control Theory of Self-Regulation

The control theory of self-regulation is, on first glance, an optimistic theory, illustrating how we can improve the self through a combination of self-awareness and self-regulation. However, an intriguing study conducted by Baumeister, Bratslavsky, Muraven, and Tice showed that self-regulating one aspect of the self makes it subsequently more difficult to self-regulate other aspects of the self. Participants who had signed up to take part in a study which they were led to believe was about taste perception were instructed to make sure they had not eaten for at least Three hours when they came to the laboratory. On arrival, participants entered a room with a small oven in which chocolate chip cookies had just been baked, ensuring that the delicious aroma of chocolate and baking filled the room. They were then seated at a table which had a stack of chocolate cookies on one side and a bowl of radishes, on the other. In the radishes condition, participants were asked to eat at least two or three radishes, while in the chocolate condition, participants were asked to eat at least two or three cookies. In both conditions, participants were reminded that they should only eat the food assigned to them.

They were left for five minutes and observed through a one-way mirror to ensure that they had followed the instructions given to them by the experimenter. After completing this task, participants were asked if they minded helping out the experimenter by taking part in an unrelated experiment on problem-solving. In actual fact, this was part of the same study. Participants were instructed to complete a problemsolving task, taking as much time as they wanted, and were told that they would not be judged on how long they took, only on whether or not they managed to solve the puzzle. In reality, the task had actually been prepared so that it was impossible to solve. The dependent measure in the study was how long participants kept working on the task before giving up. Participants gave up on the problem-solving task much more quickly in the radishes condition, after an average of just 8 minutes, than in the chocolate condition, where participants spent on average 19 minutes on the task. In sum, participants who had previously had to exert self-control – by eating the radishes and ignoring the chocolate – were less able to persist on the difficult and frustrating puzzle task. On the basis of these and similar findings, Baumeister and colleagues argued that we have limited cognitive resources at our disposal to self-regulate. As a result, when we selfregulate in one domain, the resources we have left to self-regulate in another domain are temporarily depleted.

SELF-DISCREPANCY THEORY

Higgins proposed a theory which also argues that people compare the self to a relevant standard. However, self-discrepancy theory focuses not only on the awareness of discrepancies between actual and ideal identity, but also on people's emotional response to such discrepancies. Higgins argued that people possess three types of selfschema. The actual self reflects how we are at present. The ideal self is a point of reference which reflects how we would really like to be.

The ought self, in contrast, represents the traits or characteristics that an individual believes they should possess, based on a sense of duty, responsibility or obligation. People are motivated to ensure that their actual self matches their ideal and ought self; the greater the discrepancy between the actual self and a self-guide, the greater the psychological discomfort that will be experienced. To give a specific example of this, imagine that you work in a supermarket, but you are an aspiring artist. Your parents, however, are keen for you to pursue a medical career. In this case, your actual self differs from both your ideal self and your ought self.

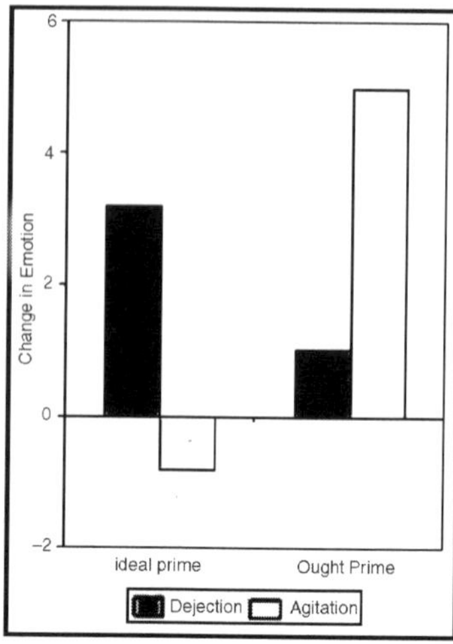

Fig. Evidence for Self-discrepancy Theory

The two types of self-discrepancy are thought to be related to unique emotional responses. An actual-ideal discrepancy is associated with the absence of positive outcomes, which results in dejection-related emotions like disappointment and sadness. Thus, if you are doing a painting on your day off from work, causing you to think about the fact that although you are a checkout assistant you would rather be a professional artist, you may feel somewhat depressed.

Actual-ought discrepancies, on the other hand, are associated with the presence of negative outcomes, which results in agitation-related emotions like anger, fear, and nervousness. So, if you visit your parents on your day off from work, this may remind you that you are failing to meet their high expectations for you to become a doctor, making you feel anxious or annoyed.

Higgins, Bond, Klein, and Strauman identified participants who had previously reported either a low or a high discrepancy between their ideal and their actual and ought selves. Several weeks later, these participants completed a task in which they either had to focus on and describe the difference between their ideal or ought self, and their actual self.

Participants with a high level of discrepancy showed an increase in dejection-related emotions after thinking about their actual-ideal discrepancies, and an increase in agitation-related emotions after thinking about their actual-ought discrepancies.

In contrast, participants with low discrepancies showed no significant changes in either emotion.

	Strategy	**Example**
1.	Exaggerate the ability of successful target	"They are more successful than me because they are a genius. But I am still really clever"

2.	Change the target of comparison	"I am much more clever and successful than many other people on my psychology course"
3.	Distance the self from successful target	"We are very different people with different interests, so I no longer sit with her in class"
4.	Devalue the dimension of comparison	"She may get better grades than me, but I have a better social life – and being popular is more important."

Self-discrepancy theory implies that by generating negative arousal, discrepancies will motivate people to reduce the discomfort they are experiencing by making changes that reduce discrepancies. However, this may not always be the case. Negative emotions often hinder successful self-regulation because if people feel upset they are more likely to give in to their immediate impulses to make themselves feel better rather than working towards a more distant goal.

For instance, if we ideally want to be slimmer than we actually are, we may reduce our calorie intake in an attempt to reduce this actual-ideal discrepancy. However, if we look in the mirror one day and are reminded of the difference that still remains between our actual self and our ideal self, we may give in to our impulses, providing ourselves with instant comfort by eating a large piece of cake. This will reduce unhappiness and discomfort in the short term, but makes our overall goal a more distant prospect.

THEORIES OF INDIVIDUAL COMPARISON

We saw how people can develop a sense of who they are from observing their own behaviour and from comparing themselves to "better" versions of the self. Social comparison theory and self-evaluation maintenance theory argue, in contrast, that we learn about the self by comparing ourselves with other individuals.

Social Comparison Theory

Social comparison theory, we learn how to define the self by comparing ourselves with those around us. Although comparing ourselves with different ideal and ought version of ourselves, and comparing ourselves with other people, are not mutually exclusive processes, there is one crucial difference. Social comparison theory argues that beliefs, feelings, and behaviours are subjective; they are, in isolation, simply the product of our own ruminations. In other words, there is no objective benchmark against which we can compare them. As such, while comparing ourselves with notions of how we should be or how we would like to be can lead to changes in the self-concept, the resulting self-definition remains subjectively defined: that is, without any feeling of external validation.

In contrast, comparing ourselves with others provides an external, objective benchmark against which to compare our thoughts, feelings and behaviours—providing people with a sense of validation for the way they are. Where behaviour is concerned, rather than always comparing the self to someone who is very similar, people may sometimes make upward comparisons or downward comparisons comparing themselves to someone who they believe to be worse than them.

People who are motivated by a desire for an accurate self-evaluation may make both upward and downward comparisons as both types of comparison are useful for deriving the most precise estimate of, for instance, academic ability. The self-evaluation maintenance model tries to explain how we maintain a positive self-esteem when comparing ourselves to others.

Self-Evaluation Maintenance Model

Imagine an acquaintance on your psychology course who always seems to get a higher grade than you on essays and projects. How would you deal with this situation? Tesser's self-evaluation maintenance model explains what we do when we are faced with someone whose success has implications for our own self-esteem.

People respond to the success of someone else in one of two ways. Social reflection is when we derive our selfesteem from the accomplishments of those who are close to us, without considering our own achievement in that domain. This may help to explain why parents are often so proud of their children's achievements. However, knowing someone who is successful can also evoke an upward social comparison, comparing our own achievements with the achievements of the target person. When someone we know is doing very well in a particular domain, what determines whether we engage in social reflection or social comparison? We are only likely to engage in social reflection with the successful individual under two conditions.

First, the domain on which the individual is successful must be irrelevant to us. When this is the case, the success of someone else does not threaten our self-concept in any way. As such, we can enjoy their success because it adds to our abilities rather than challenging them.

Second, we must be certain about our abilities in that particular domain. If we are confident that we are also very successful, the success of someone else should pose no threat to us. Instead, their success should actually add to our perception of success. If, for example, you are certain that you are excellent at psychology, the success of another student is unlikely to concern you. Instead, knowing that someone else is also very good should lead you to reflect on the fact that you are on a top psychology course where the students tend to be excellent, enhancing rather than threatening your self-concept. When the domain on which another person is successful is relevant, however, this evokes an upward comparison. If the success of the other person is on a dimension that is important to how we see the self, this will challenge our view of the self as being successful on this domain and will have a negative impact on our self-esteem.

Uncertainty about our own abilities will also evoke an upward comparison. If we are uncertain about our own abilities and we are then confronted by someone who is very able on a particular domain, this is likely to further increase our uncertainty in our own abilities. Again, this is likely to have a negative impact on our self-esteem.

In sum, when we compare ourselves to a successful person on a domain that is relevant to our self-concept but on which we are uncertain about our own abilities, we are making an upward comparison which can have a detrimental effect on our self-esteem. But how can we maintain a positive self-concept in such circumstances? The self-evaluation maintenance model, we have four strategies at our disposal. *First*, we can exaggerate the ability of the person who is outperforming us. In the case of the clever psychology student, if you reclassify that student as "a genius", the comparison is no longer relevant—the student is essentially in a different league from you.

Second, we can switch the target of comparison to someone who we know to be less successful than us, creating a downward comparison that is good for self-esteem. So, you might compare yourself to someone else on your psychology course who generally does less well on essays and exams than you do. By making this new and different comparison, it is now you who is the success.

Third, we can downplay our similarity to the target of comparison or physically and emotionally distance ourselves from them. You might, for example, stop sitting with or talking to the clever student.

Fourth and *finally*, we can maintain positive self-esteem by devaluing the dimension of comparison. You might, for example, argue that academic success is not important to you, but that having a good social life is much more important.

THEORIES OF GROUP COMPARISON

Although early researchers investigating the self perceived the self to be a unique identity which we share with no-one else, social psychologists now have a more flexible notion of the self. The self-concept is thought to be made up of many selfschemas, some of which reflect individual aspects of the self, such as personality, but others which reflect our relationships with family, friends, and social groups.

Although in combination these self-schemas make us unique because no other person is likely to have exactly the same configuration, we certainly share aspects of our identity with others. More broadly, being either female or male is part of all of our self-concepts, but it is a part that we share with millions of other people. Brewer and Gardner proposed three types of self that reflect these shared and non-shared aspects.

The individual self consists of attributes and personality traits that differentiate us from other individuals. The relational self is defined by our relationships with significant others. Finally, the collective self reflects our membership in social groups. We focus on the collective self, and how our membership in social groups contributes towards the definition of our self-concept.

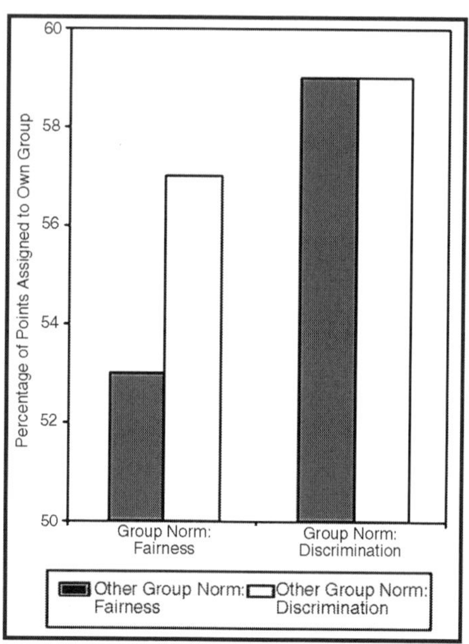

Fig. The Effect of Group Norms on Behaviour When Social Identity is Salient

Social Identity Approach

Aspects of the self, just as to social identity theory can be divided into those that reflect our personal identity and those that reflect our social identity. Personal identities are those that reflect idiosyncratic aspects of the self, such as personality traits. In contrast, our social identity reflects the broader social groups to which we belong. The organization of our self-schemas means that each identity we hold is associated with a range of associated concepts that guide our thoughts, feelings and behaviour. However, given that we hold many different identities it would be impossible, and indeed impractical, for us to use every identity to guide our behaviour. Instead, our sense of self at any particular point in time depends upon which of our many personal or social identities is psychological salient. Which identity is salient at any given time depends on the context. Imagine, for example, that you are chatting to a close friend on your college campus. At this point in time, it is your personal identity that is likely to be salient, as you talk about your personal experiences with another individual. Imagine now that you arrive at the college soccer pitch to watch a match between your college and a rival college. Because you are here to support your college team, your social identity as a member of that college will now be salient.

Each social identity is associated with a range of attributes that characterize the prototypical group member. They are also associated with a set of group norms a collection of shared beliefs about how group members should think and behave. Self-categorization theory is an extension of social identity theory that focuses on the set of group norms that define collective identities. When an individual's social identity becomes salient, their perceptions of themselves and others become depersonalized.

In other words, rather than seeing themselves as a unique individual, they will perceive themselves more in terms of the shared features that define group membership, thinking and behaving more in line with the norms of that group. Group members also obey what is referred to as the meta-contrast principle, which means that they exaggerate similarities within the group and differences with other groups. Jetten, Spears, and Manstead showed the effect of social identity on adherence to group norms.

Participants first had their social identity made salient by being told they were being assigned to one of two groups, based on the technique they had used during an initial task in which they were required to estimate the number of dots on a computer screen. To increase identification with their group, they then took part in what they believed was a "group task", although in actual fact there were no other group members. In this task, they estimated the number of black squares appearing on a screen and were given false feedback about the estimates of three other group members. They were then asked to distribute money between members of their own group and members of another group. To manipulate the group norm, participants learned that 10 out of 15 members of their group who had already taken part in the study had either distributed money equally between the two groups or had given more money to their own group.

The norm of the other group was also manipulated, so that participants believed that the other group tended to distribute money equally or fairly. Participants were strongly influenced by the norms of their own group, giving a greater proportion of money to members of their own group when there was a norm of discrimination but distributing money more equally between the two groups when there was a group norm of fairness. In contrast, they paid somewhat less attention to the norms of the other group.

There are many real-life examples of how group norms can affect our attitudes and behaviour. People who are normally perfectly reasonable and non-violent sometimes become aggressive and anti-social when they act as a group member rather than as an individual. A clear example of this is the fights and riots that sometimes erupt at football matches between the supporters of different teams. Similarly, research has shown that women perform more poorly on maths tests than men when their gender identity is made salient because they conform to the negative stereotypes associated with their group membership.

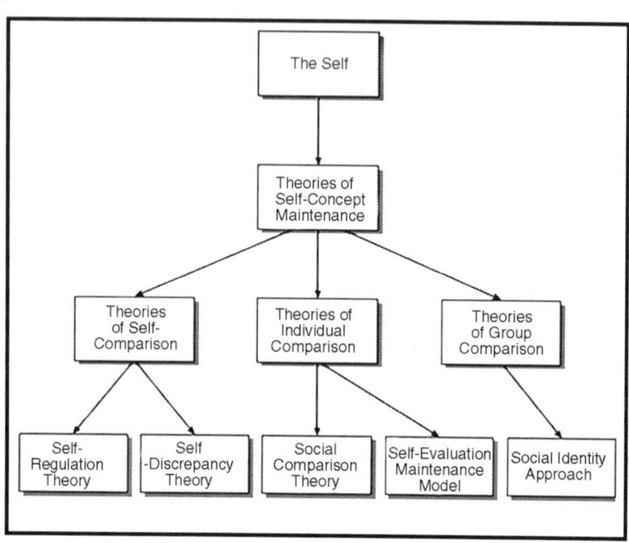

SELF-MOTIVES

Give that the self-concept is central to every individual, guiding attitudes and behaviour and determining whether people feel positive or negative about themselves, we might expect it to be a key guiding principle in motivating our behaviour. We discuss three of these motivations.

- *First,* we hold a motive for self-assessment, a desire to know who we truly are, regardless of whether the truth is positive or negative. We are motivated to have an accurate self-perception to reduce uncertainty about our abilities or personal characteristics. For this reason, people like to complete diagnostic tests, which evaluate the performance of an individual and distinguish their performance from the performance of others, when evaluating the self.
- *Second,* we are motivated to seek information that enables self-verification. Put another way, we want to confirm what we already believe to be true about our self-concept, even if we see ourselves in a negative light. If our search for information confirms what we already believe, this reassures us that we have an accurate self-perception and provides us with a sense of security and stability. To demonstrate the self-verification motivation, Swann, Stein-Seroussi, and Giesler asked people who had either a positive or a negative self-concept

whether they would prefer to interact with evaluators who had a favourable impression of them, or an unfavourable impression of them. They found that people with a positive self-concept were more likely to choose the evaluator who viewed them positively, but people with a negative self-concept tended to choose the evaluator who viewed them negatively.

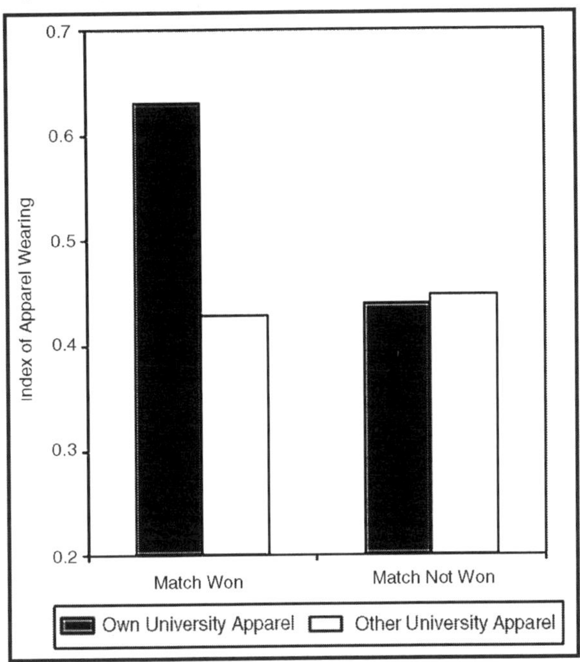

Fig. Basking in Reflected Glory

- *Third*, we have a motivation for self-enhancement, a desire to seek out information about ourselves that allows us to see the self in a positive light. Which of these three motives are the most important for guiding people's behaviour? This is not such an easy question, because the three can be somewhat contradictory, particularly for people with lower self-esteem. Self-enhancement would involve looking for positive self-knowledge whereas self-verification would involve seeking out negative self-knowledge. However, some research has suggested that individuals with lower self-esteem seek a compromise between these two motives, seeking out individuals who make them feel better about themselves without completely disconfirming their existing negative self-concept. Despite some inventive compromises to enable people to satisfy all three motives, ultimately one appears to come out on top. Sedikides conducted a series of studies in which the motives of self-assessment, self-verification and self-enhancement were pitted against each other.

Participants completed a self-reflection task in which they could pick questions to ask themselves in order to learn what sort of person they were. Participants' strongest tendency was to ask themselves questions that focused on positive rather than negative aspects of the self. They were much less likely to ask themselves questions that focused on core aspects of themselves that they already know a lot about or peripheral aspects of themselves that they didn't know much about. In sum, self-enhancement appears to be the most powerful self-motive. As such, it has received most of the attention of researchers seeking to understand how self-motives shape our behaviours.

SELF-ENHANCEMENT

Why is self-enhancement so important to us? It is clear from the work on self-esteem discussed earlier that it is adaptive to have high self-esteem, provided it is not too high, and is stable rather than extreme and unstable. We self-regulate more effectively, and therefore cope with negative and positive life events in a more constructive way, when we have high self-esteem. But, given its usefulness, how can we maintain positive self-esteem? The types of strategies employed can be divided into two broad classes, depending on whether they involve deriving a positive self-concept from personal or social aspects of the self.

Strategies to Enhance the Personal Self

Self-affirmation theory when self-esteem has been damaged or threatened in some way, people often compensate by focusing on and publicly affirming positive aspects of themselves, thereby allowing them to maintain a positive self-concept. Steele demonstrated this effect in a study conducted among Mormon women, for whom community cooperation is an important ethic. These participants were first rung by a researcher who claimed she was conducting a poll. In the self-concept threat condition, the researcher commented that Mormons were typically uncooperative with community projects, whilst in the self-concept irrelevant threat condition they were told that Mormons were typically unconcerned with driver safety and care.

Finally, in a self-concept affirmation condition participants were told that Mormons were typically cooperative with community projects. Two days later, participants received an apparently unrelated phone call from a researcher posing as a member of the local community asking them if they would be willing to list the contents of their kitchen as part of some research to help develop a community food cooperative.

Steele found that compared to 65 per cent who agreed to help in the self-concept affirmation condition, approximately 95 per cent of participants in both threat conditions agreed to help. Presumably participants who felt threatened wanted to reaffirm a positive aspect of their self-concept, and did so by publicly demonstrating their community spirit. Another phenomenon that highlights people's tendency to self-enhance is the self-serving attribution bias.

There is considerable evidence that when people are making attributions about themselves on the basis of their behaviour, they show self-serving biases. When we are successful, we tend to show a self-enhancing bias, attributing our success to internal characteristics; for example, we might think "I got an A grade in the examination because I am clever". When we fail, however, we tend to show a self-protecting bias, attributing our failure to external characteristics. We might, for example, think "I got a D grade because I wasn't feeling well on the day of the examination". People also have a memory bias in favour of self-enhancing information. Mischel, Ebbesen, and Zeiss exposed participants to an equal amount of positive and negative information about their personality and then tested their memory of that information.

They found that participants had better memory for the positive information than for the negative information. Other research suggests that people are more critical of information that criticises them than information that praises them. Wyer and Frey had participants complete an intelligence test and then gave them either positive or negative feedback. Participants were then given the opportunity to read a report on the validity of intelligence tests which contained a mix of supportive and critical information. Participants who had been told they had performed poorly subsequently judged intelligence tests to be less valid than did participants who had received positive feedback.

Strategies to Enhance the Social Self

In addition to these individual self-enhancement strategies, people also derive a positive self-image from their group memberships. The social identity approach when people's social self is salient, they incorporate in their selfconcept any traits that are thought to be part of the group, regardless of whether those traits are positive or negative.

It is therefore understandably important to group members that their group is evaluated positively. In the same way that people try to maintain a positive personal identity by comparing themselves favourably to other individuals group members are also motivated to hold a positive social or collective identity. They do so by comparing themselves favourably with members of other groups. The desire to maintain a positive social identity can explain why group members show ingroup bias, a preference for their own group over outgroups, groups to which they do not belong. By expressing how good your group is compared to others, by implication, the self as a group member reaps the benefits of this positive intergroup comparison. Given the importance of the link between the self and the ingroup, but not the outgroup, in promoting disharmony between groups, some researchers have focused on the self as a way of improving intergroup relations.

In particular, if it is the absence of a link between the self and outgroup that is partly responsible for intergroup bias then perhaps forging such links can reduce such bias. So the groups to which we belong can provide an important source of self-esteem, and we are motivated to create a positive image of them because this then reflects well on us. But our ingroups can sometimes be seen as either positive or negative, depending upon factors beyond our control.

Under these circumstances, group members use a number of strategies to both maintain a positive social identity and buffer themselves from the potentially damaging self-esteem implications of being a member of a low status group. It is easy for high status groups to maintain a positive social identity because they can compare themselves favourably with low status groups.

However, low status group members have to resort to other strategies, particularly if they are not willing or able to leave their group to join a higher status group. They may attempt a social change strategy, where they compete with the high status group to improve their status relative to that group. Alternatively, they may attempt a social creativity strategy, finding new dimensions on which they compare more favourably.

Members of a college that is academically poor, for example, may maintain a positive social identity when being compared to a top academic college by saying that they are better at sport, or throw better parties. Finally, members of low status groups may simply dis-identify with the group, disregarding that membership as an important part of their identity.

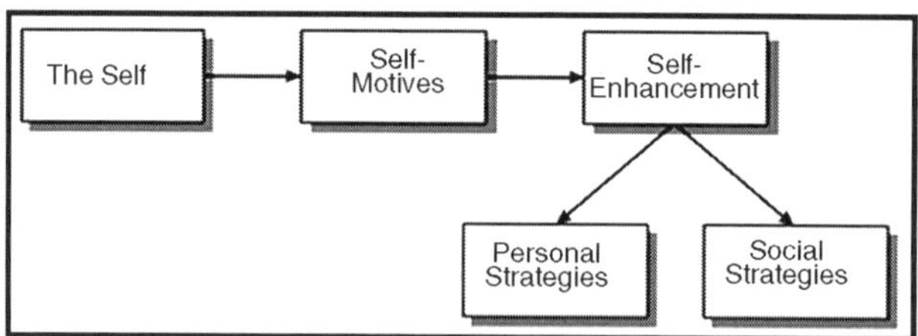

Fig. Memory Map

Robert Cialdini and colleagues showed this dis-identification strategy when they investigated the behaviour of fans of college American football teams. During the 1973 collegiate football season, students at seven universities were covertly monitored every Monday during an introductory psychology class.

The proportion of students at the class wearing apparel that identified their university name, insignia or emblem was recorded. Researchers then considered whether students' apparel differed depending on whether their university's football team had won or not won at the weekend. Students wore more apparel that displayed the name or insignia of their university when their university football team had been recently successful than when their team had not been successful. Cialdini *et al*. called *this phenomenon basking in reflected glory*. Essentially, people derive a positive self-concept from the achievements of other group members even if they were not personally instrumental in those achievements. When one's group is performing poorly, however, group members often use a very different strategy, which is showed by the lack of apparel seen in Cialdini's study when the team had lost.

SELF-ESTEEM

The amount of time we spend thinking about the self and comparing it to others it is not surprising that the self has an important evaluative component. We not only think about what our self-concept is, but also whether aspects of our self-concept are positive or negative. An individual's self-esteem is their subjective appraisal of themselves as intrinsically positive or negative and can have significant implications for psychological functioning.

Our level of self-esteem inevitably varies from time to time, depending on the context we find ourselves in. Getting a good mark for your psychology coursework is likely to elevate your self-esteem; getting a poor mark is likely to depress it.

However, it is quite easy to bring to mind some people who always seem to be self-confident and others who display more self-doubt and pessimism about their lives. We talk about such chronic individual differences in self-esteem, how they develop and what consequences they have.

DEVELOPMENT OF SELF-ESTEEM

How positive our self-concept is in later life appears to depend, at least to some extent, on the parenting style of our primary caregivers. There are three parenting styles which differ on two dimensions: how demanding and how responsive the parent is towards the child. Children with the highest self-esteem are typically brought up by authoritative parents. This type of parent has a style high on both of these dimensions. They place a lot of demands on their child, imposing rules on them and disciplining them for disobedience.

However, they are also responsive, supportive and warm. Children with lower self-esteem and less confidence in their abilities are often brought up with one of two less effective styles of parenting. Authoritarian parents are overly strict and demanding, failing to be responsive to the child's needs. At the opposite end of the spectrum, permissive parents are responsive, but not strict enough, indulging their child's every desire. Although the level of chronic self-esteem people have may be determined during childhood, a meta-analysis of 50 self-esteem studies conducted by Robins and colleagues showed that over the course of people's lifespan general tendencies to have either high or low self-esteem can vary.

They found that self-esteem among children aged between 6 and 11 was relatively unstable. This may be because young children are still in the process of developing their self-concept. Self-esteem was most stable among people in their 20s and remained relatively stable until mid-adulthood, probably because by this point in time, people have a fully developed sense of self and are less affected by temporary life changes. By the age of 60, however, self-esteem stability declines. Trzesniewski and colleagues explained that this might reflect the life changes that occur later in life, for example, retirement, declining health and the death of others from their generation.

CONSEQUENCES OF SELF-ESTEEM

Many researchers have investigated the consequences of having low or high self-esteem. However, before we go any further, it is important to note that a review by Baumeister and colleagues showed that the "low self-esteem" individuals in most studies do not have low levels of self-esteem in absolute terms. Instead, they simply have lower selfesteem, in relative terms, compared to high self-esteem individuals. Nevertheless, as we shall see, there is evidence that people with lower self-esteem deal with life events quite differently from individuals with higher self-esteem.

Mood Regulation

There is a general assumption that everyone wants to feel positive about themselves and their lives and, to this end, do everything possible to maintain a positive outlook. However, recent research by Joanne Wood and her colleague indicates that people with lower self-esteem are less likely to make the effort to feel good than people with higher self-esteem.

Two studies succinctly demonstrate how people with higher and lower self-esteem differ in their reactions to positive and negative life events. Wood, Heimpel, and Michela recorded participants' memories of positive events. They found that people with lower self-esteem were more likely to "dampen" the good feelings they experienced, by distracting themselves, trying to make themselves feel less good, and trying to calm themselves, than were people with higher self-esteem.

Heimpel, Wood, Marshall, and Brown got participants who had reported a failure in their everyday life to list their immediate plans and reasons for those plans. Participants with lower self-esteem were less likely to express goals to improve their mood than were participants higher in self-esteem. Heimpel and colleagues also found that having a goal to improve one's mood was associated with a greater improvement in mood the following day.

Together, these findings indicate that people with lower self-esteem make less effort to regulate their mood; they do not try and maintain a good mood after a positive life event, neither are they motivated to elevate their mood after a negative life event. These findings demonstrate that having lower self-esteem can be maladaptive, and explain why people with lower selfesteem tend to feel worse than those with higher self-esteem after a negative event.

Narcissism

One of the major criticisms of the study of self-esteem has been the over-emphasis on the negative consequences of lower self-esteem. Clearly, having lower self-esteem can be maladaptive for that individual. However, lower self-esteem is also frequently cited as an antecedent of anti-social behaviour, including the violent behaviour of youth gangs, perpetrators of domestic violence, armed robbers, murderers and terrorists.

Despite these claims, there is actually very little supportive evidence for this. Baumeister, Smart, and Boden put forward the alternative argument that it is in fact higher self-esteem that is associated with higher levels of aggression and violence, although only under certain circumstances. Specifically, they proposed that people with higher self-esteem who have their ego threatened in some way, for example someone contradicting their viewpoint or their positive self-appraisal, will react aggressively to defend their higher self-esteem.

Clearly, not all people with higher self-esteem behave aggressively when they feel threatened, so what determines who becomes aggressive? It seems that individuals who respond with aggression to an ego-threat are narcissistic. In other words, they tend to have extremely high self-esteem, believing that they are somehow special and superior to others, but at the same time, their self-esteem is unstable. As a result, they are reliant on validation from others in order to maintain their fragile positive self-concept.

This may explain why criticism may generate such an explosive response from these individuals. In contrast, people with normal, stable higher levels of self-esteem are typically no more aggressive than individuals with lower self-esteem. Bushman and Baumeister showed the relationship between narcissism and the tendency to be aggressive. Participants were told they were taking part in a study on how people respond to feedback from others and that they would be working with another participant.

They then wrote a one paragraph essay which was subsequently taken away to be shown to the other participant. Participants marked and gave feedback on the essay of the "other participant" and were then given feedback on their own essay, supposedly from that other participant. In the praise condition, participants were given positive ratings and the comment "Great essay!", whilst in the threat condition, they were given negative ratings and the comment "This is one of the worst essays I have read!" Finally, participants were told that they would take part in a competitive reaction time task with the other participant, in which they would have to press a button as fast as possible on each trial. Whoever failed the trial would then receive a blast of noise from the other participant, which could be varied in intensity, and which therefore determined how much discomfort it would cause the recipient.

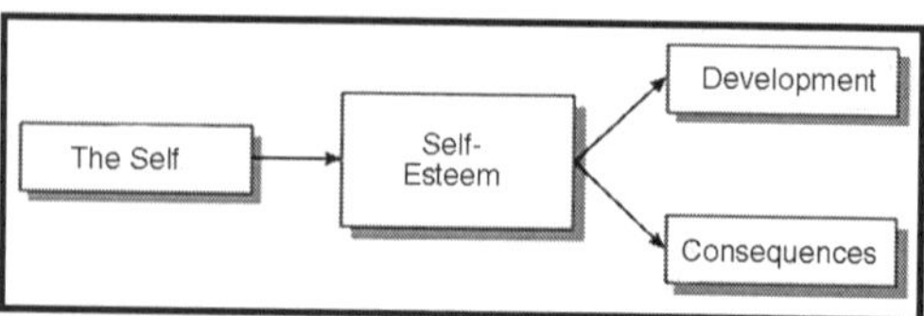

There was a positive relationship between narcissism and aggression but this relationship was particularly strong when there was an ego threat. In other words, individuals higher in narcissism were even more aggressive than individuals lower in narcissism when they felt their ego was threatened.

5

Non-Formal Education and Extension Education

FORMAL EDUCATION

A formal education programme is the process of training and developing people in knowledge, skills, mind, and character in a structured and certified programme.

SYSTEMS OF FORMAL EDUCATION

Education is a concept, referring to the process in which students can learn something:

- Instruction refers to the facilitating of learning towards identified objectives, delivered either by an instructor or other forms.
- Teaching refers to the actions of a real live instructor designed to impart learning to the student.
- Learning refers to learning with a view towards preparing learners with specific knowledge, skills, or abilities that can be applied immediately upon completion.

PRESCHOOL EDUCATION

Preschool education or Infant education is the provision of education for children before the commencement of statutory and obligatory education, usually between the ages of zero or three and five, depending on the jurisdiction. In British English, nursery school or simply "nursery" or playgroup is the usual term for preschool education. In the United States preschool and Pre-K are used, while "nursery school" is an older term. Preschool work is organized within a framework that professional educators create. The framework includes structural, process and alignment components that are associated with each individual unique child that has both social and academic outcomes. Arguably the first pre-school institution was opened in 1816 by Robert Owen in New Lanark, Scotland. The Hungarian countess Theresa Brunszvik followed in 1828.

In 1837, Friedrich Fröbel opened one in Germany, coining the term "kindergarten".

Developmental Areas

The areas of development which preschool education covers varies from country to country. However, the following main themes are represented in the majority of systems.

- Personal, social, economical, and emotional development
- Communication, including sign language, talking and listening
- Knowledge and understanding of the world
- Creative and aesthetic development
- Educational software
- Mathematical awareness and development
- Physical development
- Playing
- Self-help skills
- Social skills

Allowing preschool aged children to discover and explore freely within each of these areas of development is the foundation for developmental learning. While the National Association for the Education of Young Children and the National Association of Child Care Professionals have made tremendous strides in publicizing and promoting the idea of developmentally appropriate practice, there is still much work to be done. It is widely recognized that although many preschool educators are aware of the guidelines for developmentally appropriate practice, putting this practice to work effectively in the classroom is more challenging. The NAEYC published that although 80% of Kindergarten classrooms claim to be developmentally appropriate, only 20% actually are.

Age and Importance

Preschool is generally considered appropriate for children between zero or three and five years of age, between the baby or toddler and school stages. During this stage of development, children learn and assimilate information rapidly, and express interest and fascination in each new discovery. It is well established that the most important years of learning are begun at birth.

A child's brain at this age is making connections that will last the rest of their life. During these early years, a human being is capable of absorbing more information at a time than they will ever be able to again. The environment of the young child influences the development of cognitive skills and emotional skills due to the rapid brain growth that occurs in the early years.

Studies have shown that high quality preschools have a short and long term effect in improving the outcomes of a child, especially a disadvantaged child. However, some more recent studies dispute the accuracy of the earlier results which cited benefits to preschool education, and actually point at preschool being detrimental to a child's cognitive and social development. A study by UC Berkeley and Stanford University on 14,000 Kindergarteners revealed that while there is a temporary cognitive boost in pre-reading and math, preschool holds detrimental effects on social development and cooperation. The Universal Preschool movement is an international effort to make access to preschool available to families in a similar way to compulsory primary education. Various jurisdictions and advocates have differing priorities for access, availability and funding sources. There has been a shift from preschools that operated primarily as controlled play groups to educational settings in which children learn specific, if basic, skills. It examines several different perspectives on teaching in kindergarten, including those of the developmentally appropriate practice, the academic approach, the child-centered approach, and the Montessori approach to the curriculum.

Gratuity

The gratuity of infant education has been established in some countries, as Spain, beginning in the second cycle but extending to the first cycle.

Methods of Preschool Education

Some preschools have adopted specialized methods of teaching, such as Montessori, Waldorf, Head Start, HighReach Learning, High Scope, The Creative Curriculum, Reggio Emilia approach, Bank Street, Forest kindergartens, and various other pedagogies which contribute to the foundation of education. Creative Curriculum has an interactive web site where parents and teachers can work together in evaluating preschool age children. The web site is very user friendly and prints off many reports that are helpful in evaluating children and the classroom itself.

The web site has a variety of activities that are targeted to each of the fifty goals on the continuum. The International Preschool Curriculum adopted a bilingual approach to teaching and offers a curriculum that embraces international standards and recognizes national requirements for preschool education. In the United States most preschool advocates support the National Association for the Education of Young Children's Developmentally Appropriate Practices. Family childcare can also be nationally accredited by the National Association of Family Childcare if the provider chooses to go through the process. National accreditation is only awarded to those programmes who demonstrate the quality standards set forth by the NAFCC.

Funding for Preschool Programmes

While a majority of American preschool programmes remain tuition-based, support for some public funding of early childhood education has grown over the years. As of 2008, 38 states and the District of Columbia invested in at least some pre-kindergarten programmes, and many school districts were providing preschool services on their own, using local and federal funds. The benefits and challenges of a public preschool are closely tied to the amount of funding provided. Funding for a public preschool can come in a variety of sources. According to Levin and Schwartz funding can range from federal, state, local public allocations, private sources, and parental fees. The problem of funding a public preschool occurs not only from limited sources but from the cost per child. The average cost across the 48 states is $6,582.

There are four categories that determine the costs of public preschools: personnel ratios, personnel qualifications, facilities and transportation, and health and nutrition services. According to Levin and Schwartz these structural elements depend heavily on the cost and quality of services provided. The main personnel factor related to cost is the qualifications each preschool require for a teacher. Another determinate of cost is the length of a preschool day. The longer the session, the more increase in cost. Therefore, the quality of programme accounts presumably for a major component of cost. Collaboration has been a solution for funding issues in several districts. Wilma Kaplan, principal, turned to collaborating with the area Head Start and other private preschool to fund a public preschool in her district. "We're very pleased with the interaction. It's really added a dimension to our programme that's been very positive". The National Head Start Bureau has been looking for more opportunities to partner with public schools. Torn Schultz of the National Head Start Bureau states, "We're turning to partnership as much as possible, either in funds or facilities to make sure children get everything necessary to be ready for school". The goal for funding is to develop a variety of sources that provide for all children to benefit from early learning within a public preschool.

Special Education in Preschool

In the United States, students who may benefit from special education receive services in preschools. Since the inception of the Individuals with Disabilities Education Act Public Law 101-476 in 1975 and its amendments, PL 102-119 and PL 105-17 in 1997, the educational system has moved away from self-contained classrooms and progressed to inclusion. As a result, there has been a need for special education teachers to practice in various settings in order to assist children with special needs, particularly by working with regular classroom teachers when possible to strengthen the inclusion of children with special needs. As with other stages in the life of a child with special needs, the Individualized Education Plan or an Individual Family Service Plan is an important way for special education teachers, regular classroom teachers, administrators and parents to set guidelines for a partnership to help the child succeed in preschool.

PRIMARY EDUCATION

Primary education is the first stage of compulsory education. It is preceded by pre-school or nursery education and is followed by secondary education. In North America this stage of education is usually known as elementary education and is generally followed by middle school. In most countries, it is compulsory for children to receive primary education, though in many jurisdictions it is permissible for parents to provide it. The transition to secondary school or high school is somewhat arbitrary, but it generally occurs at about eleven or twelve years of age.

Some educational systems have separate middle schools with the transition to the final stage of education taking place at around the age of fourteen. The major goals of primary education are achieving basic literacy and numeracy amongst all pupils, as well as establishing foundations in science, mathematics, geography, history and other social sciences. The relative priority of various areas, and the methods used to teach them, are an area of considerable political debate. Typically, primary education is provided in schools, where the child will stay in steadily advancing classes until they complete it and move on to high school/secondary school.

Children are usually placed in classes with one teacher who will be primarily responsible for their education and welfare for that year. This teacher may be assisted to varying degrees by specialist teachers in certain subject areas, often music or physical education. The continuity with a single teacher and the opportunity to build up a close relationship with the class is a notable feature of the primary education system. Traditionally, various forms of corporal punishment have been an integral part of early education. Recently this practice has come under attack, and in many cases been outlawed, especially in Western countries. The National Council of Educational Research and Training is the apex body for school education in India. The NCERT provides support and technical assistance to a number of schools in India and oversees many aspects of enforcement of education policies. In India, the various bodies governing school education system are:

- The state government boards, in which the majority of Indian children are enrolled.
- The Central Board of Secondary Education board.
- The Council for the Indian School Certificate Examinations board.
- The National Institute of Open Schooling.
- International schools affiliated to the International Baccalaureate Programme and/or the Cambridge International Examinations.
- Islamic Madrasah schools, whose boards are controlled by local state governments, or autonomous, or affiliated with Darul Uloom Deoband.
- Autonomous schools like Woodstock School, Auroville, Patha Bhavan and Ananda Marga Gurukula.

Primary school teaching in India consists of 12 grade levels. These are:

- Kindergarten: nursery - 3 years, Lower Kindergarten (LKG) -4 years, Upper Kindergarten (UKG) - 5 years
- 1st class: 6 years
- 2nd class: 7 years
- 3rd class: 8 years
- 4th class: 9 years
- 5th class: 10 years
- 6th class: 11 years
- 7th class: 12 years
- 8th class: 13 years
- 9th class: 14 years
- 10th class: 15 years
- 11th class: 16 years
- 12th class: 17 years

SECONDARY EDUCATION

Secondary education is the stage of education following primary school. Secondary education is generally the final stage of compulsory education. However, secondary education in some countries includes a period of compulsory and a period of non-compulsory education. The next stage of education is usually college or university. Secondary education is characterized by transition from the typically compulsory, comprehensive primary education for minors to the optional, selective tertiary, "post-secondary", or "higher" education for adults. Depending on the system, schools for this period or a part of it may be called secondary schools, high schools, gymnasia, lyceums, middle schools, colleges, vocational schools and preparatory schools, and the exact meaning of any of these varies between the systems.

In India

In India, Before The Indian Constitutional Amendment in 2002, Article 45 of the Constitution was- "Art.45. Provision for free and compulsory education for children.—The State shall endeavour to provide,within a period of ten years from the commencement of this Constitution, for free and compulsory education for all children until they complete the age of fourteen years." But that Constitutional obligation was time and again deferred - first to 1970 and then to 1980,1990 and 2000. The 10th Five-year Plan visualizes that India will achieve the Universal Elementary Education by 2007. However, the Union Human Resource Development Minister announced in 2001 that India will achieve this target only by 2010. Bill, 2002, renumbered as the Constitution Act, 2002, which was passed on 12 Dec 2002 stated: An Act further to amend the Constitution of India. BE it enacted by Parliament in the Fifty-third Year of the Republic of

India as follows:- 1. Short title and commencement. This Act may be called the Constitution Act, 2002. It shall come into force on such date as the Central Government may, by notification in the Official Gazette, appoint. 2. Insertion of new article 21A.- After article 21 of the Constitution, the following article shall be inserted, namely Right to education.- "Art.21A. The State shall provide free and compulsory education to all children of the age of six to fourteen years in such manner as the State may, by law, determine.". 3. Substitution of new article for article 45.- For article 45 of the Constitution, the following article shall be substituted, namely:- Provision for early childhood care and education to children below the age of six years.

"Art.45. The State shall endeavour to provide early childhood care and education for all children until they complete the age of six years.". 4. Amendment of article 51A. - In article 51A of the Constitution, after clause (J), the following clause shall be added, namely:- "Art.(k) who is a parent or guardian to provide opportunities for education to his child or, as the case may be, ward between the age of six and fourteen years.". On the basis of Constitutional mandate provided in Article 41, 45, 46, 21A and various judgments of Supreme Court the Government of India has taken several steps to eradicate illiteracy, improvement the quality of education and make children back to school who left the school for one or the reasons. Some of these programmes are National Technology Mission, District Primary Education Programme, and Nutrition Support for Primary Education, National Open School, Mid- Day Meal Scheme, Sarva Siksha Abhiyan and other state specific initiatives.

Besides, this several states have enacted legislation to provide free and compulsory primary education such as- the Kerala Education Act 1959, the Punjab Primary Education Act 1960, the Gujarat Compulsory Primary Education Act 1961, U.P. Basic Education Act 1972, Rajasthan Primary Education Act 1964, etc. However, the Constitution of India and Supreme Court have declared that the education is now a fundamental right of the people of India,

Historical background

India has a long tradition of organized education. As a historian has put it, "There is no other country where the love of learning had so early an origin or has exercised so lasting and powerful an influence." However, educational effort in the country has come a long way from this traditional position in its definition, coverage as well as impact. The current educational system in the country operates in an altogether different context from the classical past. The country's commitment to the provision of education for all and its endeavor to achieve this goal in a speedy fashion has to be seen in this complex milieu within which the educational system is currently functioning. As the veteran educationist Shri J.P.Naik put it: "The Indian Society, especially the Hindu Society has been extremely inegalitarian, and this is the one value on the basis of which the society can be humanized and strengthened. In fact, the issue is so crucial that the Indian society cannot even hope to survive except on the basis of an egalitarian reorganization". Between 1813 and 1921, the British administrators laid the foundations of the modern educational system. The principal positive contribution of the British administrators to equality was to give all citizens open access to educational institutions maintained from or supported by public funds. For instance, the worst difficulties were perhaps encountered when the problem of educating the "untouchable" castes came up. The first test case arose in 1856 when a boy from an untouchable caste applied for admission to the government school at Dharwar.

He was refused admission on the ground that it would result in the withdrawal of all the caste Hindu children from the school and thus in the closure of the school itself. But the decision was sharply criticized by the Governor General of India as well as by the Court of Directors in the East India Company and a clear policy was laid down that no untouchable child should be refused admission to a government school even if it meant the closure of the school. The British administrators thus established, firmly and unequivocally, the right of every child irrespective of caste, sex or traditional taboos, to seek admission to all schools supported or aided by public funds. The British administrators refused to accept the principle of compulsory elementary education. The Indian nationalist thought, however, was firmly of the view that the provision of equality of educational opportunity must include a certain minimum general education to be provided to all children on a free and compulsory basis.

A demand that four years of compulsory education should be provided to all children was put forward, for the first time before the Indian Education Commission by the Grand Old Man of India, Dadabhai Naoroji in 1881. Gopal Krishna Gokhale who moved a resolution on the subject in the Central Legislative Assembly in 1910 and again took the proposal vide a bill in 1912, neither of which achieved their objective. At this stage, it is illuminating to read the then announced Indian Educational Policy, In 1913. It begins as under: "His Most Gracious Imperial Majesty the King Emperor, in replying to the address of the Calcutta University on the 6th January 1912, said: -

- "It is my wish that there may be spread over the land a network of schools and colleges from which will go forth loyal and manly and useful citizens, able to hold their own in industries and agriculture and all the vocations in life. And it is my wish too, that the homes of my Indian subjects may be brightened and their labour sweetened by the spread of knowledge with all that follows in its train, a higher level of thought, comfort and of health. It is through education that my wish will be fulfilled, and the cause of education in India will ever be very close to my heart."

The Government of India, have decided, with the approval of the Secretary of State, to assist Local Governments, by means of large grants from imperial revenues as funds become available', to extend comprehensive systems of education in the several provinces. Each province has its own educational system, which has grown up under local conditions and become familiar to the people as a part of their general well being. In view of the diverse social conditions in India there cannot in practice be one set of regulations and one rate of progress for the whole of India. Even within provinces there is scope for greater variety in types if institutions that exists today.

The Government of India have no desire to deprive Local Governments of interest and initiative in education. But it is important at intervals to review educational policy in India as a whole. Principles, bearing on education in its wider aspects and under modern conditions and conceptions, on orientalia and on the special needs of the domiciled community, were discussed at three important conferences of experts and representative non-officials held within the last two years. These principles are the basis of accepted policy. How far they can at any time find local application must be determined with reference to local conditions.

On the question compulsory and free elementary education, the Policy stated: The public demand for compulsory primary education continued however to grow, and between 1918 and 1931 compulsory education laws were passed for most parts of the country by the newly elected State legislatures in which Indians were in majority. In 1937, Mahatma Gandhi put forward his scheme of Basic Education under which education of seven or eight years duration was to be provided for all children and its content was to be revolutionized by building it round a socially useful productive craft.

As a result of all these efforts, the idea that it was the duty of the state to provide free and compulsory education to all children till they reached the age of 14 years was nationally accepted as an important aspect of the overall effort to provide equality of opportunity. Under the wise leadership of Sir John Sargent, the then educational adviser to the Government of India, these ideas were accepted by the British administrators and the Post-war Plan of educational development in India known popularly as the Sargent Plan, put forward proposals to provide free and compulsory basic education to all children in the age group 6-14 over a period of 40 years.. The nationalist opinion did not accept this long period, and a committee under the chairmanship of B.G.Kher proposed that this goal could and should be achieved in a period of 16 years. It was this recommendation that was eventually incorporated in the Constitution as a Directive Principle of State Policy. It was thus not a mere statement of an ideal, but a well-thought out enunciation of a policy, which is yet to be implemented though a substantial component was sought to be achieved by 2000 under the Education for All plan.

A core curriculum is emphasized at the elementary school level. This is a carefully planned curriculum that in content it compares favourably with those adopted in a number of other countries. A common core can help in overcoming discrepancies between the educational opportunities of urban and rural people, and that of men and women, but it cannot eliminate those difficulties unless literacy rates improve, greater participation occurs in school and other changes take place in society. In addition to the regular statistical return system, which is regularly compiled and published under the heading Education in India each academic year, there are also two expert institutions under the aegis of the Ministry of Human Resource Development, viz.

National Council of Educational Research and Training and National Institute of Educational Planning and Administration which carry out regular research and surveys, and in-depth analyses.

Adult Education – Historical Background and Review of Achievements

Eradication of illiteracy has been one of the major national concerns of the Government of India since independence. During the first Five Year Plan, the programme of Social Education, inclusive of literacy, was introduced as part of the Community Development Programme. Efforts of varied types were made by the States for the spread of literacy. Among these, the Gram Shikshan Mohim initiated in Satara District of Maharashtra in 1959 was one of the successful mass campaigns. It aimed at completing literacy work village-by-village within a short period of 3 to 6 months, through the honourary services of primary teachers and middle-school and high school students, supported by the entire community. It achieved a good deal of success but suffered from the lack of follow-up due to financial constraints and some of its good work was lost as a consequence. In spite of these varied initiatives the programme of adult literacy did not make much headway.

The topic was dealt at length by the Kothari Commission which emphasized the importance of spreading literacy as fast as possible. The Commission also observed that "literacy if it is to be worthwhile, must be functional". It suggested the following measures:

- Expansion of universal schooling of five-year duration for the age group 6 - 11.
- Provision of part-time education for those children of age group 11 - 14 who had either missed schooling or dropped out of school prematurely.
- Provision of part-time general and vocational education to the younger adults of age group 15 – 30.
- Use of mass media as a powerful tool of environment building for literacy.
- Setting up of libraries.
- Need for follow up programme.

- Active role of universities and voluntary organisation at the State and district levels. The National Policy on Education in 1968 not only endorsed the recommendations of the Education Commission but also reiterated the significance of universal literacy and developing adult and continuing education as matters of priority.

While the formal elementary education programme was supplemented by a Non-formal Education system, it was also decided to undertake Adult Literacy programmes culminating in the Total Literacy mission approach. A multi-pronged approach of universalization of elementary education and universal adult literacy has been adopted for achieving total literacy. The National Policy on Education has given an unqualified priority to the following three programmes for eradication of illiteracy, particularly among women:-

- Universalization of elementary education and universal retention of children up to 14 years of age.
- A systematic programme of non-formal education in the educationally backward states.
- The National Literacy Mission which aims at making 100 million adults literate by 1997.

The major thrust of these programmes is on promotion of literacy among women, members belonging to Scheduled Castes and Scheduled Tribes particularly in the rural areas. The Adult Education Programme consists of three components: basic literacy, functionality and civic awareness. The programme covers different schemes so that finally it aims at helping learners achieve a 'reasonable degree of self-reliance in literacy and functionality and better appreciation of the scope and value of science. Of course, even before Independence, there were adult education programmes.

Mahatma Gandhi had education as one of his constructive programmes, and as a mass campaign had through his movement, tried to make districts completely literate. Some success was also achieved. For instance Surat District, in erstwhile Bombay Presidency had been totally literate, but again relapsed into illiteracy for lack of follow-up. There were efforts at spreading by the Baroda Rulers, supplemented by a live library movement. Here again lack of follow-up and sustained efforts caused a relapse into illiteracy among the vulnerable sections. There were voluntary agencies working in the field.

Some agencies as the Karnataka Adult Education Council, Gujarat Social Education Committee and Bombay City Social Education Committee has had large programmes extending to the whole state or a metropolitan city. Literacy House of Lucknow did commendable work in this field. It came into existence in 1953 when its founder, Mrs. Welthy H. Fisher established it in small verandah at Allahabad, with a view to eradicate illiteracy and promote education in India. It was shifted to Lucknow in 1956. The University Grants Commission, at its meeting held in 5 May 1971, considered the general pattern of development and assistance towards adult education in the university and agreed that "assistance to universities for programme of adult education be made on a sharing basis of 75:25 and that the Commission's assistance to university would not exceed Rs. 3 lakhs for the Fourth Plan period." Departments of Continuing Education took up the work of "University goes to Masses".

The slogan "Each One, Teach One" caught the imagination of not only the students, but also a large number of educated individuals, and it looked like these programmes will meet a major success. However, like most enthusiastically launched programmes, they also fell by the wayside. A Farmers Training and Functional literacy project was launched in 1968-69, coordinating the activities of Ministries of Education, Agriculture and Information and Broadcasting. The Central Advisory Board of Education in its November 1975 meeting asked that the exclusive emphasis on formal system of education should be given up and a large element of non-formal education should be introduced within the system. In one sense, though the Non-formal education system was launched with its own set of objectives, the main purpose was to tackle the problem of dropouts from the formal system. The dropout from the formal system continues to hover around 50% and have not shown any great variation in the last four decades.

It is not difficult to guess the collective identities of the victims, children who fail to survive at school. They are children of landless agricultural labourers and subsistence peasants. Caste-wise, a substantial proportion of them belongs to the Scheduled Castes that have been granted special rights including reservation in higher education and representative bodies, in the Constitution. The situation of children belonging to many of the Scheduled Tribes is worse, especially in the central Indian belt. Forest-dwelling tribal communities have had to bear the brunt of State initiatives in dam construction, development of tourism with the help of game sanctuaries and mining. Apart from such destabilizing experiences, bias against tribal cultures and languages also makes the school curriculum and the teacher a deterrent for the advancement of tribal education. There are about 40 million rural artisans in India. For them, the current standard school curriculum is trivial, and in a sense irrelevant and demeaning. No wonder, one realizes in a rather simple, unscientific way, these children stop coming to school early.

Finally, the child residing in a slum, living in conditions of uncertainly and violence is always a likely case of early withdrawal or elimination. In keeping with recent trends in the international literacy movement, the emphasis of mass literacy programmes in India shifted from 'literacy' to 'adult education' through the intermediate phases of 'functional literacy' and 'non-formal education' during the last fifty years. The Policy Statement of the present programme highlights the development of functional competencies and awareness of the adult learners as two of the three equally important components of the National Adult

Education Programme. The third component is obviously literacy. Our Universities had also been roped into this activity.

The National Adult Education Programme was inaugurated on October 2, 1978. In a statement in the Parliament on April 5, 1977, the Union Education Minister declared that "along with universalization of elementary education, highest priority in educational planning would be accorded to adult education." The objective of the NAEP is "to organise adult education programmes, with literacy as an indispensable component, for approximately 100 million illiterate persons in the age-group 15-35 with a view to providing them with skills for self-directed learning leading to self-reliant and active role in their own development and in the development of their environment." In concrete terms, three R's, social awareness and functionality are the three basic components of the NAEP. In spite of careful planning before the launch of this programme, the Sardar Patel Institute of Social and Economic Research, after a survey carried out in the initial flush of enthusiasm, observed about the progress of the programme in a progressive state like Gujarat: "On the whole, while the NAEP in Gujarat was generally found to be addressed to the target groups kept in view under the NAEP and it was found to have some other commendable aspects, all things considered, its achievement in terms of spread of literacy is rather modest, and more so in terms of social awareness and functionality".

The report had gone on to say: "The more crucial aspects like the content of education, pedagogy, etc. can be probed into only if longer time is available, or ideally, on an ongoing basis. It is these aspects which have contributed most to the continuing stagnation of even the spread of literacy in the country.

This study is not sufficient to indicate whether breakthrough in these areas is being made, and whether the adult education programme is assuming the character of a Mass Movement as would be desirable and is clearly the intent of NAEP". Then came the National Literacy Mission. For a short while during the era of the high profile technology missions, some attention was given to issues like immunization, safe drinking water and literacy along with talk of people's participation and social audit of these programmes. In 1989, the district-based Total Literacy Campaigns emerged as a programme strategy for the National Literacy Mission against this background. While it was correctly envisaged that the initial social mobilization for a time-bound campaign provides the inspiration to spark for a mass participation of people, volunteering their time and energy for a cause like literacy, the follow-up programme was not worked out clearly. However, admitting and recognizing the many flaws and failures of the 'campaign approach', even as early as1994, NLM continued with the same TLC strategy and tried to bolster it with better monitoring, internal evaluation and presently with a revival effort through what is called 'Operation Restoration'. Reviewing the functioning of these programmes, Avik Ghosh concludes: "The present focus of NLM on literacy has to shift, and similarly the mission-mode-time-bound thrust of NLM should give way to a more durable and sustained programme of adult education that responds to the needs of adults as individuals and also as members of the disadvantaged groups".

The Total Literacy Campaigns, initially at least, helped in fostering a participatory approach in dealing with this issue, though here again, the problem of sustaining the momentum has remained. In the budget for 1999–2000, allocation for the Rural Functional Literacy Project does not find a special mention. The overall allocation to adult education has, however, been increased by about 40%.Unless it be in the context of revolutionary social transformation, the lack of spectacular success in a programme like Adult Education and of sustaining its momentum is understandable. It is after all a far distant cousin in terms of financial outlays to the formal system.

Further, there is the very real problem of pedagogy. For instance, as Prof. Jalaluddin says: "While 1652 mother tongues have been identified in the recent censuses in India, only 15 major literary languages have been accorded political status under the Eighth Schedule of the Indian Constitution. Then there is the problem of script. In the context of a nationwide adult literacy and education programme, the question of the acquisition of more than one writing system or even script by linguistic minorities becomes an important area of language planning. The term biliteracy is used in this context in India." Further in countries like India which have a long tradition of transmission of ideas and wisdom orally, such individual and societal transformations through a mass literacy campaign, are rather a form of renewal in nature than being additive or extensive". There is also the problem continued sustenance of the campaign approach. There are some hopeful signs of ICT-supported services being used to bridge the gulf. Some collaborative partnership of the Government of India and non-governmental agencies in partnership with International Organizations and private sector has been mooted and the results of such collaborative efforts may perhaps show a way. And yet, the importance of this component cannot be gainsaid. "In our country, numerous persons enter adulthood without proper education and consequently their self-confidence is shaky.

In a fast-changing environment of economic and cultural change, they will continue to be edged out unless their capacities are actively consolidated and improved so as to encounter the world outside on equal terms". This programme can be in the nature of a Sunset programme; but till then, *i.e.* literacy becomes self-sustaining fact with self-arising demand for its very usefulness and need for a fuller life, no Government should be allowed to ignore this aspect.

Into The Future

The need to go into a learning mode as also conditions for creating capabilities in the education system to meet the needs of knowledge growth, communication expansion, reinforcement of cultural roots is indicated. Changing needs of Educational Technology and entry of computers and Integration of Information and Communication Technology demand new structures, which the system should be able to assimilate. Renewal of education also calls for provision for regular reviews, which reckons also changing scenarios and developments in emerging technologies.

In a UNESCO publication, "Education in Asia and the Pacific", Raja Roy Singh has rightly written: "The dynamics of education and its role in each society in development and transformation make it essential that education continuously renews itself in order to prepare for a future rather than for obsolescence. This renewal process derives from a variety of sources which include: the growth of human knowledge, which is the basic component of education; the heritage of collective experience and values which education transmits to the new generations; the means and methods of communication by which knowledge and values are transmitted and the new values and aspirations which the human spirit adds to the collective experience and wisdom of the past or by which the heritage of the past is reinterpreted and reassessed."

Current Literacy Programmes

- Rural Functional Literacy Project: Adult Education Centres are set up by RFLP in all the States and Union Territories. They are fully funded by the Central Government although the State Governments and Union Territory Administrations are responsible for its implementation.
- State Adult Education Programme: Funded fully by the State Governments, this programme aims at strengthening ongoing Adult Education Programmes and expanding its coverage to ensure that the programmes reach women and other underprivileged groups.
- Adult Education through Voluntary Agencies: A Central Scheme of Assistance to Voluntary Agencies exists to facilitate the participation of Voluntary Agencies. The Government of India provides financial grants to Voluntary Agencies on programme basis.
- Involvement of students and youth in Adult Education Programmes. The University Grants Commission provides 100 per cent financial assistance to colleges and universities to support their active involvement in literary and adult education activities. Specifically, 50,000 adult education centres are expected to be organized under this programme. Simul-taneously with the adult education programme, the college and university students will be engaged in spreading universal primary education among non-school-going children.
- Nehru Yuvak Kendras: This non-student youth organization has been developing training programmes to educate young people according to their identified felt needs.

- Non-Formal Education for Women and Girls: This project puts special emphasis on improving women's socio-economic status by ensuring their participation in development programmes in addition to efforts for family planning and promotion of welfare of children. This programme is a joint effort of the Government of India and UNICEF.
- Shramik Vidyapeeths: This programme has been established and ever since funded by the Government of India with the aim to provide integrated education to urban and individual workers and their families in order to raise their productivity and enrich their present life.
- Central Board for Workers Education : This programme aims at providing literacy to unskilled and semi-skilled persons as well as raising their awareness and functionality. Its special feature is to meet the recognized needs of the workers with a specially matched programme.
- Functional Literacy for Adult Women : Started in the International Year of Women, under the sponsorship of the Government of India, this programme covers health and hygiene, food and nutrition, home management and child care, education, and vocational and occupational skills.
- Incentives Awards Scheme for Female Adult Literacy : designed to promote literacy among 15-35 year old women, this scheme presents awards to adult education centres. At the State level, the awards are intended for equipments of various kinds as well as training facilities.
- Post-Literacy and Follow-up Programme : The programme has been in operation since 1984-1985. The Directorate of Adult Education has developed broad guidelines for the preparation of neo-literate materials for the State Governments and State Resource Centres. Prototype neo-literate materials have also been produced.

The listed activities reflect India's determination to make the entire population literate by involving the other Government agencies related to development as well Universities and Voluntary Organization in literary activities. The responsibility for planning and financing these activities, however, rests with the Central and State Governments.

Education System in India

The education system in India has savored a special bond between the teacher and the pupil since time unknown. In fact, India was the country to have established what we know as the 'gurukul' system of education. However, with the coming of the Britishers, English has become a part and parcel of Indian education system. Today English is the third major medium of instruction in India after Hindi and Marathi. The present education system in India mainly comprises primary education, secondary education, senior secondary education and higher education. Elementary education consists of eight years of education. Each of secondary and senior secondary education consists of two years of education. Higher education in India starts after passing the higher secondary education or the 12th standard. Depending on the stream, doing graduation in India can take three to five years. Post graduate courses are generally of two to three years of duration. After completing post graduation, scope for doing research in various educational institutes also remains open. With more than 17,000 colleges, 400 universities, 13 institutes of national importance and various other vocational institutes, the higher education system in India is one of the largest in the world. However, it is the fast integrating world economy and corresponding rise of students mobility that have made studying in India an attractive option. There are a large number of Indian as well as foreign students who apply every year to Indian universities and colleges.

For all those who wish to study in India, it is very important to get prior and correct information about the courses that you would like to undertake, the university you want to apply to and how to go about the application procedure. For an international student, it is also important to know the accommodation facilities, weather conditions, food habits and cost of living in the city in which he or she intends to study.

Education for the Marginalized in India

As education is the means for bringing socio- economic transformation in a society, various measures are being taken to enhance the access of education to the marginalized sections of the society. One such measure is the introduction of the reservation system in the institutes of higher education. Under the present law, 7.5% seats in the higher educational institutes are reserved for the scheduled tribes, 15% for scheduled castes and 27% for the non creamy layers of the Other Backward Classes.

Under the Indian constitution, various minority groups can also set up their own educational institutes. Efforts are also being taken to improve the access to higher education among the women of India by setting up various educational institutes exclusively for them or reserving seats in the already existing institutes. The growing acceptance of distance learning courses and expansion of the open university system is also contributing a lot in the democratization of higher education in India.

Facilities for International Students in India

Surprises are always waiting as you enter any new place. One may take time adjusting him/ her in the new environment. It is normal to feel excited, confused and even overwhelmed. These problems are mainly faced by the international students when they arrive in India. They may face problems like language problem, accommodation problem and food problem and so on. But international student's offices at most of the institutes provide facilities for International Students in India that can ease their woes.

Moreover the Government of India has also set up the Education Consultants of India to cater to the needs of the growing number of International Students in India. Colleges and institutes The international students are required to carry the necessary documents along with them such as admission letter, passport, residence permit etc. The international students can avail the residential permit after registering themselves at the Foreigner's Registration Office within a period of seven days from their arrival. All over the country offer different courses for the international students. International students can apply for medical courses, engineering courses, applied arts courses etc. The government has reserved some seats for foreign students and students from other developing countries.

International students can get admission through this reserved quota. For more information related to these admissions, the students can contact the Indian High Commission located in their countries. Self-financing international students looking for admission to postgraduate courses can also choose from the various courses that are offered by the Indian universities.

Apart from the Government of India, there are some private educational institutes that provide various facilities for international students in India. The Government of India offers various scholarships annually to international students. These scholarships are offered to those who are interested in pursuing their studies in India. Some of the scholarships offered by the government are Cultural Exchange Programme, Commonwealth Scheme, SAARC Scholarship Scheme and ICCR Scholarship Scheme.

Advantages of Studying in India

India is fast becoming a major economic power in the world today. And if its growth trend continues for some more years, it would soon be playing a major role in the world economy along with China.

This itself has been a major cause of attraction for many international students. Moreover, India's successful stint with democracy has also been a major magnetic force for scholars around the world. However, apart from knowing India well, there are some other advantages that are attracting students to study in India

- Low Cost: The cost of education in India is quite low as compared to many other countries of the world.
- Quality Education: Quality of education is not uniform throughout the length and breath of the country. However, there are some educational institutes in India that provide world class education.Indian Institutes of Technology,All India Institute of Medical Science - AIIMS, Delhi. Armed Forces Medical College, Pune. Christian Medical

College, Vellore. JIPMER, Puducherry. Jawaharial Nehru Medical College, AMU, Aligarh. National Institute of Fashion Technology NIFT – New Delhi. Maulana Azad Medical College, Delhi. Loyola College, Chennai. Indian Institutes of Management, Indian Institutes of Science, National Law Schools, Jawaharlal Nehru University, Presidency College, Chennai. Anna University, Chennai National Institute of Technology Tiruchirapalli Tamil Naidu, Madras University, Hyderabad University, Campus Law Center, Delhi University, Delhi. Faculty of Law,National Law School of India Univ, Bangalore. NALSAR University of Law, Hyderabad. National Law Institute University, Bhopal. National Law University, Jodhpur, Allahabad University Allahabad, Kumaon-University of Uttarakhand. Garwal-University of Uttarakhand. Banaras Hindu University Of Varanasi. CIHTS Sarnath. Delhi University and are some such Institutes.The government of India is also speeding up the efforts to establish more such institutes that can offer quality education in India.

- Financial Assistance: Various scholarships, education loans and other financial aids are now available for studying in India today.
- Consultation Service: The government of India provides consultation service to the interested international students through Education Consultants of India. Thus one can get all the information about the Indian education system, cost of education, duration, visa, accommodation facilities even before landing up in India.
- Unique Courses: One can also study some unique courses that were discovered and developed by the traditional knowledge system of India. Ayurveda, Sankrit, Yoga, Hindi are some such courses that enthuse many international students.

Note-The right to education will be meaningful only and only if the all the levels education reaches to all the sections of the people otherwise it will fail to achieve the target set out by our Founder Father to make Indian society an egalitarian society.

HIGHER EDUCATION

Higher education or post-secondary education refers to a level of education that is provided at academies, universities, colleges, seminaries, institutes of technology, and certain other collegiate-level institutions, such as vocational schools, trade schools, and career colleges, that award academic degrees or professional certifications. Since 1950, Article 2 of the first Protocol to the European Convention on Human Rights obligates all signatory parties to guarantee the right to education. At the world level, the United Nations International Covenant on Economic, Social and Cultural Rights of 1966, guarantees this right under its Article 13, which states that "higher education shall be made equally accessible to all, on the basis of capacity, by every appropriate means, and in particular by the progressive introduction of free education".

ADULT EDUCATION

Adult education is the practice of teaching and educating adults. Adult education takes place in the workplace, through 'extension' or 'continuing education' courses at secondary schools, or at colleges or universities. Other learning places include folk high schools, community colleges, and lifelong learning centers. The practice is also often referred to as 'Training and Development'and is often associate with workforce or professional development. It has also been referred to as andragogy. Adult education is different from vocational education, which is mostly workplace-based for skill improvement; and also from non-formal adult education, including learning skills or learning for personal development.

ALTERNATIVE EDUCATION

Alternative education, also known as non-traditional education or educational alternative, includes a number of approaches to teaching and learning other than mainstream or traditional education. Educational alternatives are often rooted in various philosophies that are fundamentally different from those of mainstream or traditional education. While some have strong political, scholarly, or philosophical orientations, others are more informal associations of teachers and students dissatisfied with some aspect of mainstream or traditional education.

Educational alternatives, which include charter schools, alternative schools, independent schools, and home-based learning vary widely, but often emphasize the value of small class size, close relationships between students and teachers, and a sense of community.

India

In India, from the early 20th century, some educational theorists discussed and implemented radically different forms of education. Rabindranath Tagore's Visva-Bharati University, Sri Aurobindo's Sri Aurobindo International Centre of Education and Mahatma Gandhi's ideal of "basic education" are prime examples. In recent years many new alternative schools have formed including Kanavu in Wyanadu, Kerala, and Timbaktoo Collective. A traditional system of learning in India is now regarded as a basis for developing new methods of alternative schooling. Students used to stay in Gurukulas, where they received free food and shelter, and education from a "guru". Progress was not based on examinations and marks; tests were given by the gurus but not ranks. This system aimed to nurture the students' natural creativity and all-round personality development. While the mainstream education system in India is still based on that introduced by Lord Macaulay, a few projects aim to rejuvenate the early system, Some students in these and similar projects take up research work in the field of Sanskrit studies, Vedic studies, Vedic science, Yoga and Ayurveda. Others after completing their education in a Gurukula continue into regular mainstream education such as Bachelor degrees in Commerce, Science, Engineering etc.

INFORMAL EDUCATION

Some see informal education as the learning that goes on in daily life. As friends, for example, we may well encourage others to talk about things that have happened in their lives so that they can handle their feelings and to think about what to do next. As parents or carers we may show children how to write different words or tie their laces. As situations arise we respond. Others may view informal education as the learning projects that we undertake for ourselves. We may take up quilting, for example, and then start reading around the subject, buying magazines and searching out other quilters.

Many view informal education as the learning that comes as part of being involved in youth and community organizations. In these settings there are specialist workers / educators whose job it is to encourage people to think about experiences and situations. Like friends or parents they may respond to what is going on but, as professionals, these workers are able to bring special insights and ways of working. Informal education can be all of these things. It is a process - a way of helping people to learn.

SO WHAT IS INFORMAL EDUCATION

In the examples above we can see that whether we are parents or specialist educators, we teach. When we are engaged in learning projects we teach ourselves. In all of these roles we are also likely to talk and join in activities with others. Some of the time we work with a clear objective in mind - perhaps linked to some broader plan *e.g.* around the development of reading. At other times we may go with the flow - adding to the conversation when it seems right or picking up on an interest.

These ways of working all entail learning - but informal education tends to be unpredictable - we do not know where it might lead. In conversation we have to catch the moment where we can say or do something to deepen people's thinking or to put themselves in touch with their feelings. 'Going with the flow' opens up all sorts of possibilities for us as educators. On one hand we may not be prepared for what comes, on the other we may get into rewarding areas. There is the chance, for example, to connect with the questions, issues and feelings that are important to people, rather than what we think might be significant. Picking our moment in the flow is also likely to take us into the world of people's feelings, experiences and relationships. While all educators should attend to experience and encourage people to reflect, informal educators are thrown into this. For the most part, we do not have lesson plans to follow; we respond to situations, to experiences. Such conversations and activities can take place anywhere.

These contrasts with formal education which tends to take place in special settings such as schools. However, we should not get too tied up with the physical setting for the work. Formal education can also take place in almost any other location - such as teaching someone to add up while shopping in the market. Here it is the special sort of social setting we have to create that is important. We build an atmosphere or grab an opportunity, so that we may teach.

Obviously, informal educators work informally - but we also do more formal things. We spend time with people in everyday settings - but we also create opportunities for people to study experiences and questions in a more focused way. This could mean picking up on something that is said in a conversation and inviting those involved to take it further. For example, we may be drinking tea with a couple of women in a family or health centre who are asking questions about cervical cancer.

We may suggest they look at some materials that we have and talk about they see. Alternatively, it could mean we set up a special session, or organize a course. We may also do some individual tutoring, for example, around reading and writing. Just as school teachers may work informally for part of their time, so informal educators may run classes or teach subjects. The difference between them lies in the emphasis they put on each. So what is informal education? From what we have looked at so far we can say the following. Informal education:

- Works through, and is driven by, conversation.
- Involves exploring and enlarging experience.
- Can take place in any setting.

At one level, the purpose of informal education is no different to any other form of education. In one situation we may focus on, say, healthy eating, in another family relationships. However, running through all this is a concern to build the sorts of communities and relationships in which people can be happy and fulfilled. John Dewey once described this as educating so that people may share in a common life. Those working as informal educators have a special contribution to make here. A focus on conversation is central to building communities.

The sorts of values and behaviours needed for conversation to take place are exactly what are required if neighbourliness and democracy are to flourish. What is more, the sorts of groups informal educators such as youth and social action workers work with - voluntary, community-based, and often concerned with mutual aid - are the bedrock of democratic societies. It comes as no surprise then, that those working as informal educators tend to emphasize certain values. These include commitments to:

- Work for the well-being of all.
- Respect the unique value and dignity of each human being.
- Dialogue.
- Equality and justice.
- Democracy and the active involvement of people in the issues that affect their lives.

As informal educators we have to spend a lot of time thinking about the values that run through our work. We do not have a curriculum or guiding plan for a lot of the work, so we have to consider how we should respond to situations. This involves going back to core values. Reflecting on these allows us to make judgements about what might best help people to share in a common life.

WHY HAVE SPECIALIST INFORMAL EDUCATORS, WHAT SETS THEM APART

Everyone is an educator - but some people are recognized or appointed to teach and to foster learning. There are three main reasons why specialist informal educators may be needed. First, it may be that some situations demand a deeper understanding or wider range of skills than many of us develop in our day to day lives. Through reflection and training specialists can become sophisticated facilitators of groups and of conversations with individuals. They can also develop a certain wisdom about people and situations because of the opportunities they have.

In many communities the role may be fulfilled and developed by 'elders' or by those who are recognized to be wise. In other situations, often linked to the development of capitalism, there has been an increased division of labour. Additional or alternative forms of learning and teaching are needed. Second, it may be that people do not have the time to spend exchanging and learning with others in the ways they wish or need. Because of their situation, they may not have a chance to engage in the sorts of conversations they find fulfilling. Where we, for example, have to work some distance from home, deal with complex systems or have so much to do simply to get by, the amount of time we can spend in open talk can shrink.

In addition, we may choose not to spend time in conversation or doing things with others. With our increased use of different entertainment media such as television, the amount of time we spend directly engaging with others may well be lessened. Third, a good deal of the work that informal educators engage in is with other professionals. For example, an informal educator working in a school will have to spend a lot of their time deepening and extending the understanding and orientation of teachers and other staff. With the pressure to produce results and to achieve good test scores, relationships and processes can be easily neglected. Furthermore, there can be a narrowing of educational focus. In these situations, while informal educators may be appointed to work with students, they have to encourage and educate staff so that the needs of students can be recognized and, hopefully, met. To do this informal educators will often need both to develop a detailed understanding of the situation, and have some sort of professional qualification. So what sets informal educators apart? If we examine what they are doing, a number of characteristics emerge. They:

- Place conversation at the centre of their activities.
- Operate in a wide range of settings - often within the same day. These include centres, schools and colleges, streets and shopping malls, people's homes, workplaces, and social, cultural and sporting settings.
- Look to explore and enlarge experience.
- Put a special emphasis on building just and democratic relationships and organizations.
- Use a variety of methods including groupwork, casual conversation, play, activities, work with individuals and casework. While their work for much of the time is informal - they also make use of more formal approaches to facilitate learning.
- Work with people of all ages although many will specialize around a special age range *e.g.* children, young people or with adults. In other words informal education is lifelong education.
- Develop particular special interests such as in children's play and development; community development and community action; literacy and basic education; advice; outdoor and adventure activities; arts and cultural work; and youth work.

INFORMAL EDUCATION AND OTHER FORMS

What we are talking about as 'informal education' may well be described in Scotland as community education or community learning, in Germany as social pedagogy, and in France as animation. Similarly, informal educators' concern for justice and democracy may well bring them close to popular educators in South America. Another possible way of describing this way of working is as 'non-formal education'. We can get into all sorts of side alleys if we spend too much time arguing for our own way of naming the work. We can focus too much on difference and not enough of what is common. However, there is a serious point in thinking about these things. Naming the work in this way or that brings out different qualities, emphasizes different things.

Non-formal education. Some may contrast informal with non-formal education. The people who do this tend to present:

- Informal education as the lifelong process in which people learn from everyday experience; and

- Non-formal education as organized educational activity outside formal systems.

The distinction made is largely administrative. Formal education is linked with schools and training institutions; non-formal with community groups and other organizations; and informal covers what is left, *e.g.* interactions with friends, family and work colleagues.

The problem with this is that people often organize educational events as part of their everyday experience and so the lines blur rapidly. These pages tend to contrast informal and formal education to bring out issues around setting, aim and process.

Community education. 'Community education' is also used to describe the work we are interested in. Community educators in Scotland and in many Southern countries have similar concerns and approaches as 'informal educators'. In fact the way that the Scottish Community Education Council defines community education is very close to our view of informal education.

The main difference may lay in the way that workers view the setting in which they operate. Community educators may see themselves as educating for community, in the community. Informal educators may also be working to further democracy and commitment to others, but they may not label the setting for their activities as being 'in the community'. A social worker in a residential home may see it as a community, but not as the community as a whole. Youth work and community work. Some youth workers and community workers describe themselves as educators. Others may view themselves, first and foremost, as organizers or as case or care workers. As a result, youth work and community work can take very different forms. To limit confusion we can focus on aim and 'client group':

- Youth work: work with young people that is committed to furthering their well-being.
- Community work: work that fosters peoples' commitment to their neighbours; and participation in, and development of, local, democratic forms of organization.

If we think about these as educational processes, then much of what is claimed to be special about youth work and community work are the very qualities we have been describing as informal education. Examples of this include a concern with conversation, reflection on experience, choice, and participation.

In other words, if workers see themselves as educators then their work can be best approached as informal education either with young people or with people in particular communities. Social pedagogy and social education. In Germany our focus here may be described as social pedagogy and associated with social work and, perhaps, a 'problem-focus'. It is a perspective, 'including social action which aims to promote human welfare through child-rearing and education practices; and to prevent or ease social problems by providing people with the means to manage their own lives, and make changes in their circumstances'. Originally, in the mid 1800s, the term was used for a way of thinking about schooling as education for community. Hence, social pedagogy is sometimes translated as 'community education'.

In North America it was talked of as 'social education' - and connected with many of John Dewey's concerns. In Britain social education has tended to be used rather more to describe the process of fostering personal development and achieving maturity. It has a more individualistic orientation and may not put 'sharing in a common life' at its core, although there has been an emphasis on working with groups. Finally, in France and Italy, and among some arts workers the processes we explore here may be described as animation. For example:

- Using theatre and play as means of self-expression with community groups, children and people with special learning needs..
- Networking with people and groups so that they participate in and manage the communities in which they live.
- Developing opportunities for pre-school and school-children such as adventure playgrounds, toy libraries, outdoor activity centres, and organized sports activities.

At one level, we can talk of animation as 'making things move or happen' - much as animators do of cartoon pictures. In this view workers are motivators or 'inspirers'. Some animators are less keen on this emphasis as it can lead to doing things to people, rather than working with them. It is this latter strand that is closest to informal education. Animators in this sense, look to breathe life into situations rather than people. They help to build environments and relationships in which people can grow and have a care for each other.

NON-FORMAL EDUCATION

Non-formal education became part of the international discourse on education policy in the late 1960s and early 1970s. It can be seen as related to the concepts of recurrent and lifelong learning. Tight suggests that whereas the latter concepts have to do with the extension of education and learning throughout life, non-formal education is about 'acknowledging the importance of education, learning and training which takes place outside recognized educational institutions'. Fordham suggests that in the 1970s, four characteristics came be associated with non-formal education:

- Relevance to the needs of disadvantaged groups.
- Concern with specific categories of person.
- A focus on clearly defined purposes.
- Flexibility in organization and methods.

In many northern countries the notion of non-formal education is not common in internal policy debates - preferred alternatives being community education and community learning, informal education and social pedagogy.

NON-FORMAL EDUCATION IN INDIA

Development in the Education in India was seen mostly after independence. The educational system in the country was modified to a great level and it was structured. Different forms of education were introduced in the society. The 86th Constitutional Amendment Act was passed by the parliament to make education a fundamental right. Formal and non-formal educational systems were popularised in India. Non-formal education in India achieved world wide recognition. This policy of education was introduced mainly in the late 1960s and early 1970s. Non-formal education in India is the concept of recurrent and lifelong learning.

In addition to that non-formal education is about 'acknowledging the importance of education, learning and training which takes place outside recognized educational institutions'. According to Fordham four characteristics can be associated with non-formal education that includes: Relevance to the needs of disadvantaged groups, Concern with specific categories of person, a focus on clearly defined purposes and Flexibility in organization and methods. The notion of Non-formal education in India refers to education that mainly takes place outside of the schools that are formally organized. Moreover, non-formal is term which is used to refer to adult literacy and continuing education for adults.

This educational policy is preferred by the rural as well as urban communities as it is not compulsory and does not lead to a formal certification. The non-formal education is likely to be state-supported. The programme Non-Formal education in India was launched by the Government of India during 1979-80. According to the Non-Formal Education or NFE is designed to provide education to the children of 6-14 years age group and to those who have constrains in attending regular schools.

The non-formal education policy also helps those students who are school drop-outs, working children and children from areas without easy access to schools. This policy of education is extended to all parts of the country including urban slums as well as hilly, tribal and desert areas. The programme is functional in all the states and Union territories of India with voluntary assistance to centers offering non-formal education.

NON-FORMAL EDUCATION FOR SUSTAINABLE DEVELOPMENT

The Indian Institute of Education (IIE), Pune, India, which is one of the ten member institutes of the APPEAL Research and Training Consortium (ARTC), has undertaken an investigation of projects in India that emphasize innovative approaches to non-formal education for sustainable development. These projects focus on disadvantaged members of rural society (women, tribal minorities, lower castes) and (in addition to local empowerment) address literacy and primary education, vocational education, health education, improvement of the environment, and the decentralization of financial and administrative powers to local levels. The IIE has been engaged over the last quarter of a century in experimenting with innovative ideas for the spread of literacy and primary education through formal and non-formal modes and for the empowerment of rural women and other oppressed people.

Its model of non-formal primary education (called PROPEL or Promotion of Primary and Elementary Education) has been used in other parts of the country. The model is considered an appropriate replicable alternative for bringing primary education within the reach of all children with due regard to community lifestyles and people's expectations. Two other IIE projects, the Vigyan Ashram and the Centre for Education and Development of Rural Women, have been widely acclaimed and are also covered by this survey. The former project provides vocational education on the principle of *learning while working* and the latter is an action research project for the education and development of rural women with a view to empowering them to become agents of rural reconstruction. India is a vast country and there are many projects in rural areas oriented towards improving both formal and non-formal education. However, there are three in particular that deserve special attention because of their focus on previously unserved or underserved populations:

- Agragamee and its rural education programmes for the tribal people of Orissa
- Lok Jumbish and its programmes for literacy, education and the empowerment of rural women in Rajasthan
- The Integrated Abujhmarh Tribal Development Project undertaken by the Ramakrishna Mission for the development of tribal people in Madhya Pradesh.

The survey of these six programmes was conducted by an IIE research team under the leadership of its Director General, Dr. S.K. Gandhe. Outside agencies provided assistance in the case of two of the projects (Abujhmarh and Agragamee) The research team obtained data from available documents and supplemented their interviews of students and staff with first-hand observation of project activities.

THE PROPEL PROJECT (PROMOTION OF PRIMARY AND ELEMENTARY EDUCATION)

IIE believes that education and development are closely interrelated and that the people at the grassroots level are the makers of development while government agencies are merely facilitators. The PROPEL project assumes that *Education for All* can best be organized through community mobilization. PROPEL has evolved through three phases with an emphasis on action research and the mobilization of rural communities for educational development. During

Phase I of the project (1979-1985), nearly 4,500 children from 110 villages in different agro-climatic zones were reached under the non-formal education programme involving local leadership and communities. For this purpose 263 NFE centres were established. Phase II (1985-1988) covered 669 children in 40 NFE centres at 35 newly selected villages in poor, drought-prone and hilly areas. Emphasis in this phase was on testing measures for community involvement by strengthening village education committees as local motivators and managers of primary education.

In the third phase, there have been attempts to develop a replicable planning and development model to facilitate training programmes in community-level planning for education that can be set up by voluntary agencies and government officials. During this phase more than 5,500 out-of-school children were brought into the stream of primary education through 178 NFE centres and learning camps. Emphasis has been on reaching girls, the largest group excluded from schooling because of the household division of labour and deep-rooted social prejudices. Currently, PROPEL serves a population of 120,000 living in approximately 18,000 households scattered over 4 *blocks* or sub-districts in Maharashtra State southeast of the city of Pune.

BASIC PHILOSOPHY

PROPEL believes in teamwork, good governance, and responding to local needs. It has encouraged micro-planning, thus passing responsibility for the project operation to people at the grassroots level. It acts as a catalyst and attempts to support community ownership of the project. Collaboration and participation of the villagers are prerequisites for all activities. From the very beginning local community members are made aware of education problems in their community and participate in surveys of specific educational needs and facilities available. After the surveys have been analyzed and the community decides to take action, a village education committee is activated to help project staff set up an NFE centre, organize classes, and mobilize the community to serve the educational cause. The village education committees (VECs) have been the chief vehicle ensuring community participation in the PROPEL project. Since 1992 these VECs have received legal sanction as well as political and administrative support. VECs are established by consensus at village council meetings and are expected to play a major role in convincing parents to place their out-of-school children in NFE centres.

CURRICULUM AND MATERIALS

The NFE community centre and its curriculum are the heart of the project's programmes in non-formal education. The curriculum espoused by PROPEL attempts to cover the basic content of the first four grades of the formal primary school curriculum. In addition, the curriculum emphasizes skills needed for everyday life in the community rather than securing entrance to further education. Local relevance is imperative as far as curriculum content is concerned, as all non-formal learners are poor, and most are older than children who attend formal schools. Curriculum content is designed to further the following ideals:

- All children should become cultured, educated and self-respecting citizens.
- Children should become aware of the social conditions around them as well as the need for social change.
- Children's scientific temper should be nurtured.
- The habit of self-learning should be encouraged.
- The poverty in which children live should be countered by enabling them to organize their worksystematically and learn new skills.

The PROPEL project's NFE curriculum proposed in the 1990s includes such subjects as language studies, mathematics, general and developmental knowledge, science, aesthetics, social skills, and physical fitness and relaxation. In particular, it emphasizes opportunities for girls to express themselves freely in speech, drawing, singing, drama, and other activities that help them to become socially competent, culturally creative citizens. Unlike the formal system of education, PROPEL emphasizes locally relevant learning materials. The staff have regularly consulted local communities as well as specialists (linguists and psychologists) regarding the content and language of primers and readers. Many NFE materials are designed for self-learning and peer tutoring. Consequently, the materials have proven quite useful and efficient in the hands of semiprofessional teachers. Materials belong to an NFE class, and are collectively shared by all students, which keeps the costs down. All materials are meant to improve literacy skills, as well as disseminate useful and practical information for everyday life.

STUDENT EVALUATION

One noteworthy innovation in the NFE programme is the absence of formal examinations. Evaluation of learning is based on the NFE teacher's daily diaries and students' continuous self-evaluation as well as testing of learning by peers during the students' group work activities. Self-testing is made possible by the preparation of graded evaluation materials, particularly in literacy (language) and arithmetic. Students are also encouraged to demonstrate their learning achievements daily to family members and periodically to the rest of the community. Particularly useful for public demonstrations of achievement are the community meetings during which the students can give speeches and thus show off what they have learned.

In addition, there are the biannual *bal jatras* (children's fairs). These events, which take place in a centrally located village, provide opportunities for singing, storytelling and games, and are thus settings for both recreation and informal evaluation of children's accomplishments. Students display their skills in the *three Rs* and are evaluated with simple test materials by teachers other than their own. The rationale for this innovation was the assumption that tests administered in the class would be neither useful nor relevant, because teachers might be tempted to pass all students to show good results, and the students might be constrained to copy one another's answers.

This is what often happens in formal schooling due to the anxiety of both teachers and students. However, to continue studies in the formal school, NFE students may take the formal Grade III or IV examinations. Several former non-formal education students have been admitted to formal schools. Achievement tests show that the competence of these students in many subjects is on par with, if not better than, the competence of formal education students.

THE CENTRE FOR EDUCATION AND DEVELOPMENT OF RURAL WOMEN (CEDRW)

In 1993, IIE's priorities – action research, social and economic development, improvement of the status of women – led to the establishment of the Centre for Education and Development of Rural Women (CEDRW) in the village of Shivapur about 25 kilometres southeast of Pune in Maharashtra State. The centre not only focuses on education and empowerment of rural women and girls, but also attempts to make them both participants in development as well as subjects of development. A significant feature of the projects undertaken here is that they adopt an ethnological research approach combining the ideas of Paulo Freire on education and Gandhian principles of education for the rural masses. Freire argued that oppressed people had to reflect on their existing social condition and subsequently take action to bring about required changes. The Gandhian principles urge modification of the Anglo-Saxon model of education to include more participation by learners themselves. The CEDRW is at present engaged in the operation of various activities, such as women's savings and credit groups, vocational programmes for dropout girls and for women 15-45 years of age, camps promoting health, nutrition and personality development, and the training of local farmers and artisans through *farmers clubs*.

THE CENTRE

The CEDRW, which became functional in 1994, occupies one hectare of land outside the village of Shivapur. The infrastructure is simple and designed to harmonize with the rural setting. It consists of a workshop, administrative office, lecture-cum-dining hall, agro-exhibition hall and a preschool or child recreation centre. Apart from this, hostel facilities for 40 trainees, two self-contained guestrooms for visiting faculty, quarters for two academic staff and a residence for support staff are available. From the total land allotted, one third is for the building and the remainder is used for a tree plantation and as experimental plots for various kinds of horticulture, including the cultivation of flowers, vegetables and medicinal plants.

OBJECTIVES

The Centre has the following objectives:

- To develop a new system of rural education that will empower women to become agents of rural transformation
- To evolve integrated activities for community development
- Overall socio-economic change in the villages for sustainable development
- Women's educational development
- women's personal development

ASSUMPTIONS

- Education that goes beyond schooling has a major role to play in the process of development. This education, which is a lifelong process, is required to preserve human dignity and stimulate creativity among individuals.
- The process of development must be given a holistic perspective and hence the community as a whole must be involved in this process.
- Women's development cannot be considered in isolation from the development of men.

MODE OF PARTICIPATION

During informal meetings and discussions, community members initially identify the local problems faced by the community. The identified problems are prioritized according to the needs of the community. Subsequently, local representatives or *animators* are chosen from the community in order to establish linkages between the institute and the community. With the assistance of the animators and the community, and in consultation with the research team, an intervention or strategy is selected to tackle the problems. After implementation, the community itself evaluates the intervention on the basis of its success.

VOCATIONAL EDUCATION PROGRAMME

The CEDRW, in response to the demand from many villagers, developed a vocational education programme for school dropout girls and women aged 15 to 45 years. The programme was introduced in 1997 and is presently being conducted at the Centre with assistance from the Department of Education of the Ministry of Human Resource Development, Government of India. The minimum qualification for the course is literacy and numeracy skills equivalent to Grade 3. At present, 34 students are attending the course, which lasts 6 months. The course focuses on developing skills related to sewing, tailoring, embroidery, hand and machine knitting, and the preparation of items such as bags, purses and coverlets. In addition, there are lectures and discussions on topics related to social legislation, women's rights, work ethics, budget and accounts maintenance, marketing skills (communication), personal health and hygiene, family education, environmental health and labour law.

SELF-HELP (SAVINGS AND CREDIT) GROUPS

Another major achievement of the CEDRW is the formation of savings and credit groups for women, which have now spread to 17 villages. The success of these groups has led to the formation of a consortium, where two members, the chairman and treasurer of each group, meet occasionally to review the work and provide guidance to the others. It is interesting to note that the success of the women's groups has motivated the men to form their own.

HEALTH EDUCATION CAMPS

These camps were arranged especially for women who experience health problems. Simultaneously, there were attempts to make the community aware of the requirements of basic personal as well as environmental health and hygiene. For this purpose, doctors at the Primary Health Centre as well as private physicians offered their assistance. Later on, the villagers themselves requested information related to vision and oral hygiene, areas that posed special problems in the village. Village women, who volunteered and worked in teams, were responsible for convening the health education camp for these topics.

CHILD RECREATION CENTRE

In 1997 the CEDRW set up this centre to show that the parents and the community play a major role in the integrated development of children during the pre-school stage. In addition to preschool activities for young children (*i.e.*, storytelling, games), the Centre also has a training programme for rural women to serve as preschool staff members. Parents are actively involved through regular parent meetings.

FARMERS CLUB

This club, established by villagers in Shivapur and nearby communities, arranges meetings with visiting experts in order to keep up with advances in agricultural technology, especially as related to the cultivation of rice, a major crop in the area.

THE VIGYAN ASHRAM

The Vigyan Ashram near the village of Pabal in Maharashtra State has developed a system capable of educating and empowering school dropouts through training in basic science and technology at affordable cost and in an acceptable time frame. (The word vigyan means çscienceé and ashram denotes a place of simple living and high thinking.) The experimental project initiated by Dr. S.S. Kalbag in 1983, under the auspices of IIE, has developed a skills training programme that emphasizes *learning while doing* and *serving the community*. In 1985 this programme was approved by the Board of Secondary Education, Maharashtra, as a rural technology course and is still implemented in schools as a part of the technical stream. The course adopted in the school caters to both formal as well as non-formal education students. A similar course is also conducted exclusively for non-formal learners on a full-time basis at the ashram.

PRINCIPLES

- The basic principle governing the Vigyan Ashram model is *learning while doing*. It is based on the assumption that working with your hands stimulates the intellect.
- Technology is the application of science, and is the collaboration of head and hand.
- Basic scientific procedures such as observation, measurement, recording, classification, documentation, and formulating and testing hypotheses are essential for everyone and can also be easily practised in everyday life.
- Education means training for real life.
- All labour is worthy of dignity and there are no such things as *white collar* or *blue collar* jobs.
- Any education system to become relevant and life-based must enable learners to offer services to their community.

GENERAL OBJECTIVES

- To integrate education with development
- To stimulate the intellect in order to enable learners to reach their highest potential
- To provide a broad spectrum of technical education through access to many modern technologies
- To develop new opportunities in the rural economy through local support

SPECIFIC OBJECTIVES

- To provide skill training in the areas of agriculture, animal husbandry, food processing, food preservation, soil science, sewing and knitting, electrical assembly, and equipment maintenance
- To develop the ability to take appropriate management decisions, to quantify and document, and to do simple accounting, quality measurement and quality analysis

- To develop individual self-confidence and self-respect

MAJOR ACHIEVEMENTS

- A survey conducted in an area 25 kilometres around Pabal revealed that a large number of ex-ashramites have started small enterprises, workshops and poultry farms. These include welding works, fabricators, a photocopy shop, and women entrepreneurs who raise poultry. Other graduates have acquired sewing machines and become tailors.
- Schools in the vicinity have benefited from offering the rural technology course. There have been increases in enrollment due to the entry of students from the neighbouring villages. The students have performed better in technical subjects as well as the subjects in the formal curriculum. There has also been an increase in the percentage of students passing the high school standard examinations administered throughout the state. Finally, the contributions of students to their home communities have facilitated closer co-operation between these communities and the schools.

THE LOK JUMBISH PROJECT: EDUCATION FOR GIRLS

If primary education is a matter of concern for the whole of India, it is a major worry for the state of Rajasthan, whose literacy rates are the lowest in the country. In 1991, the literacy rate for men was around 60 per cent but only 19 per cent for women. In other words, only one of five women in Rajasthan was able to read and write. In rural Rajasthan the situation is even worse, with only 11.6 per cent of the women being literate. In this context, a project like Lok Jumbish becomes essential.

The Lok Jumbish Project aims at achieving the goal of Education for All through people's involvement and participation. (The name, *lok jumbish*, combines the Hindi word for *people* and the Urdu word for *movement.*) While many evaluations and reports have appeared dealing with Lok Jumbish and its success in the spread of primary education, here we focus on its work with respect to innovative programmes for the spread of education among girls. Although the project's efforts in improving enrollment and retention through intervention in the formal education process have been widely recognized, the emphasis here is on the various *non-formal methods* of education that are used to target marginalized populations, especially girls.

PROJECT OBJECTIVES

The Lok Jumbish Project (LJP), an offshoot of earlier efforts, began in 1992 with funding from SIDA and support from the state and federal governments.

The philosophy of the project is based on the belief that the mere provision of physical inputs is not sufficient for ensuring universal access to primary education. Instead, a strong partnership between parents, children and teachers is essential. The basic aim of this project is the universalization of primary education, with emphasis on both formal and non-formal education for all children up to 14 years of age. Non-formal education was indeed considered as a necessary tool for the spread of literacy to remote villages and socially conservative communities. The LJP has developed a three-fold approach: 1) improving the quality of education through training teachers and overhauling the curriculum, 2) changing attitudes and developing trust in education among communities that are resistant to education due to socio-cultural values, and 3) creating an environment for women to participate in the system, thereby increasing girls' access to education. The long-term objectives of the LJP are:

- To bring girls to the same level as boys and make education an instrument of women's equality
- To effectively involve people in education management
- To emphasize the quality of education
- To enable the poorest sections of society to participate equally in basic education
- To ensure that all children complete primary schooling
- To provide access to primary education for all children below age 14
- To provide opportunities for lifelong education

The LJP's primary strategy has been to mobilize and involve the local community in the demand for better delivery of education services. The idea behind this is that in the course of time it becomes the community's own agenda and therefore sustainable. The LJP achieved these objectives by *environment building*, school mapping and micro-planning, improving existing school facilities, producing and supplying textbooks and learning materials, training teachers, and promoting non-formal education and women's development. The village education committee (initially the *village core team*) in each community is ultimately the body responsible for the long-term education of its children.

Starting up in 1992, the LJP completed its first phase in 1995. The second phase began in 1995 and ended in 1998. Unfortunately, the third phase, which was planned to begin in 1998, is still not yet under way. The total project expenditure over the five-year period amounted to Rs.1,524 million of which the SIDA contributed half, the Government of India one third and the State Government the rest. The project is implemented through *blocks* or sub-districts, each block divided into clusters of 25-35 villages and with an average population of 150,000.

Altogether, 75 blocks were covered under the Lok Jumbish Project by October 1999 comprising more than 12,000 villages, 305 clusters and about 11 million people. By that time, 529 new primary schools and 540 Shiksha Karmi schools were opened, 268 primary schools were upgraded to upper primary schools and 5,010 NFE centres were opened to supplement the formal system. At present, LJP is winding up its activities in some areas, which will be soon taken over by the Government. After the SIDA stopped funding, activities have almost come to a standstill. Another international funding agency has already agreed in principle to take its place.

LOK JUMBISH STRATEGIES FOR EDUCATING GIRLS

The LJP has tried to influence formal schooling in the area it serves through teacher training and curriculum revision. Specifically, the aim has been to make both teachers and curricula much more gender sensitive than before, so that schooling becomes a more positive experience for girls. In addition, the LJP has introduced a number of innovative institutions related to non-formal education. In addition to village NFE centres, these include education camps and forums just for girls and workshops for adolescent girls and boys together. In all these efforts, the principle of gender sensitivity is woven into the fabric of the Lok Jumbish educational approach. It serves the cause of education for girls indirectly by changing attitudes, challenging social stereotypes, and redefining girls' roles paving the way to the empowerment of women through education.

BREATHING LIFE INTO SCHOOLS: INTERVENTION IN FORMAL EDUCATION

- Lok Jumbish took over malfunctioning government schools in backward areas for implementation of its agenda. The schools remained as they were in terms of structure and personnel. The intervention took the form of teacher training and introduction of a revised curriculum. The entire exercise was intended to improve the quality of education in government primary schools and make them attractive to village children and parents. At the same time, village committees and core groups worked to raise awareness of the importance of education amongst the villagers. One important outcome of these efforts was an increase in participation, especially of girls in primary education. The average percentage of overall participation in primary education increased from 46.7 per cent in 1994 to a substantial 76.8 per cent in 1998. The girls' participation rate also jumped from 29.4 to 68.1 per cent. Other data show improved school retention rates among girls attending LJP schools, as well as higher test scores in Hindi language and mathematics. In addition, it appeared that the single most important component was teacher training, which not only led to better teaching techniques, but also increased the motivation of teachers to perform well. Along with the new curriculum, this motivation contributed a great deal to improvement in quality.

BRINGING LEARNING TO THE VILLAGE COURTYARD: SAHAJ SHIKSHA CENTRES

These NFE centres initially started in 6 blocks and eventually spread to around 33 blocks, with an increase in enrollment from 8,336 in 1993 to 45,839 by the end of 1997. By October 1999 there were 5,010 centres serving children who could not attend formal schools. The dropout rate was negligible. It was heartening to find that 6,835 (out of the initial 8,336) moved on to formal schools after completing the nonformal curriculum. The ratio of enrollment of boys to girls was 3:5, which indicated that the girls benefited more from this non-formal education opportunity than boys. In addition, an evaluation study found that the programme had been successful in attracting the target segment, namely girls belonging to scheduled tribes and castes.

The *Sahaj Shiksha* centres, unlike formal schools, were usually located within the boundaries of the hamlets and literally brought learning to the doorsteps of the girls. Most of these centres operated for two or two-and-a-half hours in the evening. Parents or grandparents were often present, which imparted seriousness to teaching-learning activities at the centres. Smaller children too young to go to school sat nearby with their sisters and became familiar with the process of learning. The teachers were members of the local community who spoke the children's own dialect. They were recruited for the job by the village education committee or core team, who was also responsible for enrolling the children at the centres.

SHORT-TERM INTERVENTIONS

In addition to the regular ongoing education programmes, the LJP also organized education camps of shorter duration. For example, the *Balika Shiksan Sirvirs* were camps held for adolescent girls who could afford neither formal nor non-formal education. The first camps were four months in duration but as they became more popular their length increased to six-and-a-half months. In addition to teaching the girls how to read and write, the camps provided opportunities for them to increase their self-confidence. One positive result was that 75 to 80 per cent of the girls from the camps went on to formal schooling. In addition, the LJP held workshops attended by both adolescent girls and boys. The purpose of these residential workshops, which lasted five days, was to help girls overcome their shyness, develop selfconfidence, learn about their situation in society, question social stereotypes, and acquire information about the emotional and physical changes occurring during adolescence. Girls involved themselves in a number of activities, including traditional male ones like riding bicycles and playing cricket. They also participated in public excursions and mock elections. By the end of the workshops, most participants had developed the capacity to enter into dialogue with their peers (including boys) and had begun to acquire a new self-image. Finally, the Lok Jumbish organized a variety of activities and institutions for specific purposes. These included arts forums for adolescent girls, camps for children with disabilities, empowerment forums for women teachers, hostels for girls, and the Women's Residential Institute for Training and Evaluation (set up in 1994), whose purpose was to train women in rural areas to be teachers.

THE INTEGRATED ABUJHMARH TRIBAL DEVELOPMENT PROJECT

The Bastar District is a remote plateau located in the extreme southeastern part of Madhya Pradesh State. The western part of the district, rugged and watered by numerous streams, is known as the Abujhmarh Hills. If any part of India is still *terra incognita* to nearly all travellers, it is Abujhmarh, which has the reputation of a land free from rules and regulations, inhabited by the *Hill Marias* as popularized in the anthropological literature. Abujhmarh, comprising 250 villages, is described as a *tangled knot of hills*, a back-of-beyond that remains cut off from the rest of the world for nearly half the year. Because of their extreme geographical isolation, the Hill Marias have a very primitive economy, their mainstay being the slash-and-burn cultivation practised on the steep hill slopes. Traditionally, they have bartered forest products (resin, cocoons) for trade goods like salt, chillies, tobacco and cloth. The barter system is still prevalent, and the tribal people are most unscrupulously and liberally exploited by traders. The main problems of Abujhmarh, apart from extremely poor communication, are 1) the lack of medical facilities and a high mortality rate, especially among infants; 2) the lack of education facilities and extremely low literacy; 3) economic exploitation by various agencies; and 4) unwillingness on the part of government officials to work in the area. In August 1985, the Ramakrishna Mission established a *base camp* or ashram at Narainpur, an adminstrative headquarters in Bastar District which is also the gateway to Abujhmarh. The objective of this centre was to direct activities aimed at eradicating illiteracy, ill health and economic deprivation amongst the Hill Marias of Abujhmarh, enabling them to eventually join the mainstream of the nation. With this objective in view, the Mission set up the Integrated Abujhmarh Tribal Development Project at Narainpur.

The project serves an area of 3,905 square miles and a population of about 26,000. Despite adverse circumstances, the Mission has successfully started making major inroads against poverty, ignorance, sickness and economic exploitation. In addition to its own resources, the Mission relies on liberal grants-in-aid provided by both the state and federal governments. A 60-acre plot of land provided by the state government is the setting for the Mission's model school, a 100-bed hostel for boys, a fully equipped modern 30-bed hospital, a vocational and agricultural training centre, an NFE centre, and a *fair price shopping complex* for local people.

PROJECT ACTIVITIES

The activities of the Mission, using innovative approaches, fall into the general areas of literacy and education, health, and economic development.

LITERACY AND EDUCATION

Missionaries of the Ramakrishna Ashram (both men and women), assisted by a devoted band of qualified and dedicated staff members, look after a number of education institutions that serve the needs of the tribespeople. Foremost amongst these is a model residential school exclusively for tribal students, whose current enrollment is 341 boys and 161 girls. In addition, the Mission operates five residential co-educational schools currently serving 325 boys and 123 girls. Students at all six of these schools receive training in agriculture and horticulture using land that is part of the school premises.

The Mission also provides services for younger children. In collaboration with VISHWAS, a sister organization managed by devotees of the Ramakrishna Mission, the Narainpur centre administers 69 preschools located in the far-off villages of the Abujhmarh Hills. The purpose of these preschools is to prepare children 3 to 6 years of age to enter the regular school environment. Many of these preschools also have classes for girls and women between 11 and 65 years of age. Here they learn the *three Rs* and skills needed for everyday life.

It is an outstanding feature of the Mission schools that once students are admitted they continue to study uninterruptedly until the completion of their studies. This dedication, which includes taking on additional schoolwork during summer vacations, may account for their success in formal examinations at both primary and middle levels. In the last five years, the examination pass results have been almost 100 per cent, extremely positive for ethnic minority students. It was also heartening to note that out of 66 students who completed their studies in the Mission school, as many as 15 of them sought admission to engineering courses and 4 of them succeeded in securing admission to medical, veterinary, polytechnic and Ayurvedic courses respectively. About 20 entered graduate courses in arts, science and commerce, and 9 obtained regular employment.

HEALTH AND NUTRITION

Activities in this area include maintenance of a 30-bed hospital and health centre, 5 clinics located throughout the district, a mobile dispensary, and a project in community health services for remote villages not reached by any of these.

ECONOMIC IMPROVEMENT

Project activities in this area include the operation of a tribal youth vocational training centre, an agricultural training and demonstration farm, and the Central Sector Scheme for Agricultural Extension.

The purpose of the latter (begun in 1994) is to introduce the tribal people to modern, scientific methods of farming, thereby reducing their reliance on traditional shifting cultivation. In addition to the standard functions of extension services (demonstrating and supplying new inputs such as seeds, fertilizer, technology, etc.), the Project is involved in organizing village self-help groups, training farmers to use new technology, and promoting linkages between farmers and agricultural institutions in India (government agencies, universities, research centres).

Finally, in connection with agricultural development in the Abujhmarh Hills, there is the Rajiv Gandhi Watershed Project. The purpose of this project, which covers an area of 3,140 hectares, is to improve irrigation and reduce the effects of flooding. Since 1995, 54 tanks, 11 percolation tanks, 14 check dams and 6 stone weirs have been constructed. In addition, a number of trees were planted and fruit tree saplings distributed amongst 3,400 villagers.

THE AGRAGAMEE KISHIPUR PROJECT

In another corner of India, other ethnic minorities struggle with hunger, disease, landlessness, illiteracy and a situation characterized by a lack of basic services, leadership, and political will. The present-day district of Rayagada in the state of Orissa is inhabited by a mixed population of tribal groups (Kondhas, Parajas, Souras, etc.) and scheduled castes. In 1981, the NGO Agragamee undertook its first experiment in the *block* (sub-district) of Kashipur, fascinated by the overwhelming response and initiatives on the part of tribal people towards economic development opportunities. A group of tribal youths supported the project team and joined them during the second year of project activities. At present, the Agragamee Kashipur Project carries out a variety of education and economic development activities in six blocks of the district. Some of these have been replicated in other tribal districts of Orissa State.

General objectives:

- To develop an alternative model of education for tribal areas to be replicated elsewhere
- To encourage community participation in order to sustain programmes in the future
- To increase literacy and classroom learning
- To link education with development
- To make education a medium for the empowerment of tribal students
- To make elementary education universal throughout inaccessible tribal areas

Specific objectives:

- To develop and implement a child-centered curriculum
- To ensure community involvement and participation in operating village schools by forming village ducation committees to assume responsibility
- To generate, with the people's co-operation, the initial capital for sustaining schools and NFE centres in he future
- To help children develop a spirit of co-operation and mutual self-help
- To introduce children to basic economic activities
- To strengthen classroom learning through practical experience
- To use both traditional and mass media to generate awareness in the community

SIGNIFICANT ACTIVITIES

rprovided by the Government due to a combination of reasons, including poverty, the need to work and the inadequacy of government schools. In response the project has initiated a variety of programmes to meet the needs and priorities as identified by local tribal communities. These programmes include Non-Formal Education for Elementary Children (70 NFE centres in two remote blocks), Innovative Education in Remote Tribal Areas (100 additional centres with curricula focusing on village economic development), district resource units for NFE teacher training and materials development, an *education complex* to improve the literacy rate amongst tribal girls, *children's festivals*, creative workshops for children, vocational training, science exhibitions, parent-teacher workshops, health checkup camps, and *Bal Sansad*, which is a programme to educate tribal children about the existing political system in India and their rights in regard to voting and other forms of participation.

ELEMENTS OF INNOVATION

Ethnic minority communities have found it difficult to relate to the prevailing system of formal schooling. They require a different model of education that meets their own needs and priorities. The Agragamee Kashipur Project has attempted to provide such a model that includes a number of innovative features.

- First of all, members of the community are involved in selecting their own teachers for the NFE centre serving their children. This enables better rapport and communication between teachers and pupils, and bridges the language barrier. Parents and other village elders are encouraged to come to the classroom to share and learn. The village is also expected to provide a building where children can study.
- Second, the curriculum is relevant to the local situation of the children. Teachers do refer to the formal school syllabus, in so far as

it facilitates the learning process. But they also make use of additional material relating to the lives of the tribal people. Regular feedback from the teachers ensures that the material is being used and is acceptable to both the students and the community.

- Third, teachers are encouraged to use the folk media of songs, dance and legends to enliven teaching and help the children learn faster. This method also helps to ensure the perseverance of tribal folk traditions, as well as helping the people identify more positively with the education model they are adopting. In addition, the teachers encourage children to participate more actively in the teaching-learning process by teaching each other, with older boys taking charge of small groups of younger children.
- Finally, realizing that the process of education cannot be taken up in isolation, Agragamee's intervention combines economic activities with education and there are attempts to link education with the socioeconomic change and development activities in the villages. Children are encouraged to participate, even if as observers, in the planning processes, and issues related to development are incorporated into the NFE centre's curriculum. The teachers introduce topics concerning the children and their surroundings. They are not only teachers as such but have also received training to initiate participatory action for social change in the village.

Achievements

At present, Agragamee is managing 233 NFE centres in 7 tribal districts of Orissa. All of these institutions are operating with the active participation of the village communities. Currently, 7,584 children are enrolled, of whom 3,293 (about 45%) are girls. Village education committees have been formed and are responsible for the regular functioning of the centres. Of the 1,351 members of these committees, 559 are women. The educational process has helped to increase the self-confidence and capability of students to a great extent. In many of the villages where the NFE centres function, former students have taken over the teaching duties. In many instances, these people are doing much better than their counterparts who have undergone formal schooling. In some of the villages, youths who studied at the centres have now organized youth clubs. Currently, there are 48 youth clubs and village development committees, 18 irrigation user societies, 15 education organizations at the *panchayat* level, 5 such organizations at the block level, and one at the state level. At each level of these forums, Agragamee tries to ensure people's co-operation. The youth clubs and village committees closely monitor the education programmes run by Agragamee in the villages. They also take initiatives for increasing enrollment at the centres. At the *panchayat* level, members of the forum work together as a pressure group to ensure that the government schools in their own area are run more efficiently. They are also mobilizing parents to send their children to school. The state-level forum, the Adibasi Shakti Sangathan, tries to influence policy matters related to education in the tribal areas of Orissa.

CONCLUSIONS AND RECOMMENDATIONS

These six examples of NFE programmes in India demonstrate the success of using innovative, unconventional methods to reach populations mostly excluded from formal schooling.

This success rests largely on two factors. First, the programmes feature non-standardized, locally developed curricula that correspond to the priorities and life ways of both children and adult learners. Second, innovations in programme content and delivery occur directly in response to the needs of the local community. Instead of directives from government bureaucrats, demand as expressed by local community members largely determines the input of the NFE programmes.

The six projects and their activities clearly show the urgent need to contextualize and decentralize education, especially in the rural areas. In this connection, there should be rural development centres established at the grassroots level to facilitate decentralization and to make the education system more relevant for sustainable development. Similarly, more funding is needed for materials development at the local level, especially in regard to the preparation of appropriate science materials. Finally, these projects illustrate the importance of reaching out to those who have previous been neglected or under-served. Whether they are ethnic minorities in remote parts of Orissa or Madhya Pradesh, or rural women and girls in conservative Rajasthan, the marginal sections of society deserve the same opportunities for education and social betterment that others in more favourable circumstances already receive.

Bibliography

Anita Sharma: *Distance Education*, Global Pub, 2010.

Anju Desai: *Distance Education*, Alfa Publications, 2010.

Brijkishore Dayal: *Educational Planning and Development*, Wisdom Press, Delhi, 2013.

Brijkishore Dayal: *Educational Planning and Development*, Wisdom Press, Delhi, 2013.

C.K. Pathak: *Distance Education : Prospects and Constraints*, Rajat Pub, 2003.

C.K. Pathak: *Distance Education : Prospects and Constraints*, Rajat Pub, 2003.

Deepesh Chandra Prasad: *Distance Education*, KSK Pub, 2007.

Dhaneswar Harichandan: *Distance Education And Student Support Services*, Deep and Deep, 2009.

Husain: *Distance Education : Theory and Practice*, Anmol, 2004.

M.U. Qureshi: *New Media and Educational Planning*, Anmol Publication, Delhi, 2006.

Madhulika Sharma: *Distance Education : Concepts and Principles*, Kanishka, 2006.

Maitreya Balsara: *Educational Planning and Socio Economic Equality*, Kanishka, 1996.

Mujibul Hasan Siddiqui: *Distance Education : Theory and Research*, APH Publication.

Pramod Pathak: *Management Education* , Delhi 2004.

R K Raghuram: *Encyclopaedia of Educational Planning and Development*, Crescent Publishing Corporation, 2008.

Raghuram, R K: *Educational Planning* , Crescent Publication, Delhi, 2009.

Ramesh Chandra: *Socio-Educational Planning and Development in India*, Shree Publication, Delhi, 2009.

S. Venkataiah: *Distance Education : Challenge and Response*, Anmol, 2001.

S.K. Bhargava: *A Textbook of Distance Education,* Dominant, 2005.

S.K. Panneer Selvam: *Distance Education For National Development*, A.P.H. Pub, 2009.

S.K. Panneer Selvam: *Higher Education*, A.P.H. Publication, 2009.

S.M. Paul Khurana and P.K. Singhal: *Higher Education : Quality and Management*, Gyan, 2010.

S.R. Sharma: *A Handbook of Educational Policy*, Sarup, 2008.

Sameer Pralhad Narkhede: *Challenges of Higher Education in India*, Delhi, 2005.

Sandeep Anand: *Encyclopaedia of New Educational Policy*, Anmol, Publication, Delhi, 2008.

Saroj and S.P. Sharma: *Higher Education and Economic Reforms*, Vista International Publication, 2012.

Satish Deshpande and Usha Zacharias: *The Practice of Equal Access in Indian Higher Education,* Delhi, 2005.

Shalini Wadhwa, Sarup: *Aspects of Teaching and Learning in Higher Education*, Delhi 2006.

Sita Ram Sharma: *A Handbook of Schemes for Technical and Management Education* , Delhi, 2007.

Suresh K. Chadha: *Quality of Management Education,* Delhi, 2007.

V.K. Rao: *Crisis in World Higher Education* , Rajat Publication, Delhi, 2009.

V.P. Matheswaran: *Distance Education : Student Support Services*, Anmol, Publication, Delhi, 2005.

Vanita Singh and Nirmala Sharma: *Curriculum Development in Indian Higher Education*, Alfa Publication, 2008.

Vanita Singh and Nirmala Sharma: *Development of Higher Education in India*, Alfa Publication, Delhi, 2008 .

Vanita Singh and Nirmala Sharma: *Higher Education and Social Empowerment*, Alfa Pub, 2008.

Vijender Sharma: *Educational Planning* , Lakshay Publication, Delhi, 2011.

Vinita Agarwala and Sushma Srivastava: *Changing Scenario of Values in Society and Higher Education,* Delhi, 2004

Vinod Kumar Bansal: *Challenges in Higher Education in 21st Century*, DPS Publication, Delhi 2011.

Wasim Ahmad Khan: *Distance Education*, Prerna Parkashan, 2011.

Wiley: *A Blueprint for Change in Management Education* , Delhi, 2006.

Yogesh Rana: *Distance Education In India*, Saurabh Pub, 2010.

Zoya Hasan and Martha Nussbaum: *Equalizing Access : Affirmative*

Index